Fodor's 07

MONTRÉAL & QUÉBEC CITY

Where to Stay and Eat for All Budgets

Must-See Sights and Local Secrets

Ratings You Can Trust

Fodor's Travel Publications New York, Toronto, London, Sydney, Auckland

www.fodors.com

FODOR'S MONTRÉAL & QUÉBEC CITY 2007
Editor: Rachel Klein

Editorial Production: Tom Holton
Editorial Contributors: Chris Barry, Michèle Thibeau, Julie Waters, Paul Waters
Maps: David Lindroth, *cartographer;* Rebecca Baer and Bob Blake, *map editors*
Design: Fabrizio La Rocca, *creative director*; Guido Caroti, *art director*; Moon Sun Kim, *cover designer*; Melanie Marin, *senior picture editor*
Production/Manufacturing: Angela L. McLean
Cover Photo (Grande Allée, Québec City): Yves Tessier/Productions Tessima Ltée

COPYRIGHT

ISBN 978-1-4000-1735-5

ISSN 1525-5867

SPECIAL SALES

This book is available for special discounts for bulk purchases for sales promotions or premiums. Special editions, including personalized covers, excerpts of existing books, and corporate imprints, can be created in large quantities for special needs. For more information, write to Special Markets/Premium Sales, 1745 Broadway, MD 6-2, New York, New York 10019, or e-mail specialmarkets@randomhouse.com.

AN IMPORTANT TIP & AN INVITATION

Although all prices, opening times, and other details in this book are based on information supplied to us at press time, changes occur all the time in the travel world, and Fodor's cannot accept responsibility for facts that become outdated or for inadvertent errors or omissions. So **always confirm information when it matters,** especially if you're making a detour to visit a specific place. Your experiences—positive and negative—matter to us. If we have missed or misstated something, **please write to us.** We follow up on all suggestions. Contact the Montréal & Québec City editor at editors@fodors.com or c/o Fodor's at 1745 Broadway, New York, New York 10019.

PRINTED IN THE UNITED STATES OF AMERICA

10 9 8 7 6 5 4 3 2 1

Be a Fodor's Correspondent

Your opinion matters. It matters to us. It matters to your fellow Fodor's travelers, too. And we'd like to hear it. In fact, we *need* to hear it.

When you share your experiences and opinions, you become an active member of the Fodor's community. That means we'll not only use your feedback to make our books better, but we'll publish your names and comments whenever possible. Throughout our guides, look for "Word of Mouth," excerpts of your unvarnished feedback.

Here's how you can help improve Fodor's for all of us.

Tell us when we're right. We rely on local writers to give you an insider's perspective. But our writers and staff editors—who are the best in the business—depend on you. Your positive feedback is a vote to renew our recommendations for the next edition.

Tell us when we're wrong. We're proud that we update most of our guides every year. But we're not perfect. Things change. Hotels cut services. Museums change hours. Charming cafés lose charm. If our writer didn't quite capture the essence of a place, tell us how you'd do it differently. If any of our descriptions are inaccurate or inadequate, we'll incorporate your changes in the next edition and will correct factual errors at fodors.com *immediately.*

Tell us what to include. You probably have had fantastic travel experiences that aren't yet in Fodor's. Why not share them with a community of like-minded travelers? Maybe you chanced upon a bistro or bed-and-breakfast that you don't want to keep to yourself. Tell us why we should include it. And share your discoveries and experiences with everyone directly at fodors.com. Your input may lead us to add a new listing or highlight a place we cover with a "Highly Recommended" star or with our highest rating, "Fodor's Choice."

Give us your opinion instantly at our feedback center at www.fodors.com/feedback. You may also e-mail editors@fodors.com with the subject line "Montréal & Québec City Editor." Or send your nominations, comments, and complaints by mail to Montréal & Québec City Editor, Fodor's, 1745 Broadway, New York, NY 10019.

You and travelers like you are the heart of the Fodor's community. Make our community richer by sharing your experiences. Be a Fodor's correspondent.

Bon voyage!

Tim Jarrell, Publisher

CONTENTS

PLANNING YOUR TRIP

MAPS

ABOUT THIS BOOK

Our Ratings

Sometimes you find terrific travel experiences and sometimes they just find you. But usually the burden is on you to select the right combination of experiences. That's where our ratings come in.

As travelers we've all discovered a place so wonderful that its worthiness is obvious. And sometimes even superlatives don't do it justice: you just have to be there to know. These sights, properties, and experiences get our highest rating, **Fodor's Choice,** indicated by orange stars throughout this book.

Black stars highlight sights and properties we deem **Highly Recommended,** places that our writers, editors, and readers praise again and again for consistency and excellence.

By default, there's another category: any place we include in this book is by definition worth your time, unless we say otherwise. And we will.

Disagree with any of our choices? Care to nominate a place or suggest that we rate one more highly? Visit our feedback center at www.fodors.com/feedback.

Budget Well

Hotel and restaurant price categories from ¢ to $$$$ are defined in the opening pages of each chapter. For attractions, we always give standard adult admission fees; reductions are usually available for children, students, and senior citizens. Want to pay with plastic? **AE, D, DC, MC, V** following restaurant and hotel listings indicate if American Express, Discover, Diners Club, MasterCard, and Visa are accepted.

Restaurants

Unless we state otherwise, restaurants are open for lunch and dinner daily. We mention dress only when there's a specific requirement and reservations only when they're essential or not accepted—it's always best to book ahead.

Hotels

Hotels have private bath, phone, TV, and air-conditioning unless stated otherwise. They may operate on the European Plan (aka EP, meaning without meals), the Continental Plan (CP, with a Continental breakfast), Breakfast Plan (BP, with a full breakfast), or Modified American Plan (MAP, with breakfast and dinner). We always list facilities but not whether you'll be charged an extra fee to use them, so when pricing accommodations, find out what's included.

Many Listings

- ★ Fodor's Choice
- ★ Highly recommended
- ⊠ Physical address
- ✥ Directions
- Mailing address
- Telephone
- Fax
- On the Web
- E-mail
- Admission fee
- Open/closed times
- Ⓜ Metro stations
- Credit cards

Hotels & Restaurants

- Hotel
- Number of rooms
- Facilities
- Meal plans
- ✕ Restaurant
- Reservations
- Dress code
- Smoking
- BYOB
- Hotel with restaurant that warrants a visit

Outdoors

- Golf
- Camping

Other

- Family-friendly
- Contact information
- ⇨ See also
- Branch address
- ☞ Take note

WHAT'S WHERE

MONTRÉAL	Montréal and the island on which it stands both take their name from Mont-Royal, a stubby plug of tree-covered igneous rock that rises high above the surrounding cityscape. Although its height is unimpressive, "the mountain" forms one of Canada's finest urban parks, and its summit offers visitors a grand overview of what North America's only French-speaking metropolis has to offer. The views of the city from the Chalet du Mont-Royal in the Parc du Mont-Royal provide an excellent orientation to the city's layout and major landmarks. Vieux-Montréal, the city's cultural center, holds museums, the municipal government, and the beautiful Basilique Notre-Dame-de-Montréal within its network of narrow, cobbled streets. Although Montréal's *centre-ville,* or downtown, bustles like many major metropolises on the surface, it is unusually active below street level as well. The trendy neighborhoods of the Quartier Latin Plateau Mont-Royal Mile-End, the Village, Westmount, and Outremont are abuzz with restaurants, nightclubs, art galleries, and cafés. The greener areas of town are composed of the Parc du Mont-Royal and the Jardin Botanique, where you can walk, bike, or take a horse-drawn carriage ride through miles of paths. Much of the city is easily accessible on foot; the rest can be reached via the Métro system. The grid layout is easy to navigate, once you remember that street numbers run north from the river and that the long spine of boulevard St-Laurent splits Montréal neatly into east and west sides.
MONTRÉAL SIDE TRIPS	The Laurentians (les Laurentides) encompass thousands of miles of wilderness, but for many people the draw is Mont-Tremblant and its world-class slopes. At just 1½–2 hours from Montréal, the area has become a favorite weekend ski destination. If being 3,150 feet high doesn't make you feel close enough to the heavens, you can turn your attention to the stars at the Mont-Mégantic observatory in the Eastern Townships. Also known as les Cantons de l'Est, the townships have the architecture and rolling hills of the New England countryside to their south.
QUÉBEC CITY	Québec City, the capital of Québec Province, is widely considered to be the most French city in North America; roughly 90% of the people who live here claim French as their mother tongue. Vieux-Québec (Old Québec) is split into two tiers, sep-

	arated by steep rock against which are more than 25 *escaliers* (staircases) and a funicular. Along the banks of the St. Lawrence River is the Lower Town, or Basse-Ville, the oldest neighborhood in North America. Its timeworn streets brim with up-to-the-minute shops, charming restaurants, and art galleries, as well as touristy stores, all housed in former warehouses and residences. You can see the rooftops of the Lower Town from the Terrasse Dufferin boardwalk in Vieux-Québec's Upper Town, or Haute-Ville. One often-photographed landmark is the castlelike Fairmont Le Château Frontenac, a hotel with copper-roof towers and a commanding view of the St. Lawrence River. Many military sites—fortifications and battlements—and a number of museums and other attractions encircle the city. Beyond the town walls, old and new government buildings intermingle with the structures of a modern metropolis that grew up in the 20th century. Rue St-Jean is one of the city's trendiest neighborhoods, home to many eclectic and affordable restaurants, as is the newly hip St-Roch.
QUÉBEC CITY SIDE TRIPS	Ile d'Orleans is called "The Garden of Québec," as it provides many area restaurants with local produce. Made up of six small villages, this charming island has B&B's, crafts, and wineries. Cote de Beaupré is opposite the north coast of Ile d'Orleans, and features the thundering Montmorency Falls and the impressive Ste-Anne-de Beaupré. Valleys and plateaus, cliffs cut by waterfalls, and mountains that brush the St. Lawrence River characterize the Charlevoix region. This "Switzerland of Québec" has infused the art of painters, poets, and musicians for generations.

WHEN TO GO

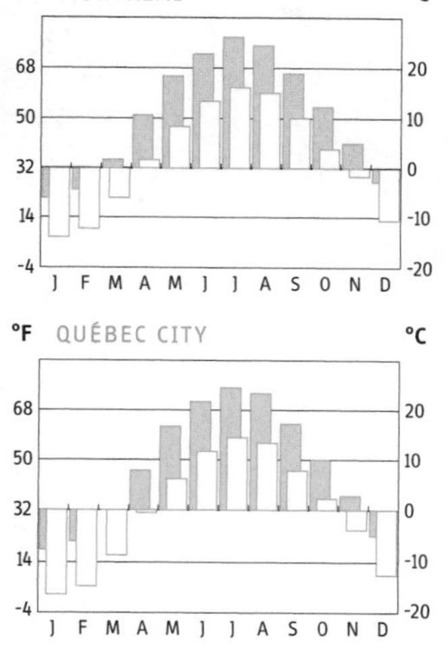

Montréal and Québec City are great in summer, when the weather is warm and festivals kick in by the dozen. Nights can be chilly. The long winter is cold, snowy, and slushy. In Montréal, it's a good opportunity to explore the underground malls that run beneath the city. In Québec City, do as the locals do: bundle up and get on with your business. Winter festivals, some of the best in the world, help take the edge off the season. Spring is short and normally chilly, while fall can be either beautifully crisp or gray, dull, and rainy.

Hilly and mountainous regions, such as the Eastern Townships and the Laurentians, tend to be colder and windier than Montréal, as befits their higher elevations.

Climate

At left are average daily maximum and minimum temperatures for Montréal and Québec City.

Forecasts **Weather Channel** (www.weather.com)

Montréal &
Québec City
Lac Kempt
CANADA
QUÉBEC
Montréal
Québec City
St-Michel-des-Saints
Parc du Mont Tremblant
Labelle
Lac Gagnan
Papineau
Lac Simon
St-Jovite
Ste-Agathe-des-Monts
Joliette
Sorel
Tracy
St-Jérome
Lachute
Hawkesbury
Montréal
Boloeil
Chambly
ONTARIO
Alexandria
Moncklan
Châteaugay
St-Jean
Salaberry-de-Valleyfield
Lac St-François
Cornwall
St. Lawrence R.
NEW YORK
Lac Champlain
117
131
125
50
31
40
133
323
158
25
15
148
30
116
17
34
13
40
10
417
20
34
15
138
401

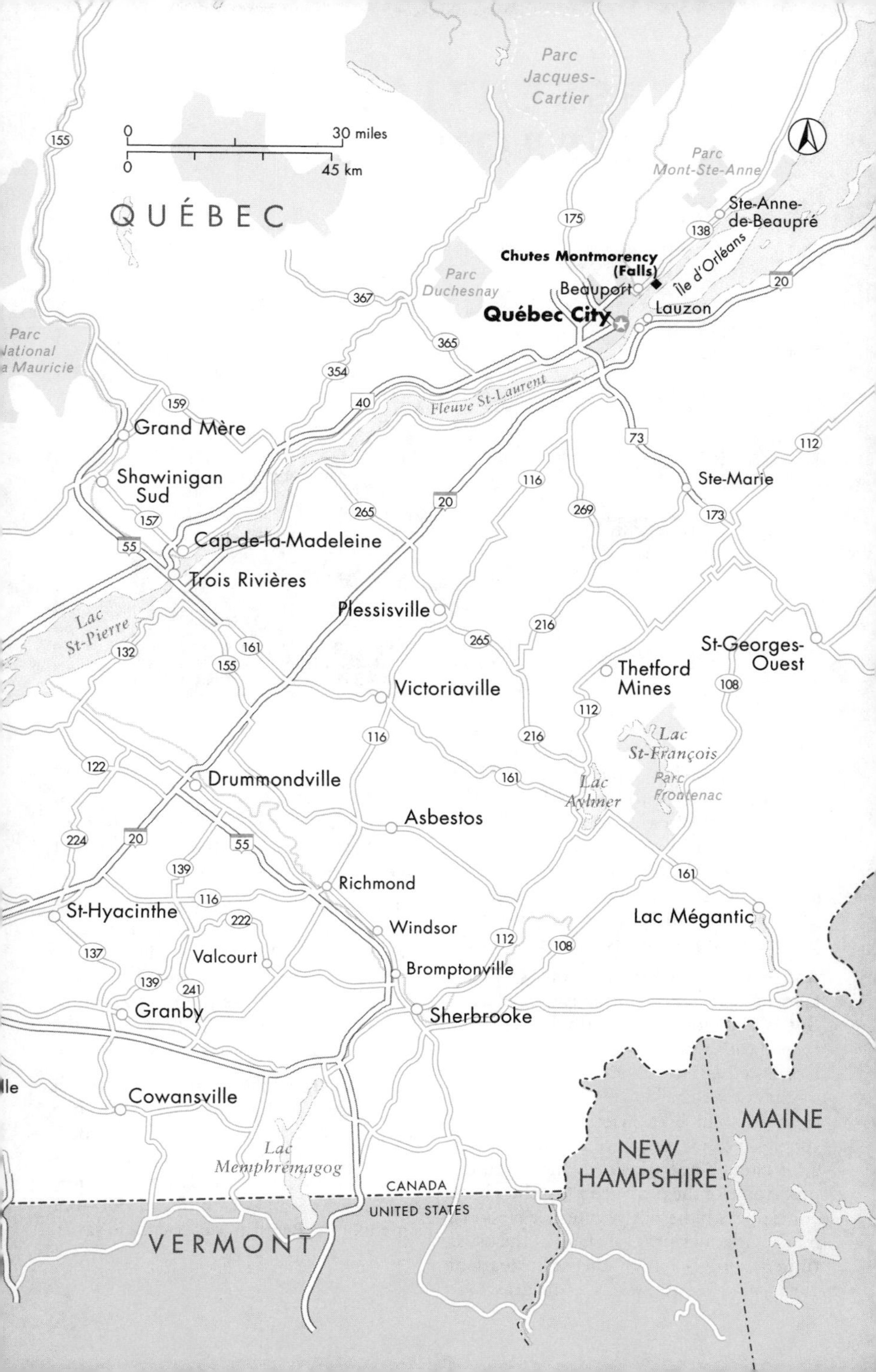

QUÉBEC
0
30 miles
0
45 km
Parc Jacques-Cartier
Parc Mont-Ste-Anne
Ste-Anne-de-Beaupré
Chutes Montmorency (Falls)
Parc Duchesnay
Beauport
Île d'Orléans
Québec City
Lauzon
Parc National de la Mauricie
Fleuve St-Laurent
Grand Mère
Shawinigan Sud
Cap-de-la-Madeleine
Trois Rivières
Lac St-Pierre
Plessisville
Ste-Marie
St-Georges-Ouest
Thetford Mines
Victoriaville
Lac St-François
Parc Frontenac
Lac Aylmer
Drummondville
Asbestos
Richmond
St-Hyacinthe
Windsor
Valcourt
Lac Mégantic
Bromptonville
Granby
Sherbrooke
Cowansville
Lac Memphremagog
CANADA
UNITED STATES
VERMONT
NEW HAMPSHIRE
MAINE
155
175
138
20
367
365
354
40
159
73
112
116
269
173
265
157
55
216
161
132
108
122
224
139
137
222
241

QUINTESSENTIAL QUÉBEC PROVINCE

Poutine

The legend is that sometime in 1957, a customer walked into Le Café Idéal in the little village of Warwick, Québec, and asked owner Fernand Lachance to add a handful of cheese curds to his order of frites. He shoved the result in front of his customer and muttered "Quel poutine"—which could be roughly translated as "What a mess."

And so was born what has become Québec's favorite fast food. Poutine is everywhere. But it's no longer just hot french fries topped with a ladleful of thick brown gravy. Dozens of variations have sprung up. You might want to try poutine Michigan, for example, which replaces the gravy with spaghetti sauce, or poutine poulet, which adds chunks of barbecued chicken to the mix. Some of the province's top chefs have come up with their own gourmet versions, made with duck gravy instead of the usual tinned goop, or blue cheese instead of curds, and sometimes even foie gras.

Hockey

What soccer is to Brazilians and baseball is to Americans, hockey is to Québecois. It's not a game, it's a religion, and its winter-long rites are celebrated in hundreds of arenas across the province.

In the mornings, bleary-eyed parents hunker down in the stands watching their children practice. At 10 PM the beer leagues take over the ice—men (and increasingly women) with full-time jobs as lawyers, accountants, and lab technicians, who strap on the skates and pads just for the fun of it.

If you can afford the scalpers' prices (or if you have a friend with connections), then get a ticket to a game at the Centre Bell. The Montréal Canadiens—the province's only National Hockey League team—hasn't won a Stanley Cup since 1993—but a night at the Bell is an experience to savor.

Sidewalk Cafés

There's something about surviving one of the harshest winters on the planet that makes it particularly sweet to spend long summer evenings sipping drinks under the open sky. And make no mistake: despite global warming, Québec still endures a fierce and unforgiving winter.

Alfresco dining begins in the southern part of the province as early as May or even late April—when it can still be quite chilly, especially at night. But if you've been cooped up eating indoors for months, a few buds on the trees or a few crocuses in the garden are enough to bring out the tables.

Restaurants and snack bars pack as many tables as they can on the sidewalks. Some have elaborate *terrasses*— fenced-in decks often with retractable awnings—perfect for one of the great treats of dining or drinking outside: watching the passing show.

Cinq-à-sept

If someone invites you to what sounds like a "sank-a-sett," it has nothing to do with swimming or tennis. It's a cocktail party that's supposed to happen between 5 PM and 7 PM but which rarely starts before 6 PM and usually ends around 8 or 8:30 PM.

The true 5-à-7 is not to be confused with the vulgar happy hour. It does not involve thirsty hordes packing away as many cheap drinks as they can before heading home. It's a more refined affair, at which conversation is at least as important as the drinks.

One of the essential skills you should master before attending your first 5-à-7, is the two-cheek kiss. The secret to perfecting this Québec-style greeting is to find a middle ground between the air-kiss and the enthusiastic smack of long-separated lovers. Something that expresses delight without possession is just about right.

IF YOU LIKE...

Everything French

One of the very best reason to visit Québec is to experience its unique culture. Steeped in traditions inherited from its former mother country France, the province remains distinctly North American yet is unlike anything else to be found on this side of the pond. Where else in America can you relax on a terrace, sipping café au laits while listening to the artist couple beside you debate politics in the language of Molière? Or treat your taste buds to that perfect foie gras, or crème brûlée, pleasantly served up by a French-speaking waiter who probably couldn't indulge you in your own language even if he wanted to?

Québec truly is like the European country next door, the France you can drive to in less than a day from your home in, say, Ohio, or New Jersey, yet separated by a million miles of difference from anything like it just south, or north, or east, or west, of its borders. The people who reside in this relatively laid-back part of the world, both French and English, share an approach to life that is uniquely Québecois, a work-to-live attitude as opposed to the live-to-work ethic found in most North American cities. It's a truly wonderful thing to experience, and the inhabitants of Québec, warm, intriguing, by all accounts a distinct society, are as interesting a people as they are gracious hosts. From the magnificent architecture of the grand basilicas to the trendy terraces lining the bohemian enclaves of Montréal's Plateau district, the French face of Québec is delightfully ubiquitous, and one of the most charming elements of this most charming of destinations.

Fabulous Festivals

Perhaps it has something to do with the Québecois joie de vivre, or maybe it's only about commerce and tourism dollars, but one thing is certain: Québec is the land of festivals. Hardly confined to the cities, even the tiniest Québec villages are apt to sponsor at least one festival over the course of the calendar year. From huge events like February's world-famous Québec City Winter Carnival in the provincial capital, to the somewhat lesser-known Carrefour mondial de l'accordéon in Montmagny, where locals and international accordion enthusiasts assemble for five days in early September to celebrate all things accordion, Québecois don't need much of an excuse to throw a party and call it a festival.

One festival of note is Les FrancoFolies de Montréal, a 10-day event held in late July and early August, celebrating Québec song and culture. French Québec has always had its own music scene replete with its own "vedettes" and personalities, virtually independent of the established Canadian music industry, with Les FrancoFolies providing an excellent opportunity to catch some of Québec's most cherished stars.

For another, slightly different taste of Québecois musical culture, there's the annual La fête des chants de marins (literally translated as sea chantey festival) in the beautiful riverside town of St-Jean-Port-Joli. Celebrating the many faces of maritime culture, storytellers, sailors, singers, and craftsmen gather for two days in mid-August for this unique event. For a detailed list of the various festivals taking place in Québec over the course of the year, go to www.bonjourQuebec.com.

Good Eats

It would be an understatement to say Québec has a wide variety of unique food tastes to sample. Of course, Québecois take their French food very seriously and traveling through most towns you won't have to look too hard to find a fab restaurant serving traditional French fare and regional specialties. Some of the best meals in the province can be had at the inns and dining rooms of the tourist-heavy regions located outside the major urban centers.

A far cry from fine dining is the time-honored and much-cherished *casse croûte.* Sure, on the surface a casse croûte doesn't seem like much more than your run-of-the-mill hot dog and hamburger joint—although hot chicken and green-pea sandwich plates are a staple of any self-respecting casse-croûte operation.

Another Québecois institution anyone with a sweet tooth will certainly appreciate are the traditional *cabanes à sucre* (maple-sugaring shacks), which open every spring come the maple syrup harvest. Québec is one of the largest maple syrup producers in the world, and there's no better way to sample the province's wares than by stopping by one of these rural establishments for a home-cooked meal of omelets, baked beans, smoked maple syrup ham and sausages, topped off with a dessert of maple sugar pie, or perhaps a side plate of maple taffy on snow. Many cabanes à sucre can be found within a short range of Montréal and Québec City.

Romping in Snow

Québecois have little choice but to embrace the winter season. After all, from early December until mid-April the province is covered in snow, with subarctic temperatures being the rule rather than the exception in the bitterly cold months of January and February.

With much of the landscape covered in the white stuff five months of the year, it's not surprising Québec has taken great pains to nurture its reputation as one of the top winter vacation destinations in North America. In the Eastern Townships region, alpine skiers can enjoy a day on the slopes at the strikingly beautiful Owl's Head ski resort for a mere C$36, with even better promotional rates during the week. Compare that to Colorado or the resorts just over the border in nearby Vermont, where a day of downhill skiing will easily run you upwards of US$65, and you realize just how good a deal Québec is when it comes to winter activities.

Of course there's more to winter in Québec than simply skiing, or snowshoeing, or ice-skating, or sipping cognac by the fireplace in the dining area of your 150-year-old rural inn. One activity steadily growing in popularity is dogsledding, with several operators around the province, like Globe-Trotter Aventure Canada Tours (888/598–7688, www.aventurecanada.com), offering backwoods dogsledding excursions lasting as long as a few hours to a full seven days. Cold as it may sound, most operators will provide the appropriate protective clothing upon request, and the faint of heart can take comfort in the knowledge that evenings are always spent sleeping and dining in cozy, heated cabins.

ON THE CALENDAR

	Québec has always been able to find a reason to party. Québec City celebrates one of the world's most brutal winters with a carnival that includes a boat race across an ice-choked river. Throughout the province, the rest of the year is full of festivals celebrating jazz, international folklore, film, classical music, fireworks, comedy, and hot-air balloons. The provincial tourist board has more information about these and other festivals.
WINTER January–February	**La Fête des Neiges** (☎ 514/872–6120 🌐 www.fetedesneiges.com) is Winter Carnival in Montréal. It lasts about two weeks and takes place at Parc Jean Drapeau on the river, in the east end of the city.
	Québec City's **Carnaval de Québec** (🌐 www.carnaval.qc.ca), a festival of winter-sports competitions, ice-sculpture contests, and parades, spans three weekends. The Plains of Abraham are the main stage.
	Festival Montréal en Lumière (🌐 www.montrealhighlights.com), a festival of mostly classical music, takes place on Montréal's Place des Arts during the last two weeks of February.
SPRING April	**Sugaring-off parties** celebrate the maple-syrup season throughout the province but especially north and east of Montréal.
	The **Blue Metropolis Montréal International Literary Festival** (☎ 514/932–1112 🌐 www.blue-met-bleu.com) presents more than 200 writers for readings, discussions, and other events in English, French, and other languages.
SUMMER June	The **Fringe Festival** (🌐 www.montrealfringe.ca) brings world-renowned playwrights, acting troupes, dancers, and musicians to Montréal.
June–August	**International Flora Montréal** (🌐 www.floramontreal.ca) presents gardens of all kinds—city, water, display, and avant-garde—in Jardin des Écluses in Montréal's Vieux-Port.
July	**Festival International de Jazz de Montréal** (☎ 514/790–1245 or 800/361–4595 in Canada, 800/678–5440 in U.S.) draws more than 1,000 musicians from all over the world for an 11-day series.
	The 11-day **Québec City International Summer Festival** (☎ 418/523–4540 or 888/992–5200 🌐 www.infofestival.com) offers music and other entertainment in the streets and parks of Old Québec City.
	Montréal's world-famous **Juste pour Rire** (Just for Laughs) (☎ 514/845–2322 🌐 www.hahaha.com) comedy festival hosts international comics, in French and English, from the second through third weeks of July.

	At Festival Orford (☎ 888/310–3665 🌐 www.arts-orford.org), international artists perform in Orford Park's music center (about an hour east of Montréal) throughout August.
	The Coupe Rogers AT&T (☎ 514/273–1515 🌐 www.tenniscanada.com) tennis tournament brings top professional players to Montréal.
	The first World Outgames Montréal (☎ 514/252–5858 🌐 www.montreal2007.org), a weeklong series of sports and cultural activities that begins in late July, celebrates individuals of all backgrounds, orientations, and abilities.
August	Montréal's World Film Festival (☎ 514/848–3883 🌐 www.ffm-montreal.org) continues to grow in popularity.
	St-Jean-sur-Richelieu's Hot-Air Balloon Festival (☎ 450/347–9555 🌐 www.montgolfieres.com) is the largest gathering of hot-air balloons in Canada.
	In early or mid-August, the Fêtes de la Nouvelle France (☎ 418/694–3319 🌐 www.nouvellefrance.qc.ca) re-creates the days of the French regime with markets and artisans in the Old Town district of Québec City.
FALL September	The Gatineau Hot-Air Balloon Festival (🌐 www.montgolfieresgatineau.com), held Labor Day weekend, brings together hot-air balloons from across Canada, the United States, and Europe.
October	Farmers' markets, arts-and-crafts fairs, and activities such as weekend hikes are part of the Festival of Colors, which celebrates autumn throughout the province of Québec.
	A week of parties hosted by Bad Boy Club Montréal draws more than 80,000 people to the Black and Blue Festival, honoring gay culture.

Montréal

WORD OF MOUTH

"The Plateau/Latin Quarter—to me this is the 'real' Montreal. Very French, very lively. Lots of outdoor cafés, small shops, byob restaurants, ethnic neighborhoods. It gets a bit run down as you get into the lower end, near St. Catherine, but much of it is quiet tree-lined streets."

–zootsi

"You must go to the Jazz Festival—it is a superb, world-class event. Lots of outdoor concerts, music is not all jazz (if you are not a fan). Held on St. Catherine St. East, they block off the streets around the multiple stages. Easy access by Metro."

–Michel_Paris

www.fodors.com/forums

By Paul and Julie Waters and Chris Barry

CANADA'S MOST DIVERSE METROPOLIS, Montréal is an island city that favors grace and elegance over order and even prosperity, a city where past and present intrude on each other daily. In some ways it resembles Vienna—well beyond its peak of power and glory, perhaps, yet still vibrant and beautiful.

But don't get the wrong idea. Montréal's always had a bit of an edge. During Prohibition, thirsty Americans headed north to the city on the St. Lawrence for booze, jazz, and a good time, and people still come for the same things. Festivals all summer long celebrate everything from comedy and French songs to beer and fireworks, and, of course, jazz. And on those rare weeks when there isn't a planned event, the party continues. Clubs and sidewalk cafés are abuzz from late afternoon to the early hours of the morning. More extraordinarily, Montréal is a city that knows how to mix it up even when it's 20 below zero. Rue St-Denis is almost as lively on a Saturday night in January as it is in July, and the festival Montréal en Lumière, or Montréal Highlights, enlivens the dreary days of February with concerts, balls, and gourmet food.

Montréal is the only French-speaking city in North America and the second-largest French-speaking city in the Western world, but it's not only Francophone culture that thrives here. About 14% of the 3.3 million people who call Montréal home claim English as their mother tongue. The two cultures, however, are not as separate as they were. Chatter in the bars and bistros of rue St-Denis east of boulevard St-Laurent still tends to be French, and crowds in clubs and restaurants on rue Crescent downtown speak, argue, and court in English. But the lines have definitely blurred.

Both major linguistic groups have had to come to grips with no longer being the only players on the field. So called *allophones*—people whose mother tongue is neither French nor English—make up fully 19% of the city's population, and to them the old, French–English quarrels are close to meaningless. Some—Jews, Italians, Greeks, and Portuguese—have been here for generations, while others—Arabs, Haitians, Vietnamese, and Latin Americans—are more recent ar-

MONTRÉAL'S TOP 5

- **Get to Church.** The Basilique Notre-Dame is not to be missed.
- **Indulge in Art.** Montréal has a flurry of fabulous museums and galleries, including the Musée des Beaux-Arts and the McCord Museum.
- **Party Till Dawn.** There's a strong history of late-night revelry in this city. Stroll along rue St-Denis or rue Crescent at about 10:30 PM and look for the place with the longest line and the rudest doorman.
- **Sample World Cuisine.** Swoon over culinary innovations at Toqué! and Cube, but don't leave without trying the local eats: smoked meat, barbecued chicken, and soggy *stimés* (steamed hot dogs).
- **Shop Till You Drop.** Thanks to Cité Souterraine (the Underground City), shopping is a year-round sport. Add in the trendy boutiques on Avenue Monkland, St-Laurent, and St-Denis, and your Visa will get a workout.

GREAT ITINERARIES

Getting a real feel for this bilingual, multicultural city takes some time. An ideal stay is five, but even three days of walking and soaking up the atmosphere is enough time to visit Mont-Royal, explore Vieux-Montréal, do some shopping, and perhaps visit the Stade Olympique (recommended for children). It also includes enough nights for an evening of bar-hopping on rue St-Denis or rue Crescent and another for enjoying a long, luxurious dinner at one of the city's excellent restaurants.

IF YOU HAVE 3 DAYS

Any visit to Montréal should start with the peak of Mont-Royal, the city's most enduring symbol. Afterward wander down to avenue des Pins and then through McGill University to downtown. Make an effort to stop at the Musée des Beaux-Arts de Montréal and St. Patrick's Basilica. On Day 2, explore Vieux-Montréal, with special emphasis on the Basilique Notre-Dame-de-Montréal, the Chapelle Notre-Dame-de-Bon-Secours, and the Musée d'Archéologie et d'Histoire Pointe-à-Callière. On Day 3 you can either visit the Stade Olympique or stroll through the Latin Quarter.

IF YOU HAVE 5 DAYS

Start with a visit to Parc du Mont-Royal. After viewing the city from the Chalet du Mont-Royal, visit the Oratoire St-Joseph. You should still have enough time to visit the Musée des Beaux-Arts before dinner. On Day 2, get in some shopping as you explore downtown, with perhaps a visit to the Centre Canadien d'Architecture. Spend all of Day 3 in Vieux-Montréal, and on Day 4 stroll through the Latin Quarter. On Day 5, visit the Stade Olympique and then do one of three things: visit the islands, take a ride on the Lachine Rapids, or revisit some of the sights you missed in Vieux-Montréal or downtown.

rivals. But together they've changed the very nature of the city, and are still doing so.

The best way to see Montréal is to walk and take public transportation. Streets, subways (Métro), and bus lines are clearly marked. The city is divided by a grid of streets roughly aligned east–west and north–south. North–south street numbers begin at the St. Lawrence River and increase as you head north; east–west street numbers begin at boulevard St-Laurent, which divides Montréal into east and west halves.

VIEUX-MONTRÉAL

Vieux-Montréal is a center of cultural life and municipal government. Most of the summer activities revolve around Place Jacques-Cartier, which becomes a pedestrian mall full of street performers and outdoor cafés, and the Vieux-Port, one of the city's most popular recreation spots. The

Orchestre Symphonique de Montréal performs summer concerts at Basilique Notre-Dame-de-Montréal, and English-language plays are staged in the Centaur Theatre in the old stock exchange building. This district has museums devoted to history, religion, and the arts.

Main Attractions

3 Fodor'sChoice ★ **Basilique Notre-Dame-de-Montréal** (Our Lady of Montréal Basilica). Few churches in North America are as wow-inducing as Notre Dame. Everything about the place, which opened in 1829, seems designed to make you gasp—from the 228-foot twin towers out front to the tens of thousands of 24-karat gold stars that stud the soaring blue ceiling. Nothing in a city renowned for churches matches Notre-Dame for sheer grandeur—or noisemaking capacity: its 12-ton bass bell is the largest in North America and its 7,000-pipe Cassavant organ can make the walls tremble. **Chapelle Notre-Dame-du-Sacré-Coeur** (Our Lady of the Sacred Heart Chapel), behind the main altar, was destroyed by a fire in 1978 and the backdrop for the altar is now a huge modern bronze sculpture that you either love or hate. The pulpit is a work of art in itself, with an intricately curving staircase and fierce figures of Ezekiel and Jeremiah crouching at its base. The whole place is so overwhelming it's easy to miss such lesser features as the stained-glass windows from Limoges and the side altars dedicated to St. Marguerite d'Youville, Canada's first native-born saint; St. Marguerite Bourgeoys, Canada's first schoolteacher; and a group of Sulpician priests martyred in Paris during the French Revolution. For a peek at the magnificent baptistery, decorated with frescoes by Ozias Leduc, you'll have to tiptoe through the glassed off prayer room in the northwest corner of the church.

In the evening, the nave of the main church is darkened for "La Lumière Fut" ("There Was Light"), a light-and-sound show that depicts the history of Montréal and showcases the church's extraordinary art.

Notre-Dame is an active house of worship, so dress accordingly (i.e., no shorts or bare midriffs). The main church is closed to tours on Sunday during the 9:30 AM, 11 AM, and 5 PM masses. The chapel can't be viewed weekdays during the 12:15 PM and 5 PM masses and is often closed Saturday for weddings. ✉ *110 rue Notre-Dame Ouest, Vieux-Montréal* ☎ *514/842–2925 or 866/842–2925* 🌐 *www.basiliquenddm.org* 🎫 *C$4, including guided tour; "La Lumière Fut" C$10* ⏲ *Daily 7–5; 20-min tours in French and English every ½ hr July–Sept., weekdays 8–4:30, Sat 8–3:15, Sun 12:30–3:15; every 2 hrs (or by prior arrangement) Oct.–June* Ⓜ *Place-d'Armes.*

The stone residence on the west side of the basilica is the **Vieux Séminaire** (Old Seminary), Montréal's oldest building. It was built in 1685 as a headquarters for the Sulpician priests who owned the island of Montréal until 1854. It's still a residence for the Sulpicians

SAVVY IN THE CITY

If you're lucky enough to wander into the Basilique Notre-Dame when the Orchestre Symphonique is rehearsing for its summer season, grab a pew and enjoy. The music and the—um—frank exchanges between conductor and musicians are free.

MONTRÉAL HISTORY

The first European settlement on Montréal island was Ville-Marie, founded in 1642 by 54 pious men and women under the leadership of Paul de Chomedey, sieur de Maisonneuve, and Jeanne Mance, a French noblewoman, who hoped to create a new Christian society.

But piety wasn't Ville-Marie's only raison d'être. The settlement's location on the banks of the St. Lawrence and Ottawa rivers meant a lucrative trade in beaver pelts, as the fur was a staple of European hat fashion for nearly a century.

The French regime in Canada ended with the Seven Years' War—what Americans call the French and Indian War. The Treaty of Paris ceded all of New France to Britain in 1763. American troops under Generals Richard Montgomery and Benedict Arnold occupied the city during their 1775–76 campaign to conquer Canada, but their efforts failed and the troops withdrew. Soon invaders of another kind—English and Scottish settlers, traders, and merchants—poured into Montréal. By 1832, the city became a leading colonial capital. But 1837 brought anti-British rebellions, and the unrest led to Canada becoming a self-governing dominion in 1867.

The city's ports continued to bustle until the St. Lawrence Seaway opened in 1957, allowing ships to sail from the Atlantic to the Great Lakes without having to stop in Montréal to transfer cargo.

The opening of the Métro in 1966 changed the way Montrealers lived, and the next year the city hosted the World's Fair. But the rise of Québec separatism in the late 1960s under the charismatic René Lévesque created political uncertainty, and many major businesses moved to Toronto. By the time Lévesque's separatist Parti Québecois won power in Québec in 1976—the same year the summer Olympics came to the city—Montréal was clearly No. 2.

Uncertainty continued through the 1980s and '90s, with the separatist Parti Québecois and the federalist Liberals alternating in power in Québec City. Since 1980, the city has endured four referenda on the future of Québec and Canada. In the most recent—the cliff-hanger of 1995—just 50.58% of Québecois voted to remain part of Canada. Montréal bucked the separatist trend and voted nearly 70% against independence.

who administer the basilica. The clock on the roof over the main doorway is the oldest (pre-1701) public timepiece in North America. ✉ *116 rue Notre-Dame Ouest, behind wall west of Basilique Notre-Dame-de-Montréal, Vieux-Montréal* Ⓜ *Place-d'Armes.*

★ ⓱ **Chapelle Notre-Dame-de-Bon-Secours** (Our Lady of Perpetual Help Chapel). Mariners have been popping into Notre-Dame-de-Bon-Secours for centuries to kneel before a little 17th-century statue of the Virgin Mary and pray for a safe passage—or give thanks for one. Often, they've expressed their gratitude by leaving votive lamps in the shape of small ships, many of which still hang from the barrel-vaulted ceiling. This is why

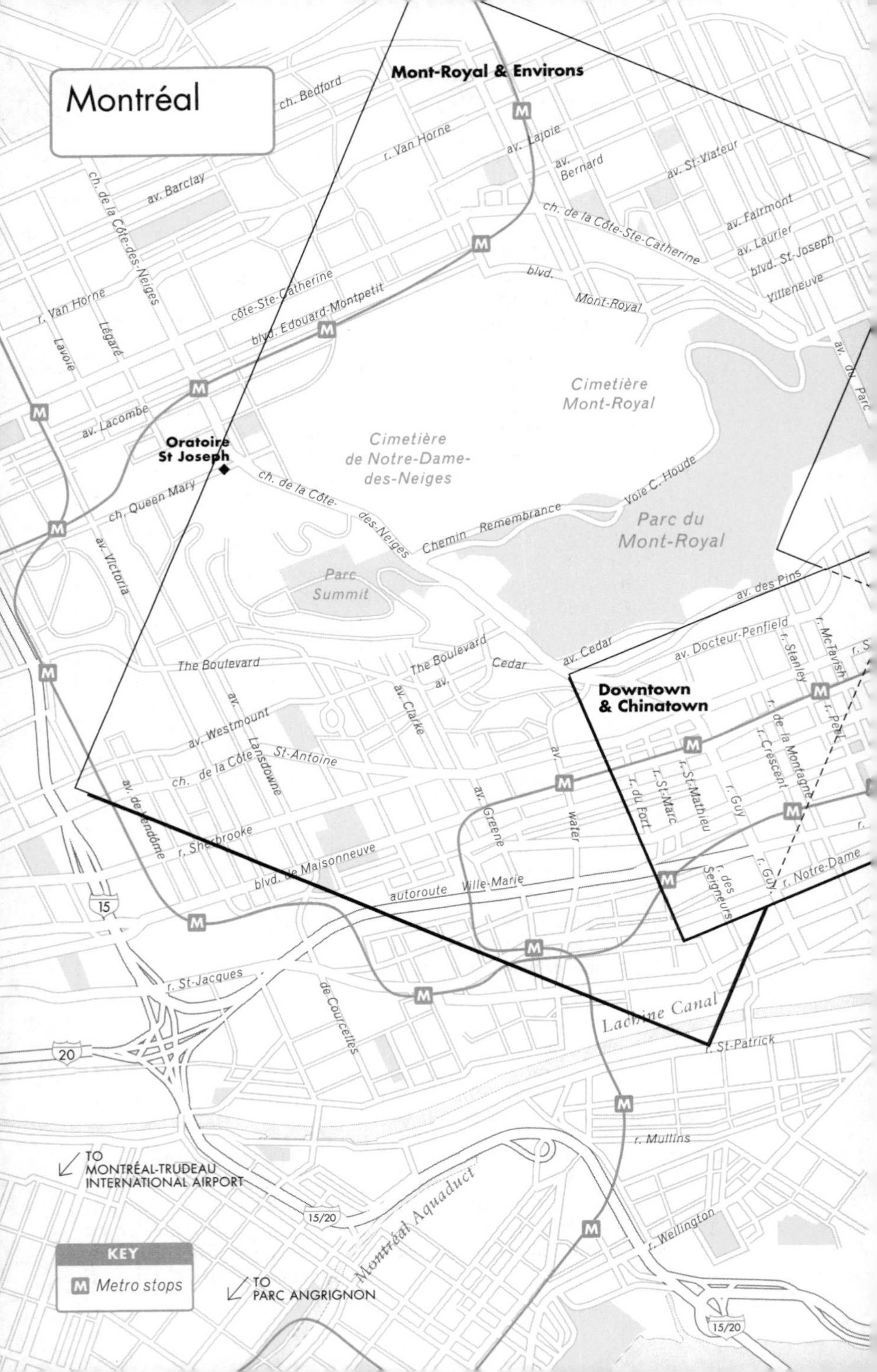
Montréal
Mont-Royal & Environs
Downtown & Chinatown
Oratoire St Joseph
Cimetière de Notre-Dame-des-Neiges
Cimetière Mont-Royal
Parc du Mont-Royal
Parc Summit
Lachine Canal
Montréal Aquaduct
TO MONTRÉAL-TRUDEAU INTERNATIONAL AIRPORT
TO PARC ANGRIGNON
KEY
Metro stops

The Plateau & Environs
Vieux-Montréal
TO HOCHELAGA-MAISONNEUVE
Parc Lafontaine
La Ronde
Stewart Museum at the Fort
Île Ste-Hélène
Biosphère
Parc Jean-Drapeau
Casino de Montréal
Parc Floral
Île Notre-Dame
Plage de l'Île Notre-Dame
Fleuve Saint-Laurent
Pont Jacques-Cartier
Pont de la Concorde
Pont Victoria
autoroute Bonaventure
av. Pierre-Dupuy
r. Mill
r. Peel
St-Jacques
r. University
côte du Beaver Hall
r. de Bleury
blvd. René-Lévesque
r. de la Gauchetière
r. St-Antoine
av. Viger
r. Notre-Dame
r. Ste-Catherine
r. Sherbrooke
r. Ontario
r. Milton
r. Prince-Arthur
r. Jeanne-Mance
r. Aylmer
av. des Pins
St-Urbain
blvd. St-Laurent
r. Roy
av. Duluth
av. Laval
r. de Bullion
r. Marie-Anne
av. du Mont-Royal
r. Villeneuve
r. St-Denis
r. Rachel
av. Christophe-Colomb
r. de Lanaudière
r. Fabre
av. du Parc Lafontaine
av. Calixa-Lavallée
av. Papineau
av. de Lorimier
Parthenais
r. d'Iberville
r. Sherbrooke
r. Hochelage
r. Chapleau
r. Amherst
Panet
blvd. de Maisonneuve
r. Notre-Dame
r. Ste-Catherine
r. Hogan
r. Ontario
r. Bercy
r. de Rouen
r. Davidson
r. Moreau
20
112
0
1/2 mile
0
500 meters

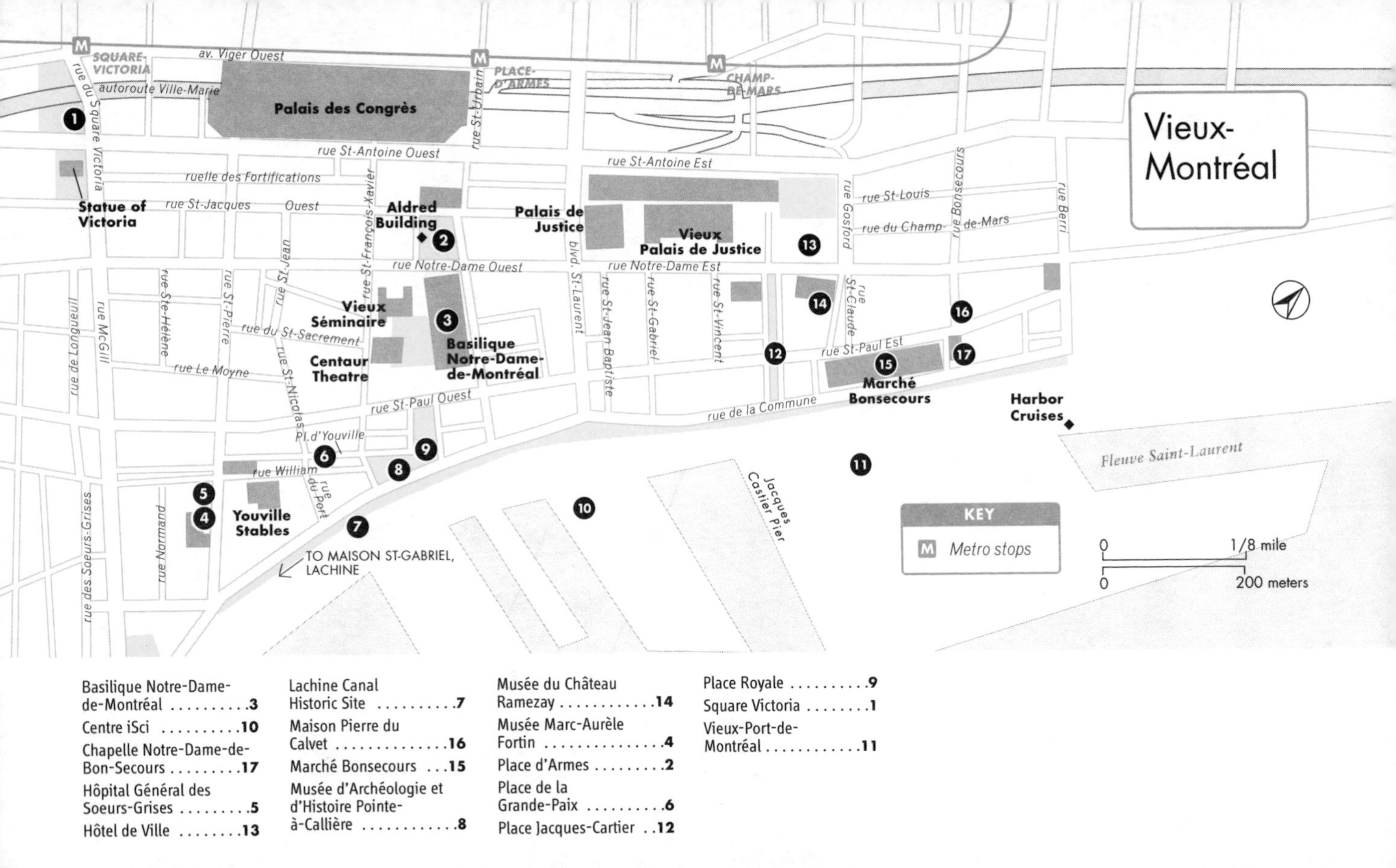
Vieux-Montréal
KEY
M Metro stops
0 1/8 mile
0 200 meters
SQUARE-VICTORIA
PLACE-D'ARMES
CHAMP-DE-MARS
av. Viger Ouest
autoroute Ville-Marie
Palais des Congrès
rue du Square Victoria
rue St-Antoine Ouest
ruelle des Fortifications
rue St-Jacques Ouest
Statue of Victoria
rue St-Urbain
rue St-François-Xavier
Aldred Building
Palais de Justice
Vieux Palais de Justice
rue St-Antoine Est
rue Notre-Dame Ouest
rue Notre-Dame Est
blvd. St-Laurent
rue St-Jean-Baptiste
rue St-Gabriel
rue St-Vincent
rue Gosford
rue St-Louis
rue du Champ-de-Mars
rue Bonsecours
rue Berri
rue St-Claude
rue St-Paul Est
rue St-Paul Ouest
rue de la Commune
Marché Bonsecours
Harbor Cruises
Fleuve Saint-Laurent
Jacques Castier Pier
Vieux Séminaire
Basilique Notre-Dame-de-Montréal
Centaur Theatre
rue St-Jean
rue du St-Sacrement
rue St-Nicolas
rue Le Moyne
rue St-Pierre
rue Ste-Hélène
rue McGill
rue de Longueuil
rue des Soeurs-Grises
rue Normand
Pl. d'Youville
rue William
rue du Port
Youville Stables
TO MAISON ST-GABRIEL, LACHINE
Basilique Notre-Dame-de-Montréal 3
Centre iSci 10
Chapelle Notre-Dame-de-Bon-Secours 17
Hôpital Général des Soeurs-Grises 5
Hôtel de Ville 13
Lachine Canal Historic Site 7
Maison Pierre du Calvet 16
Marché Bonsecours . . .15
Musée d'Archéologie et d'Histoire Pointe-à-Callière 8
Musée du Château Ramezay 14
Musée Marc-Aurèle Fortin 4
Place d'Armes 2
Place de la Grande-Paix 6
Place Jacques-Cartier . .12
Place Royale 9
Square Victoria 1
Vieux-Port-de-Montréal 11

most Montrealers call the chapel the Église des Matelots (the Sailors' Church), and why many still stop by to say a prayer and light a candle before leaving on a long trip. These days, the statue of Our Lady of Perpetual Help guards the remains of St. Marguerite Bourgeoys, who had the original chapel built in 1657 and is entombed in the side altar next to the east wall of the chapel. The current chapel dates from 1771; a renovation project in 1998 revealed some beautiful 18th-century murals that had been hidden under layers of paint. The steep climb to the top of the steeple is worth the effort for the glorious view of the harbor, as is the equally steep climb down to the archaeological excavations under the chapel for a glimpse into the chapel's history and the neighborhood. The dig is accessible through the adjacent **Musée Marguerite Bourgeoys,** which also has exhibits on the life of St. Marguerite and the daily lives of the colonists she served. The chapel is closed mid-January through February except for the 10:30 AM mass on Sunday. ✉ *400 rue St-Paul Est, Vieux-Montréal* ☎ *514/282–8670* 🌐 *www.marguerite-bourgeoys.com* 🎫 *Museum C$6, museum plus archaeology site with guide C$8* ⏲ *May–Oct., Tues.–Sun. 10–5:30; Nov–mid-Jan., Tues.–Sun. 11–5:30; Mar. and Apr., Tues.–Sun. 11–3:30* Ⓜ *Champ-de-Mars.*

OFF THE BEATEN PATH

Fodor's Choice ★

MAISON ST-GABRIEL – Walk into the big, low-ceiling kitchen of the Maison St-Gabriel, close your eyes, and you can almost hear the squeals and giggles of the *filles du roy* (king's daughters) as they learn the niceties of 17th-century home management. The filles du roy were young women without family or money but plenty of spunk who volunteered to cross the Atlantic on leaky wooden boats to become the wives and mothers of New France. At the Maison, they learned from St. Marguerite Bourgeoys and her religious order how to cook and clean, how to pray and read, and how to survive the rigors of colonial life. It can't have been easy—long hours, hard little beds, and cold stone walls—but it had its rewards and the prize at the end was a respectable, settled life. St. Marguerite also had some state-of-the-art domestic equipment—the latest in looms and butter churns, labor-saving spit turners for roasting meat, and an ingenious granite sink with a drainage system that piped water straight out to the garden. This little island of New France is well off the beaten path, deep in the working-class Pointe-St-Charles neighborhood. But it's certainly worth the 10-minute taxi ride from Vieux-Montréal. ✉ *2146 pl. Dublin, Pointe St-Charles* ☎ *514/935–8136* 🌐 *www.maisonsaint-gabriel.qc.ca* 🎫 *C$8* ⏲ *June 25–early Sept., Tues.–Sun. 11–6 (guided tours every hr); early-Sept.–mid-Dec. and late Apr.–June 24, Tues.–Sun. 1–5* Ⓜ *Charlevoix, 57 bus.*

Fodor's Choice ★

8 **Musée d'Archéologie et d'Histoire Pointe-à-Callière** (Pointe-à-Callière Archaeology and History Museum). The modern glass building is impressive and the audiovisual show is a breezy romp through Montréal's history from the Ice Age to the present, but the real reason to visit the city's most ambitious archaeological museum is to take the elevator ride down to the 17th century. It's dark down there, and just a little creepy thanks to the 350-year-old tombstones teetering in the gloom, but it's worth the trip. This is a serious archaeological dig that takes you to the very foundations of the city. You begin on the banks of the long-vanished Rivière St-Pierre, where the first settlers built their homes and traded

CLOSE UP

Art in the Métro

OPERATING SINCE 1966, the Métro is among the most architecturally distinctive subway systems in the world, with each of its 65 stations individually designed and decorated. The largest of these is Berri-UQAM, a cross-shape station with many corridors filled with artworks. The most memorable pieces include a huge black granite bench; three Expo '67 murals depicting science, culture, and recreation; a 25th-anniversary plaque and time capsule; a statue of Montréal heroine Mother Émilie Gamelin, a 19th-century nun who worked with the poor; and a vibrant red-and-blue stained-glass mural depicting three founders of Montréal.

The newer stations along the Blue Line are all worth a visit as well, particularly Outremont, with a glass-block design from 1988. Even Place-d'Armes, one of the least visually remarkable stations in the system, includes a treasure: look for the small exhibit of archaeological artifacts representing each of Montréal's four historical eras (Aboriginal, French, English, and multicultural).

with the Native American inhabitants. From there, you climb up toward the present, past the stone foundations of an 18th-century tavern and a 19th-century insurance building. Along the way, filmed figures representing past inhabitants appear on ghostly screens to chat to you about their lives and times. A more lighthearted exhibit explores life and love in multicultural Montréal. For a spectacular view of the Vieux-Port, the river, and the islands, ride the elevator to the top of the tower, or stop for lunch in the museum's glass-fronted café.

In summer, there are re-creations of period fairs and festivals on the grounds near the museum. ✉ *350 pl. Royale, Vieux-Montréal* ☎ *514/872–9150* 🌐 *www.pacmuseum.qc.ca* 🎫 *C$10* ⏲ *July and Aug., weekdays 10–6, weekends 11–6; Sept.–June, Tues.–Fri. 10–5, weekends 11–5* Ⓜ *Place-d'Armes.*

★ ⓬ **Place Jacques-Cartier.** The cobbled square at the heart of Vieux-Montréal is part carnival, part flower market, and part sheer fun. You can pause here to have you portrait painted or to buy an ice cream or to watch the buskers perform. If you have more time, try to get a table at one of the sidewalk cafés, order a beer or a glass of wine, and watch the passing parade. The 1809 monument honoring Lord Nelson's victory over Napoléon Bonaparte's French navy at Trafalgar angers some modern-day Québec nationalists, but the campaign to raise money for it was led by the Sulpician priests, who were engaged in delicate land negotiations with the British government at the time and were eager

SAVVY IN THE CITY

If you have a ghoulish streak, Vieux-Montréal offers three after-dark walking tours you'll love—the Ghosts of New France, the Ghosts of the Vieux-Port, and Historic Crimes. For information call 514/868-0303.

to show what good subjects they were. ✉ *Bordered by rues Notre-Dame Est and de la Commune, Vieux-Montréal* Ⓜ *Champ-de-Mars.*

★ 11 **Vieux-Port-de-Montréal** (Old Port of Montréal). Montréal's favorite waterfront park is your ideal gateway to the St. Lawrence River. You can rent a pedal boat, take a ferry to **Île Ste-Hélène,** sign up for a dinner cruise, or, if you're really adventurous, ride a raft through the turbulent Lachine Rapids. If you're determined to stay ashore, however, there's still plenty do. You can rent a bicycle or a pair of in-line skates at one of the shops along rue de la Commune and explore the waterfront at your leisure. If it's raining, the iSci science center on **King Edward Pier** will keep you dry and entertained, and if your lungs are in good shape, you can climb the 192 steps to the top of the **Clock Tower** for a good view of the waterfront and the islands; it was erected at the eastern end of the waterfront in memory of merchant mariners killed during World War I. Every couple of years or so, Montréal's Cirque du Soleil comes home to pitch its blue-and-yellow tent in the Vieux-Port. ✉ *Vieux-Montréal* ☎ *514/496–7678 or 800/971–7678* 🌐 *www.oldportofmontreal.com* Ⓜ *Place-d'Armes or Champ-de-Mars.*

Also Worth Seeing

10 **Centre iSci.** You—or more likely, your kids—can design an energy-efficient bike, decode an electronic message, analyze data from satellite photos, try using an MRI image to make a diagnosis, or just watch an IMAX movie on a giant screen at Montréal's interactive science center. Games, puzzles, and hands-on experiments make it an ideal place for rainy days or even fair ones. The center also includes Porto Fiorentino, a 1,000-seat family restaurant that overlooks the harbor and presents cooking demonstrations and piano concerts. In the neighboring food court, staff members give lessons about nutrition and agriculture. ✉ *Quai King Edward, Vieux-Montréal* ☎ *514/496–4724 or 877/496–4724* 🌐 *www.isci.ca* 🎫 *Exhibit halls C$10, IMAX C$12, combined ticket C$17* 🕘 *Weekdays 9:30–4, weekends 10–5* Ⓜ *Place-d'Armes.*

5 **Hôpital Général des Soeurs-Grises** (General Hospital of the Gray Nuns). A few jagged stone walls are all that's left of Montréal's first general hospital. The ruins—which once formed the west wing and the transept of the chapel—have been preserved as a memorial to Canada's first native-born saint, Marguerite d'Youville (1701–71), who took over the hospital in 1747 and ran it until a fire destroyed the building in 1765. The gold script on the wall facing the street is a copy of the letters patent signed by Louis XIV establishing the hospital. St. Marguerite's life was no walk in the park, as you'll find out if you visit the **Maison de Mère d'Youville** next door to the ruins. Marguerite started looking after the city's down-and-outs after the death of her abusive and disreputable husband—a man who made his living selling booze to the Hurons. Amused that the widow of

SAVVY IN THE CITY

Want to lose the kids—literally? Drop them off at the Shed 16 Labyrinthe, which is an indoor maze located in the Vieux-Port just east of the Centre iSci, and see if they can find their way out again.

a whiskey trader should be helping the town drunks, locals took to calling Marguerite and her Soeurs de la Charité (Sisters of Charity) the Soeurs Grises (Gray Nuns), slang for "tipsy nuns." The Maison has some remarkable reminders of her life, such as the kitchen where she worked, with its enormous fireplace and stone sink. Call ahead for tours of the house (ask for Sister Thérèse Pelletier or Sister Marguerite Daoust). ✉ *138 rue St-Pierre, Vieux-Montréal* 🎫 *Free* ⏲ *By appointment only, Tues.–Sun. 9–4* ☎ *514/842–9411* Ⓜ *Square-Victoria.*

⓭ **Hôtel de Ville** (City Hall). President Charles de Gaulle of France marked Canada's centennial celebrations in 1967 by standing on the central balcony of Montréal's ornate city hall on July 24 and shouting "*Vive le Québec libre*" ("Long live free Québec"), much to the delight of the separatist movement, and to the horror of of the federal government that had invited him over in the first place. Perhaps he got carried away because he felt so at home: the Second Empire–style city hall, built in 1878, is modeled after the one in Tours, France. Free guided tours are available daily 9–5 in June, July, and August. ✉ *275 rue Notre-Dame Est, Vieux-Montréal* ☎ *514/872–3355* 🎫 *Free* ⏲ *Daily 9–5* Ⓜ *Champ-de-Mars.*

★ ❼ **Lachine Canal Historic Site.** If you want to work up an appetite for lunch—or just get some exercise—rent a bike on rue de la Commune and ride west along the 14-km (9-mi) Lachine Canal through what used to be Montréal's industrial heartland. You could stop at the Marché Atwater to buy some cheese, bread, wine, and maybe a little pâté for a picnic in the lakefront park at the end of the trail. If that sounds too energetic, hop aboard an excursion boat and dine more formally in one of the century-old homes that line the waterfront.

The Lachine Canal is all about leisure now, but it wasn't always so. It was built in 1825 to get boats and cargo around the treacherous Lachine Rapids, and quickly became a magnet for all sorts of industries. That lasted until 1959, when the St. Lawrence Seaway opened and large cargo ships were able to go straight from the Atlantic to the Great Lakes without stopping in Montréal. The Lachine Canal was subsequently closed to navigation and became an illicit dumping ground for old cars and the victims of underworld killings, while the area around it degenerated into an industrial slum.

The federal government rescued the place in 1988. Lawns and trees along the old canal were planted, and it was transformed into a long, thin park. The abandoned canneries, sugar refineries, and steelworks have since been converted into desirable residential and commercial condominiums. The bicycle path, which in winter hosts cross-country skiers, is the first link in the more than 97 km (60 mi) of bike trails that make up the **Pôle des Rapides**(☎ 514/364–4490 🌐 www.poledesrapides.com). A permanent exhibition at the **Lachine Canal Interpretation Centre** explains the history and construction of the canal. The center, on the western end of the canal, is open daily (except Monday morning) mid-May through August, 10–noon and 1–6. ✉ *Lachine* ☎ *514/637–7433* 🌐 *www.parkscanada.gc.ca* 🎫 *Free* ⏲ *Sunrise–sunset* Ⓜ *Square Victoria (at the eastern end).*

WHERE TO REFUEL

Finding a quick bite in a food-mad city like Montréal is pretty easy. For local flavor try either La Belle Province or Lafleur fast-food restaurants, two popular Québec casse croute (snack-bar) chains offering up the very finest in authentic poutine.

Several steps up the fast-food chain are the Barbecue St-Hubert restaurants for Montréal-style chicken with crispy french fries and spicy gravy, and Chez Cora restaurants for sumptuous and–if you stick to the fruity side of the menu–healthful breakfasts.

For a picnic lunch, two local bakery chains–Première Moisson and Pain Doré–make terrific sandwiches on really good fresh bread.

16 **Maison Pierre du Calvet.** Merchant Pierre du Calvet was everything Roman Catholic, British-ruled Montréal didn't like—a notorious republican, an admirer of Voltaire, a pal of Benjamin Franklin, and a fierce supporter of the American Revolution. But he was also prosperous enough in 1725 to build a fine residence with thick stone walls and multipane casement windows. His home now houses a restaurant and a small but opulent bed-and-breakfast (called Pierre du Calvet AD 1725), where you can enjoy the same hospitality Franklin did in the mid-18th century. ✉ *405 rue Bonsecours, Vieux-Montréal* ☎ *514/282–1725* 🌐 *www.pierreducalvet.ca* Ⓜ *Champ-de-Mars.*

15 **Marché Bonsecours** (Bonsecours Market). You can't buy fruits and vegetables in the Marché Bonsecours anymore, but you can shop for local fashions and crafts in the row of upscale boutiques that fill its main hall, or lunch in one of several restaurants opening onto the Vieux-Port or rue St-Paul. But the Marché is best admired from the outside. Built in the 1840s as the city's main market, it is possibly the most beautifully proportioned neoclassical building in Montréal, with its six cast-iron Doric columns and two rows of meticulously even sashed windows, all topped with a silvery dome. In fact, the Marché was always too elegant to be just a farmers' market. It was also Montréal's premier gathering place for balls and galas, and served as city hall for 25 years. The parliament of Canada even met briefly in the market's upper hall in the late 1800s. ✉ *350 rue St-Paul Est, Vieux-Montréal* ☎ *514/872–7730* 🌐 *www.marchebonsecours.qc.ca* Ⓜ *Champ-de-Mars.*

★ 14 **Musée du Château Ramezay.** Claude de Ramezay, the city's 11th governor, was probably daydreaming of home when he built his Montréal residence. Its thick stone walls, dormer windows, and steeply pitched roof make it look like a little bit of 18th-century Normandy dropped into the middle of North America—although the round, squat tower is a 19th-century addition. The extravagant mahogany paneling in the Salon de Nantes was installed when Louis XV was still king of France. The

British used the château as headquarters after their conquest in 1760, and so did the American commanders Richard Montgomery and Benedict Arnold. Benjamin Franklin, who came north in a failed attempt to persuade the Québecois to join the American Revolution, stayed here during that winter adventure. Most of the château's exhibits are a little staid—guns, uniforms, and documents on the main floor and tableaux depicting colonial life in the cellars—but they include some unexpected little eccentricities. One of its prized possessions is a bright-red automobile the De Dion-Bouton Co. produced at the turn of the 20th century for the city's first motorist. ✉ *280 rue Notre-Dame Est, Vieux-Montréal* ☎ *514/861–3708* 🌐 *www.chateauramezay.qc.ca* 🎫 *C$7.50* ⏲ *June–Sept., daily 10–6; Oct.–May, Tues.–Sun. 10–4:30* Ⓜ *Champ-de-Mars.*

WORD OF MOUTH

"In Old Montréal, there is a strip of nice galleries between St. Sulpice and St. Laurent Street."

–mitchdesi

NEED A BREAK?

Step out the back door of the Musée du Château Ramezay and into 18th-century tranquillity. The *jardins* are laid out just as formally as Mme. de Ramezay might have wished, with a *potager* (an ornamental garden), for vegetables, and a little *verger* or orchard. You can sit on a bench in the sun, admire the flowers, and inhale the sage-scented air from the herb garden.

★ ❹ **Musée Marc-Aurèle Fortin.** Heavy clouds, higgledy-piggledy villages, and lush, fantastic trees crowd Marc-Aurèle Fortin's lively canvases. One of the local pioneers of modern art, Fortin (1888–1970) experimented wildly with different techniques. He painted some of his works on canvases that he'd prepainted gray to emphasize the warm light of the countryside; others he painted on black backgrounds to create dramatic contrasts. Fortin painted cityscapes, but he is known for his rich and bountiful landscapes of the Laurentians, the Gaspésie, and the Charlevoix region. ✉ *118 rue St-Pierre, Vieux-Montréal* ☎ *514/845–6108* 🌐 *www.museemafortin.org* 🎫 *C$5* ⏲ *Tues.–Sun. 11–5* Ⓜ *Square-Victoria.*

❷ **Place d'Armes.** When Montréal was under attack, citizens and soldiers would rally at Place d'Armes, but these days, the only rallying is done by tourists, lunching office workers, calèche drivers, and flocks of voracious pigeons. The pigeons are particularly fond of the triumphant statue of Montréal's founder, Paul de Chomedey, with his lance upraised, perched above the fountain in the middle of the cobblestone square. He slew an Iroquois chief in a battle here in 1644 and was wounded in return. Tunnels beneath the square protected the colonists from the winter weather and provided an escape route; unfortunately, they are too small and dangerous to visit. ✉ *Bordered by*

SAVVY IN THE CITY

The best place to find a calèche for a horse-drawn tour of the old city is on the south side of Place d'Armes. And be careful what you pay. Fares are set by the city. In 2006 they were C$45 for a 30-minute ride and C$75 for an hour.

rues Notre-Dame Ouest, St-Jacques, and St-Sulpice, Vieux-Montréal Ⓜ *Place-d'Armes.*

6 **Place de la Grande-Paix.** If you're looking for peace and quiet, the narrow strip of grass and trees on Place d'Youville just east of Place Royale is an appropriate place to find it. It was here, after all, that the French signed a major peace treaty with dozens of aboriginal nations in 1702. It was also here that the first French colonists landed their four boats on May 17, 1642. An obelisk records the names of the settlers. ✉ *Between pl. d'Youville and rue William, Vieux-Montréal* Ⓜ *Place-d'Armes.*

9 **Place Royale.** The oldest public square in Montréal, dating to the 17th century, was a public market during the French regime and later became a Victorian garden. The neoclassical Vielle Douane (Old Customs House) on its south side serves as the gift shop for the Musée d'Archéologie et d'Histoire Pointe-à-Callière. ✉ *Bordered by rues St-Paul Ouest and de la Commune, Vieux-Montréal* Ⓜ *Place-d'Armes.*

1 **Square Victoria.** The perfect Montréal mix: an 1872 statue of Queen Victoria on one side and an authentic Parisian Métro entrance on the other. Both are framed by a two-block stretch of trees, benches, and fountains that makes a great place to relax and admire the handsome 1920s business buildings on the east side. The art nouveau Métro entrance, incidentally, was a gift from the French capital's transit commission. ✉ *Rue Square Victoria, between rues Viger and St-Jacques, Vieux-Montréal* Ⓜ *Square-Victoria.*

DOWNTOWN & CHINATOWN

Rue Ste-Catherine—and the Métro line that runs under it—is the main cord that binds together the disparate, sprawling neighborhoods that comprise Montréal's **downtown,** or *centre-ville.* It's a long, boisterous, sometimes seedy, and sometimes elegant street that runs from rue Claremont in Westmount to rue d'Iberville in the east end. The downtown stretch—usually clogged with traffic and lined with department stores, boutiques, bars, restaurants, strip clubs, amusement arcades, theaters, cinemas, art galleries, bookstores, and even a few churches—is considerably shorter, running from avenue Atwater to boulevard St-Laurent, where downtown morphs into the Latin Quarter and the Village, the center of Montréal's gay and lesbian community.

But vibrant as the street is, much of the downtown action happens on such cross streets as rues Crescent, Bishop, de la Montagne, and Peel, which are packed with some of the district's best clubs, restaurants, and boutiques. If you're looking for a little nighttime excitement, you won't find a livelier block in the city than the stretch of rue Crescent between rue Ste-Catherine and boulevard de Maisonneuve.

Walk even farther north on rue Crescent to the lower slopes of Mont-Royal and you come to what used to be the most exclusive neighborhood in Canada—the Golden Square Mile. During the boom years of the mid-1800s, the families who lived in the area—most of them Scottish and Protestant—controlled about 70% of the country's wealth. Their

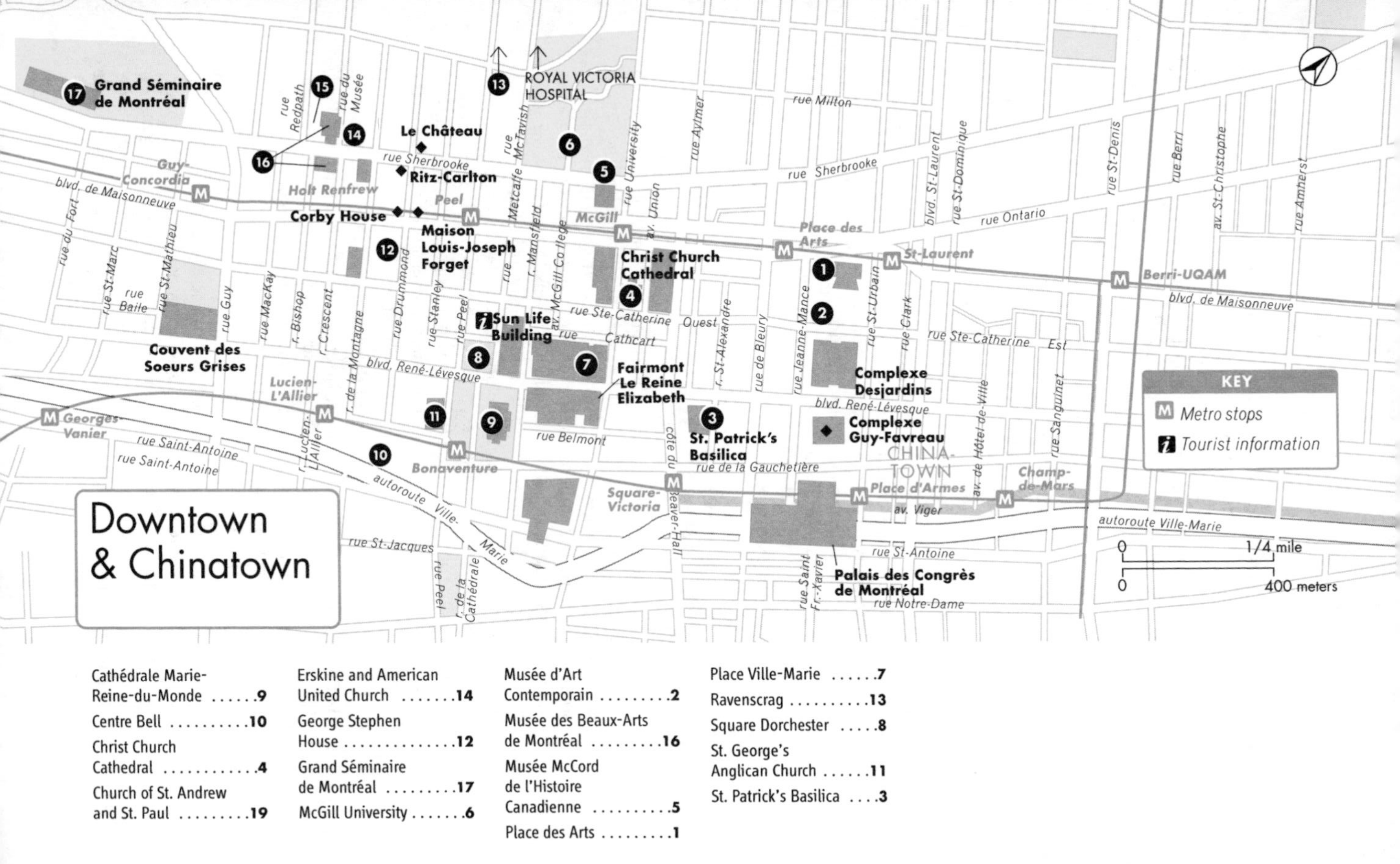

Cathédrale Marie-Reine-du-Monde 9
Centre Bell 10
Christ Church Cathedral 4
Church of St. Andrew and St. Paul 19
Erskine and American United Church 14
George Stephen House 12
Grand Séminaire de Montréal 17
McGill University 6
Musée d'Art Contemporain 2
Musée des Beaux-Arts de Montréal 16
Musée McCord de l'Histoire Canadienne 5
Place des Arts 1
Place Ville-Marie 7
Ravenscrag 13
Square Dorchester 8
St. George's Anglican Church 11
St. Patrick's Basilica 3

baronial homes and handsome churches covered the mountain north of rue Sherbrooke roughly between avenue Côte-des-Neiges and rue University. Incidentally, the descendants of those old families always call the neighborhood simply the Square Mile, and sneer at the extra adjective. Many of the old homes are gone—replaced by high-rises or modern town houses—but there are still plenty of architectural treasures for you to admire, even if most of them are now foreign consulates or university institutes.

At the other end of the downtown area is **Chinatown,** an 18-block area between boulevard René-Lévesque and avenue Viger to the north and south, and near rue de Bleury and avenue Hôtel de Ville on the west and east. Chinese people first came to Montréal in large numbers after 1880, following the construction of the transcontinental railroad. Their legacy is a shrinking but lively neighborhood of mainly Chinese and Southeast Asian restaurants, food stores, and gift shops.

Main Attractions

9 **Cathédrale Marie-Reine-du-Monde** (Mary Queen of the World Cathedral). When Bishop Ignace Bourget (1799–1885) decided to build his cathedral in the heart of the city's Protestant-dominated commercial quarter, many fellow Catholics thought he was crazy. But the bishop was determined to assert the Church's authority—and its loyalty to Rome—in the British-ruled city. So he built a quarter-scale replica of St. Peter's Basilica, complete with a magnificent reproduction of Bernini's ornate baldachin (canopy) over the main altar and an ornately coffered ceiling. Bourget didn't live to see the cathedral dedicated in 1894, but his tomb holds place of honor among those of his successors in the burial chapel on the east side of the nave. ✉ *1085 rue de la Cathédrale (enter through main doors on blvd. René-Lévesque), Downtown* ☎ *514/866–1661* 🌐 *www.cathedralecatholiquedemontreal.org* 🎫 *Free* 🕒 *Weekdays 6:30 AM–6:30 PM, Sat. 7 AM–6:30 PM, Sun. 7 AM–6:30 PM* Ⓜ *Bonaventure or Peel.*

4 **Christ Church Cathedral.** The gargoyles and Gothic doors of Montréal's Anglican (Episcopalian) cathedral might look like a welcome break in the unrelenting strip of shops and department stores lining rue Ste-Catherine, but in a way it's just an illusion. The church actually sits on top of **Les Promenades de la Cathédrale,** a major downtown mall that was constructed in 1988. The builders had to mount the church on pillars while they dug out the ground underneath it. But still, if you're looking for a little bit of England and a little spiritual uplift, Christ Church has both. Built in 1859, it's modeled on Snettisham Parish Church in Norfolk, England, with some distinctly Canadian touches. The steeple, for example, is made with aluminum plates molded to simulate stone, and inside, the Gothic arches are crowned with carvings of the types of foliage growing on Mont-Royal when the church was built. The stained-glass windows behind the main altar, installed in

SAVVY IN THE CITY

You can skate all year round at the Atrium le Mille de la Gauchetière in the office tower behind Cathédrale Marie-Reine-du-Monde. Phone 514/395–0555 for information.

CLOSE UP

The Other "Down" Town

WHEN PLACE VILLE-MARIE, the cruciform skyscraper designed by I. M. Pei, opened in the heart of downtown in 1962, the tallest structure of the time also signaled the beginning of Montréal's subterranean city. Montrealers were skeptical that anyone would want to shop or even walk around in the new "down" town, but more than four decades later, they can't live without it. About half a million people use the 30-km (19-mi) underground pedestrian network daily. The tunnels link 10 Métro stations, seven hotels, two hundred restaurants, seventeen hundred boutiques, and sixty office buildings—not to mention movie theaters, concert halls, convention complexes, the Bell Centre, two universities and a college, and subway, commuter rail, and bus stations. Montrealers who live in one of more than 2,000 apartments connected to the Underground City can pop out to buy a liter of milk on a February day and never have to change out of shirtsleeves and house slippers.

Most of the Underground City parallels the Métro lines. The six-block sector of continuous shopping between La Baie (east of the McGill station) and Les Cours Montréal (west of the Peel station) is perhaps the densest portion of the network. Montréal was ahead of the curve in requiring all construction in the Métro system to include an art component, resulting in such dramatic works as Frédéric Back's mural of the history of music in Place-des-Arts and the dramatically swirling stained-glass windows by Marcelle Ferron in Champs-de-Mars. The art nouveau entrance to the Square Victoria station, a gift from the city of Paris, is the only original piece of Hector Guimard's architectural-design work outside the City of Light.

—By Patricia Harris and David Lyon

the early 1920s as a memorial to the dead of World War I, show scenes from the life of Christ. On the wall just above and to the left of the pulpit is the Coventry Cross; it's made of nails taken from the ruins of Britain's Coventry Cathedral, destroyed by bombing in 1940. But the uplift doesn't stop with the architecture. The cathedral offers a series of free noontime concerts and organ recitals that are very popular with downtowners and visitors alike. ✉ *635 rue Ste-Catherine Ouest, Downtown* ☎ *514/843–6577* 🌐 *www.montreal.anglican.org/cathedral* 🎫 *Free* 🕑 *Mon–Sat 8–5:15, Sun. 10–5:15* Ⓜ *McGill.*

★ ❷ **Musée d'Art Contemporain** (Museum of Contemporary Art). If you have a taste for pastoral landscapes and formal portraits, you might want to stick with the Musée des Beaux-Arts. But for a walk on the wild side of art, see what you can make of the jagged splashes of color that cover the canvases of the "Automatistes," as Québec's rebellious artists of the 1930s styled themselves. Their works form the core of this museum's collection of 5,000 pieces. One of the leaders of the movement, Jean-Paul Riopelle (1923–2002), often tossed his brushes and palette knives aside and just squeezed the paint directly on to the canvas—sometimes several tubes at a time. In 1948, Riopelle and his friends fired the first

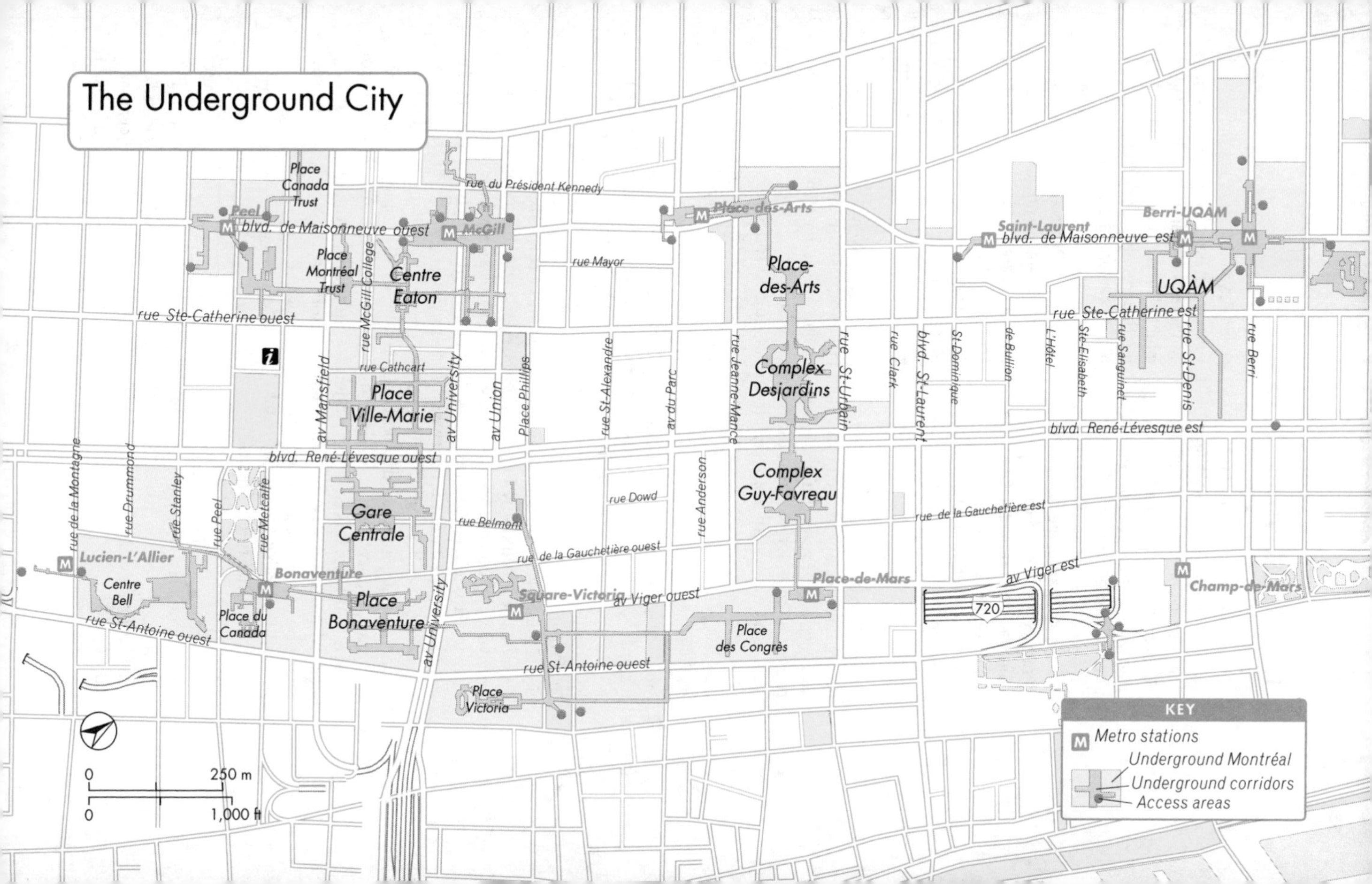
The Underground City
Place Canada Trust
rue du Président Kennedy
Peel
blvd. de Maisonneuve ouest
McGill
Place Montréal Trust
rue McGill College
Centre Eaton
rue Ste-Catherine ouest
rue Cathcart
Place Ville-Marie
av Mansfield
av University
av Union
Place Phillips
rue St-Alexandre
av du Parc
rue Jeanne-Mance
Place-des-Arts
rue Mayor
Complex Desjardins
rue St-Urbain
rue Clark
blvd. St-Laurent
St-Dominique
de Bullion
L'Hôtel
Ste-Elisabeth
rue Sanguinet
rue St-Denis
rue Berri
Saint-Laurent
blvd. de Maisonneuve est
Berri-UQÀM
UQÀM
rue Ste-Catherine est
blvd. René-Lévesque est
blvd. René-Lévesque ouest
rue de la Montagne
rue Drummond
rue Stanley
rue Peel
rue Metcalfe
Gare Centrale
rue Belmont
rue Dowd
rue Anderson
Complex Guy-Favreau
rue de la Gauchetière est
rue de la Gauchetière ouest
Lucien-L'Allier
Centre Bell
Bonaventure
Place du Canada
Place Bonaventure
rue St-Antoine ouest
Square-Victoria
av Viger ouest
Place-de-Mars
av Viger est
720
Champ-de-Mars
Place des Congrès
Place Victoria
0
250 m
0
1,000 ft
KEY
Metro stations
Underground Montréal
Underground corridors
Access areas

UNDERGROUND CITY TIPS

To get the optimum use of the whole network of tunnels, shops, and Métro lines that make up the Underground City, buy a Métro pass. Daily and weekly passes are available. Start at Place Ville-Marie. This was the first link in the system and is still part of the main hub. From here you could cover most of the main sites—from the Centre Bell to Place des Arts—without ever coming up and without having to take the Métro. But the network is so large, you'll want to use the subway system to save time, energy, and wear and tear on your feet. You might also want to explore some of the Underground City's more remote centers—the Grande Bibliothèque or Westmount Square, for example. Remember: it's easy to get lost. There are no landmarks and routes are seldom direct, so keep your eyes on the signs (a Métro map helps), and if you start to feel panicky, come up for air.

shot in Québec's Quiet Revolution by signing *Le Refus Global,* a manifesto that renounced the political and religious establishment of the day and revolutionized art in the province. The museum often has weekend programs and art workshops, some of which are geared toward children, and almost all are free. Hours for guided tours vary. ✉ *185 rue Ste-Catherine Ouest, Downtown* ☎ *514/847–6226* 🌐 *www.macm.org* 🎫 *C$8, free Wed. after 6 PM* ⏲ *Tues. and Thurs.–Sun. 11–6, Wed. 11–9* Ⓜ *Place-des-Arts.*

16 Fodor's Choice ★ **Musée des Beaux-Arts de Montréal** (Montréal Museum of Fine Arts). Canada's oldest museum has been accumulating art from all over the world since 1860. Its permanent collection includes everyone from Rembrandt to Renoir, and not surprisingly, one of the best assemblies of Canadian art anywhere, with works by such luminaries as Paul Kane, the Group of Seven, and Paul-Émile Borduas. You can trace the country's history from New France to New Age through the museum's decorative art, painting, and sculpture. But it's not all serious: in 2001, the museum absorbed the Musée des Arts Décoratifs, so you can also take a look at some fanciful bentwood furniture designed by Frank Gehry, a marvelous collection of 18th-century English porcelain, and 3,000—count 'em—Japanese snuffboxes collected by, of all people, Georges Clémenceau, France's prime minister during World War I. All this is housed in two buildings linked by an underground tunnel—the older, neoclassical **Michal and Renata Hornstein Pavilion,** on the north side of rue Sherbrooke, and the glittering, glass-fronted **Jean-Noël-Desmarais Pavilion,** across the street. The museum also has a gift shop, a bookstore, a restaurant, a cafeteria, and a gallery where you can buy or even rent paintings by local artists. ✉ *1380 rue Sherbrooke Ouest, Square Mile* ☎ *514/285–2000* 🌐 *www.mmfa.*

WORD OF MOUTH

"The Metro is really easy to navigate in Montréal. You will be able to get a map at all Metro booths."

—Jojonana

qc.ca 🎫 *Permanent collection free, special exhibits C$15, C$7.50 Wed.* ⏲ *Mon., Tues., Thurs., and Fri. 11–6, Wed. 11–9, weekends 10–6* Ⓜ *Guy-Concordia.*

★ ❺ **Musée McCord de l'Histoire Canadienne** (McCord Museum of Canadian History). David Ross McCord (1844–1930) was a wealthy pack rat with a passion for anything that had to do with Montréal and its history. His collection of paintings, costumes, toys, tools, drawings, and housewares provides a glimpse of what city life was like for all classes in the 19th century. If you're interested in the lifestyles of the elite, however, you'll love the photographs that William Notman (1826–91) took of the rich at play. One series portrays members of the posh Montréal Athletic Association posing in snowshoes on the slopes of Mont-Royal, all decked out in Hudson Bay coats and woolen hats. Each of the hundreds of portraits was shot individually in a studio and then painstakingly mounted on a picture of the snowy mountain to give the impression of a winter outing. There are guided tours (call for schedule), a reading room, a documentation center, a gift shop, a bookstore, and a café. ✉ *690 rue Sherbrooke Ouest, Square Mile* ☎ *514/398–7100* 🌐 *www.mccord-museum.qc.ca* 🎫 *C$10* ⏲ *June 25–early Sept., Mon. and weekends 10–5, Tues.–Fri. 10–6; early Sept.–June 24, Tues.–Fri. 10–6, weekends 10–5* Ⓜ *McGill.*

★ ❸ **St. Patrick's Basilica.** St. Pat's—as most of its parishioners call it—is to Montréal's Anglophone Catholics what the Basilique Notre-Dame is to their French-speaking brethren—the mother church and a monument to faith and courage. The church, built in 1847, is also one of the purest examples of the Gothic Revival style in Canada with a high vaulted ceiling glowing with green and gold mosaics. The tall, slender columns are actually pine logs lashed together and decorated to look like marble, so that if you stand in one of the back corners and look toward the altar you really do feel as if you're peering at the sacred through a grove of trees. One of the joys of visiting the place is that you'll probably be the only tourist there, so you'll have plenty of time to check out the old pulpit and the huge lamp decorated with six 6-foot-tall angels hanging over the main altar. And if you're named after some obscure saint like Scholastica or Aeden of Fleury, you can search for your namesake's portrait among the 170 painted panels on the walls of the nave. ✉ *460 blvd. René-Lévesque Ouest, Downtown* ☎ *514/866–7379* 🌐 *www.stpatricksmtl.ca* 🎫 *Free* ⏲ *Daily 8:30–6* Ⓜ *Square-Victoria.*

NEED A BREAK?

On the west side of St. Patrick's Basilica (✉ 460 blvd. René-Lévesque Ouest, Downtown Ⓜ Square-Victoria) is a small but delightful green space with picnic tables and shady trees. The Van Houtte coffee shop in the nearby office tower has a patio that opens on to the park, so refreshments are available.

Also Worth Seeing

❿ **Centre Bell.** There was a time when the Montréal Canadiens almost seemed to own the National Hockey League's Stanley Cup. After each winning season in the 1960s and '70s, city hall would put out a press release announcing the "Stanley Cup parade will follow the usual route." Those days are long gone. *Les Glorieux* (or "the glorious ones"), as the fans call the team, haven't won a cup since 1993, and the superstitious blame it on their 1996 move from the hallowed Forum to the brown-brick Centre Bell. Despite a dearth of championship seasons, the Canadiens remain the city's favorite professional sports team. Guided tours usually include a visit to the Canadiens' dressing room. ✉ *1260 rue de la Gauchetière Ouest, Downtown* ☎ *514/925–2582 tours, 514/925–5656 tickets* 🎫 *Tour C$8* ⏲ *Tours daily at 11:15 and 2:45 in English, 9:45 and 1:15 in French* Ⓜ *Bonaventure.*

⓳ **Church of St. Andrew and St. Paul.** If you want to see the inside of Montréal's largest Presbyterian church—sometimes affectionately called the A&P—you'll have to call the secretary and make arrangements, or simply show up for Sunday services. Either way, it's worth the effort, if only to see the glorious stained-glass window of the risen Christ that dominates the sanctuary behind the white-stone communion table. It's a memorial to members of the Royal Highland Regiment of Canada (the Black Watch) who were killed in World War I. One of the advantages of showing up for the Sunday service is that you get a chance to hear the church's fine, 6,911-pipe Cassavant organ and its 50-voice choir. ✉ *Rue Sherbrooke Ouest at rue Redpath, Square Mile* ☎ *514/843–3431* 🌐 *www.standrewstpaul.com* 🎫 *Free* ⏲ *Sun. service at 11 AM, other times by arrangement* Ⓜ *Guy-Concordia.*

⓮ **Erskine and American United Church.** If you love Tiffany glass, go to the Erskine and American's avenue du Musée entrance, ring the bell, and ask politely—beg if you have to—to be allowed in to the side chapel where you can bask in the light streaming through 24 of Louis Comfort Tiffany's windows—the largest collection of them outside the United States. "Heavenly" is not too strong a word. The Musée des Beaux-Arts de Montréal is in the process of buying the church as an exhibition space for religious art, but until that happens, you'll have to make your own arrangements. ✉ *Rue Sherbrooke Ouest at av. du Musée, Square Mile* ☎ *514/849–3286* 🎫 *Free* ⏲ *Sun. service at 11 AM, other times by arrangement* Ⓜ *Guy-Concordia.*

OFF THE BEATEN PATH

EXPORAIL – You can rattle around Canada's largest railway museum in a vintage tram specially built in the 1950s for sightseeing tours in Montréal when the city still had a streetcar system. The museum has more than 150 locomotives, but if you're a steam buff, you won't want to miss CPR 5935, the largest steam locomotive built in Canada, and CNR 4100, the most powerful in the British Empire when it was built in 1924. To see how the rich and powerful traveled, take a look at Sir William Van Horne's luxurious private car. Of special interest to the kids will be the car that served as a mobile classroom. The museum is south of the city in the town of St-Constant. On several summer Saturdays, rail buffs can take the Museum Express, which leaves from the Lucien-L'Allier suburban train station, in the west end of Centre Bell. Trains depart at 11 AM and return at 4 PM. ✉ *110 rue St-*

SAVVY IN THE CITY

There are 4,500 cabs cruising the streets of Montréal, so finding one in the downtown core is usually as easy as holding up your hand (except on Christmas Eve, of course).

Pierre, St-Constant J5A 1G7 ☎ 450/632–2410 🌐 www.exporail.org 🎫 C$12, with Museum Express excursion C$32 ⏲ Mid-May–early Sept., daily 10–6; early Sept.–Oct., Wed.–Sun. 10–5; Nov.–mid-May, weekends 10–5.

⓬ **George Stephen House.** Scottish-born Sir George Stephen (1829–1921) was in his way as grandiose as Donald Trump is today. He founded the Canadian Pacific Railway, and in 1882, he spent C$600,000—an almost unimaginable sum at the time—to build a suitable home for himself and his family. He imported artisans from all over the world to panel its ceilings with Cuban mahogany, Indian lemon tree, and English oak and to cover its walls in marble, onyx, and gold. It's now a private club, but you can get a glimpse of all this grandeur on Saturday evening when the dining room is open to the public for dinner (C$30 for three courses, C$70 for seven) and on Sunday when it's open for brunch (C$42, including a guided tour). The dining room is closed from July to mid-September. *✉ 1440 rue Drummond, Square Mile ☎ 514/849–7338 🌐 www.clubmountstephen.net ✍ Reservations essential Ⓜ Peel or Guy-Concordia.*

⓱ **Grand Séminaire de Montréal.** Education goes way back at the Grand Séminaire. In the mid-1600s, St. Marguerite Bourgeoys used one of the two stone towers in the garden as a school for First Nations (Native American) girls while she and her nuns lived in the other. The 1860 seminary buildings behind the towers are now used by men studying for the priesthood. In summer there are free guided tours of the towers, the extensive gardens, and the college's beautiful Romanesque chapel. The chapel is open for Sunday mass from September through June. *✉ 2065 rue Sherbrooke Ouest, Square Mile ☎ 514/935–1169 Ext. 239 📠 514/935–5497 🌐 www.gsdm.qc.ca 🎫 By donation ⏲ Guided tours June–Aug., Tues.–Sat. at 1 and 3 PM; mass Sept.–June, Sun. at 10:30 AM Ⓜ Guy-Concordia.*

❻ **McGill University.** Merchant and fur trader James McGill would probably be horrified to know that the university that he helped found in 1828 has developed an international reputation as one of North America's best party schools. The administration isn't too happy about it, either. But there's no real cause for alarm. McGill is still one of the two or three best English-language universities in Canada, and certainly one of the prettiest. Its campus is an island of grass and trees in a sea of traffic and skyscrapers. If you take the time to stroll up the drive that leads from the Greek Revival Roddick Gates to the austere neoclassical Arts Building, keep an eye out to your right for the life-size statue of McGill himself, hurrying across campus clutching his tricorn hat. If you have an hour or so, drop into the temple-like **Redpath Museum of Natural History** to browse its eclectic collection of dinosaur bones, old coins, African art, and shrunken heads. *✉ 859 rue Sherbrooke Ouest, Square Mile ☎ 514/398–4455, 514/*

> **SAVVY IN THE CITY**
>
> If you're traveling alone at night by bus, you can by law, ask to be dropped off anywhere between stops. Who said chivalry was dead?

398–6655 tours, 514/398–4086 museum ⊕ *www.mcgill.ca* 🎫 *Free* ⏲ *Museum weekdays 9–5, Sun. 1–5 (June–Aug., closed Fri.)* Ⓜ *McGill.*

NEED A BREAK?

Sit in the shade of one of McGill University's (⊠ 859 rue Sherbrooke Ouest, Square Mile ☎ 514/398-4455 Ⓜ McGill) 100-year-old maples and read a chapter or two of a Montréal classic like Hugh MacLennan's *Two Solitudes*, or just let the world drift by.

6 **Place des Arts.** Step backstage at Place des Arts—Montréal's primary performing-arts center—and you can learn the secrets behind the magic of modern theater. The experienced guide might even let you try your hand at lighting a stage or raising a curtain. The 90-minute tours for groups of 15 to 30 take in all five of the complex's theaters and auditoriums. Call ahead to schedule a tour. ⊠ *175 rue Ste-Catherine Ouest, Downtown* ☎ *514/842–2112 tickets, 514/285–4270 information, 514/285–4200 tours* ⊕ *www.pda.qc.ca* 🎫 *C$8.50 per person for groups of 15–25, C$7.50 per person for groups of 25–30* ⏲ *By appointment only* Ⓜ *Place-des-Arts.*

7 **Place Ville-Marie.** The cross-shape 1962 office tower was Montréal's first modern skyscraper; the mall complex underneath it was the first link in the Underground City. The wide expanse of the building's plaza, just upstairs from the mall, makes a fine place to relax with coffee or a snack from the food court below. Benches, potted greenery, and fine views of Mont-Royal make it popular with walkers, tourists, and office workers. ⊠ *Bordered by blvd. René-Lévesque and rues Mansfield, Cathcart, and University, Downtown* ☎ *514/866–6666* Ⓜ *McGill or Bonaventure.*

13 **Ravenscrag.** If you're up for a bit of a climb, walk up rue Peel to avenue des Pins for a look at a grand example of the kind of palaces Montréal's industrial barons built for themselves in the 19th century. From Ravenscrag's lofty perch, Sir Hugh Allan—who pretty much controlled Canada's transatlantic transport—could watch his ships come and go. The 60-room mansion, which looks like Tuscany dropped onto the slopes of Mont-Royal, is one of the finest bits of neo-Renaissance architecture in North America. ⊠ *1025 av. des Pins, Square Mile* Ⓜ *Peel.*

8 **Square Dorchester.** On sunny summer days, you can join the office workers, store clerks, and downtown shoppers who gather in Square Dorchester to eat lunch under the trees and perhaps listen to an open-air concert. If there are no vacant benches or picnic tables, you can still find a place to sit on the steps at the base of the dramatic monument to the dead of the Boer War. Other statues honor Scottish poet Robert Burns (1759–96) and Sir Wilfrid Laurier (1841–1919), Canada's first French-speaking prime minister. ⊠ *Bordered by blvd. René-Lévesque and rues Peel, Metcalfe, and McTavish, Downtown* Ⓜ *Bonaventure or Peel.*

11 **St. George's Anglican Church.** St. George's is possibly the prettiest Anglican (Episcopalian) church in Montréal. Step into its dim, candle-scented interior and you'll feel you've been transported to some prosperous market town in East Anglia. The double hammer-beam roof, the rich stained-glass windows, and the Lady Chapel on the east side of the main altar all add to the effect. It certainly seems a world away from Centre Bell,

the modern temple to professional hockey just across the street. On the other hand, several prominent National Hockey League players and game announcers regularly drop in for a few minutes of quiet meditation before joining the action on the ice. ✉ *1101 rue Stanley, Downtown* ☎ *514/866–7113* 🌐 *www.st-georges.org* *Free* ⏲ *Tues.–Sun. 9–4; Sun. services at 9 and 10:30* AM Ⓜ *Bonaventure.*

THE PLATEAU & ENVIRONS

The Plateau—as it's more commonly called these days—is still home to a vibrant Portuguese community, but much of the housing originally built for factory workers has been bought up and renovated by artists, performers, and academics eager to find houses that are also close to all the action. The **Quartier Latin** or the **Latin Quarter** just south of the Plateau has been drawing the young since the 1700s, when Université de Montréal students gave the area its name. Both the Latin Quarter and the Plateau have rows of French and ethnic restaurants, bistros, coffee shops, designer boutiques, antiques shops, and art galleries. When night falls, these streets are full of omnilingual hordes—young and not so young, rich and poor, established and still studying.

The gentrification of the Plateau inevitably pushed up rents and drove students, immigrant families, and single young graduates just starting out farther north to **Mile-End,** an old working-class neighborhood that is now full of inexpensive restaurants and funky little shops selling handicrafts and secondhand clothes. Farther north is **Little Italy,** which is still home base to Montréal's enormous Italian community. Families of Italian descent live all over the greater-Montréal area now, but many come back here every week or so to shop, eat out, or visit family and friends.

The lively strip of rue Ste-Catherine running east of the Latin Quarter is the backbone of the **Village**—Montréal's main gay community. Its restaurants, antiques shops (on rue Amherst), and bars make it a popular destination for visitors of all persuasions.

Many of the older residences in these neighborhoods have graceful wrought-iron balconies and twisting staircases that are typical of Montréal. They were built that way for practical reasons. The buildings are what Montrealers call duplexes or triplexes—that is, two or three residences stacked one atop another. To save interior space, the stairs to reach the upper floors were put outside. The stairs and balconies, treacherous in winter, are often full of families and couples gossiping, picnicking, and partying come summer. If Montrealers tell you they spend the summer in Balconville, they mean they don't have the money or the time to leave town and won't get any farther than their balconies.

Main Attractions

❷ **Boulevard St-Laurent.** A walk along boulevard St-Laurent is like a walk through Montréal's cultural history. The shops and restaurants, synagogues and churches, that line the 10-block stretch north of rue Sherbrooke reflect the various waves of immigrants who have called it home. Keep your eyes open and you'll see Jewish delis, Hungarian sausage shops,

WHAT'S FREE WHEN?

There's never a charge to visit any of Montréal's numerous historic churches, and some, like **St. Joseph's Oratory** (✉ 3800 Queen Mary, Côte-des-Neiges Ⓜ Côte-des-Neiges), one of the world's most visited shrines, offer free guided tours weekdays at 1 PM and 4 PM.

During the last weekend in May, admission to every museum in Montréal is free. A complimentary bus service leaving from the Info-Tourist office at 1001 Dorchester Square will shuttle you from one museum to another, but be prepared for long waits. Also, many museums offer free admission to their permanent exhibits year-round, including the **Redpath** (✉ 859 Sherbrooke Ouest ⏲ Weekdays 9–5, Sun. 1–5, closed Fri. in summer) and the **Montréal Firefighters Museum** (✉ 5100 St-Laurent ⏲ Sun. 1:30–4:30 PM). The **McCord Museum of Canadian History** (✉ 690 Sherbrooke Ouest) offers free admission between 10 AM and noon the first Saturday of every month.

Keep in mind that it's free to skate on any of the municipally run outdoor skating rinks—including Beaver Lake in Parc Mont-Royal—and that while the municipal pools are technically only free for residents, there's no admission to take a dip on weekdays.

Chinese grocery stores, Portuguese favelas, Italian coffee bars, Greek restaurants, Vietnamese sandwich shops, and Peruvian snack bars. You'll also spot some of the city's trendiest restaurants and nightclubs. The first immigrants to move into the area in the 1880s were Jews escaping pogroms in Eastern Europe. It was they who called the street "the Main," as in Main Street—a nickname that endures to this day. Even Francophone Montrealers sometimes call it "Le Main." Ⓜ *St-Laurent, Sherbrooke, or Mont-Royal.*

NEED A BREAK?

Wilensky's Light Lunch (✉ 34 av. Fairmount Ouest, Plateau Mont-Royal ☎ 514/ 271-0247 Ⓜ Laurier) hasn't changed its decor, menu, or 'tude since 1932. Stop in for bologna on a kaiser roll and a cherry Coke. The food's cheap and the nostalgia's free.

❹ **Chapelle Notre-Dame-de-Lourdes** (Our Lady of Lourdes Chapel). Artist and architect Napoléon Bourassa called the Chapelle Notre-Dame-des-Lourdes *l'oeuvre de mes amours,* or a labor of love—and it shows. He designed the little Byzantine-style building himself and set about decorating it with the exuberance of an eight-year-old making a Mother's Day card. He covered the walls with murals and encrusted the altar and pillars with gilt and ornamental carving. It's not Montréal's biggest monument to the Virgin Mary, but it's the

SAVVY IN THE CITY

Boulevard St-Laurent divides Montréal into western and eastern halves. Street numbers for east-west streets start at St-Laurent.

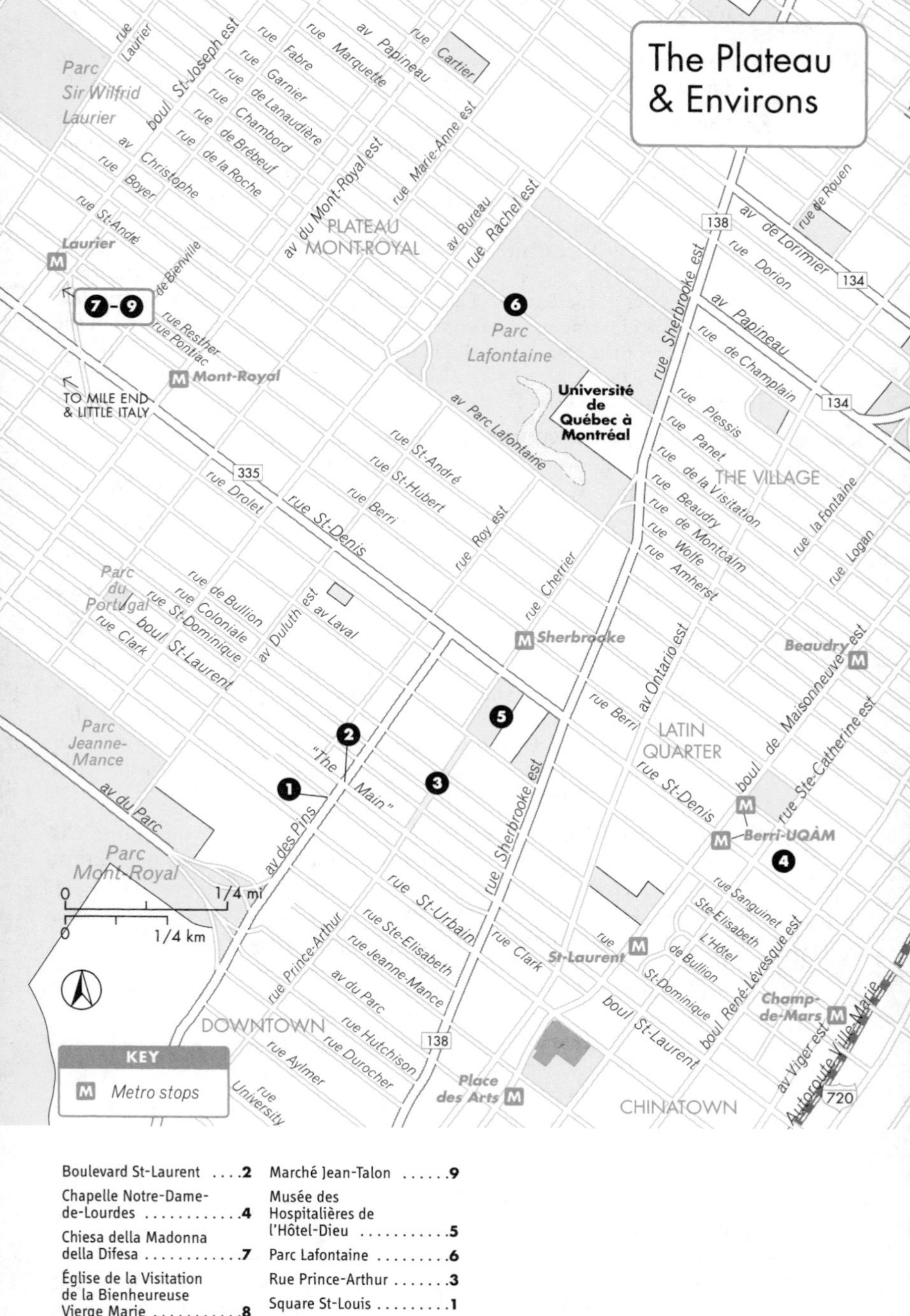

Boulevard St-Laurent 2
Chapelle Notre-Dame-de-Lourdes 4
Chiesa della Madonna della Difesa 7
Église de la Visitation de la Bienheureuse Vierge Marie 8
Marché Jean-Talon 9
Musée des Hospitalières de l'Hôtel-Dieu 5
Parc Lafontaine 6
Rue Prince-Arthur 3
Square St-Louis 1

most unabashedly sentimental. ✉ *430 rue Ste-Catherine Est, Latin Quarter* 🎫 *Free* ⏲ *Mon.–Sat. 7:30–6, Sun. 9–6:30* Ⓜ *Berri-UQAM.*

7 **Chiesa della Madonna della Difesa.** If you look up at the cupola behind the main altar of Little Italy's most famous church, you'll spot Montréal's most infamous piece of ecclesial portraiture. Yes, indeed, that lantern-jaw fellow on horseback who looks so pleased with himself is Benito Mussolini, the dictator who led Italy into World War II on the wrong side. In fairness, though, the mural, by Guido Nincheri (1885–1973), was completed long before the war and commemorates the signing of the Lateran Pact with Pope Pius XI, one of Il Duce's few lasting achievements. The controversy shouldn't distract you from the beauties of the rest of the richly decorated church. ✉ *6800 av. Henri-Julien, Little Italy* ☎ *514/277–6522* 🎫 *Free* ⏲ *Daily 10 AM–6 PM* Ⓜ *Beaubien or Jean-Talon.*

OFF THE BEATEN PATH

ÉGLISE DE LA VISITATION DE LA BIENHEUREUSE VIERGE MARIE – You have to ride the Métro to its northern terminus at the Henri-Bourassa station, and then walk for 15–20 minutes through some pretty ordinary neighborhoods to reach the Church of the Visitation of the Blessed Virgin Mary, but it's worth the trek to see the oldest extant church on the
8 island. Its stone walls were raised in the 1750s, and the beautifully proportioned Palladian front was added in 1850. Decorating lasted from 1764 until 1837, with stunning results. The altar and the pulpit are as ornate as wedding cakes but still delicate. The church's most notable treasure is a rendering of the Visitation attributed to Pierre Mignard, a painter in the 17th-century court of Louis XIV. Parkland surrounds the church, and the nearby Îles de la Visitation (reachable by footbridge) make for a very good walk. ✉ *1847 blvd. Gouin Est, Sault-au-Récollet* ☎ *514/388–4050* 🎫 *Free* ⏲ *Daily 10–11:30 and 1–4* Ⓜ *Henri-Bourassa.*

9 **Marché Jean-Talon.** If you're trying to stick to a diet, stay away: the smells of grilling sausages, roasting chestnuts, and fresh pastries will almost certainly crack your resolve. And if they don't, there are dozens of tiny shops full of Québec cheeses, Lebanese sweets, country pâtés, local wines, and handmade chocolates that will. Less threatening to the waistline are the huge mounds of peas, beans, apples, carrots, pears, garlic, and other produce on sale at the open-air stalls. On Saturday mornings in particular it feels as if all Montréal has come out to shop. ✉ *7015 rue Casgrain, Little Italy* ☎ *514/277–1588* Ⓜ *Jean-Talon.*

SAVVY IN THE CITY

For lunch-on-the-run in Little Italy: try a freshly barbecued spicy sausage from one of the stands in Marché Jean-Talon.

3 **Rue Prince-Arthur.** In the 1960s, rue Prince-Arthur was the Haight-Ashbury of Montréal, full of shops selling leather vests, tie-dyed T-shirts, recycled clothes, and drug paraphernalia. It still retains a little of that raffish attitude, but it's much tamer and more commercial these days.

CLOSE UP

Mile-End

HISTORICALLY THE HOME TO MONTRÉAL'S working-class Jewish community, in recent years the Mile-End section of the Plateau Mont-Royal has become one of the hippest neighborhoods in town. By day it's a great place to take a stroll or simply hang out on the terraces of its numerous cafés to watch the colorful mix of locals—artsy bohemians, Hasidic Jews, Greeks, and rock and rollers—pass by. The closest Metró to Mile-End is Laurier.

Lingering testaments to the still considerable Jewish population include **Wilensky's** (✉ 34 Fairmount Ouest), whose highly celebrated salami sandwiches were immortalized in Mordecai Richler's novel *The Apprenticeship of Duddy Kravitz,* as well as the **Fairmount** (✉ 74 Fairmount Ouest) and **St-Viateur** (✉ 263 St-Viateur Ouest) bagel emporiums. Baked in wood ovens, Montréal's bagels are as unique, if not as famous as, its smoked meat sandwiches, and locals will insist you've never really eaten a bagel until you've tried one from either of these culinary institutions.

At night, Mile-End comes alive with the sound of rock and roll, with **Casa del Popolo** (✉ 873 St-Laurent), the **Playhouse** (✉ 5656 Park Av.), the **Main Hall** (✉ 5390 St-Laurent), and the **Green Room** (✉ 5386 St-Laurent), all hosting local and international indie bands most nights of the week. Montréal's indie music scene has been booming for several years now, and, if you spend a little time in any of these venues you might get a glimpse as to why the *New York Times* and *Spin* magazine (among others) have all recently championed Montréal as "the new Seattle," i.e., the latest mecca for aspiring indie rock sensations. It's also, without question, the best neighborhood in town to find reasonably priced Greek food, with **le Coin Grec** (✉ 4903 Park Av.) and **Arahova** (✉ 256 St-Viateur Ouest) being choice favorites among discerning Mile-End-ers.

The blocks between avenue Laval and boulevard St-Laurent are a pedestrian mall, and the hippie shops have metamorphosed into inexpensive Greek, Vietnamese, Italian, Polish, and Chinese restaurants and neighborhood bars. So grab a table, order a coffee or an *apéro,* and watch the passing parade. Ⓜ *Sherbrooke.*

❶ **Square St-Louis.** The prosperous bourgeois families who built their comfortable homes around Square St-Louis's fountain and trees in the late 1870s would probably be dismayed to see the kind of people who congregate in their little park these days. It's difficult to walk through the place without dodging a skateboarder or a panhandler, or without being offered a sip of something from a bottle in a paper bag. But they're generally a friendly bunch, and the square is still worth a visit just to see the elegant Second Empire–style homes that surround it. ✉ *Bordered by av. Laval and rue St-Denis between rue Sherbrooke Est and av. des Pins Est, Latin Quarter* Ⓜ *Sherbrooke.*

CLOSE UP

Little Italy

AT FIRST GLANCE, you'll have a hard time differentiating Montréal's Little Italy from other working-class neighborhoods in the city's north end–a few little parks, a shopping strip, and rows of brick buildings with outdoor staircases and two or three flats each. But just glance at the gardens and you'll know where you are. Those tiny patches of soil full of tomato plants, fruit trees, and–wonder of wonders in this semifrozen city–grapevines, are a dead giveaway.

You'll see, hear, and smell plenty of other signs of the area's heritage, as well: the sausages and tins of olive oil in the windows of Milano's supermarket, the occasional Ferrari rumbling in the stalled traffic along rue Jean-Talon, the tang of pizza and sharp cheese, the Italian voices in the trattoria, and of course, the heady smell of espresso from the dozens of little cafés along rue Dante and boulevard St-Laurent.

The best time to visit the neighborhood is on the weekend, when hundreds of Italian-Canadians "come home" to visit family, to sip coffee or dine with friends, and to shop for produce and cheese at the Marché Jean-Talon. If you're lucky you'll spot a young couple getting married at the Madonna della Difesa church (whose frescoes include a portrait of Benito Mussolini).

Montréal's Italian community–at nearly a quarter of a million people–might have outgrown Little Italy, but those 30-odd blocks bounded by rues Jean-Talon, St-Zotique, Marconi, and Drolet remain its heart and soul.

Also Worth Seeing

❺ **Musée des Hospitalières de l'Hôtel-Dieu.** The nuns of the Religieuses Hospitalières de St-Joseph ran Montréal's Hôpital Hôtel-Dieu for more than 300 years until the province and the Université de Montréal took it over in the 1970s. The first sisters—girls of good families caught up in the religious fervor of the age—came to New France with Jeanne Mance in the mid-1600s to look after the poor, the sick, and the dying. The order's museum—tucked away in a corner of the hospital the nuns built but no longer run—captures the spirit of that age with a series of meticulously bilingual exhibits. Just reading the excerpts from the letters and diaries of those young women helps you to understand the zeal that drove them to abandon the comforts of home for the hardships of the colonies. The museum also traces the history of medicine and nursing in Montréal. ✉ *201 av. des Pins Ouest, Plateau Mont-Royal* ☎ *514/849–2919* 🌐 *www.museedeshospitalieres.qc.ca* 🎫 *C$6* ⏲ *Mid-June–mid-Oct., Tues.–Fri. 10–5, weekends 1–5; mid-Oct.–mid-June, Wed.–Sun. 1–5* Ⓜ *Sherbrooke.*

SAVVY IN THE CITY

Bargain-hunter alert: twice a year–in mid-June and at the end of August–the Main Madness street sale transforms boulevard St-Laurent into an open-air bazaar.

CLOSE UP

The Village

FORMERLY KNOWN AS THE GAY VILLAGE, the area bordering rue Ste-Catherine Est from Amherst to de Lorimier, and on the north-south axis from René-Lévesque to Sherbrooke, is a thriving part of town, replete with restaurants, bars, bathhouses, boutiques, and cafés. Montréal has one of the most vibrant gay communities in the world, widely supported by residents of this proudly liberal, open-minded city. In recent years, the municipal, federal, and provincial governments have taken it upon themselves to aggressively promote the Village and Montréal's gay-friendly climate as a reason for tourists to visit, including those who wish to wed. In recognition of the Village's importance to the city, the downtown borough of Ville-Marie hangs a rainbow flag in its council chambers, and the recently rebuilt entrance to the Beaudry Métro station, essentially the gateway to the neighborhood, is now adorned with rainbow pillars.

The best way to explore the area is on foot, getting off at the Beaudry Métro station and heading east along rue Ste-Catherine. No trip to the Village would be complete without stopping by **Le Drugstore** (✉ 1366 rue Ste-Catherine Est), the largest gay entertainment complex in the world, or **Cabaret Mado** (✉ 1115 rue Ste-Catherine Est), which, operated by legendary local drag queen Mado, regularly plays host to the city's swankiest drag entertainers.

❻ **Parc Lafontaine.** You could say that Parc Lafontaine is a microcosm of Montréal: the eastern half is French, with paths, gardens, and lawns laid out in geometric shapes; the western half is English, with meandering paths and irregularly shaped ponds that follow the natural contours of the land. In summer you can take advantage of bowling greens, tennis courts, an open-air theater (Théâtre de Verdure) where there are free arts events, and two artificial lakes with paddleboats. In winter one lake becomes a large skating rink. The park is named for Sir Louis-Hippolyte Lafontaine (1807–64), a pioneer of responsible government in Canada. His statue graces a plot on the park's southwestern edge. ✉ *3933 av. Parc Lafontaine, Plateau Mont-Royal* ☎ *514/872–9800* ⏲ *Daily 9 AM–10 PM* Ⓜ *Sherbrooke or Mont-Royal.*

MONT-ROYAL & ENVIRONS

Fodor's Choice ★

In geological terms, Mont-Royal is a mere bump—a plug of basaltlike rock that has been worn down by several ice ages to a mere 760 feet. But in the affections of Montrealers it's a Matterhorn. Without a trace of irony, they call it simply *la Montagne* or "the Mountain," and it's easy to see why it's so well loved. For Montrealers it's a refuge in the middle of the city, a semitamed wilderness you can get to by bus or, if you have the lungs for the climb, simply by walking. It's where you go to get away from it all—to walk, to jog, to ski, to feed the squirrels, and to admire the view—and sometimes to fall in love. And even when you can't get away, you can see the mountain glimmering beyond the skyscrapers and the high-rises—green in summer, gray and white in winter, and gold and crimson in fall.

The heart of all this is Parc Mont-Royal itself—nearly 500 acres of forests and meadows laid out by Frederick Law Olmsted (1822–1903), the man responsible for New York City's Central Park. Olmsted believed that communion with nature could cure body and soul, so much of the park has been left as wild as possible, with narrow paths meandering through tall stands of maples and red oaks. In summer, it's full of picnicking families and strolling couples; in winter, cross-country skiers and snowshoers take over. If you want to explore with minimum effort, you can hire the services of a horse-drawn carriage (or sleigh in winter).

Just outside the park's northern boundaries are the city's two biggest cemeteries and beyond that the campus of the Université de Montréal. Not far away from the park and perched on a neighboring crest of the same mountain is the Oratoire St-Joseph, a shrine that draws millions every year. North of the oratory is the busy Côte-des-Neiges neighborhood, teeming with shops and restaurants—Thai, Russian, Korean, Indian, Peruvian, and Filipino, to name a few. South of the oratory, on the other side of the mountain, is **Westmount,** one of the wealthiest Anglophone neighborhoods on the island. Its Francophone twin—the equally prosperous **Outremont**—skirts the mountain's northeastern slopes.

Main Attractions

★ ❹ **Chalet du Mont-Royal.** No trip to Montréal is complete without a visit to the terrace in front of the Chalet du Mont-Royal. It's not the only place to go to get an overview of the city, the river, and the countryside beyond, but it's the most spectacular. On clear days you can see not just the downtown skyscrapers, but Mont-Royal's sister mountains—Monts St-Bruno, St-Hilaire, and St-Grégoire—as well. These isolated peaks, called the Montérégies, or Mountains of the King, rise dramatically from the flat countryside. Beyond them, you might be able to see the northern reaches of the Appalachians. Be sure to take a look inside the chalet, especially at the murals depicting scenes from Canadian history. There's a snack bar in the back. ✉ *Off voie Camillien-Houde, Plateau Mont-Royal* ☎ *No phone* 🎫 *Free* ⏲ *Daily 9–5* Ⓜ *Mont-Royal.*

★ ❿ **Oratoire St-Joseph** (St. Joseph's Oratory). Two million people from all over North America and beyond visit St. Joseph's Oratory yearly. The most devout Catholics climb the 99 steps to its front door on their knees. It is the world's largest and most popular shrine dedicated to the earthly father of Jesus (Canada's patron saint), and it's all the work of a man named Brother André Besette (1845–1937). By worldly standards Brother André didn't have much going for him, but he had a deep devotion to St. Joseph and an iron will. In 1870, he joined the Holy Cross religious order, and was assigned to work as a doorkeeper at the classical college the order oper-

> **SAVVY IN THE CITY**
>
> If you're looking for an exotic lunch, the Côte-des-Neiges neighborhood north of Mont-Royal is a maze of world cuisine restaurants.

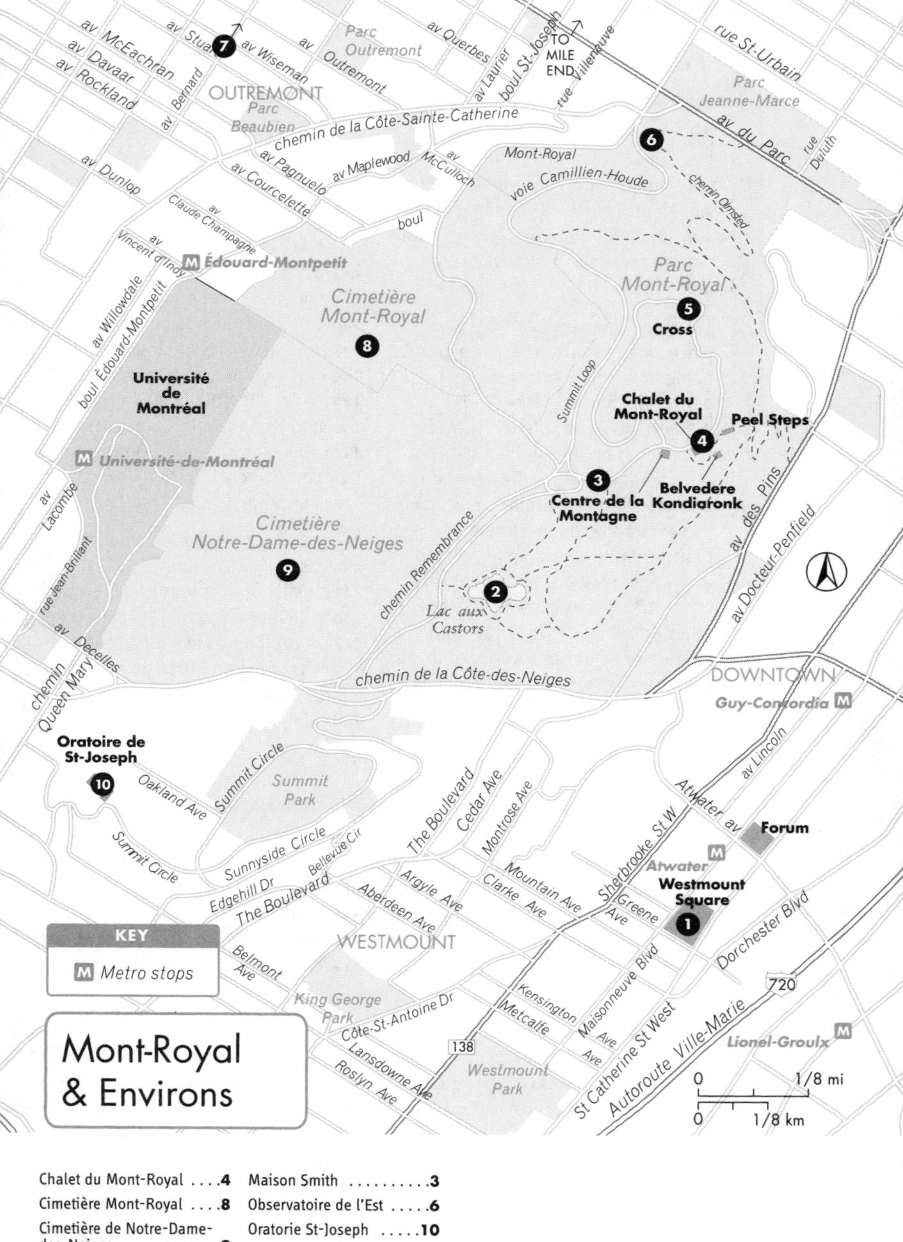

Mont-Royal
& Environs
KEY
Metro stops
Parc Mont-Royal
Cross
Chalet du Mont-Royal
Peel Steps
Belvedere Kondiaronk
Centre de la Montagne
Cimetière Mont-Royal
Cimetière Notre-Dame-des-Neiges
Lac aux Castors
Université de Montréal
Édouard-Montpetit
Université-de-Montréal
OUTREMONT
Parc Outremont
Parc Beaubien
Parc Jeanne-Marce
TO MILE END
DOWNTOWN
Guy-Concordia
Forum
Atwater
Westmount Square
WESTMOUNT
King George Park
Westmount Park
Summit Park
Oratoire de St-Joseph
Lionel-Groulx
chemin de la Côte-Sainte-Catherine
chemin de la Côte-des-Neiges
voie Camillien-Houde
chemin Remembrance
Summit Loop
av du Parc
av des Pins
av Docteur-Penfield
Sherbrooke St W
Maisonneuve Blvd
St Catherine St West
Autoroute Ville-Marie
Dorchester Blvd
Atwater av
720
138
0 1/8 mi
0 1/8 km

CLOSE UP

Westmount & Outremont

ON THE ISLAND OF MONTRÉAL, the names "Westmount" and "Outremont" are synonymous with wealth and power. If–as some people say–the neighborhoods are two sides of the same coin, that coin has to be a gold one.

The similarities between the two places are obvious. Both have grand homes, tree-shaded streets, and perfectly groomed parks. Both are built on the slopes of Mont-Royal–Westmount on the southwest and Outremont on the northeast–and both are close to the city center. Each has its own trendy–or, in Outremont, branché–area for shopping, dining, and sipping lattes. Westmount's is concentrated along avenue Greene and Outremont's is centered on the western ends of rues Laurier and Bernard. Less well-known, perhaps, is that both places are not uniformly wealthy. The southern stretch of Westmount is full of immigrant, working-class families, and the eastern fringes of Outremont are home to Montréal's thriving Hasidic community.

The two neighborhoods may appear mirror images of each other, but they have one essential difference. Although the barriers between Francophones and Anglophones in the city might be eroding, Westmount remains stubbornly English–right down to its neo-Gothic churches and lawn-bowling club–and Outremont is stubbornly French, with a distinct preference for Second Empire homes.

If you want to get a feel for what novelist Hugh MacLennan called Montréal's "two solitudes," there's no more pleasant way to do it than to take a stroll down avenue Green on one afternoon and then go shopping on rue Laurier the next. Vive la difference.

ated just north of Mont-Royal. In 1904 he began building a little chapel to honor his favorite saint on the mountainside across the road, and the rest is history. Thanks to reports of miraculous cures attributed to St. Joseph's intercession, donations started to pour in, and Brother André was able to start work replacing his modest little shrine with something more substantial.

The result, which wasn't completed until after his death, is one of the most triumphalist pieces of church architecture in North America. The oratory and its extensive gardens dominate Mont-Royal's northwestern slope. Its octagonal copper dome—one of the largest in the world—can be seen from miles away in all directions. Under that dome, the interior of the main church is equally grand, but its austerity is almost frigid. The best time to visit it is on Sunday for the 11 AM solemn mass, when the sanctuary is brightly lighted and the sweet voices of Les Petits Chanteurs de Mont-Royal—the city's best boys' choir—fill the nave with music.

The crypt is shabbier than its big brother upstairs but more welcoming. In a long, narrow room behind the crypt, 10,000 votive candles glitter

1

before a dozen carved murals extolling the virtues of St. Joseph; the walls are hung with crutches discarded by those said to be cured. Just beyond is the simple tomb of Brother André, who was beatified in 1982. His preserved heart is displayed in a glass case upstairs in one of the several layers of galleries sandwiched between the crypt and the main church.

High on the mountain, east of the main church, is a beautiful garden commemorating the Passion of Christ with life-size representations of the 14 traditional stations of the cross. On the west side of the church is Brother André's original chapel, with pressed-tin ceilings and plaster saints that is, in many ways, more moving than the church that overshadows it. ✉ *3800 chemin Queen Mary, Côte-des-Neiges* ☎ *514/733–8211* 🌐 *www.saint-joseph.org* 🎫 *Free* ⏲ *Mid-Sept.–mid-May, daily 7 AM–8:30 PM; mid-May–mid-Sept., daily 7 AM–9 PM* Ⓜ *Côte-des-Neiges.*

NEED A BREAK?

A sinfully light croissant or decadent pastry from the Duc de Lorraine (✉ 5002 Côte-des-Neiges, Côte-des-Neiges ☎ 514/371-4128 Ⓜ Côte-des-Neiges) is just the antidote to the sanctity of the Oratoire St-Joseph. If it's lunchtime, try one of the Duc's meat pies or a quiche, followed by coffee and a scoop of homemade ice cream.

Also Worth Seeing

8 **Cimetière Mont-Royal.** If you find yourself humming *Getting to Know You* as you explore Mont-Royal Cemetery's 165 acres, blame it on the graveyard's most famous permanent guest, Anna Leonowens (1834–1915). She was the real-life model for the heroine of the musical *The King and I.* The cemetery—established in 1852 by the Anglican, Presbyterian, Unitarian, and Baptist churches—is laid out like a terraced garden with footpaths that meander through crab apple trees and past Japanese lilacs. ✉ *1297 chemin de la Forêt, Plateau Mont-Royal* ☎ *514/279–7358* 🌐 *www.mountroyalcem.com* ⏲ *Daily 8–7* Ⓜ *Edouard-Montpetit.*

9 **Cimetière de Notre-Dame-des-Neiges** (Our Lady of the Snows Cemetery). At 343 acres, Canada's largest cemetery is not much smaller than the neighboring **Parc Mont-Royal,** and as long as you just count the living, it's usually a lot less crowded. You don't have to be morbid to wander the graveyard's 55 km (34 mi) of tree-shaded paths and roadways past the tombs of hundreds of prominent artists, poets, intellectuals, politicians, and clerics. Among them is Calixa Lavallée (1842–91), who wrote "O Canada," the country's national anthem. Many of the monuments are the work of such leading Québecois artists as Louis-Philippe Hébert and Alfred Laliberité. The cemetery offers some guided tours in summer. Phone ahead for details. ✉ *4601 chemin de la Côte-des-Neiges, Plateau Mont-Royal* ☎ *514/735–1361* 🌐 *www.cimetierenddn.org* ⏲ *Daily 8–7* Ⓜ *Université-de-Montréal.*

OFF THE BEATEN PATH

COSMODOME – Replicas of rockets and spaceships and a full-size mock-up of the space shuttle *Endeavor* are among the kid-pleasing exhibits that make the 30-minute drive to the Cosmodome in suburban Laval a worthwhile trek for families—especially on a rainy day. There are also films, demonstrations, and games. Next door to the Cosmodome is the

Space Camp (☎ 800/565–2267), a training center for amateur astronauts age nine or older. It is affiliated with the U.S. Space Camp in Georgia. ✉ *2150 autoroute des Laurentides, Laval* ☎ *450/978–3600* 🌐 *www.cosmodome.org* *C$11.50* ⏲ *Late June–Aug., daily 10–6; Sept.–late June, Tues.–Sun. 10–6.*

SAVVY IN THE CITY

Montréal's summer rituals include the Tam Tam, an informal drum festival that takes place every Sunday afternoon when the sun shines around the Sir George-Etienne Cartier Monument on the eastern slopes of the mountain near avenue du Parc. Bring your bongos.

5 **Croix sur la Montagne.** The 102-foot-high steel cross at the top of Mont-Royal has been a city landmark since it was erected in 1924, largely with money raised through the efforts of 85,000 high-school students. In 1993, the 249 bulbs used to light the cross were replaced with an ultramodern fiber-optic system.

2 **Lac aux Castors** (Beaver Lake). Mont-Royal's single body of water is actually a reclaimed bog, but it's a great place for kids to float model boats in the summertime or take a ride on a pedal boat. In winter it makes a fine skating rink. ✉ *Off chemin Remembrance, Plateau Mont-Royal* Ⓜ *Edouard-Montpetit.*

3 **Maison Smith.** If you need a map of Mont-Royal's extensive hiking trails or want to know about the more than 150 kinds of birds here, the old park keeper's residence is the place to go. It's also a good for getting a snack, drink, or souvenir. The pretty little stone house—built in 1858—is the headquarters of Les Amis de la Montagne (The Friends of the Mountain), an organization that offers various guided walks on the mountain and in nearby areas. ✉ *1260 chemin Remembrance, Plateau Mont-Royal* ☎ *514/843–8240* 🌐 *www.lemontroyal.qc.ca* ⏲ *Late June–early Sept., weekdays 9–6, weekends 9–8; early Sept.–late June, weekdays 9–5, weekends 9–6* Ⓜ *Mont-Royal.*

6 **Observatoire de l'Est.** If you're just driving across the mountain, be sure to stop at least briefly at the mountain's eastern lookout for a spectacular view of the Stade Olympique and the east end of the city. Snacks are available. ✉ *Voie Camillien-Houde, Plateau Mont-Royal* Ⓜ *Mont-Royal.*

7 **Rue Bernard.** If your taste runs to chic and fashionable rather than bohemian and eccentric, there is simply no better street for people-watching than rue Bernard. Its wide sidewalks and shady trees make it ideal for the kind of outdoor cafés that attract the bright and the beautiful. ✉ *Outremont* Ⓜ *Outremont.*

1 **Westmount Square.** You be the judge: were the skylights cut into the terrace of Westmount Square in 1990 a desecration, as the architectural community claimed at the time, or a necessary step to bring some light into the gloomy, high-end shopping mall beneath? What infuriated the architects is that the square—a complex of three towers, a two-story office building, and a shopping concourse—was the work of the sainted

Ludwig Mies Van der Rohe and should be left untouched by mere mortals lest Van der Rohe's vision of pure forms rising from a flat plain be blighted. But Van der Rohe himself showed some flexibility in the design of this building. For one thing, he clothed it in dark granite instead of his beloved travertine marble—a sensible concession to Montréal's harsh climate. ✉ *Corner of av. Wood and blvd. de Maisonneuve, Westmount* ☎ *514/932–0211* 🎫 *Free* Ⓜ *Atwater.*

HOCHELAGA-MAISONNEUVE

The Stade Olympique that played host to the 1976 Summer Olympics and the leaning tower that supports the stadium's roof dominate the skyline of Hochelaga-Maisonneuve. But there's much more to the area than the stadium complex, including the Jardin Botanique (Botanical Garden); the Insectarium, which houses the world's largest collection of bugs; and Parc Maisonneuve, an ideal place for a stroll or a picnic. The rest of the area is largely working-class residential, but there are some good restaurants and little shops along rue Ontario Est.

Until 1918 when it was annexed by Montréal, the east-end district of Maisonneuve was a city unto itself, a booming, prosperous industrial center full of factories making everything from shoes to cheese. The neighborhood was also packed with houses for the almost entirely French-Canadian workers who kept the whole machine humming.

Maisonneuve was also the site of one of Canada's earliest experiments in urban planning. The Dufresne brothers, a pair of prosperous shoe manufacturers, built a series of grand civic buildings along rue Morgan, including a theater, public baths, and a bustling market, all of which you can still see today. The Dufresne administration also opened Parc Maisonneuve, a 155-acre green space that is now home to the Jardin Botanique de Montréal and a municipal golf course. All this was supposed to make working-class life more bearable, but World War I put an end to the brothers' plans and Maisonneuve became part of Montréal, twinned with the east-end district of Hochelaga.

Main Attractions

6 **Insectarium.** If you're a little squeamish about beetles and roaches, you might want to give the bug-shape building in the middle of the **Jardin Botanique** a pass, but kids especially seem to love it. Most of the more than 250,000 insects in the Insectarium's collection are either mounted or behind panes of glass thick enough to minimize the shudder factor—a good thing when you're looking at a tree roach the size of a wrestler's thumb. There is, however, a room full of free-flying butterflies, and in February and May, the Insectarium releases thousands of butterflies and moths into the Jardin Botanique's main greenhouse. At varying times during the year, the Insectarium brings in chefs to prepare such delicacies as deep-fried bumblebees and chocolate-dipped locusts—protein-rich treats that most adults seem able to resist. ✉ *4581 rue Sherbrooke Est, Hochelaga-Maisonneuve* ☎ *514/872–1400* 🌐 *www.ville.montreal.qc.ca/insectarium* 🎫 *May–Oct. C$12.75, Nov.–Apr. C$9.75 (includes*

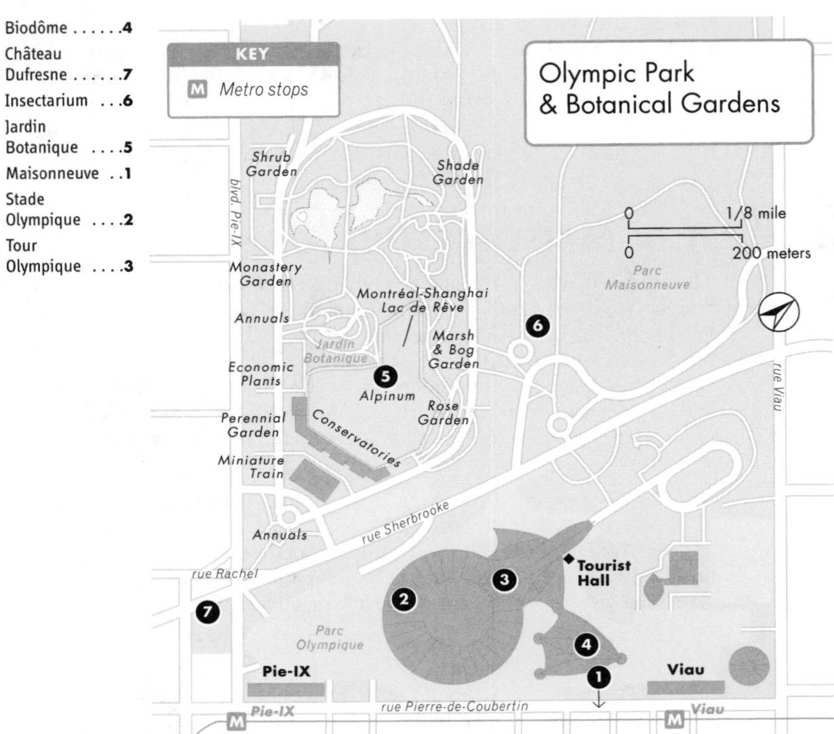

Jardin Botanique) ⏲ May–Aug., daily 9–6; Sept. and Oct., daily 9–9; Nov.–Apr., Tues.–Sun. 9–5 Ⓜ Pie-IX or Viau.

5 Fodor's Choice ★ **Jardin Botanique** (Botanical Garden). Creating one of the world's great botanical gardens in a city with a winter as harsh as Montréal's was no mean feat, and the result is that no matter how brutal it gets in January, there's one corner of the city where it's always summer. With 181 acres of plantings in summer and 10 greenhouses open all year, Montréal's Jardin Botanique is the second-largest attraction of its kind in the world (after England's Kew Gardens). It grows more than 26,000 species of plants, and among its 30 thematic gardens are a rose garden, an alpine garden, and—a favorite with the kids—a poisonous-plant garden. You can attend traditional tea ceremonies in the Japanese Garden, which has one of the best bonsai collections in the West, or wander among the native birches and maples of the Jardin des Premières-Nations (First Nations Garden). The Jardin de Chine (Chinese Garden), with its pagoda and waterfall, will transport you back to the Ming Dynasty. Another highlight is the **Insectarium.** ✉ *4101 rue Sherbrooke Est, Hochelaga-Maisonneuve* ☎ *514/872–1400* 🌐 *www.ville.montreal.qc.ca/jardin* 🎟 *May–Oct. C$12.75, Nov.–Apr. C$9.75 (includes Insectarium)* ⏲ *May–Aug., daily 9–6; Sept. and Oct., daily 9–9; Nov.–Apr., Tues.–Sun. 9–5* Ⓜ *Pie-IX.*

❷ **Stade Olympique.** Montrealers finished paying for their Olympic stadium in the spring of 2006—30 years after the games it was built for—but they still call it the Big Owe, and not very affectionately, either. It certainly looks dramatic, squatting like a giant flying saucer in the middle of the east end. But the place is hard to heat, it's falling apart, and the saga of the retractable roof—it worked precisely three times—is a running joke for local comics. Abandoned by the baseball and football teams it was supposed to house, the stadium is now used for trade shows, motorcycle races, and monster-truck competitions. ✉ *4141 av. Pierre-de-Coubertin, Hochelaga-Maisonneuve* ☎ *514/252–8687* 🌐 *www.rio.gouv.qc.ca* Ⓜ *Pie-IX or Viau.*

SAVVY IN THE CITY

No Montréal street name puzzles visitors more than Pie IX. It's pronounced Pee-Neuf in French, which doesn't sound at all like its English equivalent, Pius IX.

❸ **Tour Olympique.** The world's tallest tilting structure—eat your heart out, Pisa—is the 890-foot tower that was supposed to hold the Stade Olympique's retractable roof. It looked great on paper, but it never worked in practice. But if you want a great view of the city, ride one of the cable cars that slide up the outside of the tower to the observatory at the top. On a clear day you can see up to 80 km (50 mi). Daily guided tours of the Olympic complex leave from the **Tourist Hall** (☎ 514/252–8687) in the base of the Tour Olympique. Tours at 12:40 and 3:40 are in English, and tours at 11 and 2 are in French. ✉ *4141 av. Pierre-de-Coubertin, Hochelaga-Maisonneuve* ☎ *514/252–4141 Ext. 5246* 🎫 *Tower C$5.50, tower and tour of Olympic complex C$13* ⏲ *Mid-June–Labor Day, daily 9–7; Labor Day–mid-June, 9–5* Ⓜ *Pie-IX or Viau.*

Also Worth Seeing

❹ **Biodôme.** Not everyone thought it was a great idea to transform an Olympic bicycle-racing stadium into a natural-history exhibit, but the result is one of the city's most popular attractions, albeit one that's begun to show some wear and tear. Four ecosystems—a boreal forest, a tropical forest, a polar landscape, and the St. Lawrence River—are under one climate-controlled dome. You follow protected pathways through each environment, observing indigenous flora and fauna. A word of warning: the tropical forest is as hot and humid as the real thing, and the Québec and arctic exhibits can be quite frigid. If you want to stay comfortable, dress in layers. ✉ *4777 av. Pierre-de-Coubertin, Hochelaga-Maisonneuve* ☎ *514/868–3000* 🌐 *www.biodome.qc.ca* 🎫 *C$19* ⏲ *Late June–early Sept., daily 9–6; early Sept.–late June, Tues.–Sun. 9–5* Ⓜ *Viau.*

SAVVY IN THE CITY

If you grew up watching Maurice (Rocket) Richard storm down the ice in the red jersey of the Montréal Canadiens, you'll want to visit the little shrine set up to his memory in the Aréna Maurice Richard at 2800 rue Viau just east of the Stade Olympique.

❼ **Château Dufresne.** The adjoining homes of a pair of shoe manufacturers, Oscar and Marius Dufresne, provide a revealing glimpse into the lives of Montréal's Francophone bourgeoisie in the early 20th century. The brothers built their beaux arts palace in 1916 along the lines of the Petit-Trianon in Paris and lived in it with their families—Oscar in the eastern half and Marius in the western half. Worth searching out are the delicate domestic scenes on the walls of the Petit Salon, where Oscar's wife entertained her friends. Her brother-in-law relaxed with his male friends in a smoking room decked out like a Turkish lounge. During the house's incarnation as a boys' school in the 1950s, the Eudist priests, who ran the place, covered the room's frieze of frolicking nymphs and satyrs with a modest curtain that their charges lifted at every opportunity. ✉ *2929 rue Jeanne-d'Arc, Hochelaga-Maisonneuve* ☎ *514/259–9201* 🌐 *www.chateaudufresne.qc.ca* 🎫 C$7 ⏲ *Thurs.–Sun. 10–5* Ⓜ *Viau.*

❶ **Maisonneuve.** At the beginning of the 20th century, civic leaders wanted to transform this industrial center into a model city with broad boulevards, grandiose public buildings, and fine homes. World War I and the Depression killed those plans, but a few fine fragments of the grand dream survive, just three blocks south of the Olympic site. The magnificent beaux arts public market, which has a 20-foot-tall bronze statue of a farm woman, stands at the northern end of tree-lined avenue Morgan. Farmers and butchers have moved into a modern building next door; the old market is now a community center and the site of summer shows and concerts. Monumental staircases and a heroic rooftop sculpture embellish the public baths across the street. The **Théâtre Denise Pelletier,** at the corner of rue Ste-Catherine Est and rue Morgan, has a lavish Italianate interior; **Fire Station No. 1,** at 4300 rue Notre-Dame Est, was inspired by Frank Lloyd Wright's Unity Temple in suburban Chicago; and the sumptuously decorated **Église Très-Saint-Nom-de-Jésus** has one of the most powerful organs in North America. The 60-acre **Parc Maisonneuve,** stretching north of the botanical garden, is a lovely place for a stroll. Ⓜ *Pie-IX or Viau.*

NEED A BREAK?

If you're feeling a bit peckish and want to soak up a little neighborhood ambience, drop into the cash-only Chez Clo (✉ 3199 rue Ontario Est, Hochelaga-Maisonneuve ☎ 514/522–5348 Ⓜ Pie-IX or Viau) for a bowl of the best pea soup in the city, followed—if you have the room for it—by a slab of *tourtière* (meat pie) with homemade ketchup. The dessert specialty is *pudding au chomeur* (literally, pudding for the unemployed), a kind of shortcake smothered in a thick brown-sugar sauce. The service is noisy and friendly, and the clientele mostly local, but there are often lines.

THE ISLANDS

Expo '67—the World's Fair staged to celebrate the centennial of the Canadian federation—was the biggest party in Montréal's history, and it marked a defining moment in the city's evolution as a modern metropolis. That party was held on two islands in the middle of the St. Lawrence River—Île Ste-Hélène, formed by nature, and Île Notre-Dame, created with the stone rubble excavated from the construction of Montréal's Métro. Both are very accessible. You can drive to them via the Pont de la Concorde or the Pont Jacques-Cartier, or take the Métro from the Berri-UQAM station.

Main Attractions

Biosphère. Nothing captures the exuberance of Expo '67 better than the geodesic dome designed by Buckminster Fuller (1895–1983) as the American Pavilion. It's only a skeleton now—the polymer panels that protected the U.S. exhibits from the elements were burned out in a fire long ago—but it's still an eye-catching sight, like something plucked from a science-fiction film. There's nothing particularly fanciful about the environmental center the federal government has built in the middle of the dome, however. Its purpose is to heighten awareness of the problems faced by the St. Lawrence River system, whose water levels have dropped dramatically in recent decades. But despite its earnestness, the museum manages to make the whole thing fun. Visitors of all ages—especially kids—can use games and interactive displays arranged around a large model of the waterway to explore how shipping, tourism, water supplies, and hydroelectric power are affected. ✉ *160 chemin Tour-de-l'Île, Île Ste-Hélène* ☎ *514/283–5000* 🌐 *www.biosphere.ec.gc.ca* *C$10* ⏲ *June–Sept., daily 10–6; Oct.–May, Tues.–Fri. noon–5* Jean-Drapeau.

Casino de Montréal. You have to be at least 18 to visit Montréal's government-owned casino, but you don't have to be a gambler. You can come for the bilingual cabaret theater or to sip a martini in the Cheval bar or to dine in Nuances, where the prices are almost as spectacular as the views of the city across the river. You can even come just to look at the architecture—the main building was the French pavilion at Expo '67. But if you do want to risk the family fortune, there are more than 3,200 slot machines, a keno lounge, a high-stakes gaming area, and 120 tables for playing blackjack, baccarat, roulette, craps, and various types of poker. ✉ *1 av. du Casino, Île Notre-Dame* ☎ *514/392–2746 or 800/665–2274* 🌐 *www.casino-de-montreal.com* Ⓜ *Jean-Drapeau (then Bus 167).*

Fodor'sChoice ★

Parc Jean-Drapeau. Île Ste-Hélène and Île Notre-Dame now constitute a single park named, fittingly enough, for Jean Drapeau (1916–99), the visionary (and spendthrift) mayor who built the Métro and brought the city both the 1967 World's Fair and the 1976 Olympics. The park includes a major amusement park, acres of flower gardens, a beach with filtered water, and the Casino de Montréal. There's history, too, at the Old Fort, where soldiers in colonial uniforms display the military methods used in ancient wars. In winter you can skate on the old Olympic rowing basin or slide down iced trails on an inner tube. ☎ *514/872–6120* 🌐 *www.parcjeandrapeau.com/en.*

★ **Stewart Museum at the Fort.** Each summer the grassy parade square of the Old Fort comes alive with the crackle of colonial muskets and the skirl of bagpipes. The French are

SAVVY IN THE CITY

A ferry carries foot passengers and their bikes from the Bassin Jacques-Cartier in the Vieux-Port to Île Ste-Hélène—much the nicest way to get to the islands.

represented by the Compagnie Franche de la Marine and the British by the kilted 78th Fraser Highlanders, one of the regiments that participated in the conquest of Québec in 1759. The two companies of colonial soldiers raise the flag every day at 11 AM, practice maneuvers at 1 PM, put on a combined display of precision drilling and musket fire at 3 PM, and lower the flag at 4:30 PM. Children are encouraged to take part. The fort itself, built between 1820 and 1824 to protect Montréal from an American invasion that never came, is now a museum that tells the story of colonial life in the city through displays of old firearms, maps, and uniforms. ✉ *West of Pont Jacques-Cartier, Île Ste-Hélène* ☎ *514/861–6701* 🌐 *www.stewart-museum.org* 🎫 *C$10* ⏲ *Early May–mid-Oct., daily 10–5; mid-Oct.–early May, Wed.–Mon. 10–5* Ⓜ *Jean-Drapeau.*

SAVVY IN THE CITY

In winter you and the kids can visit the Old Fort and learn to curl (bowl on ice) the way the British garrison did in the 1840s—with cannonballs cut in half on outdoor rinks.

Also Worth Seeing

Circuit Gilles Villeneuve. In July you can join the glitterati of Europe and America in the Circuit Gilles Villeneuve's grandstand to watch million-dollar Formula 1 cars shriek around the 4.3-km (2.7-mi) track—if you're lucky enough and rich enough to get a ticket, that is. This is the kind of crowd that uses Perrier water to mop up caviar stains from the refreshment tables. It might all come to an end, however. Canada's national ban on tobacco-company sponsorships makes the future of the Grand Prix du Canada uncertain. ✉ *Île Notre-Dame* ☎ *514/350–0000* 🌐 *www.grandprix.ca* Ⓜ *Jean-Drapeau.*

Plage de l'Île Notre-Dame (Île Notre-Dame Beach). The dress code at the neighboring **Casino de Montréal** might ban camisoles and strapless tops, but here, anything seems to go on warm summer days, when the beach is a sea of oiled bodies. You get the distinct impression that swimming is not uppermost on the minds of many of the scantily clad hordes. If you do want to go in, however, the water is filtered and closely monitored for contamination, and there are lifeguards on duty to protect you from other hazards. A shop rents swimming and boating paraphernalia, and there are picnic areas and a restaurant. ✉ *West side of Île Notre-Dame, Île Notre-Dame* ☎ *514/872–4537* 🎫 *C$7.50* ⏲ *Late June–Aug., daily 10–7* Ⓜ *Jean-Drapeau.*

La Ronde. Every year, it seems, La Ronde adds some new and monstrous way to scare the living daylights (and perhaps your lunch as well) out of you. The most recent addition is the Goliath, a giant steel roller-coaster that opened in the summer of 2006. It dwarfs the previous favorites—the aptly named Vampire and Monstre—in both height and speed. But if the idea of hurtling along a narrow steel track at 110 kph (68 mph) doesn't appeal to you, you might prefer the boat rides or the Ferris wheel. The popular **International Fireworks Competition** is held here weekends and a couple of weeknights in late June and July. ✉ *Eastern end of Île Ste-Hélène, Île Ste-Hélène* ☎ *514/397–2000 or 800/361–4595* 🌐 *www.laronde.com/*

en C$30 *Late May, weekends 10–8; early June–late June, daily 10–8; late June–late Aug., daily 10 AM–10:30 PM; Sept., weekends 10–7; Oct., Fri. 5 PM–9 PM, Sat. noon–9, Sun. noon–8* M *Jean-Drapeau.*

WHERE TO EAT

Good restaurants can pop up just about anywhere in Montréal, and sometimes they appear in the oddest places. Toqué!, for example, long touted as one of the city's best, is on the ground floor of an office tower in the financial district. Still, there are those certain areas—such as rue St-Denis and boulevard St-Laurent between rues Sherbrooke and Mont-Royal—that have long been the city's hottest dining strips, with everything from sandwich shops to high-price gourmet shrines.

The bring-your-own-wine craze started on rue Prince-Arthur and avenue Duluth, two lively pedestrian streets in the Plateau that still specialize in good, relatively low-cost meals. Most downtown restaurants are clustered between rues Guy and Peel on the side streets that run between boulevard René-Lévesque and rue Sherbrooke. Some interesting little cafés and restaurants have begun to spring up in the heart of the antiques district along rue Notre-Dame Ouest near avenue Atwater. Vieux-Montréal, too, has a good collection of restaurants, most of them clustered on rue St-Paul and Place Jacques-Cartier.

Wherever you go to eat, be sure to watch for such Québec specialties as veal from Charlevoix, lamb from Kamouraska, strawberries from Île d'Orléans, shrimp from Matane, lobster from the Îles-de-la-Madeleine, blueberries from Lac St-Jean, and cheese from just about everywhere.

When you dine out, you can usually order à la carte, but make sure to look for the table d'hôte, a two- to four-course package deal. It's usually more economical, often offers interesting specials, and may also take less time to prepare. If you want to splurge on time and money, consider a *menu dégustation,* a five- to seven-course tasting menu executed by the chef. It generally includes soup, salad, fish, sherbet (to cleanse the palate), a meat dish, dessert, and coffee or tea. At the city's finest restaurants, such a meal for two, along with a good bottle of wine, can cost more than C$200 and last four hours.

Menus in many restaurants are bilingual, but some are only in French. If you don't understand what a dish is, don't be shy about asking; a good server will be happy to explain. If you feel brave enough to order in French, remember that in French an *entrée* is an appetizer and what Americans call an entrée is a *plat principal,* or main dish.

Dinner reservations are highly recommended for weekend dining.

WHAT IT COSTS In Canadian dollars

	$$$$	**$$$**	**$$**	**$**	**¢**
AT DINNER	over C$30	C$21–C$30	C$13–C$20	C$8–C$12	under C$8

Prices are per person for a main course at dinner (or at the most expensive meal served).

Vieux-Montréal

Café

★ $–$$ **Claude Postel.** Fast food with style is the specialty of Claude Postel's staff, and that goes down just fine with the hordes of hungry clerks and lawyers who line up at lunchtime for such ready-made meals as braised veal and poached salmon with perhaps a vegetable and orange soup to start. The bistrolike dining room is comfortable and welcoming if you want to eat in, but you can also order a sandwich—on excellent crusty bread—and eat it alfresco at the Vieux-Port, a couple of blocks south. Mid-afternoon hunger pangs? Stop by for a cone of intensely flavored gelato-style ice cream. The place closes at 7 PM. *75 rue Notre-Dame Ouest, Vieux-Montréal 514/844–8750 MC, V Place-d'Armes.*

Contemporary

$$$–$$$$ **Aix Cuisine du Terroir.** Planters of fresh flowers and semicircular banquettes provide a little privacy for romantic couples splurging on braised wild boar and grilled tilapia. Particularly good is the lamb, served here in a miniature shepherd's pie with mushrooms and parsnip puree. *711 Côte de la Place d'Armes, Vieux-Montréal 514/842–1887 Reservations essential AE, D, DC, MC, V Place-d'Armes.*

$$$–$$$$ **Cube.** If it weren't for the flickering votive candles and the few paintings hanging on the concrete-gray walls, Cube would be as austere as a prison cell, but Chef Eric Gonzalez's cooking is at the opposite end of the bland scale. Florid would be a good word to describe his creations. Sweetbreads pierced with licorice sticks, smoked duck served with cherry preserves, Angus steak topped with crisp-fried oysters, marrow, and hazelnuts—well, you get the idea. *Hôtel St. Paul, 355 rue McGill, Vieux-Montréal 514/876–2823 Reservations essential AE, DC, MC, V Square-Victoria.*

$$$–$$$$ Fodor'sChoice ★ **Toqué!** Toqué is slang for "just a little mad," and the name fit when Chef Normand Laprise catered to the überhip in a bright and funky storefront on rue St-Denis. But there's nothing mad or crazy about his current gray-and-burgundy home on the ground floor of a glass tower, or about the pin-striped, expense-account crowd it attracts. Still, Laprise—the earliest champion of home-grown Québec products—hasn't lost his touch with the food. The menu changes daily, depending on what he finds at the market, but dinner could start with ravioli stuffed with braised duck followed by lamb from the Gatineau Valley. For dessert, cross your fingers and hope the almond-crusted blueberry pie is on the menu. *900 pl. Jean-Paul-Riopelle, Vieux-Montréal 514/499–2084 Reservations essential AE, DC, MC, V Closed Mon. No lunch Square-Victoria or Place-d'Armes.*

★ $$$–$$$$ **Verses.** The setting—a stone-walled room overlooking the hubbub of rue St-Paul—is the most romantic in the old city. And the food can be poetic—especially with appetizers such as grilled shrimp with mangoes and pineapple or tuna tartare with ginger, sesame oil, and wasabi. But the reason for this restaurant's name is that it's housed on the ground floor of Hôtel Nelligan, named after the Romantic Québecois poet Émile Nelligan. For a main course try the duck breast with tamarind and caramel or the beef fillet with mashed potatoes and chives. *Hôtel*

Nelligan, 100 rue St-Paul Ouest, Vieux-Montréal ☎ *514/788–4000* ✍ *Reservations essential* ▭ *AE, DC, MC, V* Ⓜ *Place-d'Armes.*

$$–$$$ Fodor'sChoice ★ ✕ **Club Chasse et Pêche.** Don't fret—this isn't a hangout for the local gun-and-rod set. The name—which means Hunting and Fishing Club—is an ironic reference to the wood-and-leather decor Chef Claude Pelletier inherited from the previous owners. He's jazzed it up, though, with some halogen lamps that make it easier for you to see the food, which looks almost as good as it tastes. The elegant setting, Pelletier's innovative style, and impeccable service has made this a favorite with the city's serious foodies. For a different riff on an old favorite, try Pelletier's version of surf-and-turf. You get the lobster tail, but instead of steak you get a juicy lump of suckling pig, or a crispy heap of sweetbreads. ✉ *423 rue St-Claude, Vieux-Montréal* ☎ *514/861–1112* ✍ *Reservations essential* ▭ *AE, DC, MC, V* ⊗ *Closed Sun. and Mon. No lunch Sat.* Ⓜ *Champ-de-Mars.*

Eclectic

$–$$ ✕ **Pub St-Paul.** Sometimes you just want to get away from all the fancy food and reverential talk, slump into a comfortable captain's chair in a big noisy bistro, and wash down a steak and a heap of crispy frites with a couple of pints of good draft beer. And if there's room and time, you might want to follow that with a slab of apple pie or perhaps a big lump of blueberry cheesecake. When that mood hits, this is the place—and it comes with stone walls, big wooden beams, and, on weekends, live entertainment. There's also a children's menu. ✉ *124 rue St-Paul Est, Vieux-Montréal* ☎ *514/874–0485* ▭ *AE, DC, MC, V* Ⓜ *Place-d'Armes.*

French

★ $$$–$$$$ ✕ **Les Remparts.** The weathered piece of gray stone in the corner of the dining room might once have been part of the city's ramparts, but the food is as up to date as a skyscraper. To start, the seared foie gras with caramelized pears or the perfectly seasoned chicken-liver mousse are good choices, and for the main dish try the roasted venison or the seared duck breast. But it's not all meat. Chef Jannick Bouchard also prepares a nightly vegetarian dish. ✉ *93 rue de la Commune Est, Vieux-Montréal* ☎ *514/392–1649* ▭ *AE, DC, MC, V* ⊗ *No lunch weekends* Ⓜ *Place-d'Armes.*

$$–$$$$ ✕ **Bonaparte.** Book a table in one of the front window alcoves and watch the calèches clatter by over the cobblestones as you dine. You can order à la carte, but the restaurant's best deal is the six-course tasting menu, which includes such classics as lobster bisque flavored with anise, and breast of duck cooked with maple syrup and berries. Don't be intimidated by the number of courses—portions are generally smaller than main menu versions—and their delivery is gently paced by one of the city's most professional staffs. Upstairs is a small inn. ✉ *443 rue St-François-Xavier, Vieux-Montréal* ☎ *514/844–4368* ✍ *Reservations essential* ▭ *AE, DC, MC, V* ⊗ *No lunch weekends* Ⓜ *Place-d'Armes.*

★ $$–$$$$ ✕ **Chez l'Épicier.** It's a bit of a gimmick, but this is indeed an épicier (grocer). Shelves stocked with such products as Hawaiian sea salt and lobster oil fill the front part of the room, along with refrigerated displays of pâtés and terrines. The menu, printed on brown paper bags, starts with appetizers such as shepherd's pie (made with snails instead of beef and spiked with roasted garlic) and a nutty parsnip soup flavored with orange and ginger. The more-conservative main dishes might include such delicacies as poached Chilean sea bass and veal chops in sherry-vinegar sauce. ✉ *311 rue St-Paul Est, Vieux-Montréal* ☎ *514/878–2232* ▭ *AE, DC, MC, V* ⏲ *No lunch weekends* Ⓜ *Place-d'Armes.*

$$ ✕ **Bistro Boris.** Behind the restored facade of a burned-out building is one of the best alfresco dining areas in the city. At this huge, tree-shaded terrasse the French fare includes blood pudding, grilled fish, or chops, all served with salad or fries. But get there early. The locals love the place and fill up those outdoor tables quickly. ✉ *465 rue McGill, Vieux-Montréal* ☎ *514/848–9575* ▭ *AE, DC, MC, V* Ⓜ *Square-Victoria.*

Italian

$$–$$$$ ✕ **Da Emma.** The cellar of what used to be Montréal's first women's prison hardly sounds like the ideal setting for an Italian restaurant, but fear not: Mama Emma's cooking is satisfying enough to drive out any lingering ghosts from those sad days. The place's stone walls and heavy beams make an ideal, catacomb-like setting for such Roman specialties as suckling pig roasted with garlic and rosemary and, on very special occasions, tripe Romaine. You might also want to try Mama's big juicy meatballs. Johnny Depp, a regular when he's in town, loves them. ✉ *777 rue de la Commune Ouest, Vieux-Montréal* ☎ *514/392–1568* ▭ *AE, D, DC, MC, V* ⏲ *No lunch Sat.* Ⓜ *Square-Victoria.*

Polish

★ $–$$ ✕ **Café Stash.** On chilly nights many Montrealers come here for sustenance—for borscht, pork chops, pierogis, or cabbage and sausage—in short, for all the hearty specialties of a Polish kitchen. Seating is on pews from a chapel and at tables from an old convent. ✉ *200 rue St-Paul Ouest, Vieux-Montréal* ☎ *514/845–6611* ▭ *AE, MC, V* Ⓜ *Place-d'Armes.*

Steak

$–$$ ✕ **Magnan.** Everyone from dock workers to corporate executives come to this tavern in a working-class neighborhood for the unbeatable roast beef and steaks. The salmon pie is a delightfully heavy filler that makes great picnic fare. In summer Magnan adds Québec lobster to its menu and turns its parking lot into an outdoor dining area. Excellent beer from several local microbreweries is on tap. The style is upscale warehouse, with TV sets noisily tuned to sports. ✉ *2602 rue St-Patrick, Pointe St-Charles* ☎ *514/935–9647* ▭ *AE, DC, MC, V* Ⓜ *Charlevoix.*

Downtown & Chinatown

Canadian

$–$$ ✕ **Chalet Barbecue.** Fast-food restaurants across Canada sell what they call "Montréal-style barbecued chicken." The claims are laughable. For the real thing, head for Chalet Barbecue and line up with the cabbies, truck drivers, and local families for crispy, spit-barbecued chicken served with a slightly spicy, gravylike sauce and mountains of french fries. You can eat in—call the decor rustic vinyl—or order your chicken to go. ✉ *5456 rue Sherbrooke Ouest, Notre-Dame-de-Grace* ☎ *514/489–7235* ▭ *MC, V* Ⓜ *Vendôme.*

Chinese

$$–$$$$ ✕ **Orchidée de Chine.** Diners feast on such dishes as baby bok choy with mushrooms, spicy spareribs, feather-light fried soft-shell crabs with black-bean sauce, and tender strips of beef served with bell peppers and fried basil leaves. The cream-and-yellow, glassed-in dining room has a great view onto a busy, fashionable sidewalk; a more intimate room is in the back. ✉ *2017 rue Peel, Downtown* ☎ *514/287–1878* ✍ *Reservations essential* ▭ *AE, DC, MC, V* ⏲ *Closed Sun. No lunch Sat.* Ⓜ *Peel.*

$–$$ ✕ **Maison Kam Fung.** Kam Fung is no place for a romantic tête-à-tête, but it's a great place to go with a gang of friends for a noisy dim sum feast. From 7 AM until 3 PM waiters clatter up and down the aisles between tables, pushing a parade of trolleys bearing such treats as firm dumplings stuffed with pork and chicken, stir-fried squid, barbecued chicken feet, and delicate shrimp-filled envelopes of pastry. ✉ *1111 rue St-Urbain, Chinatown* ☎ *514/878–2888* ▭ *AE, DC, MC, V* Ⓜ *Place-d'Armes.*

Contemporary

$$$–$$$$ Fodor's Choice ★ ✕ **Joe Beef.** Dining at Joe Beef is a little like being invited to a dinner party by a couple of friends who just happen to be top-notch chefs. David MacMillan and Frédéric Morin were pioneers of Montréal's modern dining scene until they got tired of living on the edge and opened this little restaurant to rediscover the joy that got them cooking in the first place. Now they cook whatever they want for a bunch of diners who are more like friends than customers. There's nothing fancy or fussy about the cuisine—everything is simple and good, from the oysters to the grilled rib steak. And if you're really hungry, try the cream chicken with little onions, or the spaghetti loaded with big juicy chunks of lobster. ✉ *2491 rue Notre-Dame Ouest, Downtown* ☎ *514/935–6504* ✍ *Reservations essential* ▭ *AE, DC, MC, V* ⏲ *Closed Sun. and Mon. No lunch* Ⓜ *Lionel-Groulx.*

Continental

$$$$ ✕ **Beaver Club.** A 2003 makeover softened the fusty-men's-club look of this grand old institution: there are now tapestry banquettes, contemporary First Nations (Native American) prints, and a brown, beige, and cream color scheme. It's still pretty sumptuous, with wing chairs, starched linens, an impeccable staff, and a menu that relies on such classics as roast beef, grilled chops, poached salmon, and Cornish hens. The bar serves the best martini in the city. ✉ *Fairmont Le Reine Elizabeth, 900 blvd. René-Lévesque Ouest, Downtown* ☎ *514/861–3511* 👔 *Jacket and tie* ▭ *AE, D, DC, MC, V* ⏲ *Closed Sun. and July. No dinner Mon., no lunch Sat. or Aug.* Ⓜ *Bonaventure.*

Delicatessen

¢–$ ✕ **Ben's.** This big, brassy deli is a Montréal institution, with 1950s furnishings and green and yellow walls hung with photos of celebrity customers. Sadly, the food, primarily smoked-meat sandwiches, isn't what it once was, but Ben's remains a good place for a late-night snack. ✉ *990 blvd. de Maisonneuve Ouest, Downtown* ☎ *514/844–1000* ✍ *Reservations not accepted* ▭ *MC, V* Ⓜ *Peel.*

Where to Eat in Montréal
KEY
M Metro stops
Cimetière Mont-Royal
Parc du Mont-Royal
Parc Jeanne-Mance
Observatoire de l'Est
Stade Molson
McGill University
Place Ville-Marie
Cathédrale Marie-Reine-du-Monde
Couvent des Soeurs Grises
Sq. Dorchester
McGill
Peel
Guy-Concordia
Atwater
Lucien-L'Allier
Bonaventure
Georges-Vanier
Lionel-Groulx
ch. de la Côte-Ste-Catherine
av. Laurier
blvd. St-Joseph
Villeneuve
rue Villeneuve
Mont-Royal
av. Mont-Royal
rue Marie-Anne
blvd. St-Laurent
de Bullion
St-Urbain
av. du Parc
av. des Pins
rue Jeanne-Mance
rue Aylmer
chemin Remembrance
voie C. Houde
av. Cedar
av. Docteur-Penfield
rue Simpson
rue Redpath
rue du Musée
rue de la Montagne
rue Stanley
rue Peel
rue McTavish
av. Victoria
av. McGill Col.
Metcalfe
Mansfield
r. Cathcart
rue University
av. Union
côte du Beaver-Hall
City Councillors
av. du Président
Belmont
rue Sherbrooke
rue Drummond
rue Crescent
rue Bishop
rue MacKay
rue Guy
rue St-Mathieu
rue St-Marc
rue du Fort
av. Atwater
blvd. de Maisonneuve
rue Ste-Catherine
av. Greene
blvd. Dorchester
blvd. René-Lévesque
autoroute Ville-Marie
rue St-Antoine
rue St-Jacques
rue des Seigneurs
rue de la Montagne
rue Peel
rue Murray
rue Ottawa
rue Notre-Dame
1
2
3
4
5
6
7
8
9
10
11
12
13
14
15
16
17
18
19
47
48
53
54 - 61
62
63
64
65
66

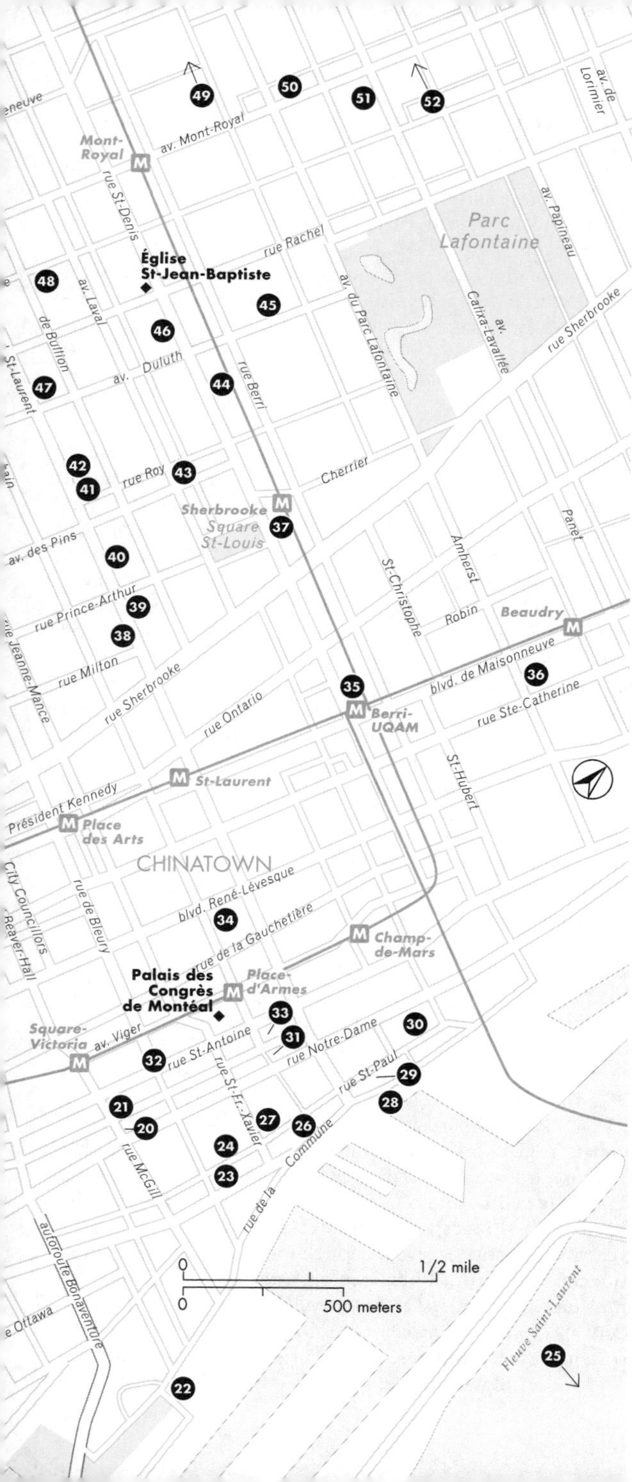

Aix Cuisine du Terroir 33
Alep .58
Anise 64
Area .36
L'Assommoir 60
Au Pied du Cochon 45
Ben's 17
Binerie Mont-Royal 49
Bistro Boris 21
Bistro Gourmet 5
Bonaparte 27
Brasserie Artisanale
& Bistro Le Reservoir 47
Brioche Lyonnaise 35
Café Ferreira 14
Café Stash 23
Cavalli 11
Le Caveau 19
Chao Phrya 63
Les Chèvres 59
Chalet Barbecue 1
Chao Phraya 65
Chez Doval 48
Chez l'Epicier 24
Club Chasse et Pêche 30
la Chronique 62
Chu Chai 46
Claude Postel 31
Le Commensal 18
Cube 20
Daou 57
Da Emma 22
Da Vinci 7
L'Express 41
Les Gâteries 37
Globe 39
Il Mulino 52
Joe Beef 4
Kaizen 3
Katsura 10
Maestro S.V.P. 40
Maison Kam Fung 34
Med Grill 38
Milos 66
Moishe's 42
Mr. Steer 15
Mythos Ouzerie 65
Nuances 25
Om .53
Orchidée de Chine 12
Le Paris 6
Pintxo 43
Pub St-Paul 29
Queue de Cheval 9
La Rapière 16
Les Remparts 28
Rosalie 8
Rotisserie Panama 55
St-Vianteur Bagel & Café 50
Schwartz's Delicatessen 41
Senzala 51,61
Tavern on the Square 2
Le Taj 13
Thai Grill 54
Toqué! 32
Tre Marie 56
Verses 26

French

$$$$ ✕ **Guy and Dodo Morali.** In the best French tradition, Guy runs the kitchen and wife Dodo handles the front room, although Guy wanders out occasionally to chat with customers and listen to complaints and compliments. The decor's classic, too—pale yellow walls hung with impressionist prints and photos of Paris—as is the cooking. The daily table d'hôte menu is the best bet, with openers such as lobster bisque followed by sweetbreads with mushrooms or lobster poached with champagne. For dessert try the tarte tatin (apples and caramel with crème anglaise). In summer, diners spill out onto a little terrace on rue Metcalfe. ✉ *Les Cours Mont-Royal, 1444 rue Metcalfe, Downtown* ☎ *514/842–3636* ✍ *Reservations essential* ▭ *AE, DC, MC, V* ⊙ *Closed Sun.* Ⓜ *Peel.*

$$$–$$$$ ✕ **La Rapière.** The musketeer D'Artagnan, master of the rapier (or *rapière*), came from southwestern France, as do most of this elegant restaurant's specialties. Start with paper-thin slices of the house-smoked goose meat or a portion of delicately pink duck foie gras, followed by a cassoulet of duck, pork, and haricots (beans). For dessert there's nougat ice with custard, crème brûlée, or an excellent cheese plate. The room itself is soothing, with terra-cotta-color walls, tapestries, and stained-glass windows. ✉ *Sun Life Building, 1155 rue Metcalfe, Downtown* ☎ *514/871–8920* ✍ *Reservations essential* ▭ *AE, DC, MC, V* ⊙ *Closed Sun. No lunch Sat.* Ⓜ *Peel.*

Fodor'sChoice ★

$$–$$$$ ✕ **Le Caveau.** Among the towers of downtown is this Victorian house where buttery sauces and creamy desserts have survived the onslaught of nouvelle cuisine. The restaurant takes its name from its warm and comfortable cellar, but if you don't like low ceilings, there's plenty of room upstairs amid the sculptures and paintings on the upper two floors. Main courses might include rabbit cooked with wine, raisins, and spices or rack of lamb crusted with bread crumbs, mustard, garlic, and herbs. A children's menu, rare in restaurants of Le Caveau's caliber, is available. ✉ *2063 av. Victoria, Downtown* ☎ *514/844–1624* ▭ *AE, DC, MC, V* ⊙ *No lunch weekends* Ⓜ *McGill.*

$$–$$$$ ✕ **Rosalie.** Rosalie's long blond-wood bar and tubular steel chairs are all very trendy, but it's the big terrasse out front that draws the crowds on late summer afternoons. The thirtysomething professionals who pour in after work for a martini or two often stay for an early supper before heading out on the town. Try the roast chicken with a white-wine sauce or, for something simpler, what is perhaps the best steak-frites in town. ✉ *1232 rue de la Montagne, Downtown* ☎ *514/392–1970* ▭ *AE, MC, V* Ⓜ *Guy-Concordia.*

$$–$$$ ✕ **Bistro Gourmet.** Yogi Berra's immortal line—"Nobody goes to that restaurant anymore, it's too crowded"—could easily be applied to Chef Gabriel Ohana's tiny yellow and blue room. It's usually so packed that service can be painfully slow, especially on weekends. But that's because the food is great and the prices are low enough to make it attractive even to college students. Try the duck breast in a citrus sauce or the tuna fillets in a sesame sauce. ✉ *2100 rue St-Mathieu, Downtown* ☎ *514/846–1553* ▭ *MC, V* ⊙ *No lunch weekends* Ⓜ *Guy-Concordia.*

$$–$$$ ✕ **Le Paris.** Nothing has changed much at Le Paris since the Poucant family opened it in 1950. And why should it? Every city needs a faded bistro with big tables, age-dimmed paint, and honest, soulful French food like grilled *boudin* (blood sausage), calves' liver, and roast chicken. It's the kind of place that makes you want to take your shoes off and relax, and maybe ask the regular at the next table what he recommends. If you do, chances are he'll suggest you start with the *brandade de morue*—a kind of spread made with salt cod, potatoes, garlic, and cream—spread on little pieces of toast. And to finish? How about stewed rhubarb or *île flottante* (meringue floating in a sea of custard)? ✉ *1812 rue Ste-Catherine Ouest, Downtown* ☎ *514/937–4898* 💳 *AE, DC, MC, V* ⏲ *No lunch Sun.* Ⓜ *Guy-Concordia.*

Indian

¢–$ ✕ **Le Taj.** The focus is the cuisine of northern India, less spicy and more delicate than that of the south. Tandoori ovens seal in the flavors of the grilled meat and fish. Among the vegetarian choices are *thali*—one vegetable entrée, lentils, and basmati rice—and *saag paneer,* spicy white cheese with spinach. A nine-course lunch buffet costs C$11, and a nightly "Indian feast" is C$27. ✉ *2077 rue Stanley, Downtown* ☎ *514/845–9015* 💳 *AE, MC, V* ⏲ *No lunch Sat.* Ⓜ *Peel.*

Italian

$$$–$$$$ ✕ **Cavalli.** The young and the beautiful like to sip cocktails by Cavalli's big front window, which in summer is open to the passing scene on busy rue Peel. The interior—a pink-and-black illuminated bar, green velvet chairs, and blond-wood paneling—makes an enticing backdrop. And the food? Italian, sort of. Seared tuna comes with bok choy and couscous, and beef carpaccio is served with Minolette cheese and slices of baby peaches preserved with white truffles. ✉ *2040 rue Peel, Downtown* ☎ *514/843–5100* ✍ *Reservations essential* 💳 *AE, DC, MC, V* ⏲ *No lunch weekends* Ⓜ *Peel.*

$$–$$$$ ✕ **Da Vinci.** If you're a hockey fan, book a table near the front of Da Vinci's Victorian dining room and keep an eye on the door. If you're lucky you might spot Sheldon Souray, Mike Ribeiro, or Michael Ryder of the Montréal Canadiens dropping in for roast veal tenderloin or crab-stuffed ravioli. Big, comfortable chairs, discreet service, and generous portions have made Da Vinci an after-practice and after-game favorite for decades. When ordering, however, keep in mind just how much professional hockey players earn these days. ✉ *1180 rue Bishop, Downtown* ☎ *514/874–2001* ✍ *Reservations essential* 💳 *AE, DC, MC, V* ⏲ *Closed Sun.* Ⓜ *Guy-Concordia.*

Japanese

$$–$$$ ✕ **Katsura.** Many Montrealers got their introduction to sushi at Katsura, the first restaurant in the city to make raw fish trendy. It has been overtaken since then, but the pretty waitresses in silk kimonos, the Japanese prints, and the deep red furnishings still attract happy crowds of twentysomethings on dates looking for a little elegance. And such delicacies as the spicy Kamikaze Roll—salmon, avocado, fried onion, and fish roe—or the *unagi* (grilled eel) are still worth a try. ✉ *2170 rue de la Montagne, Downtown* ☎ *514/849–1172* ✍ *Reservations essential* 💳 *AE, MC, V* ⏲ *No lunch weekends* Ⓜ *Peel or Guy-Concordia.*

Portuguese

★ $$$–$$$$ ✕ **Café Ferreira.** A huge mural of antique-pottery fragments decorates the pale-yellow walls of this high-ceiling room—an elegant setting for its "haute" version of Portuguese cuisine. The traditional *caldo verde,* a soup made with kale and sausage, shares space on the menu with grilled fresh sardines; baked salt cod topped with a tomato, onion, and pepper salsa; and *arroz di marisco,* a paella-like dish full of seafood, garlic, and onions. ✉ *1446 rue Peel, Downtown* ☎ *514/848–0988* ▭ *AE, MC, V* ⊙ *No lunch Sat.* Ⓜ *Peel.*

Steak

$$$$ ✕ **Queue de Cheval.** The white-aproned chefs toiling away under the 20-foot-wide copper canopy look more like pagan priests engaged in some arcane ritual than cooks grilling slabs of dry-aged, prime beef on a huge open grill. The meat is sold by the pound, and all accompaniments are extra, so the crowd is pretty much limited to people whose wallets are as thick as the steaks—say, 1½ to 3½ inches. "Go big or stay home" is Queue de Cheval's motto, so don't say you weren't warned. Herringbone brick walls and wide windows create an atmosphere that's half stable, half château. ✉ *1221 blvd. René-Lévesque Ouest, Downtown* ☎ *514/390–0090* ▭ *AE, D, DC, MC, V* Ⓜ *Peel.*

¢–$$ ✕ **Mr. Steer.** Brisk service, well-worn vinyl booths, and thick, juicy, almost spherical hamburgers, discreetly seasoned and served slightly *saignant* (rare) with heaps of curled french fries, are the hallmarks of this unpretentious spot in the downtown shopping district. Steak, too, is available at reasonable prices. ✉ *1198 rue Ste-Catherine Ouest, Downtown* ☎ *514/866–3233* ▭ *MC, V* Ⓜ *Peel.*

Vegetarian

$–$$ ✕ **Le Commensal.** You don't have to be a vegetarian to like Le Commensal. Even members of the steak-frites crowd drop in occasionally to sample the salads, couscous, and meatless versions of such favorites as lasagna and shepherd's pie that this Montréal-grown chain dishes out. The food is served buffet style and sold by weight. There are at least seven outlets on the island, all of them big and bright with modern furniture; the nicest is on the second floor of a downtown building with windows overlooking busy, fashionable rue McGill College. ✉ *1204 rue McGill College, Downtown* ☎ *514/871–1480* ▭ *AE, DC, MC, V* Ⓜ *McGill* ✉ *1720 rue St-Denis, Quartier-Latin* ☎ *514/845–2627* Ⓜ *Sherbrooke* ✉ *5199 ch. de la Côte-des-Neiges, Plateau Mont-Royal* ☎ *514/733–9755* Ⓜ *Côte-des-Neiges.*

The Plateau & Environs

Basque

$$ ✕ **Pintxo.** You don't dine at Pintxo—you graze. And what a lovely pasture it is, too, with bare brick walls, white tablecloths, and waiters in Lacoste shirts and expensive jeans. Pintxos (pronounced "pinchos") are the Basque version of tapas, tiny two-bite solutions to the hunger problem, best enjoyed with a good beer or a glass of chilled sherry. There are about 15 of them on the menu every night, ranging from tiny stacks of grilled vegetables to more substantial dishes, such as seared scallops

with black olives and tuna fillets with ratatouille. If creating your dinner one bite at a time doesn't appeal, there are more normal-size dishes on the menu, such as beef cheeks braised in wine and panfried fish with leeks and artichokes. ✉ *256 rue Roy est, Plateau Mont-Royal* ☎ *514/844–0222* ✍ *Reservations essential* ▭ *AE, DC, MC, V* ⊙ *Closed Sun. No lunch Sat.–Tues.* Ⓜ *Sherbrooke.*

Brazilian

$–$$ ✕ **Senzala.** Two homey locations serve good Brazilian fare, including such specialties as *feijoada* (a stew of pork, black beans, cabbage, and oranges). But brunch—served Thursday to Sunday—is what the locals line up for. Familiar foods like bacon and eggs are served with a tropical touch alongside fried plantains and fruit kabobs. There's also a great selection of fruity smoothies. ✉ *177 rue Bernard Ouest, Mile-End* ☎ *514/274–1464* Ⓜ *St-Laurent* ✉ *4218 rue de la Roche, Plateau Mont-Royal* ☎ *514/521–1266* Ⓜ *Mont-Royal* ▭ *AE, MC, V* ⊙ *No lunch Mon.–Wed.*

Cafés

$–$$ ✕ **Brasserie Artisanale & Bistro Le Reservoir.** A fine selection of beers—the white wheat is particularly good—is brewed up at this neighborhood pub. On the food front, it specializes in bistro lunches and weekend brunches. The evening menu provides high-end sandwiches and snacks. The crowd is a mix of local businesspeople, students, and artists. The location off boulevard St-Laurent and the second-floor terrace with a great view of the passing parade make this place hard to beat. ✉ *9 av. Duluth Est, Plateau Mont-Royal* ☎ *514/849–7779* ▭ *AE, MC, V* Ⓜ *Mont-Royal.*

$–$$ ✕ **Brioche Lyonnaise.** You'll have to go a long way to find a better butter brioche—and try saying that three times quickly—than the one at the Brioche Lyonnaise. Order one along with a steaming bowl of café-au-lait (please don't call it a latte—not here), and you've got a breakfast fit for a king. Come back in the afternoon to try one of the butter-and-cream-loaded pastries in the display case. Heartier fare is available at lunch and dinner, and the place stays open until midnight. The atrium in the back and a terrasse are open in fine weather. ✉ *1593 rue St-Denis, Latin Quarter* ☎ *514/842–7017* ▭ *AE, MC, V* Ⓜ *Berri-UQAM.*

Fodor'sChoice ★

¢–$ ✕ **Les Gâteries.** Many writers and artists take their morning espresso in this comfortable little café facing Square St-Louis. Such local favorites as bagels, muffins, maple-syrup pie, and toast with *cretons* (a coarse, fatty kind of pâté made with pork) share space with baguettes and croissants. ✉ *3443 rue St-Denis, Plateau Mont-Royal* ☎ *514/843–6235* ▭ *AE, MC, V* Ⓜ *Sherbrooke.*

¢ ✕ **St-Viateur Bagel & Café.** Even expatriate New Yorkers have been known to prefer Montréal's light, crispy, and slightly sweet bagel to its heavier Manhattan cousin. (The secret? The dough is boiled in honey-sweetened water before baking.) St-Viateur's wood-fired brick ovens have been operating since 1959. With coffee and smoked salmon, these bagels make a great breakfast. ✉ *1127 av. Mont-Royal Est, Mile-End* ☎ *514/528–6361* ▭ *No credit cards* Ⓜ *Laurier.*

Fodor'sChoice ★

Canadian

$$–$$$ Fodor'sChoice ★ ✕ **Au Pied de Cochon.** Whatever you do, don't let your cardiologist see Martin Picard's menu; if he spots the pigs' feet stuffed with foie gras, he's liable to have a stroke, and he won't be too happy about the pork hocks braised in maple syrup, either, or the *oreilles-de-crisse* (literally, Christ's ears)—crispy, deep-fried crescents of pork skin that Picard serves as appetizers. But it's foie gras that Picard really loves. He lavishes the stuff on everything, including hamburgers and his own version of poutine (french fries, gravy, and cheese curds). Oddly enough, the trendy crowd who pack his noisy tavernlike restaurant every night don't look particularly chubby. ✉ *536 av. Duluth, Plateau Mont-Royal* ☎ *514/281–1114* ✍ *Reservations essential* ▭ *AE, D, DC, MC, V* ⊙ *Closed Mon. No lunch* Ⓜ *Sherbrooke or Mont-Royal.*

¢–$ ✕ **Binerie Mont-Royal.** That rarest of the city's culinary finds—authentic Québecois food—is the specialty at this tiny restaurant. The fare includes stews made with meatballs and pigs' feet, various kinds of tourtière, and pork and beans. It's cheap, filling, and charming. ✉ *367 av. Mont-Royal Est, Plateau Mont-Royal* ☎ *514/285–9078* ▭ *No credit cards* ⊙ *No dinner weekends* Ⓜ *Mont-Royal.*

Contemporary

$$$–$$$$ ✕ **Area.** Chef Ian Perreault scrapped main courses in 2004 to join the small-plate revolution. That means you get to build your own dinner out of a tempting list of soups, *amuse-bouches,* desserts, and tiny platters of such staples as Angus beef and mashed potatoes. It can be a complicated process and a little fiddly, but it can also be a lot of fun. Think of it as a kind of Western dim-sum. Not that Perreault's food is all Western. He calls his cooking "intelligent fusion," so you're likely to find tempura shrimp right next to the mushroom risotto with sautéed wild mushrooms. ✉ *1429 rue Amherst, Village* ☎ *514/890–6691* ✍ *Reservations essential* ▭ *AE, DC, MC, V* Ⓜ *Beaudry.*

★ $$$–$$$$ ✕ **La Chronique.** It's a pretty place with scarlet walls and black-and-white pictures, but people don't come to Chef Marc de Canck's little 36-seat restaurant for the ambience or for the crowd; they come, quite simply, for the food. Without fuss or fanfare, De Canck has been cranking out the city's most adventurous dishes ever since he opened in 1995. The man doesn't seem capable of compromise or playing safe. His work seamlessly blends lightened French fare with Japanese, Chinese, and Creole touches. Starters like sashimi salmon rubbed with coarsely ground pepper, coriander, and mustard seed might precede veal sweetbreads with chorizo or panfried mahimahi with thin slices of eggplant filled with goat cheese. Weekend dinners are prix-fixe only—four courses are C$68, and six courses are C$95. ✉ *99 rue Laurier Ouest, Mile-End* ☎ *514/271–3095* ✍ *Reservations essential* ▭ *AE, DC, MC, V* ⊙ *Closed Mon. No lunch* Ⓜ *Laurier.*

★ $$$–$$$$ ✕ **Globe.** There's a persistent rumor that some people actually go to the Globe for the food, that they don't just order up braised venison or wild chinook salmon or raspberry tart so they'll have an excuse to sit at a table in one of Montréal's liveliest restaurants for a couple of hours and ogle the other slickly dressed patrons (or be ogled by them). And it's not just the patrons that are worth ogling. George Clooney, for example, fell in love—albeit briefly—with one of the Globe's waitresses back in March 2001. But that was spring, of course. ✉ *3455 blvd. St-Laurent, Plateau Mont-Royal* ☎ *514/284–3823* ▭ *AE, DC, MC, V* ⏲ *No lunch* Ⓜ *Sherbrooke.*

$$$–$$$$ ✕ **Med Grill.** Dining in the Med Grill is a little like dining in a fishbowl, which might not appeal to everyone. But if you want to see and be seen, it's pretty hard to beat a set of floor-to-ceiling windows big enough for an automobile showroom. (Tip: to look your best, dress to match the cherry-red walls.) But the Med's not all show and no eat. The food—pepper-crusted tuna with sweetbreads, for example, and a spectacular molten-chocolate cake—looks as delectable as the crowd. ✉ *3500 blvd. St-Laurent, Plateau Mont-Royal* ☎ *514/844–0027* ✍ *Reservations essential* ▭ *AE, MC, V* ⏲ *No lunch* Ⓜ *Sherbrooke.*

$$–$$$ ✕ **L'Assommoir.** A decadent menu featuring such dishes as pork braised in whiskey or hake cooked in sherry attracts a sleek and noisy crowd. But the real specialty of the house is ceviche; the menu lists 10 variations of raw fish "cooked" in citrus. The cocktails are also excellent. This is one place that has managed to modernize the martini without mangling it. ✉ *112 rue Bernard Ouest, Mile-End* ☎ *514/272–0777* ▭ *AE, MC, V* ⏲ *No lunch Mon.–Wed.* Ⓜ *St-Laurent and Bus 55.*

Delicatessen

$–$$ ✕ **Schwartz's Delicatessen.** Schwartz's has no frills. The furniture's shabby, the noise level high, and the waiters are—well, brisk would be the polite word. But its cooks do such a good job of curing, smoking, and slicing (a skill in itself) beef brisket that even when it's 20 below zero you can't see through the windows because locals line up outside to get a seat at the city's most famous deli and order a sandwich thick enough to dislocate jaws. So avoid lunch and dinner hours, and when you do get in, don't ask for a menu; there isn't one. Just order a smoked meat on rye with fries and a side order of pickles—and make it snappy. Your waiter is in a hurry. ✉ *3895 blvd. St-Laurent, Plateau Mont-Royal* ☎ *514/842–4813* ✍ *Reservations not accepted* ▭ *No credit cards* Ⓜ *Sherbrooke.*

Fodor'sChoice ★

French

$$$–$$$$ ✕ **Anise.** Chef Racha Bassoul's training is French but her roots are Lebanese. The result is cooking that keeps her trendy little 60-seat restaurant on the fringes of Mile End full of well-heeled and well-dressed Outremonters. You could start with a classic Middle Eastern dish like kebbeh nayeh (lamb tartare with cracked wheat and fresh mint), followed by something more European, like poached grouper or hangar steak. ✉ *104 rue Laurier Ouest, Mile-End* ☎ *514/276–6999* ✍ *Reservations essential* ▭ *AE, DC, MC, V* ⏲ *Closed Sun. and Mon. No lunch* Ⓜ *Laurier.*

★ **$–$$** ✕ **L'Express.** Mirrored walls and noise levels that are close to painful on weekends make L'Express the closest thing Montréal (and maybe even Canada) has to a Parisian bistro. Service is fast, prices are reasonable, and the food is good, even if the tiny crowded tables barely have room to accommodate it. Steak tartare with french fries, salmon with sorrel, and calves' liver with tarragon are marvelous. Jars of gherkins, fresh baguettes, and aged cheeses make the pleasure last longer. ✉ *3927 rue St-Denis, Plateau Mont-Royal* ☎ *514/845–5333* ✍ *Reservations essential* ▭ *AE, DC, MC, V* Ⓜ *Sherbrooke.*

Greek

$$$$ ✕ **Milos.** Don't let the nets and floats hanging from the ceiling fool you: Milos is no simple taverna—a fact reflected in the prices, which some argue are exorbitant. The main dish is usually the catch of the day grilled over charcoal and seasoned with parsley, capers, and lemon juice. Fish are priced by the pound (C$23–C$32). You can also try lamb and veal chops, cheeses, and olives. ✉ *5357 av. du Parc, Mile-End* ☎ *514/272–3522* ✍ *Reservations essential* ▭ *AE, D, DC, MC, V* ⏲ *No lunch weekends* Ⓜ *Laurier.*

$$–$$$ ✕ **Mythos Ouzerie.** Scores of fun-seeking diners come to this brick-lined semibasement every weekend to eat, drink, and be merry in a delightfully chaotic atmosphere. The food—moussaka, plump stuffed grape leaves, braised lamb, grilled squid—is always good, but go Thursday, Friday, or Saturday night, when the live and very infectious bouzouki music makes it impossible to remain seated. ✉ *5318 av. du Parc, Mile-End* ☎ *514/270–0235* ▭ *AE, DC, MC, V* Ⓜ *Laurier.*

$–$$$ ✕ **Rotisserie Panama.** Some of the best grilled meat in Montréal is what attracts big, noisy crowds to the Rotisserie Panama. The chicken and crispy lamb chops are excellent, as is the roasted baby lamb served on weekends, but if you're really feeling adventurous, order the *kokoretsi* (organ meats wrapped in intestines and grilled on a spit) or *soupa patsas,* a full-flavored tripe soup. The prices won't empty your wallet. ✉ *789 rue Jean-Talon Ouest, Mile-End* ☎ *514/276–5223* ▭ *AE, MC, V* Ⓜ *Parc or Acadie.*

Italian

$$$–$$$$ ✕ **Il Mulino.** Nothing about the decor or the location of this family-run restaurant in Little Italy hints at the good things inside. The antipasti alone—grilled mushrooms, stuffed eggplant, broiled scallops—are worth the trip. The pasta is excellent, especially the *agnolotti* (crescent-shape stuffed pasta) and the gnocchi. Main dishes include simply prepared lamb chops, veal, and excellent fish. ✉ *236 rue St-Zotique Est, Little Italy* ☎ *514/273–5776* ✍ *Reservations essential* ▭ *AE, DC, MC, V* ⏲ *Closed Sun. and Mon.* Ⓜ *Beaubien.*

★ **$$–$$$** ✕ **Tre Marie.** When a young man from Montréal's Italian community meets someone he thinks he might get serious about, this is where he often takes her. The stucco walls and dark-wood trim give the place a little class, and the food is a lot like Mama's—veal stew, for example, and veal tripe with beans and tomato sauce. And if you're feeling really hungry, there's a three-pasta dish that could feed a family of four. ✉ *6934 rue Clark, Little Italy* ☎ *514/277–9859* ✍ *Reservations essential* ▭ *AE, DC, MC, V* ⏲ *Closed Sun. and Mon.* Ⓜ *de Castelnau.*

Japanese

$$–$$$ Fodor's Choice ★ ✕ **Kaizen Treehouse.** Even if you think you've tried every possible variation on sushi, sashimi, and tempura, chances are Chef Tri Du will still be able to surprise you. Montréal's most daring master of Japanese cuisine uses traditional methods as a starting point, and then lets his considerable imagination run wild. The results can be startling. Foie gras tempura, for example, is one of his signature dishes, as is miso-marinated black cod. Also favored by the fashionable crowd that pack his restaurant on weekends are Tri's lambas—riceless maki rolls filled with king crab or sweet squid along with fish roe, cucumber, sweet potato, greens, and tempura flakes. They're listed on the menu under "Magical Food of the Elves," which sounds about right. ✉ *3527 blvd. St-Laurent, Plateau Mont-Royal* ☎ *514/845–7557* *Reservations essential* ▭ *AE, D, MC, V* ⊙ *No lunch Sat.–Mon.* Ⓜ *Mont-Royal.*

Middle Eastern

$$–$$$ ✕ **Restaurant Daou.** Heaven knows that singer Céline Dion could afford to fly her lunch in from Beirut on a chartered jet, but when she and hubby René Angelil—whose parents were both Syrians—are in town, this is where they come to get Lebanese food. The decor is nothing to write home about, but the hummus with ground meat, stuffed grape leaves, and delicately seasoned kabobs attract plenty of Middle Eastern expatriates and native-born Montrealers. ✉ *519 rue Faillon, Villeray* ☎ *514/276–8310* ▭ *AE, DC, MC, V* ⊙ *Closed Mon.* Ⓜ *Parc.*

$–$$ ✕ **Alep.** Graze on *mouhamara* (pomegranate and walnuts), *sabanegh* (spinach and onions), *fattouche* (salad with pita and mint), and *yalanti* (vine leaves stuffed with rice, chickpeas, walnuts, and tomatoes) in a pleasant, stone-walled room draped with ivy. Kebabs dominate the main courses. ✉ *199 rue Jean-Talon Est, Little Italy* ☎ *514/270–6396* ▭ *MC, V* ⊙ *Closed Sun. and Mon.* Ⓜ *Jean-Talon or de Castelnau.*

Portuguese

★ **$–$$** ✕ **Chez Doval.** Chez Doval is a neighborhood restaurant with a split personality. If you're looking for a little intimacy, book a table in the softly lighted dining room on one side of the building; if you're looking for something a little more raucous—guitar music, maybe a friendly argument about sports or politics—try the tavern on the other side. Foodwise it doesn't really matter where you sit. The chicken, sardines, grouper, and squid—all broiled à-la-Portugaise on an open grill behind the bar—are succulent, simple, and good. ✉ *150 rue Marie-Anne Est, Plateau Mont-Royal* ☎ *514/843–3390* ▭ *AE, MC, V* Ⓜ *Mont-Royal.*

Seafood

$$–$$$$ ✕ **Maestro S.V.P.** The regulars belly up to the big wooden bar and slurp down oysters by the dozen. Owner Ilene Polansky imports them from all over the world—the oysters that is, not the regulars—so you can compare the subtle differences between, say, a delicate little bivalve from Prince Edward Island's Malpeque Bay and a big meaty one from Australia's Gold Coast. A free lesson in shucking techniques comes with the order. If oysters aren't your thing, don't despair: Polansky also serves poached salmon with mango butter, a bountiful seafood *pot-au-feu* (a slow-cooked stew), and the inevitable *moules et frites* (mussels and french fries). ✉ *3615 blvd. St-Laurent, Plateau Mont-Royal* ☎ *514/842–6447* ▭ *AE, DC, MC, V* ⊙ *No lunch weekends* Ⓜ *Sherbrooke.*

Steak

$$$–$$$$ ✕ **Moishe's.** The motto says it all: "There is absolutely nothing trendy about Moishe's." And that would include the patrons, most of whom look like they would be more comfortable wearing fedoras. But if you're looking for a thick, marbled steak, perfectly grilled—preceded perhaps by a slug of premium single-malt Scotch—this is the place to come. The members of the Lighter family, who have been operating Moishe's since 1938, offer other dishes, such as lamb and fish, but people come for the beef, which the family ages in its own lockers. ✉ *3961 blvd. St-Laurent, Plateau Mont-Royal* ☎ *514/845–3509* ▭ *AE, DC, MC, V* Ⓜ *St-Laurent.*

Thai

$$–$$$ ✕ **Thai Grill.** Dishes range from the fiery—mussaman curry with beef, sautéed chicken with cashews, onions, and dried red peppers—to such fragrantly mild delicacies as *gai hor bai toey* (chicken wrapped in pandanus leaves and served with a black-bean sauce). Pale-yellow walls, rich wood trim, and traditional Thai masks decorate the elegant dining room. ✉ *5101 blvd. St-Laurent, Plateau Mont-Royal* ☎ *514/270–5566* ▭ *AE, DC, MC, V* Ⓜ *Laurier.*

$–$$ ✕ **Chao Phraya.** The huge front window of this bright, airy restaurant decorated with subtle Asian accents overlooks fashionable rue Laurier. Customers come for such classics as crunchy *poe pia* (tightly wrapped spring rolls), *pha koung* (grilled-shrimp salad), and fried halibut in a red curry sauce with lime juice. ✉ *50 rue Laurier Ouest, Laurier* ☎ *514/272–5339* ✍ *Reservations essential* ▭ *AE, DC, MC, V* ⏲ *No lunch* Ⓜ *Laurier.*

Tibetan

¢–$$ ✕ **Om.** Be careful; stepping into Om's saffron scented calm from the noise and tumult of boulevard St-Laurent can be startling enough to give you the bends. Walls the color of the Dalai Lama's robes provide the backdrop for such traditional Tibetan dishes as *momos* (beef, chicken, or vegetarian dumplings), *churu* (soup with cheese and lamb), and the fiery and sweet chicken chili. There's also an extensive list of Indian dishes. ✉ *4382 blvd. St-Laurent, Plateau Mont-Royal* ☎ *514/287–3553* ▭ *AE, MC, V* ⏲ *Closed Mon.* Ⓜ *Mont-Royal.*

Vegetarian

★ $–$$ ✕ **Chu Chai.** Vegetarians can dine well in any Thai restaurant, as vegetable dishes abound. But chefs at the rigorously vegan Chu Chai also prepare meatless versions of such classics as duck salad with pepper and mint leaves, fish with three hot sauces, and beef with yellow curry and coconut milk, substituting soy and *seitan* (a firm, chewy meat substitute made from wheat gluten) for the real thing. ✉ *4088 rue St-Denis, Plateau Mont-Royal* ☎ *514/843–4194* ✍ *Reservations essential* ▭ *AE, DC, MC, V* Ⓜ *Sherbrooke or Mont-Royal.*

Mont-Royal & Environs

Contemporary

$–$$$ ✕ **Tavern on the Square.** The business crowd sips martinis at the bar, young Westmount matrons entertain their toddlers on the terrasse, and a mixed crowd of visitors and locals—all dressed casual chic—munch on crispy shrimp and seared tuna. The Tavern's the kind of easygoing place you can take your family, your date, or your business acquaintance. ✉ *1 Westmount Sq., Westmount* ☎ *514/989–9779* ▭ *AE, DC, MC, V* ⊙ *Closed Sun. No lunch weekends* Ⓜ *Atwater.*

French

$$$–$$$$ ✕ **Les Chèvres.** Chef Stelio Perombelon thinks dining out should be fun and hassle-free—hence the color scheme (baby-blue and yellow walls trimmed with violet and orange) and the prix-fixe menu. Instead of adding up a row of *à-la-carte* items to see if they fit your budget, you just pick three courses (C$47) or five courses (C$60). And what courses they are: sweetbreads with warm asparagus salad, guinea hen with celery root and oyster mushrooms, and sweetbreads with mashed turnips. For dessert, try the cheesecake. ✉ *1201 av. Van-Horne, Outremont* ☎ *514/270–1119* ✍ *Reservations essential* ▭ *AE, DC, MC, V* ⊙ *Closed Sun. and Mon. No lunch* Ⓜ *Outremont.*

Japanese

$$–$$$$ ✕ **Kaizen.** If you like a little drama with your sushi, Kaizen's black-clad hostesses, floor-to-ceiling red curtains, and glassed-in wine cellar certainly add a dash of theater to dinner. It's a buzz place that attracts the kind of well-dressed patrons who can't bear to leave their cell phone and Blackberry at home. The sushi, maki, lambas, sashimi, and seafood soups are all well above average, and the Kobe beef is just daring enough to be interesting without being intimidating. Try the oysters Tri Afeller, mixed with spinach and shallots. ✉ *4075 rue Ste-Catherine Ouest, Westmount* ☎ *514/932–5654* ✍ *Reservations essential* ▭ *AE, DC, MC, V* ⊙ *No lunch weekends* Ⓜ *Atwater.*

The Islands

French

$$$$ ✕ **Nuances.** If you hit the jackpot on one of the slot machines downstairs or strike it rich at the baccarat table, you'll have no trouble paying the bill at the Casino de Montréal's premier restaurant. Otherwise, check the credit limit on your plastic before booking a table. And if you go ahead, make sure you get a table next to one of the windows so you can enjoy the million-dollar view of the river and Montréal's twinkling skyline while you dine on Chef Olivier Rault's loin of lamb cooked in an earthenware pot. ✉ *1 av. du Casino, Île Notre-Dame* ☎ *514/392–2708* ✍ *Reservations essential* ▭ *AE, DC, MC, V* ⊙ *No lunch* Ⓜ *Jean-Drapeau.*

WHERE TO STAY

Montréal has a wide variety of accommodations, from the big chain hotels you'll find in every city to historic inns, boutique hotels, and bargain-rate hostels. You can sleep in the room where Liz Taylor and Richard Burton got married or book a bed in an 18th-century stone inn where George Washington didn't sleep, but Benjamin Franklin did.

Keep in mind that during peak season (May through August), finding a bed without making reservations can be difficult. From mid-November to early April, rates often drop, and throughout the year many hotels have two-night, three-day, double-occupancy packages at substantial discounts.

Most of the major hotels—the ones with big meeting rooms, swimming pools, and several bars and restaurants—are in the downtown area, which makes them ideal for those who want all the facilities along with easy access to the big department stores and malls on rue Ste-Catherine, the museums of the Golden Square Mile and nightlife on rues Crescent and de la Montagne. If you want something a little more historic, consider renting a room in one of the dozen or so boutique hotels that occupy the centuries-old buildings lining the cobbled streets of Vieux-Montréal. Most of them offer all the conveniences along with the added charm of stone walls, casement windows, and period-style furnishings.

If, however, your plans include shopping expeditions to avenue Mont-Royal and rue Laurier with maybe a few late nights at the jazz bars and dance clubs of Main Street and rue St-Denis, then the place to bed down is in one of the Plateau Mont-Royal's small but comfortable hotels. Room rates in the area tend to be quite reasonable, but be careful: the hotels right in the middle of the action—on rue St-Denis for example—can be a little noisy, especially if you get a room fronting the street.

WHAT IT COSTS In Canadian dollars

	$$$$	$$$	$$	$	¢
FOR 2 PEOPLE	over C$250	C$176–C$250	C$126–C$175	C$75–C$125	under C$75

Prices are for a standard double room in high season; they exclude 7.5% provincial sales tax, 6% goods-and-services tax (GST), and a C$2.30 city tax.

Vieux-Montréal

★ $$$$ **Hôtel Le St. James.** When the Stones rolled into town in 2003, Mick and the boys took over this lavishly furnished luxury hotel. It was once the Mercantile Bank of Canada, which is why a former boardroom has 20-foot ceilings and lovingly restored murals of hydroelectric dams and waterfalls. Guest rooms include large marble bathrooms with separate tubs and showers and have Bang & Olufsen sound systems; some rooms have gas fireplaces. The hotel restaurant XO is in what used to be the main banking hall. ✉ *355 rue St-Jacques, Vieux-Montréal, H2Y 1N9* ☎ *514/841–3111 or 866/841–3111* 🖷 *514/841–1232* 🌐 *www.hotellestjames.com* *23 rooms, 38 suites, 1 apartment* *Restaurant, room service, room TVs with movies, Wi-Fi, gym, spa, bar, library, dry cleaning, laundry service, concierge, meeting rooms, parking (fee), some pets allowed* 💳 *AE, D, DC, MC, V* *EP* Ⓜ *Place-d'Armes.*

★ $$$$ **Hôtel St. Paul.** Stark white walls and huge shuttered windows give the "sky rooms" in this converted 19th-century office building on the western edge of Vieux-Montréal a light, ethereal feel. The "earth rooms" are decorated in richer, darker colors. All have separate sitting areas with sleek leather furniture. The hotel's Cube restaurant, which serves some of the city's most innovative food, is an intimate place for dinner, but the lunchtime crowd includes plenty of high-powered wheelers and dealers from the nearby financial district. ✉ *355 rue McGill, Vieux-Montréal, H2Y 2E8* ☎ *514/380–2222 or 866/380–2202* 🖷 *514/380–2200* 🌐 *www.hotelstpaul.com* *96 rooms, 24 suites* *Restaurant, room service, in-room fax, minibars, cable TV with movies, in-room broadband, in-room data ports, gym, massage, bar, dry cleaning, concierge, business services, parking (fee), no-smoking floors* 💳 *AE, D, DC, MC, V* 🍽 *BP* Ⓜ *Square-Victoria.*

$$$$ **Hôtel W.** This ultrachic, ultraluxurious chain took a risk opening its first Canadian hotel in a city whose major language is almost devoid of the letter "w." The famed "whatever, whenever service," for example, becomes "service top désirs." Not as alliterative, but the idea is the same. Want rose petals in your bathtub at 3 AM? Just call. The hotel is housed in the old Bank of Canada building, but you'd never know it once you walk through those whooshing sliding doors into the modern lobby. The bright, airy guest rooms are decorated in various shades of gray highlighted with electric-blue pinstripes. Faux-fur throws on the beds allude to Montréal's commercial past, and the bathrooms have deep, square tubs and sinks. The mezzanine-level Plateau bar is popular with local professionals, while the late-night Wunder Bar attracts celebrities. ✉ *901 Square Victoria, Vieux-Montréal, H2Z 1R1* ☎ *514/395–3100* 🌐 *www.whotels.com/montreal* *152 rooms, 30 suites* *Restaurant, room service, in-room safes, minibars, cable TV with movies and video games, in-room DVD, in-room data ports, Web TV, Wi-Fi, gym, spa, 2 bars, concierge, business services, meeting rooms, some pets allowed* 💳 *AE, D, DC, MC, V* 🍽 *EP* Ⓜ *Square-Victoria.*

Fodor's Choice ★

$$$$ **Pierre du Calvet AD 1725.** Merchant Pierre du Calvet—a notorious republican and Freemason—entertained Benjamin Franklin behind the stone walls of this elegant 18th-century home in Vieux-Montréal. Today it's a B&B luxuriously decorated with antique furnishings and Oriental rugs. Its Filles du Roy restaurant specializes in such traditional Québecois dishes as tourtière (meat pie) and braised venison, while the Le Calvet dining room celebrates classic French cuisine. The glassed-in garden, filled with flowers and potted plants, is a great place for breakfast. ✉ *405 rue Bonsecours, Vieux-Montréal, H2Y 3C3* ☎ *514/282–1725 or 866/282–1725* 🖷 *514/282–0546* 🌐 *www.pierreducalvet.ca* *1 room, 8 suites* *2 restaurants, in-room data ports, library, dry cleaning, laundry service, business services, meeting room, parking (fee), no-smoking rooms; no room TVs* 💳 *AE, D, DC, MC, V* 🍽 *BP* Ⓜ *Champ-de-Mars.*

★ **$$$–$$$$** **Auberge du Vieux-Port.** Rumor has it that it was here that Suzanne took Leonard Cohen to her loft by the river and fed him oranges and tea that came "all the way from China"—a tidbit to keep in mind if you're coming to Montréal for a romantic weekend. Suzanne—actually dancer Suzanne Verdal—is long gone, but the Auberge's stone and brick walls, brass beds, and exposed beams will almost certainly please your sweetheart. The casement windows overlook either fashionable rue St-Paul or the Vieux-Port, and on warm summer nights you can sip white wine on the rooftop terrace and watch the fireworks competitions. A full breakfast is served in Les Remparts, the hotel's French restaurant. Warning: make sure that your room is in the main building and not in the St. Paul annex. ✉ *97 rue de la Commune Est, Vieux-Montréal, H2Y 1J1* ☎ *514/876–0081 or 888/660–7678* 📠 *514/876–8923* 🌐 *www.aubergeduvieuxport.com* *27 rooms* *Restaurant, room service, in-room safes, cable TV, Wi-Fi, massage, babysitting, dry cleaning, laundry service, concierge, business services, parking (fee), some pets allowed (fee); no smoking* 💳 *AE, DC, MC, V* 🍽 *BP* Ⓜ *Place-d'Armes or Champ-de-Mars.*

★ **$$$–$$$$** **Hôtel Gault.** The street is lined with gaslights and the facade dates from the 1800s, but the loft-style rooms in this boutique hotel look like something out of a modern-design magazine. Each is different: some have tile-and-concrete floors brightened by boldly patterned geometric rugs; others have sleek, blond-wood furnishings and contrasting rough-brick walls. All have CD and DVD players. Bathrooms have freestanding modern tubs and heated tile floors. ✉ *449 rue Ste-Hélène, Vieux-Montréal, H2V 2K9* ☎ *514/904–1717 or 866/904–1717* 🌐 *www.hotelgault.com* *25 rooms, 5 suites* *Room service, in-room safes, minibars, cable TV with movies, in-room DVD, in-room broadband, in-room data ports, gym, bar, dry cleaning, laundry service, business services, parking (fee), some pets allowed, no-smoking floors* 💳 *AE, MC, V* 🍽 *CP* Ⓜ *Square-Victoria.*

$$$–$$$$ Fodor'sChoice ★ **Hôtel Nelligan.** Verses by Émile Nelligan, Québec's most passionate poet, decorate the stone and brick walls of this ultraromantic hotel on fashionable rue St-Paul. The hotel, just a block south of the Basilique Notre-Dame-de-Montréal, occupies two adjoining buildings from the 1850s. Some suites have terraces with views of the river; others overlook the four-story, brick-walled atrium. At the airy bar, make sure to snag a table near the window overlooking rue St-Paul and watch the world hustle by. And for breakfast with a view of the old city and the harbor, try the rooftop terrace. Complimentary wine and cheese are served every afternoon. ✉ *106 rue St-Paul Ouest, Vieux-Montréal, H2Y 1Z3* ☎ *514/788–2040 or 877/788–2040* 📠 *514/788–2041* 🌐 *www.hotelnelligan.com* *35 rooms, 28 suites* *Restaurant, room service, in-room safes, cable TV, in-room broadband, gym, massage, bar, lounge, library, dry cleaning, laundry service, concierge, business services, meeting rooms, parking (fee), no-smoking floors* 💳 *AE, D, DC, MC, V* 🍽 *CP* Ⓜ *Place-d'Armes.*

$$$–$$$$ **Inter-Continental Montréal.** On the edge of Vieux-Montréal, this modern luxury hotel is part of the Montréal World Trade Center, a block-long retail and office complex. The 26-story brick tower is softened a bit with fanciful turrets and pointed roofs. Rooms are large, with lush carpets, pastel walls, and heavy drapes that pull back to reveal floor-to-ceiling windows overlooking downtown or Vieux-Montréal and the waterfront. Bathrooms have separate marble tubs and showers. Le Continent restaurant serves fine international cuisine. A footbridge links the hotel's main building with the 18th-century Nordheimer

Building, which houses many of its public rooms. ✉ *360 rue St-Antoine Ouest, Vieux-Montréal, H2Y 3X4* ☎ *514/987–9900 or 800/361–3600* 📠 *514/847–8550* 🌐 *www.montreal.interconti.com* *334 rooms, 23 suites* *2 restaurants, room service, minibars, room TVs with movies and video games, in-room broadband, in-room data ports, indoor pool, health club, sauna, bar, dry cleaning, laundry service, concierge, meeting rooms, parking (fee)* 💳 *AE, D, DC, MC, V* 🍽 *EP* Ⓜ *Square-Victoria or Place-d'Armes.*

$$$–$$$$ Fodor's Choice ★ **Le Place d'Armes Hôtel & Suites.** Three splendidly ornate commercial buildings dating from the Victorian era were merged in 2005 to create Vieux-Montréal's largest boutique hotel. The high-ceiling guest rooms—some with exposed brick or stone walls—combine old-fashioned grandeur with sleek modern furnishings. The large bathrooms are tiled in black granite and white marble. The 2,000-square-foot spa includes the city's first *hammam,* or Middle Eastern–style steam bath. A rooftop bar and restaurant serves sandwiches and grilled entrées at lunch, and a comfortable lobby bar serves complimentary tea in the afternoon. The Basilique Notre-Dame-de-Montréal is just across the square, and the Palais des Congrès is nearby. ✉ *701 Côte de la Place d'Armes, Vieux-Montréal, H2Y 2X6* ☎ *514/842–1887 or 888/450–1887* 📠 *514/842–6469* 🌐 *www.hotelplacedarmes.com* *83 rooms, 52 suites* *2 restaurants, room service, in-room safes, minibars, cable TV, Wi-Fi, gym, spa, 2 bars, dry cleaning, laundry service, concierge, meeting rooms, parking (fee)* 💳 *AE, DC, MC, V* 🍽 *BP* Ⓜ *Place-d'Armes.*

$$$–$$$$ **Springhill Suites.** This modern all-suites hotel with plenty of amenities fits seamlessly into one of the narrowest and oldest streets of Vieux-Montréal. The rooms are plain but large and comfortable, with pastel walls and nondescript modern furniture. This is the perfect compromise for those seeking modern amenities in antique surroundings. Busy rue St-Paul is a block south, the Vieux-Port is a five-minute walk, and Place Jacques-Cartier is three blocks east. ✉ *445 rue St-Jean-Baptiste, Vieux-Montréal, H2Y 2Z7* ☎ *514/875–4333 or 888/287–9400* 📠 *514/875–4331* 🌐 *www.springhillsuites.com* *189 suites* *Restaurant, room service, minibars, microwaves, cable TV with movies, in-room broadband, in-room data ports, indoor pool, gym, bar, laundry service, meeting rooms, parking (fee)* 💳 *AE, D, DC, MC, V* 🍽 *BP* Ⓜ *Champ-de-Mars.*

$$$–$$$$ **Le Saint-Sulpice.** The Basilique Notre-Dame-de-Montréal is next door, and the comfortable lobby lounge and bar open onto a courtyard garden that's one of the rare green spots in Vieux-Montréal's stony landscape. The lodgings—huge suites with queen-size beds piled high with feather duvets, leather armchairs, and casement windows that actually open—are in a structure built in 2002 to blend in with the rest of the neighborhood; the gym and business center are in an adjoining 19th-century building. Some suites have fireplaces and balconies. ✉ *414 rue St-Sulpice, Vieux-Montréal, H2Y 2V5* ☎ *514/288–1000 or 877/785–7423* 📠 *514/288–0077* 🌐 *www.lesaintsulpice.com* *108 suites* *Restaurant, room service, in-room safes, some kitchens, minibars, microwaves, cable TV with movies and video games, in-room* *data ports, gym, massage, babysitting, dry cleaning, laundry service, concierge, business services, meeting rooms, parking (fee), some pets allowed (fee), no-smoking rooms* ▭ *AE, D, DC, MC, V* 🍴 *BP* Ⓜ *Place-d'Armes.*

$$–$$$$ **Hôtel XIXe Siècle.** You'd think that crystal chandeliers, 14-foot ceilings, and opulent Second Empire moldings would make the Hôtel XIXe Siècle the exclusive preserve of romantic couples and dowager duchesses, but its location in the middle of the financial district and a block from the city's convention center make it a favorite with business travelers as well. ✉ *262 rue St-Jacques Ouest, Vieux-Montréal, H2Y 1N1* ☎ *514/985–0019 or 877/553–0019* 📠 *514/985–0059* 🌐 *www.hotelxixsiecle.com* ⇨ *59 rooms* ♘ *Wi-Fi, bar, parking (fee)* ▭ *AE, D, DC, MC, V* 🍴 *BP.*

$$$ **Auberge les Passants du Sans Soucy.** Daniel Soucy and Michael Banks, two of the friendliest and most urbane hosts you're likely to run into, will go out of their way to make you feel like a house guest rather than a customer—if you're lucky enough to snag one of their 10 rooms, that is. Some regulars would rather delay their vacation than stay anywhere else. And no wonder: the hotel lobby doubles as an art gallery and the rooms have brass beds, stone walls, exposed beams, whirlpool baths, and lots of fresh-cut flowers. For breakfast there are selections such as salmon omelets and French toast, all served in front of a fireplace that's full of flowers in summer and crackling logs in winter. ✉ *171 rue St-Paul Ouest, Vieux-Montréal, H2Y 1Z5* ☎ *514/842–2634* 📠 *514/842–2912* 🌐 *www.lesanssoucy.com* ⇨ *9 rooms, 1 suite* ♘ *Cable TV, lounge, dry cleaning, laundry service, meeting room; no smoking* ▭ *AE, MC, V* 🍴 *BP* Ⓜ *Square-Victoria or Place-d'Armes.*

Fodor'sChoice ★

★ **$$–$$$** **Auberge Bonaparte.** One of the finest restaurants in Vieux-Montréal, Auberge Bonaparte has converted the upper floors of its 19th-century building into an inn. Wrought-iron or Louis Philippe–style furnishings fill the guest rooms, some of which have double whirlpool baths. The rooms in the rear (some with balconies) have views over the private gardens of the Basilique Notre-Dame-de-Montréal. Breakfast is served in your room. ✉ *447 rue St-François-Xavier, Vieux-Montréal, H2Y 2T1* ☎ *514/844–1448* 📠 *514/844–0272* 🌐 *www.bonaparte.ca* ⇨ *30 rooms, 1 suite* ♘ *Restaurant, room service, cable TV with movies, in-room data ports, bar, babysitting, concierge, meeting room, parking (fee); no smoking* ▭ *AE, D, DC, MC, V* 🍴 *BP* Ⓜ *Place-d'Armes.*

★ **$$** **Auberge de la Place Royale.** What was once a 19th-century rooming house is now a waterfront B&B overlooking the Vieux-Port. A magnificent wood staircase links the floors of this stone building. Antiques and reproductions furnish the spacious guest rooms, some of which have whirlpool tubs. In warm weather, a full breakfast is served on a sidewalk terrace; in cooler months it's delivered to your room. The service is very attentive. ✉ *115 rue de la Commune Ouest, Vieux-Montréal, H2Y 2C7* ☎ *514/287–0522* 📠 *514/287–1209* 🌐 *www.aubergeplaceroyale.com* ⇨ *9 rooms, 3 suites* ♘ *Restaurant, café, cable TV, in-room data ports, babysitting, dry cleaning, laundry service, parking (fee); no smoking* ▭ *AE, MC, V* 🍴 *BP* Ⓜ *Place-d'Armes.*

¢ **Auberge Alternative.** The name says it all. You won't find any expense-account fat cats in the breakfast room sipping the fair-trade coffee and checking the stock prices. Instead you'll find earnest, young, and young-at-heart travelers from all over the world and North America—the kind of people who often speak French or try to and are eager to plunge into the local scene. They're also the kind of people who take the time to find really cheap lodgings in really desirable areas. You can get a very basic but clean room for C$55 or a dorm bed for as little as C$18. All guests can use the kitchen facilities. ✉ *358 rue St-Pierre, Vieux-Montréal, H2Y 2M1* ☎ *514/282–0869* 🌐 *www.auberge-alternative.qc.ca* *8 rooms* *Internet room, laundry facilities, shared kitchen facilities* ▭ *MC, V* 🍽 *BP* Ⓜ *Square-Victoria.*

Downtown & Chinatown

★ **$$$$** **Ritz-Carlton.** Montréal's grandest hotel successfully blends Edwardian style—all rooms have marble baths, and some suites have working fireplaces—with modern amenities. Careful and personal attention are hallmarks of the Ritz-Carlton's service: your shoes are shined, there's fresh fruit in your room, and everyone greets you by name, which is probably why guests have included such luminaries as Elizabeth Taylor and Richard Burton, who were married here in 1964. Power meals are the rule at Le Café de Paris, where politicians and business executives meet to hash out deals. The lovely garden in the courtyard is a favorite spot for afternoon tea. ✉ *1228 rue Sherbrooke Ouest, Square Mile, H3G 1H6* ☎ *514/842–4212 or 800/363–0366* 📠 *514/842–3383* 🌐 *www.ritzcarlton.com/hotels/montreal* *419 rooms, 47 suites* *Restaurant, tea shop, room service, in-room safes, minibars, cable TV with movies and video games, in-room data ports, gym, hair salon, massage, bar, piano bar, shops, babysitting, dry cleaning, laundry service, concierge, business services, convention center, parking (fee), some pets allowed (fee)* ▭ *AE, DC, MC, V* 🍽 *EP* Ⓜ *Peel or Guy-Concordia.*

$$$–$$$$ **Le Centre Sheraton.** The huge glass-fronted lobby is usually full of conventioneers and student groups from upscale schools, and in late afternoon the lobby bar fills up quickly with local businesspeople grabbing a drink before heading home to the suburbs. If that's not your idea of a holiday, stay away, but if you don't mind the hubbub, the location is right in the heart of downtown and the blandly decorated rooms are large and airy. Those on higher floors have big windows that overlook the mountain or the St. Lawrence River. ✉ *1201 blvd. René-Lévesque Ouest, Downtown, H3B 2L7* ☎ *514/878–2000 or 800/445–8667* 📠 *514/878–3958* 🌐 *www.sheraton.com/lecentre* *785 rooms, 40 suites* *2 restaurants, coffee shop, bar, room service, minibars, cable TV with movies and video games, in-room data ports, indoor pool, health club, hair salon, babysitting, dry cleaning, laundry service, concierge, business services, meeting rooms, convention center, parking (fee)* ▭ *AE, D, DC, MC, V* 🍽 *EP* Ⓜ *Bonaventure or Peel.*

$$$–$$$$ **Delta Montréal.** With a huge baronial chandelier and gold-color carpets, the two stories of public space at the Delta look a bit like a French château. Rooms are nicely proportioned, with mahogany-veneer furnishings and windows that overlook the mountain or downtown. The hotel has the city's most complete exercise and swimming facilities and an extensive business center. The Cordial bar serves lunch on weekdays. ✉ *475 av. du Président-Kennedy, Downtown, H3A 1J7* ☎ *514/286–1986 or 877/286–1986* 🖷 *514/284–4342* 🌐 *www.deltamontreal.com* ⇒ *456 rooms, 4 suites* ♖ *Restaurant, room service, minibars, cable TV with movies and video games, in-room broadband, in-room data ports, indoor pool, fitness classes, gym, health club, hot tub, sauna, spa, squash, bar, recreation room, shops, babysitting, children's programs (ages 1–13), dry cleaning, laundry service, concierge, business services, meeting rooms, parking (fee), some pets allowed (fee), no-smoking floors* ▭ *AE, D, DC, MC, V* 🍴 *EP* Ⓜ *McGill or Place-des-Arts.*

$$$–$$$$ **Fairmont Le Reine Elizabeth.** John Lennon and Yoko Ono staged their "bed in for peace" in Room 1742 of this hotel in 1969. Rooms are modern, spacious, and spotless, with lush carpeting and richly colored fabrics. The suite-level floors—20 and 21—have business services, and the Gold floors—18 and 19—have their own elevator, check-in, and concierge. The hotel is the site of many conventions. ✉ *900 blvd. René-Lévesque Ouest, Downtown, H3B 4A5* ☎ *514/861–3511 or 800/441–1414* 🖷 *514/954–2296* 🌐 *www.fairmont.com* ⇒ *939 rooms, 100 suites* ♖ *3 restaurants, room service, some microwaves, some refrigerators, cable TV with movies and video games, in-room data ports, indoor pool, health club, hair salon, 3 bars, babysitting, dry cleaning, laundry service, concierge, concierge floors, business services, meeting rooms, parking (fee), some pets allowed (fee), no-smoking rooms* ▭ *AE, D, DC, MC, V* 🍴 *EP* Ⓜ *Bonaventure.*

$$$–$$$$ **Hilton Montréal Bonaventure.** The 2½ acres of rooftop gardens and the open-air year-round swimming pool set the Bonaventure apart from the usual run of corporate hotels, and make it a great place to take the family. The location's pretty good, too—right on top of the Place Bonaventure exhibition center with easy access to the Métro and the Underground City. Modern furniture and pastel walls decorate the guest rooms. ✉ *900 rue de la Gauchetière, Downtown, H5A 1E4* ☎ *514/878–2332 or 800/267–2575* 🖷 *514/878–3881* 🌐 *www.hilton.com* ⇒ *395 rooms, 15 suites* ♖ *Restaurant, room service, minibars, room TVs with movies and video games, in-room broadband, pool, gym, bar, shops, dry cleaning, laundry service, concierge, business services, meeting rooms, convention center, parking (fee), some pets allowed (fee), no-smoking rooms* ▭ *AE, D, DC, MC, V* 🍴 *EP* Ⓜ *Bonaventure.*

★ $$$–$$$$ **Hôtel le Germain.** What was once a dowdy, outdated downtown office building is now a sleek, luxurious boutique hotel. The earth-tone rooms showcase Québec-designed bedroom and bathroom furnishings in dark, dense tropical woods. Leather armchairs add a traditional feel. All rooms have individual sound systems and huge flat-screen TVs; some have grand views of Mont-Royal or the skyscrapers along avenue du Président-Kennedy. If you need more space, there is also a pair of two-story apartments. ✉ *2050 rue Mansfield, Downtown, H3A 1Y9* ☎ *514/849–2050 or 877/333–2050* 🖷 *514/849–1437* 🌐 *www.hotelgermain.com* ⇒ *99 rooms, 2 suites* ♖ *Restaurant, room service, minibars, cable TV, Wi-Fi, gym, bar, dry cleaning, laundry facilities, concierge, business services, meeting rooms, parking (fee), some* *pets allowed, no-smoking floors* ☰ *AE, DC, MC, V* 🍽 *CP* Ⓜ *Peel or McGill.*

$$$–$$$$ **Hôtel le Square-Phillips et Suites.** The location is certainly majestic: King Edward VII entertains the pigeons in the square across the street, and La Baie department store, St. Patrick's Basilica, and Christ Church Cathedral are all within 200 yards of the front door. After a busy day of shopping and museum-hopping, you can take a relaxing swim in the glassed-in pool on the rooftop, or just take in the views from the sundeck. All the rooms and suites have fully equipped kitchens, but you might not get a chance to use them because it's easier to find a restaurant than a grocery store anywhere near here. The art deco building itself was designed by Ernest Cormier (1885–1980) and was converted to a hotel with a rooftop sundeck in 2004. ✉ *1193 rue Square-Phillips, Downtown, H3B 3C9* ☎ *514/393–1193 or 866/393–1193* 📠 *514/393–1192* 🌐 *www.squarephillips.com* *80 rooms, 80 suites* *Breakfast room, kitchens, exercise equipment, indoor pool, business services, laundry facilities, room TVs with movies, Wi-Fi, parking (fee)* ☰ *AE, DC, MC, V* 🍽 *CP* Ⓜ *McGill.*

$$$–$$$$ **Hyatt Regency Montréal.** The Hyatt is *the* place to stay during the International Jazz Festival in July—if you're a fan, that is. The 12-story hotel, built at the northern end of Complexe Desjardins shopping mall, overlooks the Place des Arts plaza where most of the festival's free concerts are staged. It's a good location the rest of the year, too. The Musée d'Art Contemporain is across the street and Chinatown is a block away (you can walk to both via the Underground City if it's raining) and the restaurants of rue St-Denis and boulevard St-Laurent are within walking distance. ✉ *1255 rue Jeanne-Mance, Downtown, H5B 1E5* ☎ *514/982–1234 or 800/233–1234* 📠 *514/285–1243* 🌐 *www.montreal.hyatt.com/property* *605 rooms, 34 suites* *Restaurant, minibars, cable TV with movies, in-room data ports, Wi-Fi, indoor pool, gym, spa, bar, dry cleaning, laundry service, business services, meeting rooms, parking (fee), no-smoking floors* ☰ *AE, D, DC, MC, V* 🍽 *EP* Ⓜ *Place-des-Arts or Place-d'Armes.*

$$$–$$$$ **Loews Hôtel Vogue.** This is where such stars as George Clooney, Julia Roberts, and Matt Damon come to stay and play. The lobby bar with its big bay window overlooking rue de la Montagne is a favorite for martinis after work, but for something a little quieter you can sip your predinner drinks by the big fireplace in the lobby lounge. Guest rooms are luxurious, with striped silk upholstered furniture and beds draped with lacy duvets. Canopy beds give many rooms a romantic touch. The bathrooms have whirlpool baths, televisions, and phones. The location—a five-minute walk from Holt Renfrew and other high-end boutiques—makes it an ideal base for serious shoppers. ✉ *1425 rue de la Montagne, Downtown, H3G 1Z3* ☎ *514/285–5555 or 800/465–6654* 📠 *514/849–8903* 🌐 *www.loewshotels.com* *126 rooms, 16 suites* *Restaurant, room service, in-room fax, minibars, cable TV, in-room data ports, gym, sauna, bar, babysitting, children's programs (ages 1–18), dry cleaning, laundry service, concierge, business services, meeting rooms, parking (fee), some pets allowed* ☰ *AE, D, DC, MC, V* 🍽 *EP* Ⓜ *Peel.*

Fodor's Choice ★

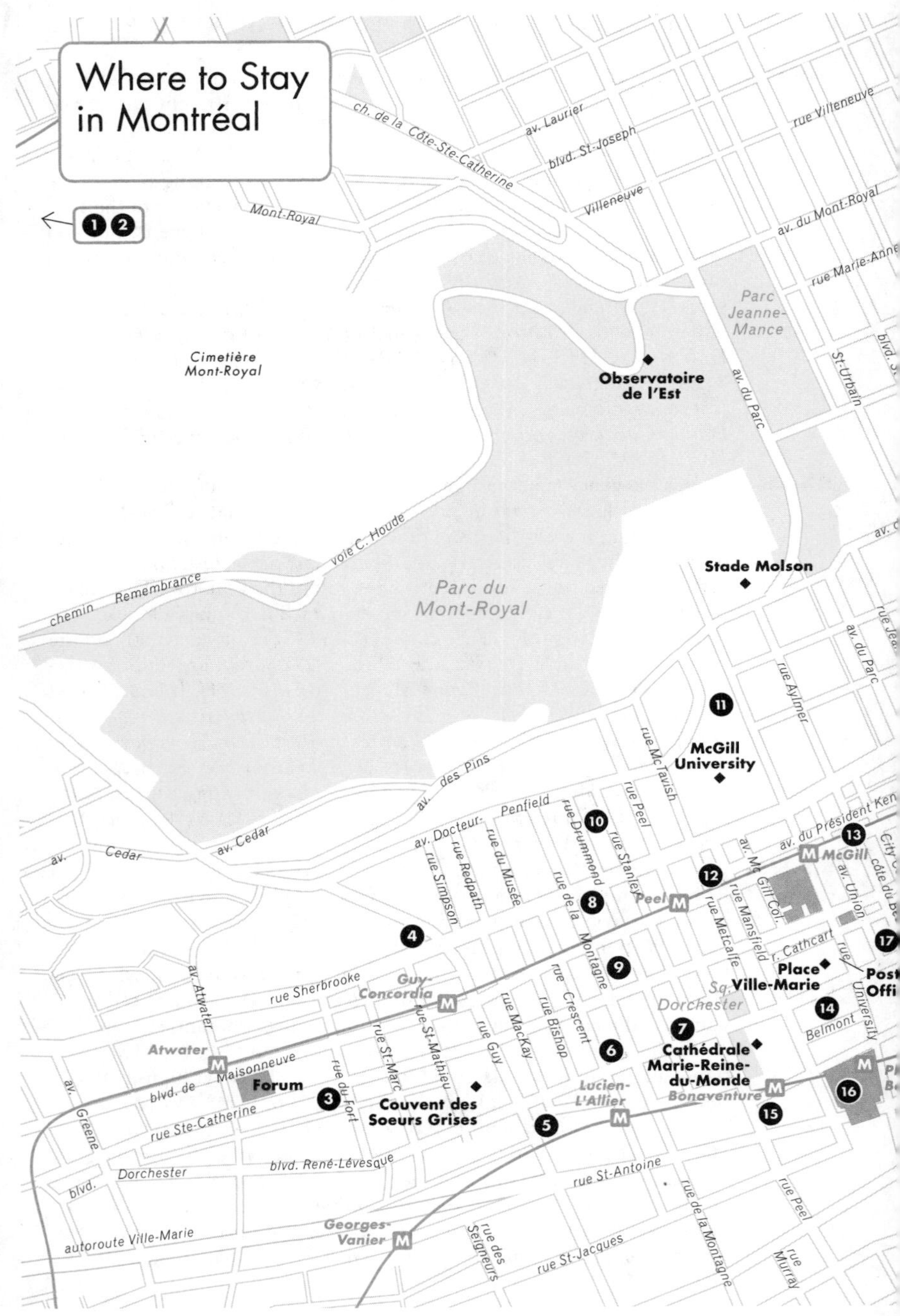
Where to Stay in Montréal
1 2
ch. de la Côte-Ste-Catherine
av. Laurier
blvd. St-Joseph
rue Villeneuve
Villeneuve
Mont-Royal
av. du Mont-Royal
rue Marie-Anne
Parc Jeanne-Mance
Cimetière Mont-Royal
Observatoire de l'Est
av. du Parc
St-Urbain
voie C. Houde
chemin Remembrance
Parc du Mont-Royal
Stade Molson
rue Aylmer
av. du Parc
11
McGill University
rue McTavish
av. des Pins
rue Peel
Penfield
av. Docteur-
rue Drummond
10
rue Stanley
av. Cedar
av. Cedar
rue Simpson
rue Redpath
rue du Musée
rue de la Montagne
8
Peel
12
av. McGill Col.
av. du Président Ken
13
McGill
av. Union
rue Mansfield
rue Metcalfe
4
r. Cathcart
rue University
17
Place Ville-Marie
Post Offi
9
rue Crescent
rue Bishop
rue MacKay
rue Guy
rue Sherbrooke
Guy-Concordia
av. Atwater
rue St-Mathieu
rue St-Marc
Sq. Dorchester
14
Belmont
7
Cathédrale Marie-Reine-du-Monde
6
Atwater
blvd. de Maisonneuve
Forum
rue du Fort
3
Couvent des Soeurs Grises
Lucien-L'Allier
Bonaventure
15
16
5
av. Greene
rue Ste-Catherine
blvd. René-Lévesque
blvd. Dorchester
rue St-Antoine
rue de la Montagne
rue Peel
Georges-Vanier
autoroute Ville-Marie
rue des Seigneurs
rue St-Jacques
rue Murray

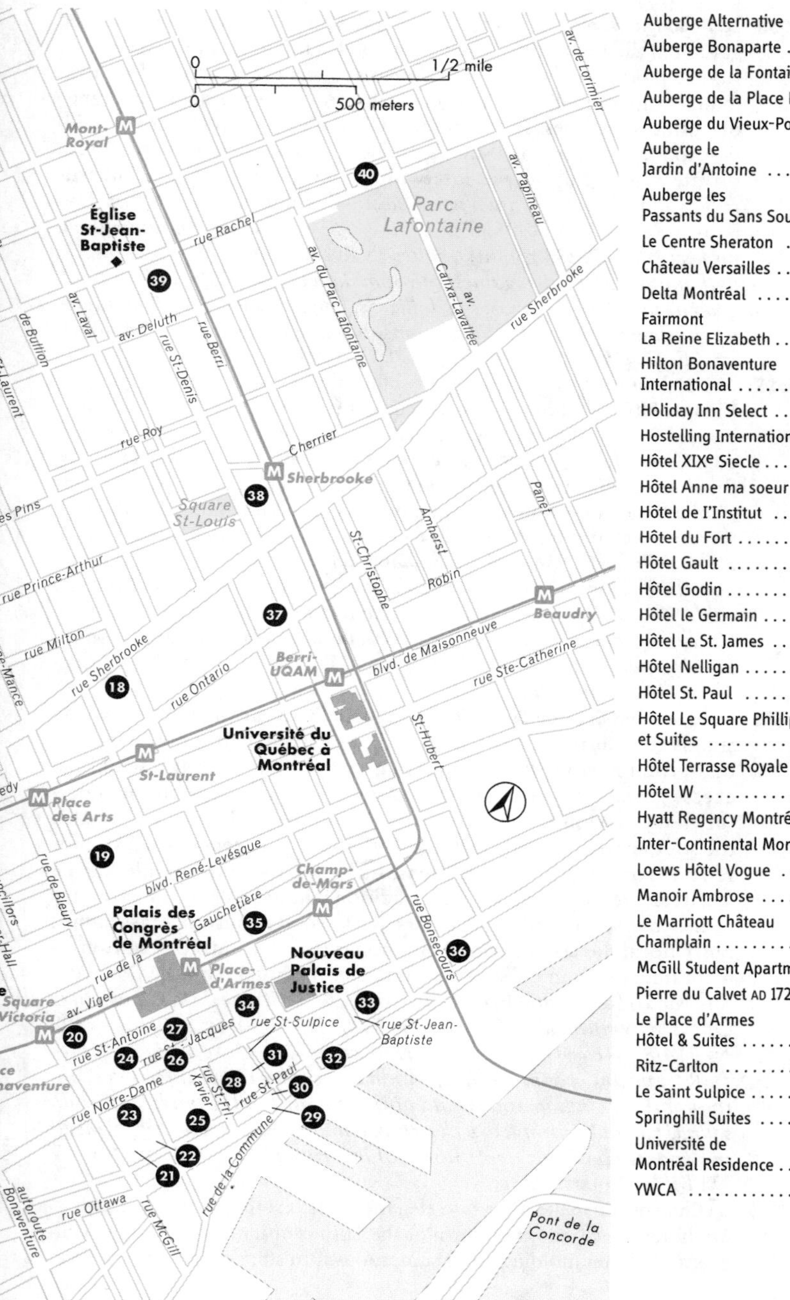

0
1/2 mile
0
500 meters
Mont-Royal
Église St-Jean-Baptiste
rue Rachel
Parc Lafontaine
av. de Lorimier
av. Papineau
av. du Parc Lafontaine
av. Calixa-Lavallée
rue Sherbrooke
av. Laval
de Bullion
av. Deluth
rue St-Denis
rue Berri
rue Roy
Cherrier
Sherbrooke
Square St-Louis
es Pins
Panet
Amherst
St-Christophe
Robin
rue Prince-Arthur
Beaudry
rue Milton
rue Sherbrooke
rue Ontario
Berri-UQAM
blvd. de Maisonneuve
rue Ste-Catherine
St-Hubert
Université du Québec à Montréal
St-Laurent
Place des Arts
rue de Bleury
blvd. René-Lévesque
Champ-de-Mars
Palais des Congrès de Montréal
Gauchetière
rue Bonsecours
Nouveau Palais de Justice
rue de la
Place-d'Armes
Square Victoria
av. Viger
rue St-Antoine
rue St-Jacques
rue St-Sulpice
rue St-Jean-Baptiste
rue Notre-Dame
rue St-Fr.-Xavier
rue St-Paul
rue de la Commune
autoroute Bonaventure
rue Ottawa
rue McGill
Pont de la Concorde

$$–$$$$ **Holiday Inn Select.** From the two pagodas on the roof to the well-tended garden in the lobby, this Chinatown hotel is full of surprises. The hotel sits catercorner to the Palais des Congrès convention center and is a five-minute walk from the World Trade Center. An executive floor has a range of business facilities. Its restaurant, Chez Chine, serves excellent Chinese food. The hotel has a small gym, but you also have access to a plush private health club downstairs with a whirlpool, saunas, a billiards room, and a bar. *99 av. Viger Ouest, Chinatown, H2Z 1E9 514/878–9888 or 888/878–9888 514/878–6341 www.yul-downtown.hiselect.com 235 rooms, 6 suites Restaurant, minibars, cable TV with movies and video games, in-room data ports, Wi-Fi, indoor pool, gym, health club, 2 saunas, spa, billiards, bar, dry cleaning, laundry service, business services, meeting rooms, parking (fee), no-smoking floors AE, D, DC, MC, V EP Place-d'Armes.*

$$–$$$$ **Hôtel du Fort.** In a residential neighborhood known as Shaughnessy Village, Hôtel du Fort is close to shopping at the Faubourg Ste-Catherine and Square Westmount and just around the corner from the Canadian Center for Architecture. All rooms here have good views of the city, the river, or the mountain. Wood furniture and pleasantly plump sofas fill the large, airy rooms, which have spacious bathrooms. Breakfast is served in a charming lounge. *1390 rue du Fort, Shaughnessy Village, H3H 2R7 514/938–8333 or 800/565–6333 514/938–2078 www.hoteldufort.com 103 rooms, 24 suites In-room safes, kitchenettes, cable TV with movies and video games, in-room data ports, gym, babysitting, dry cleaning, laundry service, business services, meeting rooms, parking (fee), no-smoking floors AE, DC, MC, V EP Atwater or Guy-Concordia.*

$$$ **Le Marriott Château Champlain.** At the southern end of Place du Canada stands this 36-floor skyscraper with distinctive half-moon windows that give it a Moorish look (although some argue that it resembles a cheese grater). Those oddly shaped windows give the rooms wonderful views of Mont-Royal to the north and the St. Lawrence River to the south and east. Although the 1960s exterior seems to call out for retro decoration, the public areas, including the comfortable Bar Le Senateur, are elegant and French traditional in style. Bedrooms are cozy rather than large, with wing chairs, dark wood furniture, brass lamps, puffy floral duvets, and small but modern marble bathrooms. Convenient underground passageways connect the hotel with the Bonaventure Métro station and Place Ville-Marie. *1050 rue de la Gauchetière Ouest, Downtown, H3B 4C9 514/878–9000 or 800/200–5909 514/878–6761 www.marriott.com 611 rooms, 33 suites Restaurant, room service, minibars, cable TV with movies, in-room broadband, in-room data ports, indoor pool, gym, health club, sauna, bar, babysitting, dry cleaning, laundry service, concierge, meeting rooms, parking (fee), no-smoking rooms AE, DC, MC, V BP Bonaventure.*

$$–$$$ **Château Versailles.** The two elegant mansions that make up this luxury hotel were built at the turn of the 20th century, and have high ceilings and plaster moldings. The sumptuous furnishings throughout reflect the beaux arts architecture. The marble fireplaces in many of the guest rooms and public rooms still work—a treat on chilly evenings. ✉ *1659 rue Sherbrooke Ouest, Square Mile, H3H 1E3* ☎ *514/933–3611 or 888/ 933–8111* 🖷 *514/933–6867* 🌐 *www.versailleshotels.com* *63 rooms, 2 suites* *Room service, in-room safes, minibars, cable TV with movies and video games, Wi-Fi, gym, bar, babysitting, dry cleaning, laundry service, concierge, business services, parking (fee), no-smoking rooms* *AE, DC, MC, V* *CP* Ⓜ *Guy-Concordia.*

$–$$ **Manoir Ambrose.** Staying at the Manoir Ambrose is like staying with an eccentric relative who just happens to have a couple of mansions halfway up the southern slope of Mont-Royal and just a few hundred yards from some of the best shopping in Canada. Despite its grand past, the Manoir is more homey than luxurious, like a comfortable pair of slippers. Within a few hours, manager Lucie Gagnon and her staff will have you feeling as if you've lived in the Golden Square Mile all your life. The two-room family suite is a great deal at C$150 a night. ✉ *3422 rue Stanley, Square Mile, H3A 1R8* ☎ *514/288–6922* 🖷 *514/288–5757* 🌐 *www.manoirambrose.com* *22 rooms, 20 with private bath, 2 with shared bath* *Cable TV with movies, Wi-Fi, laundry services, business services; no a/c in some rooms, no smoking* *AE, MC, V* *CP* Ⓜ *McGill.*

¢–$ **McGill Student Apartments.** From mid-May to mid-August, while McGill students are on summer recess, you can stay in the school's dorms on the grassy, quiet campus in the heart of the city. You can use the campus swimming pool and gym facilities for a fee. The university cafeteria is open during the week, serving breakfast and lunch. Be sure to book early. ✉ *3935 rue University, Square Mile, H3A 2B4* ☎ *514/398–6367* 🖷 *514/398–6770* 🌐 *www.mcgill.ca/residences* *1,000 rooms without bath* *Cafeteria, some kitchenettes, pool, gym* *MC, V* *Closed mid-Aug.–mid-May* *EP* Ⓜ *McGill.*

¢–$ **YWCA.** One block from rue Ste-Catherine, this lodging open to both men and women is close to dozens of restaurants, museums, nightclubs, and attractions. The auberge floor, where the rooms have sinks and shared baths, is very popular with budget travelers. The more-expensive—but still very reasonable—hotel floor has large, well-maintained rooms with private baths. It's particularly popular with couples and with female business travelers who—unlike their male counterparts—can use the gym, fitness room, and heated indoor pool. ✉ *1355 blvd. René-Lévesque Ouest, Downtown, H3G 1T3* ☎ *514/866–9941* 🖷 *514/861–1603* 🌐 *www.ydesfemmesmtl.org* *63 rooms, 30 with bath* *Restaurant, indoor pool, fitness classes, gym, sauna, shops; no TV in some rooms* *MC, V* *EP* Ⓜ *Lucien-L'Allier.*

¢ **Hostelling International.** Young travelers from around the world, as well as a smattering of families and adventurous older wanderers, flock to Hostelling International's Montréal branch. With its red awnings and friendly café-bar with a pool table, it resembles a small European hotel. There are same-sex dorm rooms that sleep 4, 6, or 10 people and private rooms suitable for couples or small groups. If you're not Canadian, you must have a Hostelling International membership to stay here

(C$35 for two years). There are kitchen facilities and lockers for valuables. Reserve early for summer lodging. ✉ *1030 rue Mackay, Downtown, H3G 2H1* ☎ *514/843–3317* 🖷 *514/934–3251* 🌐 *www.hostellingmontreal.com* *243 beds* *Café, hair salon, laundry facilities; no a/c in some rooms, no room TVs, no smoking* *AE, DC, MC, V* *EP* Ⓜ *Lucien-L'Allier.*

The Plateau & Environs

$$$ **Hôtel Godin.** You can't do better than the Hôtel Godin for either location or style if you're coming to Montréal for the nightlife on rue St-Denis and boulevard St-Laurent. Such hot spots as the Globe and the Med Grill are just across the street and it's an easy walk to Vieux-Montréal, Plateau Mont-Royal, or downtown. Style-wise, the hotel is striking: one half of the place is an art-nouveau classic from 1915; the other is a brick-and-glass contemporary completed in 2004. The uncompromisingly modern interior—exposed concrete ceilings, tile floors, stainless-steel furnishings—is flooded with natural light. (Some original details remain; check out the spiral staircase in the older wing.) The rooms, decorated in various shades of gray and hung with modern prints, have high-definition TVs and big windows with great views of the lively Latin Quarter. ✉ *10 rue Sherbrooke Ouest, Latin Quarter, H2X 4C9* ☎ *514/843–6000 or 866/744–6346* 🖷 *514/843–6810* 🌐 *www.hotelgodin.com* *126 rooms, 10 suites* *Restaurant, room service, minibars, cable TV with movies, in-room broadband, Web TV, gym, hair salon, sauna, bar, dry cleaning, laundry service, concierge, meeting rooms, parking (fee), some pets allowed, no-smoking rooms* *AE, DC, MC, V* *CP* Ⓜ *St-Laurent.*

Fodor'sChoice ★

★ **$$–$$$** **Auberge de la Fontaine.** If you're a cyclist, the Auberge de la Fontaine is an ideal place to park your bike (and yourself). Housed in two adjoining turn-of-the-20th-century residences, the hotel overlooks Parc Lafontaine and one of the city's major bicycle trails. And although it looks a little staid on the outside, the interior is what Montrealers would call *branché*—or just a little zany. One wall of your room might be bare brick, for example, another purple, and the ceiling might be green. But somehow it all works. Some rooms have whirlpool baths, and a few have private balconies with views of the park. A copious Continental breakfast is served in the dining room, and you are free to use the little ground-floor kitchen and help yourself to snacks from the refrigerator. ✉ *1301 rue Rachel Est, Plateau Mont-Royal, H2J 2K1* ☎ *514/597–0166 or 800/597–0597* 🖷 *514/597–0496* 🌐 *www.aubergedelafontaine.com* *18 rooms, 3 suites* *Dining room, cable TV, library, business services, meeting rooms, Wi-Fi, some free parking, no-smoking rooms* *AE, DC, MC, V* *CP* Ⓜ *Mont-Royal.*

$–$$$ **Hôtel Anne ma soeur Anne.** Staying at Anne ma soeur Anne is a little like having your own *pied-à-terre* in the Plateau Mont-Royal, especially if you book a back room with a view over the little tree-shaded garden (worth every penny of the extra cost). The built-in furniture adds to the effect: tip up your Murphy bed and you have a living room right on rue St-Denis. The rooms all have microkitchens—coffeemakers, microwaves, and toaster ovens—but every morning Anne or one of her staff delivers fresh coffee and a croissant to your room. ✉ *4119 rue St-Denis, Plateau Mont-Royal, H2W 2M7* ☎ *514/281–3187 or 877/281–3187* 🖷 *514/281–1601* 🌐 *www.annemasoeuranne.com* *17 rooms* *Internet room, microwaves* 💳 *AE, MC, V* *CP* Ⓜ *Mont-Royal.*

$$ **Hôtel de l'Institut.** People rave about the unbeatable location on Square St-Louis and the great views of the St. Lawrence River from the balconies, but what sets this hotel apart is the charming service. It occupies two floors of the Institut de Tourisme et d'Hôtellerie du Québec, an internationally known school that trains students seeking careers in the hospitality industry. Working in the hotel is an integral part of their education, and as a result you're cared for by squads of smiling, eager-to-please young people in crisp uniforms. Students also staff the bar and the ground-floor restaurant where student chefs sharpen their skills in the kitchen. ✉ *3535 rue St-Denis, Latin Quarter, H2X 3P1* ☎ *514/282–5120 or 800/361–5111 Ext. 5120* 🖷 *514/873–9893* 🌐 *www.ithq.qc.ca* *40 rooms, 2 suites* *Restaurant, cable TV, Wi-Fi, bar, concierge, meeting rooms, parking (fee), no-smoking rooms* 💳 *AE, DC, MC, V* *BP* Ⓜ *Sherbrooke.*

$–$$ **Auberge le Jardin d'Antoine.** Patterned wallpaper and antique-reproduction furniture give this small hotel plenty of charm, but its best selling point is its location right on rue St-Denis, among the Latin Quarter's trendy restaurants and nightclubs. Some rooms open onto a narrow, brick-paved terrace. Breakfast is served in a pleasant, stone-walled dining room. ✉ *2024 rue St-Denis, Latin Quarter, H2X 3K7* ☎ *514/843–4506 or 800/361–4506* 🖷 *514/281–1491* 🌐 *www.hotel-jardin-antoine.qc.ca* *25 rooms* *Cable TV, no-smoking rooms* 💳 *AE, D, MC, V* *CP* Ⓜ *Berri-UQAM.*

Mont-Royal & Environs

$ **Hôtel Terrasse Royale.** At first blush, the location looks remote. But the Oratoire St-Joseph and Parc Mont-Royal are just a walk away and the busy local neighborhood—Côte-des-Neiges—is full of little markets and ethnic restaurants where you can dine cheaply and well. Getting downtown is no problem, either: the Côte-des-Neiges Métro is just across the street. The hotel itself is clean and comfortable, and the rooms all have kitchen facilities. ✉ *5225 chemin de la Côte-des-Neiges, Mont-Royal, H3T 1Y1* ☎ *524/739–6391 or 800/567–0804* 🖷 *514/342–2512* 🌐 *www.terrasse-royale.com* *56 rooms* *Kitchenettes, parking (fee)* 💳 *AE, MC, V* *EP* Ⓜ *Côte-des-Neiges.*

¢–$ **Université de Montréal Residence.** The university's student housing accepts visitors from early May to mid-August. Rooms are simple but clean and well maintained. It's on the opposite side of Mont-Royal from downtown and Vieux-Montréal, but next to the Edouard-Montpetit Métro station. You have free access to the university's pool and gym facilities. ✉ *2350 blvd. Edouard-Montpetit, Mont-Royal, H3T 1J4* ☎ *514/343–6531* 🖷 *514/343–2353* 🌐 *www.resid.umontreal.ca* *800 rooms, 200 with bath* *Parking (fee), in-room Internet (fee), in-room refrigerators, laundry facilities, pool, gym* 💳 *MC, V* ⏲ *Closed late Aug.–early May* *EP* Ⓜ *Université-de-Montréal or Edouard-Monpetit.*

CLOSE UP

Festivals

The **Black and Blue Festival** (☎ 514/875-7026 🌐 www.bbcm.org) is a weeklong string of parties hosted by BBCM (Bad Boy Club Montréal) that began in 1991, and is now held annually in October. Proceeds are donated to AIDS support organizations.

Teams from around the world compete in the **Concours d'Art International Pyrotechnique** (International Fireworks Competition; ☎ 514/397-2000, 514/790-1245, 800/361-4595 in Canada, 800/678-5440 in the U.S. 🌐 www.montrealfeux.com), held in late June and July (mostly on weekends). Their launch site is La Ronde, on Île Ste-Hélène. A ticket includes an amusement-park pass and a reserved seat with a view, but thousands fill the Jacques-Cartier Bridge to watch the show for free, and hundreds more head to the Vieux-Port.

International stars show up for the **Festival International des Films du Monde** (World Film Festival; ☎ 514/848-3883 🌐 www.ffm-montreal.org), from late August to early September, usually screens about 400 films in a dozen venues.

The **Festival International de Jazz de Montréal** (Montréal International Jazz Festival; ☎ 514/790-1245, 800/361-4595 in Canada, 800/678-5440 in the U.S. 🌐 www.montrealjazzfest.com), brings together more than 1,000 musicians for more than 400 concerts over a period of nearly two weeks, from the end of June to the beginning of July. Past stars include Count Basie, Ella Fitzgerald, Lauryn Hill, Wynton Marsalis, Chick Corea, Dave Brubeck, and Canada's most famed singer-pianist, Diana Krall. About three-fourths of the concerts are presented free on outdoor stages. You can also hear blues, Latin rhythms, gospel, Cajun, and world music. Contact **Bell Info-Jazz** (☎ 514/871-1881 or 888/515-0515) for information about the festival and travel packages.

FrancoFolies (☎ 514/876-8989 🌐 www.francofolies.com) celebrates the art of French songwriting. Such major French stars as Isabelle Boulay, Paul Piché, and Michel Rivard play at packed concert halls, while lesser-known artists play free outdoor concerts. More than 1,000 musicians perform in dozens of styles, including rock, hip-hop, jazz, funk, and Latin. The festival usually starts in late July and lasts through early August.

For five days every June, the **Mondiale de la Bière** (☎ 514/722-9640 🌐 www.festivalmondialbiere.qc.ca) transforms the glass-roofed concourse of the Gare Windsor into a giant beer garden offering visitors a chance to sample more than 350 ales, lagers, and ciders from nearly 100 microbreweries. Snacks such as grilled meat, kippered herrings, Belgian chocolates, quail eggs, and an almost infinite variety of Québec cheeses are also available.

Montréal en Lumière (Montréal Highlights; ☎ 514/288-9955 or 888/477-9955 🌐 www.montrealenlumiere.com) brightens the bleak days of February. For every event, experts artfully illuminate a few historic buildings. Such leading chefs as Paul Bocuse of France come to town to give demonstrations and to take over the kitchens of leading restaurants. Concerts, ice-sculpture displays, plays, dance recitals, and other cultural events take place during the festival.

NIGHTLIFE & THE ARTS

The "Friday Preview" section of the *Gazette* (🌐 www.montrealgazette.com), the English-language daily paper, has an especially thorough list of events at the city's concert halls, theaters, clubs, dance spaces, and movie houses. The *Mirror* (🌐 www.montrealmirror.com), *Hour* (🌐 www.hour.ca), and French-language *Voir* (🌐 www.voir.ca) and *Ici* (🌐 www.icimontreal.com) also list events and are distributed free at restaurants and other public places.

For tickets to major pop and rock concerts, shows, festivals, and hockey, soccer, and football games, you can go to the individual box offices or contact **Admission** (☎ 514/790–1245 or 800/361–4595 🌐 www.admission.com). Tickets to Théâtre St-Denis and other venues are available via **Ticketmaster** (☎ 514/790–1111 🌐 www.ticketmaster.ca)

The Arts

It's hardly surprising that North America's only French-speaking metropolis should be the continent's capital of French theater. Montréal is the home of nearly a dozen professional companies and several important theater schools. But the city also has a lively English-language theater scene and one of the few Yiddish theaters in North America. Add a couple of world-renowned orchestras and some bold dance companies to the mix and you have a rich cultural stew that has something to appeal to everyone.

Circus

Fodor's Choice ★ **Cirque du Soleil.** This amazing circus is one of Montréal's great success stories. The company—founded in 1984 by a pair of street performers—has revolutionized the ancient art of circus. Its shows, now an international phenomenon, use no lions, tigers, or animals of any kind. Instead, they employ music, humor, dance, glorious (and often risqué) costumes, and spectacular acrobatics to tell a story or develop a theme. The cirque has four resident companies in Las Vegas, one in Orlando, but none in Montréal. However, every couple of years—usually odd-numbered ones—one of its international touring companies returns to where it all began, the Vieux-Port, and sets up the familiar blue-and-yellow tent for a summer of sold-out shows. ☎ *514/790–1245 or 800/361–4595* 🌐 *www.cirquedusoleil.com.*

Classical Music

For a city its size, there are a remarkable number of opportunities for fans of classical music to get their fill in Montréal. The Orchestre Métropolitain du Grand Montréal, or the MSO (Montréal Symphony Orchestra) as it's known in the Anglophone community, is undoubtedly the best known local orchestra on the international stage, but if the opportunity presents itself, classical music enthusiasts would be wise to check out the McGill Chamber Orchestra, which generally performs at the architecturally stunning and acoustically perfect Pollack Concert Hall on McGill University's downtown campus.

★ **I Musici de Montréal.** Arguably the best chamber orchestra in Canada, I Musici, under the direction of Yuli Turovsky, performs at Place des Arts and Pollack Hall, but its music is best suited to Tudor Hall atop the Ogilvy department store. ☎ *514/982–6037* 🌐 *www.imusici.com.*

The **Orchestre Métropolitain du Grand Montréal.** During their regular season, October–April, Orchestre Métropolitain perform at Place des Arts with a focus on the promotion of Canadian talent. ☎ *514/598–0870* 🌐 *www.orchestremetropolitain.com.*

Fodor'sChoice ★ **Orchestre Symphonique de Montréal.** When not on tour or in the recording studio, Montréal's internationally renowned symphony orchestra plays at the Salle Wilfrid-Pelletier at Place des Arts. The orchestra also gives holiday and summer concerts in Basilique Notre-Dame-de-Montréal and pop concerts at the Arena Maurice Richard, which is part of the Stade Olympique. For their free summertime concerts, check the *Gazette* listings. ☎ *514/842–9951* 🌐 *www.osm.ca.*

Pollack Concert Hall. McGill University's concert hall presents concerts not only by **I Musici** but also by the **McGill Chamber Orchestra,** the **Montréal Chamber Orchestra,** and the **Société de Musique Contemporaine.** ✉ *555 rue Sherbrooke Ouest, Square Mile* ☎ *514/398–4547* Ⓜ *McGill.*

Spectrum. The Spectrum is a large yet intimate concert hall that primarily books contemporary bands but also serves as a select performance spot during the Jazz Festival and Montréal's FrancoFolies. ✉ *318 rue Ste-Catherine Ouest, Downtown* ☎ *514/861–5851* 🌐 *www.spectrumdemontreal.ca* Ⓜ *St-Laurent.*

Théâtre St-Denis. The 2,500-seat, second-largest auditorium in Montréal (after Salle Wilfrid-Pelletier in Place des Arts), stages a wide range of pop-music concerts performed in English and French, including recent performances by Elvis Costello, folk singer Rita MacNeil, and Québecois rock icon Dan Bigras. ✉ *1594 rue St-Denis, Latin Quarter* ☎ *514/849–4211* 🌐 *www.theatrestdenis.com* Ⓜ *Berri-UQAM.*

Dance

Traditional and contemporary dance companies thrive in Montréal, though many take to the road or are on hiatus in summer.

Agora de la Danse. This important downtown performance and rehearsal space is affiliated with the Université du Québec à Montréal dance faculty. ✉ *840 rue Cherrier Est, Downtown* ☎ *514/525–1500* 🌐 *www.agoradanse.com* Ⓜ *Sherbrooke.*

Les Ballets Jazz de Montréal. Les Ballets Jazz has done much to popularize modern dance through their free performances at the open-air Théâtre de Verdure in Parc Lafontaine. Performances are also held at Place des Arts and Agora de la Danse. ☎ *514/982–6771* 🌐 *www.bjmdanse.ca.*

Fondation de Danse Margie Gillis. Margie Gillis, one of Canada's most exciting and innovative soloists, works with her own company and guest artists to stage performances at Place des Arts, Agora de la Danse, and other area venues. ☎ *514/845–3115* 🌐 *www.margiegillis.org.*

Les Grands Ballets Canadiens. Québec's premier ballet company performs at Place des Arts. Its seasonal offerings mix such classics as *Romeo and Juliet* and *The Nutcracker* with more-contemporary fare. The company also hosts performances by visiting international troupes. ☎ *514/849–0269 or 514/849–8681* 🌐 *www.grandsballets.qc.ca.*

LaLaLa Human Steps. Casablanca-born choreographer Édouard Lock founded LaLaLa to explore the boundaries of modern dance. The popular troupe has a heavy international schedule but also performs at Place des Arts and at Montréal festivals. ☎ *514/277–9090* 🌐 *www. lalalahumansteps.com.*

Montréal Danse. Lavish sets and dazzlingly sensual choreography have helped make Montréal Danse one of Canada's most popular contemporary repertory companies. They have a busy touring schedule but also regularly perform at Place des Arts, Agora de la Danse, Théâtre de Verdure, and elsewhere. ☎ *514/871–4005* 🌐 *www.montrealdanse.com.*

O Vertigo. O Vertigo stages innovative, contemporary performances. ☎ *514/251–9177* 🌐 *www.overtigo.com.*

Place des Arts. Montréal's main concert facility acts as a favorite venue for visiting large-scale productions. ✉ *175 rue Ste-Catherine Ouest, Downtown* ☎ *514/842–2112* 🌐 *www.pda.qc.ca* Ⓜ *Place-des-Arts.*

Tangente. Between September and June, Tangente holds weekly performances of experimental dance at Agora de la Danse. Tangente also acts as an archive for contemporary dance and experimental performance art and fosters national and international exchanges. ☎ *514/525–5584* 🌐 *www.tangente.qc.ca.*

Film

Although many of the cinemas that once lined rue Ste-Catherine have closed down in recent years to make way for new, stadium-seating megaplexes like the AMC Forum 22 and the Paramount, Montrealers remain uniquely privileged in the variety of cinema-going experiences available to them. Ranging from the ultramodern, ultrahip, Ex-Centris theater on the Main to the gorgeous art deco confines of the majestic Imperial theater on Bleury street downtown, in addition to the standard Hollywood fare consistently shown at the megaplexes, locals have the opportunity to enjoy the numerous domestic productions released each year by the province's thriving French-language film industry.

AMC Forum 22. Once the home ice of the Montréal Canadiens, the AMC Forum's 22 screens feature plenty of Hollywood biggies, but often host foreign-language and independent productions as well. The complex includes several restaurants and coffee shops, a bar, a poolroom, and a gift shop. ✉ *2313 rue Ste-Catherine Ouest, Downtown* ☎ *514/904–1274* Ⓜ *Atwater.*

Cinémathèque Québecoise. Montréal's Museum of the Moving Image has a collection of 28,000 Québecois, Canadian, and foreign films, as well as a display of equipment dating from the early days of cinema. ✉ *335 blvd. de Maisonneuve Est, Latin Quarter* ☎ *514/842–9763* 🌐 *www.cinematheque.qc.ca* Ⓜ *Berri-UQAM.*

CinéRobothèque. Cinephiles can use a robot to help them browse through the National Film Board of Canada's collection of 8,200 documentaries, dramas, short features, and animated flicks. ✉ *1564 rue St-Denis, Latin Quarter* ☎ *514/496–6887* 🌐 *www.nfb.ca/cinerobotheque* Ⓜ *Berri-UQAM.*

Ex-Centris. Cinema buffs looking for the best in independent productions—both Canadian and foreign—head for Ex-Centris. A pleasant 15-minute walk from the Mont-Royal Métro station, it's worth a visit if only to see the huge rotating clock in the lobby and its bathrooms with their reflective metal walls. Its three comfortable theaters are equipped to screen digital works. ✉ *3536 blvd. St-Laurent, Plateau Mont-Royal* ☎ *514/847–2206* 🌐 *www.ex-centris.com* Ⓜ *Sherbrooke.*

Famous Players Paramount. This major theater complex has two IMAX theaters in addition to 15 regular screens—all showing the latest Hollywood blockbusters. ✉ *707 rue Ste-Catherine Ouest, Downtown* ☎ *514/842–5828* 🌐 *www.famousplayers.com* Ⓜ *Peel.*

Grande Bibliothèque. Montréal's new library has 18 screening stations where you can view some of the 1,000 films in its collection. ✉ *475 blvd. de Maisonneuve Est, Latin Quarter* ☎ *514/873–1100* 🌐 *www.banq.qc.ca* Ⓜ *Berri-UQAM.*

Impérial. Since being renovated in 2002, the sumptuous decor dating back to the golden age of cinema has been retained at Montréal's oldest and most distinguished movie theater. It currently screens foreign and independent productions. ✉ *1432 rue Bleury, Downtown* ☎ *514/848–0300* Ⓜ *Place-des-Arts.*

Opera

Although the genre doesn't generally attract the same size crowds as, say, the Montréal Symphony Orchestra, local opera buffs will tell you the quality of productions the one major opera company in town presents each year are second to none.

L'Opéra de Montréal. L'Opéra de Montréal stages five productions a year at Place des Arts and features opera workshops as well as an annual benefit performance. ☎ *514/985–2258* 🌐 *www.operademontreal.com.*

Theater

There are at least 10 major French-language theater companies in town, some of which enjoy international reputations. The choices for Anglophones are more limited.

★ **Centaur Theatre.** Montréal's best-known English-language theater company stages everything from frothy musical revues to serious works by Eugène Ionesco and prominently features works by local playwrights. Its home is in the former stock exchange building in Vieux-Montréal. ✉ *453 rue St-François-Xavier, Vieux-Montréal* ☎ *514/288–3161* 🌐 *www.centaurtheatre.com* Ⓜ *Place-d'Armes.*

Mainline Theater. Operated by the same people who present the Montréal Fringe Festival every summer, the Mainline opened in early 2006 to serve the city's burgeoning Anglo theater community and has been going strong ever since. ✉ *3997 St-Laurent, Plateau Mont-Royal* ☎ *514/849–3378* 🌐 *www.montrealfringe.ca* Ⓜ *St-Laurent.*

Monument-National. The highly regarded National Theatre School of Canada—or the École Nationale de Théâtre du Canada—supplies world stages with a steady stream of well-trained actors and directors. It works and performs in the historic and glorious old theater that has played host to such luminaries as Edith Piaf and Emma Albani. (Québec's first feminist rallies in the early 1900s also took place here.) Graduating classes perform professional-level plays in both French and English. The theater also plays host to an assortment of touring plays, musicals, and concerts. ✉ *1182 blvd. St-Laurent, Downtown* ☎ *514/871–2224 or 800/361–4595* 🌐 *www.monument-national.qc.ca* Ⓜ *St-Laurent.*

Saidye Bronfman Centre. English-language plays can be seen at this center for the arts both for Montréal as a whole and for the Jewish community in particular. Plays in English are presented most of the year, but in May the Yiddish Theatre Group takes over the stage. ✉ *5170 chemin de la Côte Ste-Catherine, Côte-des-Neiges* ☎ *514/739–2301 or 514/739–7944* 🌐 *www.saidyebronfman.org* Ⓜ *Côte-Ste-Catherine.*

Théâtre Denise Pelletier. The Pelletier, with an objective to introduce younger audiences to theater, puts on French-language productions in a beautifully restored Italianate hall. It's is a 15-minute walk from the Métro station. ✉ *4353 rue Ste-Catherine Est, Hochelaga-Maisonneuve* ☎ *514/253–8974* 🌐 *www.denise-pelletier.qc.ca* Ⓜ *Joliette.*

Théâtre de Quat'Sous. This cerebral theater puts on modern and experimental plays in French. ✉ *100 av. des Pins Est, Downtown* ☎ *514/845–7277* 🌐 *www.quatsous.com* Ⓜ *Sherbrooke.*

Fodor's Choice ★ **Théâtre du Nouveau Monde.** In this North American temple of French and stage classics, a season's offerings can include works by locals Michel Tremblay and Robert Lepage as well as works by Shakespeare, Molière, Camus, Ibsen, Chekhov, and Arthur Miller. ✉ *84 rue Ste-Catherine Ouest, Downtown* ☎ *514/866–8667* 🌐 *www.tnm.qc.ca* Ⓜ *St-Laurent.*

Théâtre du Rideau Vert. A modern French repertoire is the specialty at this theater. ✉ *4664 rue St-Denis, Plateau Mont-Royal* ☎ *514/844–1793* 🌐 *www.rideauvert.qc.ca* Ⓜ *Mont-Royal.*

Théâtre Jean Duceppe. Named for one of Québec's most beloved actors, this theater makes its home in the smallest and most intimate of the four auditoriums in Place des Arts. It stages major French-language productions. ✉ *175 rue Ste-Catherine Ouest, Downtown* ☎ *514/842–2112* 🌐 *www.duceppe.com* Ⓜ *Place-des-Arts.*

Théâtre St-Denis. Touring Broadway productions often can be seen, especially in summer, at this multipurpose theater. ✉ *1594 rue St-Denis, Latin Quarter* ☎ *514/849–4211* Ⓜ *Berri-UQAM.*

Nightlife

Montréal has long been celebrated for its vibrant nightlife. Dozens of places to dance, listen to live music, or just kick back with a cold one abound along the streets of downtown, the Plateau Mont-Royal, and the Latin Quarter. Rue Ste-Catherine between rue Amherst and avenue Papineau—an area better known as the Village—is the heart of the gay community. Not to be overlooked, however, is Montréal's indie rock scene, which in recent years has evolved from a handful of struggling bands into one of the liveliest local music scenes on the continent. Montréal's ascendancy to indie-rock haven is often attributed to the city's relatively low cost of living and its reputation as the "hippest city in Canada." As a result, music fans can now see bands seven nights a week in any number of venues, the majority of them in the Mile End and Plateau Mont-Royal districts.

Most Montréal bars stop serving around 3 AM but stay open until at least 3:30.

Bars

There's certainly no shortage of places to go drinking in Montréal. From the hip terraces of the Plateau and the Village to the somewhat less-glamorous utilitarian watering holes along the Main, there is a wealth of drinking establishments to choose from, catering, literally, to every taste and persuasion.

Bar Godin. Bar Godin, in the lower level of the hip hotel of the same name, has cement floors and upholstered seating, a patio, and creative cocktails. ✉ *2102 blvd. St-Laurent, Latin Quarter* ☎ *514/843–6000* Ⓜ *St-Laurent.*

Bières & Compagnie. More than 100 different beers, 30 of them locally brewed, are available here, along with dining fare that includes 30 varieties of mussels, ostrich hamburger in lyonnaise sauce and, just one example of the dishes cooked in suds, filet mignon on a bed of mushrooms in Guinness sauce. ✉ *4350 rue St-Denis, Plateau Mont-Royal* ☎ *514/844–0394* Ⓜ *Mont-Royal.*

Biftek. Throughout the 1990s this busy no-frills Plateau nightspot, the former workplace of Hole bassist and celebrated local luminary Melissa Auf der Maur, was the center of the indie music scene and a choice location for those looking to mingle with visiting rock stars. Although not quite as vibrant as it was in its heyday, the Bif, as it's often referred to, still packs 'em in most nights with a clientele comprised of beer-guzzling university students and local rock musicians. ✉ *3702 blvd. St-Laurent, Plateau Mont-Royal* ☎ *514/844–6211* Ⓜ *Sherbrooke or St-Laurent.*

★ **Brutopia.** As the tongue-in-cheek name suggests, Brutopia offers a large selection of draft beers. Yummy pasta, salads, and steaks make it a popular downtown meeting place. ✉ *1219 rue Crescent, Downtown* ☎ *514/393–9277* Ⓜ *Guy-Concordia.*

Cheers. No, you won't find Sam Malone, Norm, or even Cliff Clavin here, but you might just find yourself someone to spend the night with at this hugely popular pickup bar catering to young Anglophones and tourists. Wednesday, when drinks are free for women all night long, tends to be the busiest night of the week. Lines are the rule rather than the exception so arrive early. ✉ *1260 rue Mackay, Downtown* ☎ *514/932–3138* Ⓜ *Guy-Concordia.*

Cock'n Bull Pub. It's a little low rent to be sure, but the time-honored Cock'n Bull Pub is something of an institution along the western half of the Ste-Catherine street strip. The crowd is a mix of seasoned older drinkers and college students, the drinks reasonably priced, and the vibe relaxed and friendly. ✉ *1944 rue Ste-Catherine Ouest, Downtown* ☎ *514/933–4556* Ⓜ *Guy-Concordia.*

Else's. With a good selection of beer and cider, an eclectic clientele, a first-rate staff, and a packed house for Montréal's infamous *cinq-à-sept* (happy "hour," 5–7) on Thursday and Friday, Else's is a great place to people-watch and hang with the locals. ✉ *156 rue Roy Est, Plateau Mont-Royal* ☎ *514/286–6689* Ⓜ *Sherbrooke.*

★ **Gogo Lounge.** Funky, colorful decor and a retro-café feel attract twenty- and thirtysomethings to sip kitschy-named martinis like Pussycat, LSD, and Yellow Submarine. ✉ *3682 blvd. St-Laurent, Plateau Mont-Royal* ☎ *514/286–0882* Ⓜ *Sherbrooke.*

Île Noir. Île Noir has a rich wood interior which makes it an especially cozy spot to enjoy an impressive selection of more than 100 single-malt whiskeys. ✉ *342 rue Ontario Est, Latin Quarter* ☎ *514/982–0866* Ⓜ *Berri-UQAM.*

★ **Jello Bar.** Lava lamps, love seats, more than 50 different martinis, a '60s feel, and live music every night—everything from swing and jazz to salsa and R&B—make this happenin' spot just that much more happenin'. ✉ *151 rue Ontario Est, Latin Quarter* ☎ *514/285–2621* Ⓜ *Berri-UQAM.*

Mile End Bar. Currently one of the hippest watering holes in town, the Mile End Bar is set on three floors, with deejays playing mostly electronic music. It's a favorite hangout among young, trendy, Plateau and Mile End residents. ✉ *5322 blvd. St-Laurent, Mile-End* ☎ *514/279–0200* Ⓜ *Laurier.*

Pub St-Paul. Located smack-dab in the heart of Old Montréal, the Pub St-Paul is hardly elegant, but the drinks are cheap, the food as good as it is inexpensive—at least for the neighborhood—and the atmosphere fun and relaxed. ✉ *124 rue St-Paul Est, Vieux-Montréal* ☎ *514/874–0485* Ⓜ *Champ-de-Mars.*

Le Sainte-Elisabeth. Situated in one of the arguably seedier sections of the downtown core, a stone's throw from the heart of the city's traditional red-light district, the Sainte-Elisabeth retains one of the nicest backyard terraces in town. The service is friendly, a good selection of domestic and imported beers are yours to choose from, with the crowd primarily comprised of French twentysomethings and students from the nearby UQAM campus. Monday and Tuesday nights in summer are very busy, as pints of Boréale, a popular local beer, are priced at C$3 and C$4, respectively. ✉ *1412 rue Ste-Elisabeth, Downtown* ☎ *514/286–4302* Ⓜ *St-Laurent.*

Sofa. As the name suggests, Sofa is a comfortable place to sip a port or bourbon and watch the arty-looking Plateau denizens pass by. ✉ *451 rue Rachel Est, Plateau Mont-Royal* ☎ *514/285–1011* Ⓜ *Mont-Royal.*

Stogie's Lounge. The relaxed surroundings are ripe for friendly arguments about anything—except the merits of smoking. And despite the smoking ban, you can still enjoy imported *puros* directly from Cuba in comfort. ✉ *2015 rue Crescent, Downtown* ☎ *514/848–0069* Ⓜ *Guy-Concordia.*

Vol de Nuit. A premier watering hole for McGill students, the best thing about Vol de Nuit, outside of the great two-for-one drink specials, is their large terrace on the Prince Arthur street pedestrian mall. Come the warm weather, this is one of the very best people-watching terraces in the city—if you're lucky enough to find a vacant seat. ✉ *14 rue Prince Arthur Est, Plateau Mont-Royal* ☎ *514/845–6253* Ⓜ *Sherbrooke.*

Wax Lounge. Specializing in champagne, this intimate upstairs bar has comfy couches and is an excellent spot for people-watching, lounging, or both. ✉ *3481 blvd. St-Laurent, Plateau Mont-Royal* ☎ *514/282–0919* Ⓜ *Sherbrooke or St-Laurent.*

Whiskey Café. A superb menu of 20 types of port and more than 70 kinds of Scotch, not to mention high-tech bathrooms, make this elegant bar a worthwhile destination. ✉ *3 rue Bernard Ouest, Plateau Mont-Royal* ☎ *514/278–2646* Ⓜ *Rosemont or Beaubien.*

Winnie's. Named for Winston Churchill, this Montréal institution is largely populated by young—and single—professionals who work downtown. ✉ *1459 rue Crescent, Downtown* ☎ *514/288–0623* Ⓜ *Guy-Concordia.*

Ziggy's Pub. A favorite with young Anglophones, Ziggy's has a bubbly crowd of both regulars and colorful local personalities who will keep you well entertained. ✉ *1470 rue Crescent, Downtown* ☎ *514/285–8855* Ⓜ *Guy-Concordia.*

Casino

Although there are several casinos within striking distance of Montréal, the most popular local gaming institution by far is le Casino de Montréal, which is conveniently located on Île Notre-Dame, only a few minutes by car, bicycle, or Métro from the city's downtown core.

Casino de Montréal. One of the world's largest gaming rooms, the casino has more than 3,000 slot machines and 120 tables for baccarat, craps, blackjack, and roulette. There are some quirks for those used to Vegas-style gambling: no drinking on the floor, and no tipping the croupiers. Winners may want to spend some of their gains at Nuances or one of the casino's three other restaurants. The Cabaret de Casino offers some of the best shows in town. To get to the casino, which is open around the clock, you can take a C$10 cab ride from downtown, drive (parking is free), or take the Métro to the Jean-Drapeau station and then board

Bus 167 which will deliver you right to the doorstep. ✉ *1 av. du Casino, Île Notre-Dame* ☎ *514/392–2746 or 800/665–2274* 🌐 *www.casino-de-montreal.com* Ⓜ *Jean-Drapeau.*

Comedy

The Montréal Just For Laughs Comedy festival, which takes place every July, has been the largest such festival in the world since its inception back in 1983. But Montrealers don't have to wait until summer every year to get their comedy fix, as there are several downtown clubs catering exclusively to all-things-funny.

Comedy Nest. This modest, unassuming club hosts established Canadian and international comedians but is also an excellent spot to catch some of the city's funniest up-and-comers. Dinner-and-show packages are available. ✉ *Pepsi Forum, 2313 rue Ste-Catherine Ouest, 3rd fl., Downtown* ☎ *514/932–6378* 🌐 *www.thecomedynest.com* Ⓜ *Atwater.*

Comedyworks. Comedyworks is a popular room that books both amateur and established comics and has a reputation for offering fairly risqué fare on occasion. ✉ *1238 rue Bishop, Downtown* ☎ *514/398–9661* 🌐 *www.comedyworks.com* Ⓜ *Guy-Concordia.*

Dance Clubs

Clubbing is, to say the least, huge in Montréal. Back at the height of the disco era in the 1970s, Montréal was considered one of the top five cities in the world for both the trendsetting dance music it produced, and also for the sheer volume of discotheques to be found in the city's midst. The legacy continues today, with local deejays like A-Trak enjoying tremendous international reputations, and the city hosting as many or more dance clubs than ever before.

Cactus. Thursday through Saturday, the dance floor is always packed with patrons enjoying the rigorously authentic Latin music. ✉ *4461 rue St-Denis, Plateau Mont-Royal* ☎ *514/849–0349* Ⓜ *Mont-Royal.*

Club 6/49. Open every night but Sunday, this popular Latin dance club is best for salseros. ✉ *1112 rue Ste-Catherine Ouest, Downtown* ☎ *514/868–1649* Ⓜ *Peel.*

Club 737. A sweeping panoramic view and a rooftop terrace are two of the outstanding features of this multilevel dance club. It also does the weekend disco thing and is very popular with the mid-twenties to mid-thirties office crowd. ✉ *1 pl. Ville-Marie, Downtown* ☎ *514/397–0737* Ⓜ *Bonaventure.*

Club Exit. This lively Plateau dance hall caters to the hip-hop, reggae, rap, and R&B crowds. ✉ *3553 blvd. St-Laurent, Plateau Mont-Royal* ☎ *514/285–2223* Ⓜ *Sherbrooke or St-Laurent.*

Cubano's Club. Wednesday is the choice night for salseros at Cubano's. ✉ *316 rue Ste-Catherine Ouest, Downtown* ☎ *514/878–9009* Ⓜ *Place-des-Arts.*

Electric Avenue. If you find yourself pining for the Decade of Decadence, rock down to Electric Avenue where the DJs are unapologetically nostalgic for the 1980s. It's open Thursday to Saturday from 10 PM until last call. ✉ *1469 rue Crescent, Downtown* ☎ *514/285–8885* Ⓜ *Guy-Concordia.*

Juice Nightclub. The music here is predominantly house and R&B, often provided by some of Montréal's top deejays like DJ Renegade or Miguel Graca. A simple yet comfortable club with two large dance floors and excellent drink specials, it also serves as a choice location to simply sit back and gaze at the beautiful people on the dance floor. ✉ *3603 blvd. St-Laurent, Plateau Mont-Royal* ☎ *514/282–2332* Ⓜ *Sherbrooke.*

Le Monkey. Set on two floors, one very loud with a dance floor, the other a considerably quieter lounge area, Le Monkey is a great spot to get your first taste of the St-Denis street party scene. Typical of the neighborhood, the clientele is young and overwhelmingly Francophone, possessing that special joie de vivre Québecois are so famous for. ✉ *1599 St-Denis, Latin Quarter* ☎ *514/285–1087* Ⓜ *Sherbrooke.*

Dome. This large complex is stocked with a plethora of bars, a delightful upstairs terrace, a huge dance floor, and a multitude of armchairs and comfortable sofas in which to sit back and take in all the action. The music played here tends to be rap and R&B. ✉ *32 rue Ste-Catherine Ouest, Downtown* ☎ *514/875–5757* Ⓜ *St-Laurent.*

Newtown. One of the city's hottest clubs, Newtown is named for its owner, Formula 1 race-car driver Jacques Villeneuve ("Newtown" is the literal translation of "Villeneuve"). The tri-level dance club–bar–restaurant caters to a trendy, upscale crowd. Reserve early for the private tables outside on the terrace. ✉ *1476 rue Crescent, Downtown* ☎ *514/284–6555* Ⓜ *Guy-Concordia.*

Salsathèque. Simply put, this is one of the most popular Latin clubs in town. ✉ *1220 rue Peel, Downtown* ☎ *514/875–0016* Ⓜ *Peel.*

Saphir. Offering an eclectic cross section of underground subcultures and music, Saphir's first floor leans more towards goth, punk and glam while upstairs the sounds are urban and electronica. Drinks are cheap and the clientele relatively unassuming. ✉ *3699 blvd. St-Laurent, Plateau Mont-Royal* ☎ *514/284–5093* Ⓜ *Sherbrooke or St-Laurent.*

Thursdays/Les Beaux Jeudis. The primo downtown bar and disco for the professional set, Thursdays opens at 9:30 PM. ✉ *1449 rue Crescent, Downtown* ☎ *514/288–5656* Ⓜ *Guy-Concordia.*

Tokyo Bar. A traditional Montréal discotheque located in the heart of the action along the Main, the music is loud, pumping, and either house, hip-hop, disco, or '80s retro, depending on the night. If the music gets too loud for you, head up to their rooftop terrace and watch all the goings on down below on colorful St-Laurent Boulevard. ✉ *3709 blvd. St-Laurent, Plateau Mont-Royal* ☎ *514/842–6838* Ⓜ *St-Laurent.*

Folk Music

There are numerous venues in which to catch folk music in Montréal, with the Yellow Door coffeehouse being the premier local venue for traditional folk in the vein of say, Bob Dylan, Leonard Cohen, or Joni Mitchell.

Hurley's Irish Pub. At Hurley's, there's never a cover charge to see the city's best Celtic musicians, dancers, and storytellers. ✉ *1225 rue Crescent, Downtown* ☎ *514/861–4111* Ⓜ *Guy-Concordia.*

McKibbin's Irish Pub. Celtic fiddlers from all over Canada—and, indeed, the world—put in appearances here and the Irish stew is even better than the music. ✉ *1426 rue Bishop, Downtown* ☎ *514/288–1580* Ⓜ *Guy-Concordia.*

Old Dublin. This lively and friendly Montréal institution presents Celtic bands every night of the week. The menu is made up of standard pub fare, with the notable exception of a few first-rate Indian dishes. ✉ *1219A rue University, Downtown* ☎ *514/861–4448* Ⓜ *McGill.*

Yellow Door. A Montréal folk-music institution since the 1960s and Canada's longest-running coffeehouse, the Yellow Door is an alcohol-free basement club in the heart of the McGill University student ghetto. It is a showcase for both local and international folk music acts. ✉ *3625 rue Aylmer, Downtown* ☎ *514/398–6243* Ⓜ *McGill.*

Gay Bars & Nightclubs

Most of the bars, clubs, and restaurants of the Village, the heart of Montréal's gay and lesbian community, line rue Ste-Catherine between rue Amherst and avenue Papineau. In general, the farther east you walk on rue Ste-Catherine, the greater the emphasis on saunas and strip clubs. ***Fugues*** (☎ 514/848–1854 🌐 www.fugues.com), a gay newspaper published in French with a smattering of articles in English, lists upcoming events.

Agora. An intimate and casual gay and lesbian hangout in the middle of downtown, Agora is usually quiet and perfect for intimate conversation—apart, of course, from Saturday karaoke nights. ✉ *1160 rue Mackay, Downtown* ☎ *514/934–1428* Ⓜ *Guy-Concordia.*

Bar L'Aigle Noir. At one of Montréal's premier leather/fetish bars, X-rated films are shown on TVs around the bar area while deejays spin house, dance, and techno music seven nights a week. ✉ *1315 rue Ste-Catherine Est, Village* ☎ *514/529–0040* Ⓜ *Beaudry.*

Cabaret Mado. Drag queen extraordinaire Mado holds court in this traditional cabaret-theme club that provides engaging entertainment, encourages patrons to get involved in the weekly karaoke and improv nights, and promises a memorable evening. ✉ *1115 rue Ste-Catherine Est, Village* ☎ *514/525–7566* 🌐 *www.mado.qc.ca* Ⓜ *Berri-UQAM.*

Club Bolo. Country-and-western dancing and ambience attract both men and women to this Village club staffed partly by country-lovin' volunteers. ✉ *960 rue Amherst, Village* ☎ *514/849–4777* Ⓜ *Berri-UQAM.*

Club Date Piano Bar. Styled in the Manhattan piano bar tradition, Club Date caters to a mixed clientele and has karaoke competitions seven nights a week. ✉ *1218 rue Ste-Catherine Est, Village* ☎ *514/521–1242* Ⓜ *Beaudry or Berri-UQAM.*

Club Parking. In the heart of the Village, Parking serves an interesting mix of older leather guys and young hipsters. The upstairs bar, where the music is mostly from the '80s, has a reputation of being one of the best meeting spots in town. ✉ *1296 rue Amherst, Village* ☎ *514/282–1199* Ⓜ *Beaudry.*

Club Unity 2. Unity 2 caters to a young, hip crowd. Small, semiprivate lounges are scattered throughout the two-story complex, and the beautiful rooftop terrace is one of the finest in the Village, if not the entire city. Expect to hear some of Montréal's best DJs spinning from Thursday to Saturday. Admission can be C$10 or more, but entrance is free before 11. ✉ *1171 rue Ste-Catherine Est, Village* ☎ *514/523–2777* Ⓜ *Beaudry or Berri-UQAM.*

Le Drugstore. Eight bars on eight floors make up this mammoth complex that in recent years has become an institution of the city's gay scene. There is also a café, a newsstand, a handsome rooftop terrace, and small shops. Although the crowd includes all ages and types, this is the neighborhood's most popular hangout for women, who gravitate toward the basement pool hall and the second-floor lounge. ✉ *1360 rue Ste-Catherine Est, Village* ☎ *514/524–1960* Ⓜ *Beaudry.*

Sky Pub/Sky Club. One of the busiest bars in town is two hangouts in one. Downstairs, the Sky Pub is a sprawling, mostly male bar that hosts the neighborhood's most popular happy hour; upstairs, Sky Club is a trendy disco with two small dance floors and a mixed crowd of gays and lesbians. ✉ *1474 rue Ste-Catherine Est, Village* ☎ *514/529–6969* Ⓜ *Beaudry.*

Stereo. Some of the most beautiful cross-dressers in the city gather here to bust a move on the huge dance floor of this converted theater. It's popular with both men and women. Things get started late, so don't even bother arriving before midnight. ✉ *858 rue Ste-Catherine Est, Village* ☎ *514/286–0325* Ⓜ *Beaudry or Berri-UQAM.*

Le Stud. Le Stud is loud, leather-filled, and legendary as a men-only hangout that's open until the wee hours. ✉ *1812 rue Ste-Catherine Est, Village* ☎ *514/598–8243* Ⓜ *Papineau.*

Les Talons Noir. Just a little east of the Village, this friendly neighborhood bar caters to the rapidly expanding gay community in the historically French working-class district of Hochelaga-Maisonneuve. It's a quieter alternative to the often rowdy Village scene. ✉ *3945 rue Ontario Est, Hochelaga-Maisonneuve* ☎ *514/598–1342* Ⓜ *Pie-IX.*

Jazz & Blues

House of Jazz. This is a great spot to catch live performances and chow down on some tasty ribs and chicken, too. ✉ *2060 rue Aylmer, Downtown* ☎ *514/842–8656* Ⓜ *McGill.*

Upstairs Jazz Club. Local and imported jazz musicians take the stage seven nights a week. Mahimahi and salmon are two dinner specialties in this intimate "good vibe" spot. ✉ *1254 rue Mackay, Downtown* ☎ *514/931–6808* 🌐 *www.upstairsjazzclub.com* Ⓜ *Guy-Concordia.*

Laser Tag

Laser Quest. Fog machines, music, and live-action laser-tag games on five levels—what more can you ask for? It's open until 11 PM on Friday and Saturday and until 9 PM Wednesday and Thursday. ✉ *1226 rue Ste-Catherine Ouest, Downtown* ☎ *514/393–3000* 🌐 *www.laserquest.com* Ⓜ *McGill.*

Reggae, Hip-Hop & World

Aria. Aria, one of Montréal's most established after-hours clubs, caters to an urban crowd with local and international DJs spinning most Friday and Saturday nights. Doors open at 1:30 AM on weekends. ✉ *1280 rue St-Denis, Latin Quarter* ☎ *514/987–6712* Ⓜ *Berri-UQAM.*

Le Balattou. This crowded club specializes in African, Caribbean, and World Beat music. Performances start late and last even later. ✉ *4372 blvd. St-Laurent, Plateau Mont-Royal* ☎ *514/845–5447* Ⓜ *Mont-Royal.*

Blue Dog. This popular venue offers an eclectic musical mix—from reggae to rock, drum and bass, and house progressive—with the real action taking place after 11. ✉ *3958 blvd. St-Laurent, Plateau Mont-Royal* ☎ *514/848–7006* Ⓜ *Sherbrooke.*

Rock

Barfly. Fans of blues, punk rock, country, and bluegrass jam into this tiny but tasteful hole-in-the-wall with some of the cheapest drink prices to be found anywhere on the Main (St-Laurent). ✉ *4062A blvd. St-Laurent, Plateau Mont-Royal* ☎ *514/284–6665* Ⓜ *Sherbrooke.*

Casa del Popolo. Undoubtedly one of the city's top venues for indie rock music, this scruffy bar is ideal to hear up-and-coming local acts. Casa—as it's commonly known—also books out-of-town bands. While you enjoy the music, take a look at the original art and sample some of the tasty, reasonably priced grub. ✉ *4873 blvd. St-Laurent, Plateau Mont-Royal* ☎ *514/284–0122* Ⓜ *Mont-Royal.*

Club Soda. The granddaddy of city rock clubs, Club Soda is a tall, narrow concert hall with high-tech design and 500 seats—all of them good. The club is open only for shows; phone the box office to find out what's playing. ✉ *1225 blvd. St-Laurent, Downtown* ☎ *514/286–1010 Ext. 200* 🌐 *www.clubsoda.ca* Ⓜ *St-Laurent.*

Le Divan Orange. Divan Orange is the perfect spot to get a feel for the Montréal indie music scene and to hang out with the hipsters 'round town. ✉ *4234 blvd. St-Laurent, Plateau Mont-Royal* ☎ *514/840–9090* Ⓜ *Mont-Royal.*

Foufounes Electriques. Foufs, as it's locally known, is the oldest alternative rock venue in the city, having played host to everyone from Nirvana to the Dickies. A favorite with punks, it's not for the faint of heart, which should come as no surprise from a club whose name means "electric buttocks." ✉ *87 rue Ste-Catherine Est, Downtown* ☎ *514/844–5539* Ⓜ *St-Laurent.*

Playhouse. This former strip club in Mile End is now a cabaret and features a steady diet of local indie bands. Despite the change in entertainment policy, Playhouse still manages to maintain that strip-club vibe—in a good way, of course. ✉ *5656 av. du Parc, Mile-End* ☎ *514/276–0594* Ⓜ *Laurier.*

Spectrum. The most popular performance venue for rock bands in Montréal. The sight lines as well as the sound quality here are consistently excellent. ✉ *318 rue Ste-Catherine Ouest, Downtown* ☎ *514/861–5851* Ⓜ *Place-des-Arts.*

SPORTS & THE OUTDOORS

Most Montrealers would probably claim they hate winter, but the city is full of cold-weather sports venues—skating rinks, cross-country-ski trails, and toboggan runs. During warm-weather months, residents head for the tennis courts, miles of bicycle trails, golf courses, and two lakes for boating and swimming.

Auto Racing

Grand Prix du Canada. One of only two venues in North America where Formula 1 racing can be witnessed, the Canadian Grand Prix takes place in late June at the Circuit Gilles Villeneuve on Île Notre-Dame, consistently inspiring Montréal's busiest tourist weekend. ☎ *514/350–4731, 514/350–0000 tickets* 🌐 *www.grandprix.ca.*

Biking

Despite the bitter winters (or perhaps because of them), Montréal has fallen in love with the bicycle. More than 350 km (217 mi) of cycling paths crisscross the metropolitan area, and bikes are welcome on the first car of Métro trains during off-peak hours. Ferries at the Vieux-Port take cyclists to Île Ste-Hélène and the south shore of the St. Lawrence River, where riders can connect to hundreds of miles of trails in the Montérégie region.

Féria de Vélo de Montréal (Montréal Bike Festival). Held each year at the end of May and continuing until the beginning of June, the Montréal Bike Festival is the biggest such celebration in North America. Events include a 22-km (14-mi) ride for children and challenge races of 100 km (62 mi) and 150 km (93 mi). It all culminates with as many as 50,000 cyclists taking over the streets for the **Tour de l'Île,** a 50-km (31-mi) night ride along a route encircling the city. ☎ *514/521–8356* 🌐 *www.velo.qc.ca.*

★ **Lachine Canal.** The most popular cycling trail on the island begins at the Vieux-Port and wends its way to the shores of Lac St-Louis in Lachine. **Parks Canada.** Guided cycling tours along the Lachine Canal are conducted by Parks Canada every summer weekend (☎ 514/283–6054 or 514/637–7433 🌐 www.pc.gc.ca).

La Maison des Cyclistes. Rent a bike, drop in to sip a coffee at the Bicicletta café, or browse through the cycling maps in the adjoining boutique. ✉ *1251 rue Rachel Est, Plateau Mont-Royal* ☎ *514/521–8356* 🌐 *www.velo.qc.ca* Ⓜ *Mont-Royal.*

Le Pôle des Rapides. This network of 100 km (62 mi) of bicycle trails follows lakefronts, canals, and aqueducts. ☎ *514/364–4490* 🌐 *www.poledesrapides.com.*

Vélo Montréal. The closest place to rent bicycles for a tour of Parc Maisonneuve, the Botanical Gardens, and the site of the 1976 summer Olympics, is this east-end shop. ✉ *3880 rue Rachel Est, Rosemont* ☎ *514/236–8356 or 514/259–7272* 🌐 *www.velomontreal.com* Ⓜ *Pie- IX.*

Boating

In Montréal you can climb aboard a boat at a downtown wharf and be crashing through Class V white water minutes later.

Lachine Rapids Tours. For an hour-long voyage up the river in a big aluminum jet boat, Lachine Rapids Tours offers five daily departures from May through September at a cost of C$60 per person with all gear included. Rafting trips are also available or you can opt for a half-hour jaunt around the islands in a 10-passenger boat reaching speeds up to 100 kph (62 mph). Departures are every half hour between 10 AM and 6 PM from late June until early September at a cost of C$25 for adults. Trips are narrated in French and English. ✉ *Clock Tower Pier (for jet-boating) and Jacques Cartier Pier (for speedboating) located at the Old Port of Montréal, Vieux-Montréal* ☎ *514/284–9607* 🌐 *www.jetboatingmontreal.com* Ⓜ *Champ-de-Mars.*

Football

Although there is some football played at the college level in Montréal, the quality pales in comparison to the high-stakes world of American college ball. When Montrealers think football, they think of their cherished Alouettes, who play their home games at the foot of Mont-Royal park in the wonderfully intimate Molson Stadium.

Montréal Alouettes. The 2002 national champions of the Canadian Football League play the Canadian version of the game—bigger field, just three downs, and a more wide-open style—under open skies at McGill University's Molson Stadium from June through October. With ticket prices ranging from $21 (End zones) to $125 (Super Platinum), it's one of the best sporting deals in town. ☎ *514/871–2266 information, 514/871–2255 tickets* 🌐 *www.montrealalouettes.com.*

Golf

Montréal golf enthusiasts have several excellent golf courses available to them, many less than a half-hour drive from downtown.

Tourisme Québec. For a complete listing of the many golf courses in the area, this is the best place to start. ☎ *514/873–2015 or 800/363–7777* 🌐 *www.bonjourquebec.com or www.golfquebec.org.*

Club de Golf Métropolitain Anjou. A clubhouse featuring a steak-house restaurant, a banquet hall, a snack bar, a terrace BBQ grill, and a pro shop with an indoor practice range makes this a top-notch facility—not to mention, of course, their par-72, 18-hole championship golf course (7,005 yards from the gold tees). They also have a slightly less-challenging 18-hole executive course (2,751 yards) on their grounds. Rates for 18 holes range from C$18 to C$59.50, plus C$30 for an electric cart.

Getting here is only a 20-minute drive from downtown Montréal. *(Anjou Metropolitan Golf Club)* ✉ *9555 blvd. du Golf, Anjou* ☎ *514/353–5353* 🌐 *www.golfmetropolitainanjou.com.*

Golf Dorval. A short car ride from downtown Montréal, Golf Dorval encompasses two 18-hole courses (par 70 and 72), a driving range, and two putting greens. Rates for 18 holes range from C$26 to C$40. A cart is an additional C$32. ✉ *2000 av. Reverchon, Dorval* ☎ *514/631–4653 (GOLF) for reservations* 🌐 *www.golfdorval.com.*

Meadowbrook Golf Club. A somewhat challenging par-75, 18-hole course whose main selling point is its location, Meadowbrook is only a few miles from the heart of downtown Montréal. Rates range from C$19 to C$33 for 18 holes. A cart is C$27. The closest Métro stop is Ville Marie, although it's quite a distance away. ✉ *8370 Côte St-Luc, Côte St-Luc* ☎ *514/488–4875* 🌐 *www.clubdegolfmeadowbrook.com.*

Hockey

Ice hockey is nothing short of an institution in Montréal, the city that arguably gave birth to the sport back in the late 19th century. Although variations of the game are said to have been played in other U.S. and Canadian cities as early as 1800, the first organized game of modern hockey was played in Montréal in 1875, and the first official team, the McGill University Hockey Club, was founded in Montréal in 1880. The city's beloved Montréal Canadiens is the oldest club in the National Hockey League and, as Montrealers will be keen to tell you, one of the most successful teams in North American sports history. The Habs, taken from Habitants, or early settlers, as they are affectionately referred to locally, have won 24 Stanley Cups, although they've been struggling in the standings for several years now and haven't won a cup since the 1992–93 season. Nevertheless, Les Canadiens are a great source of pride to the city's sports fans, and tickets for their local games continue to be a hot commodity.

Montréal Canadiens. The Habs meet National Hockey League rivals at the Centre Bell from October through April (and even later if they make the play-offs). Buy tickets in advance to guarantee a seat. ✉ *1260 rue de la Gauchetière Ouest, Downtown* ☎ *514/932–2582* 🌐 *www.canadiens.com* Ⓜ *Lucien-L'Allier or Peel.*

McGill University Redmen. The Redmen make up in passion what they might lack in polish—especially when they take on their cross-city rivals, the Concordia University Stingers. ✉ *475 av. des Pins Ouest, Downtown* ☎ *514/398–7006* 🌐 *www.redmenhockey.com* Ⓜ *McGill.*

Ice-Skating

Come the winter months you don't have to look very far to find an ice-skating rink in Montréal. There are municipally run outdoor—and some indoor—rinks in virtually every corner of the city.

Access Montréal. For information on the numerous ice-skating rinks (at least 195 outdoor and 21 indoor) in the city, it's best to call or check the Web sites listed. Outdoor rinks are open from January until mid-March, and admission is free. The rinks on Île Ste-Hélène and at the

Vieux-Port are especially large, but there is a C$3 admission charge to skate at the latter. ☎ *514/872–1111* 🌐 *www.ville.montreal.qc.ca or www.oldportofmontreal.com.*

Atrium le Mille de la Gauchetière. You can skate year-round at this glassed-in atrium in a downtown skyscraper. There's disco skating Friday and Saturday nights from October to April and scheduled ice shows throughout the year. It's closed Monday from Easter to Thanksgiving. Skate rental is C$5.50 per day. ✉ *1000 rue de la Gauchetière, Downtown* ☎ *514/395–1000 or 514/395–0555* 🌐 *www.le1000.com* Ⓜ *Bonaventure.*

Jogging

Most city parks have jogging paths, and you can also run the trail along the Lachine Canal.

Parc du Mont-Royal. For a panoramic view, head to the dirt track in Parc du Mont-Royal. It's a superb place for a tranquil jog surrounded by nature right in the middle of the city. ☎ *514/843–4928.*

Other Sports

Trapezium. If you've ever longed to run away and join the circus, then the Trapezium can help you fulfill that fantasy. Instructors assess your skill level and then teach you how to fly through the air with the greatest of ease. Even the faint of heart have been known to take the plunge in the center's safe and friendly environment. ✉ *2350 rue Dickson, Montréal East* ☎ *514/251–0615* 🌐 *www.trapezium.qc.ca* 🎫 *C$40* Ⓜ *l'Assomption.*

Rock Climbing

If you're planning on scaling any of the considerable mountains in the nearby Laurentian or Eastern Townships regions, you might first want to practice your technique at an indoor climbing center in Montréal.

Allez-Up. With the highest climbing walls in Montréal (48 feet), Allez-Up has 35 top ropes installed and offers more than 75 different routes. Located on the edge of downtown Montréal in a landmark, redbrick building, rates start at C$13 for the day with admission for women on Monday nights being a cool eight bucks. Hours vary depending on the season so it's best to call in advance. ✉ *1339 rue Shearer, Pointe-St-Charles* ☎ *514/989–9656* 🌐 *www.allezup.com* Ⓜ *Charlevoix.*

Escalade Horizon Roc. Located deep in the heart of the city's east end, Escalade Horizon Roc has expanded to feature more than 27,000 square feet of climbing surfaces, making it the largest climbing center in the world. It's open weekdays 5–11, Saturday 9–6, and Sunday 9–5. ✉ *2350 rue Dickson, Montréal Est* ☎ *514/899–5000* 🌐 *www.horizonroc.com* Ⓜ *l'Assomption.*

Skiing & Snowboarding

You don't have to travel far from Montréal to find good downhill skiing or snowboarding, but you do have to travel. There is a wealth of ski centers in both the Laurentian and Eastern Townships regions with pros and cons to each. The slopes in the Townships are generally steeper and slightly more challenging but it requires more time to get out to them. Also, the Townships' centers tend to be quieter and more family oriented, so if it's après-ski action you're looking for, you might prefer heading out to a Laurentian hill like Mont-Saint-Sauveur where, for many, partying is as much the experience as is conquering the slopes.

As for cross-country skiing, you needn't even leave the city to find choice locations to pursue the sport. There exists a network of trails stretching throughout Mont-Royal park, and the Lachine Canal offers a 12-km (7-mi) stretch of relatively flat terrain, making for both a scenic and relatively simple cross-country excursion.

Tourisme Québec. The "Ski-Québec" brochure available from the tourism office has a wealth of information about skiing in and around the city. ☎ *514/873–2015 or 800/363–7777* 🌐 *www.bonjourquebec.com.*

CROSS-COUNTRY

Cap-St-Jacques Regional Park. Cross-country trails crisscross most city parks, including Parcs des Îles, Maisonneuve, and Mont-Royal, but the best cross-country skiing on the island is found along the 32 km (20 mi) of trails in the 900-acre Cap-St-Jacques park in the city's west end, about a half-hour drive from downtown. To get to the park via public transportation, take the Métro to the Henri-Bourassa station and then Bus 69 west. ✉ *20099 blvd. Gouin Ouest, Pierrefonds* ☎ *514/280–7272)* Ⓜ *Henri-Bourassa (Bus 69 west).*

DOWNHILL

Mont-Bromont. About a 45-minute drive from downtown Montréal, Mont-Bromont (72 trails, 6 lifts) is the closest Appalachian hill, with a 1,329-foot vertical drop. It's in the Eastern Townships, southeast of the city. ☎ *450/534–2200.*

Mont-St-Bruno. Mont-St-Bruno (14 trails, 4 lifts), on the south shore, has a modest vertical drop of 443 feet, but it includes Québec's biggest ski school and a high-speed lift. It also offers night skiing. ☎ *450/653–3441.*

Mont-St-Sauveur. With a vertical drop of 700 feet, Mont-St-Sauveur (38 trails, 8 lifts) is the closest decent-size ski area in the Laurentian Mountains, the winter and summer playground for Montrealers. It's about an hour's drive northwest of Montréal. ☎ *514/871–0101.*

Parc du Mont-Royal. Within Montréal, "the mountain," as it's familiarly called, is essentially a toboggan run, but its modest slope makes it ideal for beginners and little ones learning to ski.

Soccer

Although soccer still isn't quite the phenomenon in Montréal as it is elsewhere around the globe, the city has been supporting one professional team, the Montréal Impact, since 1993. A new stadium built expressly for the Impact is scheduled to be completed in 2007, a strong indication of the sport's increasing popularity, and a sign that the team's local owners, the Saputo family, are firmly committed to seeing the sport prosper in Montréal.

Montréal Impact. A consistently strong member of the North American A league, the team plays from mid-May until mid-September at the Centre Sportif Claude-Robillard and is a great sports bargain. ☎ *514/790–1245 or 514/328–3668* 🌐 *www.impactmontreal.com.*

Swimming

Most of the city's municipal outdoor pools are open from mid-June through August. Admission is free weekdays and C$2.75 on weekends and holidays.

Bain Schubert. Swimming is free at this renovated art deco pool. ✉ *3950 blvd. St-Laurent, Plateau Mont-Royal* Ⓜ *Sherbrooke or St-Laurent.*

Parc-Plage l'Île Notre-Dame. The water is always clean at this sandy man-made beach, located just over the water from downtown. To get there by public transit, take Bus 167 from the Métro station. ✉ *West side of Île Notre-Dame, Île Notre-Dame* Ⓜ *Jean-Drapeau.*

Vieux-Montréal CEGEP. There is a free indoor pool, open evenings Tuesday through Friday and Saturday 9–3, on the campus of this Montréal junior college. ✉ *255 rue Ontario Est, Latin Quarter* ☎ *514/982-3457* Ⓜ *Berri-UQAM or St-Laurent.*

Tennis

The City of Montréal maintains public tennis courts in several neighborhood parks around the city. Fees vary from court to court but are generally quite reasonable.

Accès Montréal. The Jeanne-Mance, Kent, Lafontaine, and Somerled parks all have public courts. For details contact Accès Montréal. ☎ *514/872–1111* 🌐 *www.ville.montreal.qc.ca.*

Windsurfing & Sailing

Although people have been sailing it for centuries, and windsurfing it for at least a couple of decades, who would ever have thought in a city where winters can last six months there would be opportunities to actually surf the St. Lawrence River? In 1999, South African champion kayaker and river surfer Corran Addison, a recent immigrant to Montréal, discovered a heretofore unknown yet ever-present 6-foot-tall standing wave that never breaks, thus allowing for an epic ride.

L'École de Voile de Lachine. You can rent sailboards and small sailboats at the Lachine Sailing School where courses are offered as well. ✉ *3045 blvd. St-Joseph, Lachine* ☎ *514/634–4326* 🌐 *www.ecoledevoiledelachine.com* Ⓜ *Angrignon.*

SHOPPING

Montrealers *magasinent* (shop) with a vengeance, so it's no surprise that the city has 160 multifaceted retail areas encompassing some 7,000 stores. The law allows shops to stay open weekdays 9–9 and weekends 9–5. However, many merchants close evenings Monday through Wednesday and on Sunday. Many specialty service shops are closed Monday as well. Just about all stores, with the exception of some bargain outlets and a few art and antiques galleries, accept major credit cards. Most purchases are subject to a federal goods-and-services tax (GST) of 6% as well as a provincial tax of 7.5%. Non-Canadians can claim a refund of some of these taxes, however.

Montréal is one of the fur capitals of the world. If you think you might be buying fur, it's wise to check with your country's customs officials before your trip to find out which animals are considered endangered and cannot be imported. The same caveat applies to collectors of Inuit ivory carvings, which cannot be imported into the United States or other countries. If you do buy Inuit carvings, whether they're made of ivory or soapstone, look for the government of Canada's igloo symbol, which attests to the piece's authenticity.

Shopping Districts

Fodor'sChoice ★ **Avenue Laurier Ouest.** The eight blocks between boulevard St-Laurent and chemin de la Côte-Ste-Catherine make up one of the most fashionable shopping strips in the city. Shops and boutiques sell high-end fashions, home furnishings, decorative items, artwork, books, kitchenware, toys and children's ware, and gourmet food. There are plenty of restaurants, bars, and cafés to rest your feet and check your purchases. The street is about a 15-minute walk from the Laurier Métro station.

Avenue Monkland. Somewhere between 1995 and 2000, the five blocks of Monkland running west of avenue Girouard went from drab to trendy so quickly that the word "Monklandization" has entered the Montréal vocabulary as an alternative to gentrification. The strip is lined with cafés and restaurants, as well as a good selection of boutiques specializing in children's and women's clothes, shoes, toys, books, and crafts. The main shopping area begins after a five minute walk from the Villa-Maria Métro station.

★ **Boulevard St-Laurent.** Affectionately known as the Main, St-Laurent has restaurants, boutiques, and nightclubs that cater mostly to an upscale clientele. Still, the area has managed to retain its working-class immigrant roots and vitality to some degree: high-fashion shops are interspersed with ethnic-food stores, secondhand bookshops, and hardware stores. Indeed, a trip up this street takes you from Chinatown to Little Italy. Shoppers flock to the two blocks of avenue Mont-Royal just east of boulevard St-Laurent for secondhand clothing. The street is a 10-minute walk west of the Mont-Royal Métro station.

Downtown. Montréal's largest retail district takes in rues Sherbrooke and Ste-Catherine, boulevard de Maisonneuve, and the side streets between them. Because of the proximity and diversity of the stores, it's the best shopping bet if you're in town overnight or for a weekend. The area bounded by rues Sherbrooke, Ste-Catherine, de la Montagne, and Crescent has antiques and art galleries in addition to designer salons. Fashion boutiques and art and antiques galleries line rue Sherbrooke. Rue Crescent holds a tempting blend of antiques, fashions, and jewelry displayed beneath colorful awnings. To get here, take the Métro to the Peel, McGill, or Guy-Concordia station.

Plaza St-Hubert. Visit the four-block stretch of St-Hubert between rues Bellechasse and Jean-Talon in March or April and you'll probably be swamped by teenage girls buying dresses for their high-school prom. Any time of the year, you'll be dodging brides-to-be buying wedding dresses and browsing for rings with their beaux. The street also has dozens of fabric stores, independent boutiques, jewelry stores, and end-of-the-line retailers and liquidation centers like Pennington's Dex and Le Château. The Beaubien and Jean-Talon Métro stations provide easy access to the area.

Rue Amherst. Antiques shops began springing up in the Village in the early 1990s, most of them on rue Amherst between rues Ste-Catherine and Ontario. The area used to be less expensive than rue Notre-Dame, but it's not always the case these days. Use the Beaudry Métro station.

Rue Chabanel. When Montrealers say "Chabanel," they mean the eight-block stretch just west of boulevard St-Laurent, which is the heart of the city's garment district. The factories and shops here are tiny—dozens of them are crammed into each building—and the goods seem to get more stylish and more expensive the farther west you go. For really inexpensive leather goods, sportswear, children's togs, and linens, try the shops at 99 rue Chabanel; 555 rue Chabanel has more deluxe options. The manufacturers and importers at 555 have their work areas on the upper floors and have transformed the mezzanine into a glitzy mall with bargains in men's suits, winter coats, knit goods, and stylish leather jackets. Many of the city's furriers have also moved into the area. A few places on Chabanel accept credit cards, but bring cash anyway. If you pay in cash, the price will often include the tax. From the Crémazie Métro station, take Bus 53 north.

Rue Notre-Dame Ouest. The fashionable place for antiquing is a formerly run-down five-block strip of Notre-Dame between rue Guy and avenue Atwater. Most of the action is at the western end of the strip, as are many of the restaurants and cafés that have sprung up to cater to shoppers. The Lionel-Groulx Métro station is the closest.

★ **Rue St-Denis.** Perhaps Montréal's trendiest area, rue St-Denis has shops of all descriptions and some of the best restaurants in town. People-watching is a popular pastime. Cutting-edge fashions can be found both in the shops and on the shoppers. Head here via the Berri-UQAM, Sherbrooke, or Mont-Royal Métro station.

Vieux-Montréal. Like most touristy areas, the old part of the city has more than its fair share of garish souvenir shops, but shopping here can be worthwhile. Fashion boutiques and shoe stores with low to moderate prices line rues Notre-Dame and St-Jacques, from rue McGill to Place Jacques-Cartier. The area is also rich in art galleries and crafts shops, especially along rue St-Paul. During the warmer months, sidewalk cafés are everywhere, and so are street performers. Use the Place-d'Armes or Champ-de-Mars Métro station.

Department Stores

Les Ailes de la Mode. This shiny little department store is a sort of temple to the power of the clothing label. Its three floors carry a large number of those labels—Hugo Boss, Armani, Jax, Cerruti, Max Mara, Escada, Arnold Brant, Bugatti, Riviera—not to mention dozens of top lines of cosmetics, perfumes, jewelry, and housewares, plus Godiva chocolates. Despite the glitter, however, the store is hidden away at the back of a shopping mall of the same name, behind a distracting phalanx of high-price boutiques. ✉ *677 rue Ste-Catherine Ouest, Downtown* ☎ *514/282–4537* Ⓜ *McGill.*

La Baie. The Bay is a descendant of the Hudson's Bay Company, the great 17th-century fur trading company that played a pivotal role in Canada's development. La Baie has been a department store since 1891. In addition to selling typical department-store goods, it's known for its duffel coats and signature Hudson's Bay blankets, with handsome stripes of red, green, and white. ✉ *585 rue Ste-Catherine Ouest, Downtown* ☎ *514/281–4422* Ⓜ *McGill.*

Fodor's Choice ★ **Holt Renfrew.** This high-end department store is Canada's answer to Saks Fifth Avenue, with labels such as Theory, Catherine Malandrino, Marc Jacobs, and Vince. Each designer has its own miniboutique. ✉ *1300 rue Sherbrooke Ouest, Downtown* ☎ *514/842–5111* Ⓜ *Peel or Guy-Concordia.*

★ **Ogilvy.** Founded in 1865, Ogilvy still stocks items by high-end retailers such as Burberry, Louis Vuitton, and Lalique. The store is divided into individual designer boutiques. A kilted piper regales shoppers each day at noon. ✉ *1307 rue Ste-Catherine Ouest, Downtown* ☎ *514/842–7711* Ⓜ *Peel.*

Simons. This youth-oriented department store in elegant 19th-century digs specializes in high-quality clothes for men and women, including its own highly respected house label. Its sales are excellent. Simons shares its address with a 12-screen Paramount theater, an IMAX theater, a bar, and a coffee shop. ✉ *977 rue Ste-Catherine Ouest, Downtown* ☎ *514/282–1840* Ⓜ *Peel.*

Shopping Centers & Malls

Le Centre Eaton. Eaton Center has a youthful edge, with a huge Levi's outlet and some trendy sporting-goods stores. The five-story mall, the largest in the downtown core, has 175 boutiques and shops and is linked to the McGill Métro station. An instant tax refund service, for nonresidents, is on the fifth floor. ✉ *705 rue Ste-Catherine Ouest, Downtown* ☎ *514/288–3708* Ⓜ *McGill.*

Le Complexe Les Ailes. The Les Ailes flagship store in this complex attached to Le Centre Eaton sells women's clothing and accessories; the other 60 retailers include Tommy Hilfiger and Archambault, a music store. ✉ *677 rue Ste-Catherine Ouest, Downtown* ☎ *514/285–1080* Ⓜ *McGill.*

Complexe Desjardins. Splashing fountains and exotic plants create a sense of relaxation here. The roughly 80 stores range from budget-clothing outlets to the exclusive Jonathan Roche Monsieur for men's fashions. To get here, take the Métro to Place des Arts and then follow the tunnels to the multitier atrium mall. ✉ *Blvd. René-Lévesque at rue Jeanne Mance, Downtown* ☎ *514/845–4636* Ⓜ *Place-des-Arts.*

Les Cours Mont-Royal. This elegant mall caters to expensive tastes, but even bargain hunters find it an intriguing spot for window-shopping. The more than 80 shops include DKNY and Harry Rosen. Beware: the interior layout can be disorienting. ✉ *1455 rue Peel, Downtown* ☎ *514/842–7777* Ⓜ *Peel.*

Marché Bonsecours. Inaugurated in the 1840s as the city's principal public market, this neoclassical building now houses boutiques that showcase Québecois, Canadian, and First Nations artwork, clothing, and furniture. Don't miss the Institut de Design Montréal Gallery boutique. It's full of intriguing little office and home gadgets that make unique gifts. ✉ *350 rue St-Paul Est, Vieux-Montréal* ☎ *514/872–7730* Ⓜ *Champ-de-Mars.*

Le Place Montréal Trust. This complex is a gateway to Montréal's vast Underground City. Its shops tend to specialize in high-end fashion. Indigo, one of the city's better bookstores, is also here. ✉ *1500 rue McGill College, at rue Ste-Catherine Ouest, Downtown* ☎ *514/843–8000* Ⓜ *McGill.*

Place Ville-Marie. With its 42-story cruciform towers, Place Ville-Marie is where weatherproof indoor shopping first came to Montréal in 1962. It was also the start of the underground shopping network that Montréal now enjoys. Stylish shoppers head to the 100-plus retail outlets for lunchtime sprees. ✉ *Blvd. René-Lévesque and rue University, Downtown* ☎ *514/866–6666* Ⓜ *McGill or Bonaventure.*

Les Promenades de la Cathédrale. There are more than 50 shops at this complex directly beneath Christ Church Cathedral, including Canada's largest Linen Chest outlet, with hundreds of bedspreads and duvets, plus aisles of china, crystal, linen, and silver. The Anglican Church's Diocesan Book Room sells an unusually good and ecumenical selection of books as well as religious objects. ✉ *625 rue Ste-Catherine Ouest, Downtown* ☎ *514/845–8230* Ⓜ *McGill.*

Square Westmount. This mall serves the mountainside suburb of Westmount, home of wealthy Montrealers, including business execs and former prime ministers. It's hardly surprising that the city's finest shops are here. With more than 50 boutiques, as well as the exclusive Spa de Westmount, the prospects for self-indulgence are endless. ✉ *Rue Ste-Catherine Ouest and av. Greene, Westmount* ☎ *514/932–0211* Ⓜ *Atwater.*

Specialty Shops

Antiques

L'Antiquaire Joyal. Art deco furnishings and decorations have top billing at this modest little shop. ✉ *1751 rue Amherst, Village* ☎ *514/524–0057* Ⓜ *Beaudry.*

Antiquités Clément & Beaulé. Lamps and candelabras take up much of the space here, along with some lovely 18th-century European pieces. ✉ *2440 rue Notre-Dame Ouest, St-Henri* ☎ *514/931–2507* Ⓜ *Lionel-Groulx.*

Antiquités Curiosités. This shop carries well-priced Victorian-era tables and tallboys, as well as lamps and lighting fixtures. The merchandise is crammed into three rooms spread over two floors. ✉ *1769 rue Amherst, Village* ☎ *514/525–8772* Ⓜ *Beaudry.*

Antiquités Phyllis Friedman. Phyllis Friedman, who specializes in 17th- to 19th-century English and European antiques, no longer has a retail outlet, but she's been in business since 1983 and is one of the city's most knowledgeable dealers. She still has a warehouse full of English hunt tables, Empire nightstands, Anglo-Irish glass, ceramics, and crystal. By appointment only. ☎ *514/946–2480* 🌐 *www.phyllisfriedman.com.*

Antiquités Pour La Table. As the name suggests, this store specializes in making your table look perfect. There's an extensive selection of antique porcelain, crystal, and linens—all impeccably preserved and beautifully displayed. Don't bother coming here to replace missing or broken pieces, though, since most of what's on display is complete sets. ✉ *902 rue Lenoir, St-Henri* ☎ *514/989–8945* Ⓜ *St-Henri.*

Cité Déco. Nostalgic for the good old days? This is just the place to pick up a chrome-and-Arborite dining-room set and an RCA tube radio. It also has art deco furnishings and accessories from the '30s and '40s. ✉ *1761 rue Amherst, Village* ☎ *514/528–0659* Ⓜ *Beaudry.*

Coach House. This cluttered little shop in the posh suburb of Westmount is packed with antique silverware, jewelry, glassware, crystal, and lamps. ✉ *1331 av. Greene, Westmount* ☎ *514/937–6191* Ⓜ *Atwater.*

Expressions de Grace. Tibetan temple art, Thai silks, jade carvings, and teakwood furniture are among this shop's Asian treasures. ✉ *2657 rue Notre-Dame Ouest, St-Henri* ☎ *514/486–7332* Ⓜ *Lionel-Groulx.*

Galerie Tansu. The highlights here are 18th- and 19th-century porcelain and ceramic objects, furnishings from Japan and China, and Tibetan chests and carpets. ✉ *1130 blvd. de Maisonneuve Ouest, Downtown* ☎ *514/846–1039* Ⓜ *Peel.*

Lapidarius. You'll find mostly watches, jewelry, silverware, carpets, and chandeliers at this Westmount shop. ✉ *1312 av. Greene, Westmount* ☎ *514/935–2717 or 800/267–0373* Ⓜ *Atwater.*

Lucie Favreau. Autographed hockey sweaters, old baseball programs, posters, and other sports memorabilia are the specialty here, along with old promotional and advertising items, antique toys, and Christmas decorations. ✉ *1904 rue Notre-Dame Ouest, St-Henri* ☎ *514/989–5117* Ⓜ *Georges-Vanier.*

Old Times Antiques. Brass and copper lamps and decorations are highlighted in this cluttered shop. ✉ *2621 rue Notre-Dame Ouest, St-Henri* ☎ *514/931–3777* Ⓜ *Lionel-Groulx.*

Milord Antiques. Milord's has stuffed an old bank building with 18th- and 19th-century art and European furniture. The shop also has a fine collection of porcelain and crystal. ✉ *1870 rue Notre-Dame Ouest, St-Henri* ☎ *514/933–2433* Ⓜ *Lucien-L'Allier.*

Ruth Stalker. She made her reputation finding and salvaging fine pieces of early-Canadian pine furniture, but Ruth Stalker has also developed a good instinct for such folk art as exquisitely carved hunting decoys, weather vanes, and pottery. ✉ *4447 rue Ste-Catherine Ouest, Westmount* ☎ *514/931–0822* Ⓜ *Atwater.*

Viva Gallery. Asian antique furniture and art take center stage at Viva, where you'll find a wide selection of carved tables, benches, and armoires. ✉ *1970 rue Notre-Dame Ouest, St-Henri* ☎ *514/932–3200* Ⓜ *Lucien-L'Allier.*

Art

Montréal brims with art galleries that present work by local luminaries as well as international artists. The downtown area has a wide choice; Vieux-Montréal is also rich in galleries, most of which specialize in Québecois and First Nations work.

★ **Edifice Belgo.** In a nondescript building, Edifice Belgo is in essence a mall of roughly 20 art galleries showing both established and emerging artists. Galerie Roger Bellemare is one of the best galleries to look for contemporary art. Galerie Trois Points showcases the work of Montréal and Québec artists. Both galleries are on the fifth floor. ✉ *372 rue Ste-Catherine Ouest, Downtown* ☎ *514/393–9969 Galerie René Blouin, 514/866–8008 Galerie Trois Points* Ⓜ *Place-des-Arts.*

Galerie Art & Culture. Canadian landscapes from the 19th and 20th centuries are the specialty here. ✉ *227 rue St-Paul Ouest, Vieux-Montréal* ☎ *514/843–5980* Ⓜ *Place-d'Armes.*

Galerie de Bellefeuille. This Westmount gallery has a knack for discovering important new talents. It represents many of Canada's top contemporary artists as well as some international ones. Its 5,000 square feet hold a good selection of sculptures, paintings, and limited-edition prints. ✉ *1367 av. Greene, Westmount* ☎ *514/933–4406* Ⓜ *Atwater.*

Galerie de Chariot. This gallery claims to have the largest collection of Inuit soapstone and ivory carvings in Canada. It also has a wide selection of drawings and beadwork, all of which is government authenticated. ✉ *446 pl. Jacques-Cartier, Vieux-Montréal* ☎ *514/875–6134* Ⓜ *Champ-de-Mars.*

Galerie Elena Lee. This is the city's leading dealer in glassworks. It exhibits both Canadian and international artists, some working strictly in glass, others using metal, wood, and found materials. ✉ *1460 rue Sherbrooke Ouest, Square Mile* ☎ *514/844–6009* Ⓜ *Guy-Concordia.*

★ **Galerie Walter Klinkhoff.** Brothers Alan and Eric Klinkhoff specialize in Canadian historical and contemporary art. ✉ *1200 rue Sherbrooke Ouest, Square Mile* ☎ *514/288–7306* Ⓜ *Peel.*

★ **La Guilde Graphique.** The Graphic Guild has an exceptional selection of original prints, engravings, and etchings. ✉ *9 rue St-Paul Ouest, Vieux-Montréal* ☎ *514/844–3438* Ⓜ *Champ-de-Mars.*

Beauty

Bella Pella. The soaps, shampoos, and body lotions found here are all handmade by area artisans using organic ingredients such as olive oil, goats' milk, and cranberries. ✉ *3933 rue St-Denis, Plateau Mont-Royal* ☎ *514/845–7328* Ⓜ *Mont-Royal.*

S/he & Co. If you want to pamper yourself, this is the place to come for lotions, perfumes, creams, and shampoos. And if you want someone else to pamper you, there's small spa downstairs. ✉ *1361 av. Greene, Westmount* ☎ *514/932–1444* Ⓜ *Westmount Square.*

Books & Stationery

Bibliomania. It's possible to find some out-of-print gems among Bibliomania's extensive shelves of secondhand books. The store also sells engravings, postcards, and other printed collectibles. ✉ *460 rue*

Ste-Catherine Ouest, Room 406, Downtown ☎ *514/933–8156* Ⓜ *Place-des-Arts.*

L'Essence du Papier. With its selection of imported and handmade papers, the Essence of Paper is a reminder that letter-writing can be an art form. Here are pens suited to most tastes and budgets, as well as waxes and stamps with which to seal any romantic prose that you might be inspired to produce. There's also a wide selection of place cards, invitations, and journals. ✉ *4160 rue St-Denis, Plateau Mont-Royal* ☎ *514/288–9691* Ⓜ *Mont-Royal.*

Indigo. Although it is mainly about books and magazines, this chain has branched out into DVDs, cards, gifts, and housewares. This location also has a large children's section. ✉ *1500 av. McGill College, Downtown* ☎ *514/281–5549* Ⓜ *McGill.*

★ **Paragraphe.** Stubbornly independent until 2003 when it was bought out by Archambault, a Montréal chain of music stores, Paragraphe carries the usual selection of best-sellers and thrillers but also stocks Canadian works and histories. It's a favorite with visiting authors who stop by to read from their latest releases, as well as Booker Prize winner Yann Martel, who drops in from time to time. ✉ *2220 av. McGill College, Downtown* ☎ *514/845–5811* Ⓜ *McGill.*

Renaud-Bray. With 23 branches in Québec—nearly half of them in Montréal—Renaud-Bray is the largest French-language book chain in Canada. Its shops stock translated best-sellers and thrillers as well as original works from Europe and Canada. ✉ *1432 rue Ste-Catherine, Downtown* ☎ *514/876–9119* Ⓜ *Guy-Concordia.*

S. W. Welch. The old books here include meditations on religion and philosophy as well as mysteries and science fiction. ✉ *3878 blvd. St-Laurent, Plateau Mont-Royal* ☎ *514/848–9358* Ⓜ *Mont-Royal.*

★ **The Word.** Deep in the McGill University neighborhood, the Word is a timeless shop with sagging shelves that hold used books on art, philosophy, and literature. The owner here still tallies your bill by hand. ✉ *469 rue Milton, Downtown* ☎ *514/845–5640* Ⓜ *McGill.*

Cigars

Remember that U.S. law forbids Americans to bring most Cuban products, including cigars, back into the country.

Casa del Habano. This cigar shop stocks the finest cigars Cuba produces. ✉ *1434 rue Sherbrooke Ouest, Downtown* ☎ *514/849–0037* Ⓜ *Guy-Concordia.*

Davidoff. You'll find the best names in cigars here as well as a fine collection of smoking accessories and humidors. ✉ *1458 Sherbrooke Ouest, Downtown* ☎ *514/289–9118* Ⓜ *Guy-Concordia.*

H. Poupart. For more than 100 years, H. Poupart has been supplying Montrealers with the best cigars, cigarettes, chewing and pipe tobaccos, and snuff. The shop also stocks Waterman pens, Riedel glassware, and chess sets. ✉ *1474 rue Peel, Downtown* ☎ *514/842–5794* Ⓜ *Peel.*

Clothing

Aime Com Moi. Québecois designers create the exclusive women's clothing sold at this shop. ✉ *150 av. Mont-Royal Est, Plateau Mont-Royal* ☎ *514/982–0088* Ⓜ *Mont-Royal.*

BCBG MAX AZRIA. Everything here fits right into Montréal's avant-garde attitude. Max Azria's super-stylish clothing, shoes, and handbags all make a statement. ✉ *1300 rue Ste-Catherine Ouest, Downtown* ☎ *514/398–9130* Ⓜ *Peel.*

Bedo. If you want to look fashionable without going broke, this is the place to shop for men's and women's casual wear. ✉ *1256 rue Ste-Catherine Ouest, Downtown* ☎ *514/866–4962* Ⓜ *Peel.*

Betty's Bazaar. For fun feminine clothes to wear out on the town, you can't do better. ✉ *218 rue St-Paul Ouest, Vieux-Montréal* ☎ *514/285–2212* Ⓜ *Place-d'Armes.*

Bovet. If you're looking for cutting-edge men's fashion, this is definitely not the place, but if you're looking for the biggest selection of middle-of-the-road fashions the city has to offer at reasonable prices, head for this local chain's north-end branch on boulevard Métropolitain, which claims to be the biggest menswear store in the province of Québec. ✉ *4475 blvd. Métropolitain Est, North End* ☎ *514/374–4551* Ⓜ *Viau.*

Buffalo David Bitton. Buffalo jeans—and the billboards advertising them—are deliberately and daringly sexy, even for this day and age. But their fans claim they're also comfortable and they certainly go well with the belts, T-shirts, shoes, and other accessories Montrealer David Bitton designs. ✉ *1223 rue Ste-Catherine Ouest, Downtown* ☎ *514/845–1816* Ⓜ *Peel.*

Chas. Johnson & Sons. The three expert kilt makers on hand here can cut any tartan to any size. The shop also rents Highland formal gear for all occasions and sells *sporrans* (leather pouches hung from kilts), *skean-dhus* (knives worn at the top of the stocking in traditional Scottish dress), doublets, and day jackets, as well as a full line of classic British menswear. ✉ *1184 Phillips Pl., Downtown* ☎ *514/878–1931* Ⓜ *McGill.*

Club Monaco. The specialty here is urban attire—some of which might do in the office—for men and women. ✉ *Les Cours Mont-Royal, 1455 rue Peel, Downtown* ☎ *514/499–0959* Ⓜ *Peel.*

Diffusion Griff 3000. This is Anne de Shalla's showcase for leading Québecois fashion designers. ✉ *350 rue St-Paul Est, Vieux-Montréal* ☎ *514/398–0761* Ⓜ *Champ-de-Mars.*

General 54. Stores like this are what give Mile End its rep for cutting edge. The clothes—many by local designers—are very feminine and whimsical. ✉ *54 rue St-Viateur Ouest, Mile End* ☎ *514/271–2129* Ⓜ *Laurier.*

Harricana. Yesterday's old fur coats and stoles are transformed into everything from car coats and ski jackets to baby wraps and cushion covers by the artisans of this Québec City–based company named for one of the province's great northern rivers. The fashions are sold at dozens of shops, but the best place to see what's available is this combination atelier and boutique. ✉ *3000 rue St-Antoine Ouest, Downtown* ☎ *877/894–9919* Ⓜ *Lionel-Groulx.*

Henri Henri. Simply the best men's hat store in Canada, Henri Henri has a huge stock of Homburgs, Borsalinos, fedoras, top hats, and derbies, as well as cloth caps and other accessories. Hat prices range from about C$60 to well over C$1,000 for a top-of-the-line Homburg or Panama. The friendly employees delight in showing off their wares. ✉ *189 rue Ste-Catherine Est, Downtown* ☎ *514/288–0109 or 888/388–0109* Ⓜ *St-Laurent.*

Ima. Clothes with labels like Joie and Lucious fill the racks of this high-end boutique, but it also stocks some unique clothes by local designers. ✉ *24 rue Prince Arthur Ouest, Plateau Mont-Royal* ☎ *514/844–0303* Ⓜ *Sherbrooke.*

Indigo. As the name suggests, the main product here is jeans, and there's a dizzying array of brands to choose from. And this is Westmount, so you know your choices won't be cheap. ✉ *4920 rue Sherbrooke Ouest, Westmount* ☎ *514/486–4420* Ⓜ *Westmount Square.*

Jacob. Fashionable professional women shop at Jacob for office-appropriate clothes—as well as some slightly daring lingerie. ✉ *1220 rue Ste-Catherine Ouest, Downtown* ☎ *514/861–9346* Ⓜ *Peel.*

Kamkyl. If you're the kind of man who leans to blue blazers and khaki pants, you'll know as soon as you walk into Yvonne and Douglas Mandel's hushed minimalist boutique in Vieux-Montréal that you're in the wrong place. The Mandels design clothes—silky sweaters, beautifully cut jackets, patterned shirts—for men who are serious about fashion. ✉ *4393 rue St-Pierre, Vieux-Montréal* ☎ *514/281–8221 or 877/281–8221* Ⓜ *Place-d'Armes.*

Kanuk. This company's owl trademark has become something of a status symbol among the shivering urban masses. The coats designed by Kanuk could easily keep an Arctic explorer warm, but its elegant winter clothes and excellent rainwear are just as desirable. Many retailers carry Kanuk coats, but you can also buy them at the display room over the factory here. ✉ *485 rue Rachel Est, Plateau Mont-Royal* ☎ *514/527–4494* Ⓜ *Mont-Royal.*

Lola & Emily. The perfect boutique for the undecided woman: Lola's side specializes in the fun and frilly, Emily's in everything in basic black or beige. ✉ *3475 blvd. St-Laurent, Plateau Mont-Royal* ☎ *514/288–7598* Ⓜ *Mont-Royal.*

Mains Folles. You'll find tropical-print dresses, skirts, and blouses imported from Bali at this store. ✉ *4427 rue St-Denis, Plateau Mont-Royal* ☎ *514/284–6854* Ⓜ *Mont-Royal.*

MO851. Handbags, jackets, and gloves in fine supple leathers are the specialty of this Canadian-based chain. ✉ *3526 blvd. St-Laurent, Plateau Mont-Royal* ☎ *514/849–9759* Ⓜ *Mont-Royal.*

Parasuco. Montrealer Salvatore Parasuco—inventor of "ergonomic jeans"—has been making history in denim ever since he opened his first store in 1975 at the age of 19. He has since spread across the country and into the United States, but his flagship shop—completely refurbished in 2006—is still in Montréal. ✉ *1414 rue Crescent, Downtown* ☎ *514/284–2288* Ⓜ *Guy-Concordia.*

Revenge. Nearly 40 Canadian and Québecois designers create Revenge's well-crafted original fashions for women. ✉ *3852 rue St-Denis, Plateau Mont-Royal* ☎ *514/843–4379* Ⓜ *Sherbrooke.*

Rooney. Exposed brick walls, high ceilings, and polished wooden floors set off such 20-something fashion favorites as Splendid, Ella Moss, Nudie Jeans, Heatherette, Brown Sound, etc. ✉ *395 rue Notre-Dame Ouest, Vieux-Montréal* ☎ *514/543–6234* Ⓜ *Place-d'Armes.*

Roots. Its quality materials and approachable, sometimes retro look have made Roots a fashion favorite. ✉ *1035 rue Ste-Catherine Ouest, Downtown* ☎ *514/845–7995* Ⓜ *Peel.*

Scandale. The cutting-edge fashions sold here are all originals created on-site by Québecois designer Georges Lévesque. In keeping with the name, the window displays are always a bit lurid. From the St-Laurent Métro station, take Bus 55 north. ✉ *3639 blvd. St-Laurent, Plateau Mont-Royal* ☎ *514/842–4707* Ⓜ *Mont-Royal.*

Space FB. The initials stand for François Beauregard, a Montréal designer whose snug tank tops and hip-hugging pants are much loved by the younger crowd. ✉ *3632 blvd. St-Laurent, Plateau Mont-Royal* ☎ *514/282–1991* Ⓜ *Mont-Royal.*

Tilley Endurables. The famous Canadian-designed Tilley hat is sold here, along with other easy-care travel wear. ✉ *1050 rue Laurier Ouest, Outremont* ☎ *514/272–7791* Ⓜ *Laurier.*

Winners. This discount designer clothing store has turned shopping into a sport. And now that it carries housewares, leaving empty-handed is even more difficult. Suitably enough, its downtown outlet is on the lowest level of Place Montréal Trust. ✉ *1500 av. McGill College, Downtown* ☎ *514/788–4949* Ⓜ *McGill.*

CHILDREN'S **Oink Oink.** This piggy store carries fashions as well as toys and books for infants and children. It also stocks clothes for teenagers. It's fun to hear the staff answer the phone. ✉ *1343 av. Greene, Westmount* ☎ *514/939–2634* Ⓜ *Atwater.*

FURS Montréal is one of the fur capitals of the world. Close to 90% of Canada's fur manufacturers are based in the city, as are many of their retail outlets. Most stores are clustered along rue Mayor and boulevard de Maisonneuve between rues de Bleury and Aylmer.

Alexandor. Nine blocks west of the main fur-trade area, Alexandor caters to downtown shoppers. It sells wool and cashmere coats with fur trim as well as coats in mink, fox, chinchilla, and beaver. ✉ *2055 rue Peel, Downtown* ☎ *514/288–1119* Ⓜ *Peel.*

Holt Renfrew. The fur showroom here is perhaps the most exclusive in the city, with prices to match. When Queen Elizabeth II got married in 1947, Holt gave her a priceless Labrador mink. ✉ *1300 rue Sherbrooke Ouest, Downtown* ☎ *514/842–5111* Ⓜ *Peel or Guy-Concordia.*

Marcel Jodoin Fourrures. This store carries a wide selection of nearly new (less than five years old) fur coats, jackets, and stoles, most of which go for less than the cost of an imitation. ✉ *1228 rue St-Denis, Downtown* ☎ *514/288–1683* Ⓜ *Berri-UQAM.*

McComber Grosvenor. Two of Montréal's biggest fur merchants have merged to create this showroom filled with beautiful mink coats and jackets. ✉ *433 rue Mayor, Downtown* ☎ *514/288–1255* Ⓜ *Bleury.*

LINGERIE **Collange.** Lacy goods of the designer variety are sold here. ✉ *1 Westmount Sq., Westmount* ☎ *514/933–4634* Ⓜ *Atwater.*

Deuxième Peau. As its name suggests, Second Skin sells lingerie so fine you don't notice you're wearing it. While you're feeling brave and beautiful, kill two birds with one stone and try on a bathing suit. ✉ *4457 rue St-Denis, Plateau Mont-Royal* ☎ *514/842–0811* Ⓜ *Mont-Royal.*

Lyla. Lyla carries seductively lacy lingerie. ✉ *400 rue Laurier Ouest, Outremont* ☎ *514/271–0763* Ⓜ *Laurier.*

VINTAGE **Boutique Encore.** In business for about 50 years, Boutique Encore has retained its popularity by maintaining a good selection of designer labels. Although best known for its nearly new women's fashions, it also includes the big names for men. ✉ *2165 rue Crescent, Downtown* ☎ *514/849–0092* Ⓜ *Peel or Guy-Concordia.*

Eva B. If your fantasy is being a flapper, or if you want to revive the pill-box hat, turn back the clock and perk up your wardrobe with an item from the vast collection sold here. ✉ *2013 blvd. St-Laurent, Downtown* ☎ *514/849–8246* Ⓜ *St-Laurent.*

Fabrics

Créations Nicole Moisan. Miles and miles of lace are sold here, with thousands of patterns to choose from, all from Europe. Custom orders are available. ✉ *4324 rue St-Denis, Plateau Mont-Royal* ☎ *514/284–9506* Ⓜ *Mont-Royal.*

C&M Textiles. This shop's knowledgeable staff will show you a wide selection of velvets, lace, and wools. ✉ *7500 rue St-Hubert, Villeray* ☎ *514/272–0247* Ⓜ *Jean-Talon.*

Madeleine Soie & Laine. As the name suggests, silk and wool are the specialties here. ✉ *6394 rue St-Hubert, Villeray* ☎ *514/272–7391* Ⓜ *Beaubien.*

Food

Charcuterie/Boucherie Hongroise. This family-owned and -operated store smokes and cures bacon and hams and sells a wide selection of German, Polish, and Hungarian sausages. ✉ *3843 blvd. St-Laurent, Plateau Mont-Royal* ☎ *514/844–6734* Ⓜ *Mont-Royal.*

Marché Atwater. The Atwater Market is one of the city's oldest public markets. It's a favorite with downtowners looking for fresh produce, specialty meats and sausages, fresh fish, and Québec cheese. The main produce market is outdoors under shelters. Restaurants and shops are inside a two-story complex perfect for rainy-day browsing. The market's just off the Lachine Canal, so it's the ideal place for cyclists on the canal bicycle path to stop for lunch or to buy the makings of a picnic. ✉ *138 av. Atwater, Downtown* ☎ *514/937–7754* Ⓜ *Lionel-Groulx.*

Marché de Westmount. The shops at this indoor market sell pastries, cheeses, pâtés, cakes, candies, and chocolates. You can assemble a picnic and eat it at one of the little tables scattered among the stalls. ✉ *1 Westmount Sq., Westmount* ☎ *No phone* Ⓜ *Atwater.*

Fodor'sChoice ★ **Marché Jean-Talon.** This is the biggest, best, and liveliest of the city's public markets. On weekends in summer and fall, crowds swarm the half acre or so of outdoor produce stalls, looking for the fattest tomatoes, sweetest melons, and juiciest strawberries. Restaurants and shops on the periphery sell meat, fish, cheese, sausage, bread, pastries, and other delicacies. In spring, Jean-Talon is overrun with gardeners rushing to get the best plants and seeds. The market is in the northern end of the city but is easy to get to by Métro. ✉ *7070 rue Henri-Julien, Little Italy* ☎ *514/277–1588* Ⓜ *Jean-Talon.*

Milano. One of the largest cheese selections in the city as well as fresh pastas of all kinds are the highlights of this market. An entire wall is devoted to olive oils and vinegars; there's also a butcher and a sizeable produce section. ✉ *6862 blvd. St-Laurent, Little Italy* ☎ *514/273–8558* Ⓜ *Jean-Talon.*

Nino. On weekends this place gets hectic, as shoppers pack the narrow aisles scanning the shelves for spices, pickles, hams, and kitchen gadgets of all sorts. ✉ *3667 blvd. St-Laurent, Plateau Mont-Royal* ☎ *514/844–7630* Ⓜ *Mont-Royal.*

Gifts

Desmarais et Robitaille. The local clergy come here to buy vestments, chalices, altar candles, and other liturgical items, but Desmarais et Robitaille also stocks Québecois wood carvings, handicrafts, religious articles, and sacred music. ✉ *60 rue Notre-Dame Ouest, Vieux-Montréal* ☎ *514/845–3194* Ⓜ *Place-d'Armes.*

L'Empreinte Coopérative. Fine Québec handicrafts are on display here. ✉ *272 rue St-Paul Est, Vieux-Montréal* ☎ *514/861–4427* Ⓜ *Champ-de-Mars.*

Home Furnishings

L'Institut de Design de Montréal. The Montréal Institute of Design has an amusingly innovative collection of kitchen brushes, buckets, CD-storage racks, clocks, bathroom equipment, and so forth. ✉ *Marché Bonsecours, 390 rue St-Paul Est, Vieux-Montréal* ☎ *514/866–2436* Ⓜ *Champ-de-Mars.*

Ungava Factory Outlet. Canadian-made down comforters, futons, and pillows as well as sheets, curtains, and home decor are sold at wholesale prices here. Custom orders are welcome. ✉ *10 av. des Pins Ouest, Suite 112, Plateau Mont-Royal* ☎ *514/287–9276* Ⓜ *Sherbrooke.*

Housewares

Ares Kitchen & Baking Supplies. In this shop you can find just about any kitchen gadget imaginable, as well as top-of-the-line equipment that would make a professional chef's flame burn brighter. It's a 30-minute drive from downtown. ✉ *2355 Trans-Canada Hwy., Pointe Claire* ☎ *514/695–5225.*

Danesco. A manufacturer and importer of kitchen equipment and tableware, Danesco operates an outlet out of its main office, located 45 minutes from downtown. There are great deals on everything from pots and pans to cutlery and linen napkins. ✉ *18111 Trans-Canada Hwy., Kirkland* ☎ *514/694–0950.*

Faema. Coffee lovers come here for espresso machines and other paraphernalia, as well as the beans to make their favorite brew. Ice-cream machines are also available. ✉ *14 rue Jean-Talon Ouest, Little Italy* ☎ *514/276–2671* Ⓜ *Jean-Talon.*

Linen Chest. One of the city's largest selections of competitively priced china, crystal, and cutlery—affectionately known as the "Great Wall of China"—is found inside this downtown shop. Down comforters and bedding are also a specialty. ✉ *625 rue Ste-Catherine Ouest, Downtown* ☎ *514/282–9525* Ⓜ *McGill.*

Les Touilleurs. The name means "the whisks," but there's a lot more here than beats an egg—top-quality knives, gadgets, small appliances, cookbooks, and even a fully equipped kitchen where local chefs share their secrets with the public. ✉ *152 rue Laurier Ouest, Mile End* ☎ *514/278–0008* Ⓜ *Laurier.*

Zone. The collection of kitchen, table, and decorative items and gadgets here is eclectic, and prices are reasonable. ✉ *4246 rue St-Denis, Plateau Mont-Royal* ☎ *514/845–3530* Ⓜ *Mont-Royal.*

Jewelry

AmberLux. As the name suggests, amber in every kind of setting is available here. ✉ *625 rue Ste-Catherine Ouest, Downtown* ☎ *514/844–1357* Ⓜ *McGill.*

Birks. Since 1879 Birks has been helping shoppers mark special occasions, whether engagements, weddings, or retirements. ✉ *1240 Phillips Sq., Downtown* ☎ *514/397–2511* Ⓜ *McGill.*

★ **Kaufmann de Suisse.** Expert craftspeople create the fine jewelry sold here. ✉ *2195 rue Crescent, Downtown* ☎ *514/848–0595* Ⓜ *Guy-Concordia.*

Music

★ **Archambault.** Québec's oldest music store stocks musical instruments and sheet music, as well as an extensive selection of CDs, DVDs, and books. ✉ *500 rue Ste-Catherine Est, Downtown* ☎ *514/849–6201* Ⓜ *Berri-UQAM.*

Cheap Thrills. In addition to good new and secondhand CDs, Cheap Thrills has a large selection of used books at bargain prices. ✉ *2044 Metcalfe, Downtown* ☎ *514/844–8988* Ⓜ *McGill.*

HMV. This chain carries everything from Bach to Limp Bizkit, as well as a wide variety of DVDs. ✉ *1020 rue Ste-Catherine Ouest, Downtown* ☎ *514/875–0765* Ⓜ *Peel.*

Steve's Music Store. A shabby warren of five storefronts, Steve's is jammed with just about everything you need to be a rock star, from instruments to sheet music. ✉ *51 rue St-Antoine Ouest, Downtown* ☎ *514/878–2216* Ⓜ *Place-d'Armes.*

Shoes

Aldo. Aldo Bensadoun opened his first shoe store in 1972. His shoe empire now includes more than 600 stores across Canada, operating under the names Aldo, Simard et Voyer, Globo, Stoneridge, and Transit. Aldo also sells handbags, leather apparel, sandals, and backpacks. ✉ *1320 rue Ste-Catherine Ouest, Downtown* ☎ *514/866–1376* Ⓜ *Peel.*

Alibi. Alibi imports shoes for men and women from Brazil, Spain, Japan, China and Italy. ✉ *1500 rue McGill-College, Downtown* ☎ *514/843–3019* Ⓜ *McGill.*

Bellini. As the name suggests, all the shoes that you'll find in this store come from Italy. ✉ *1119 rue Ste-Catherine Ouest, Downtown* ☎ *514/288–6144* Ⓜ *Peel.*

Browns. This local institution stocks fashion footwear and accessories for men and women. As well as the store's own label, it carries DKNY, Costume National, Dolce & Gabbana, Christian Dior, and Tods. ✉ *1191 rue Ste-Catherine Ouest, Downtown* ☎ *514/987–1206* Ⓜ *Peel.*

Mona Moore. Pale-pink walls and glass shelves create the backdrop for one of the city's best selections of women's shoes, featuring such names as Marc Jacobs, Chloé, and Pierre Hardy. ✉ *1446 rue Sherbrooke Ouest, Downtown* ☎ *514/842–0662* Ⓜ *Guy-Concordia.*

Tony's. Dedicated to the finely shod foot, Tony's places stylish imports beside elegantly sensible domestic footwear for men and women. ✉ *1346 av. Greene, Westmount* ☎ *514/935–2993* Ⓜ *Atwater.*

Sporting Goods & Clothing

Canadiens Boutique Centre Bell. Hockey sticks, pucks, jerseys, posters, and other authentic memorabilia—all bearing the emblem of the world's most storied hockey team—are for sale here. ✉ *1220 rue de la Gauchetière, Downtown* ☎ *514/989–2836* Ⓜ *Bonaventure.*

Le Baron. Le Baron stocks everything the serious hiker, hunter, or fisherman would need for a trip to Québec's backwoods, from fishing rods to fly repellent. But it also has a good selection of the kind of comfort-oriented equipment favored by family campers on a road trip. ✉ *8601 blvd. St-Laurent, North End* ☎ *514/381–4231* Ⓜ *Crémazie.*

La Cordée. Montréal's trekking and hiking crowd come here to buy everything from boots and shorts to kayaks and sleeping bags. If you love the great outdoors and the gadgets that go with it, this is a great place to browse. ✉ *2159 rue Ste-Catherine Est, Village* ☎ *514/524–1106* Ⓜ *Papineau.*

Toys & Games

★ **Cerf Volanterie.** Claude Thibaudeau makes the sturdy, gloriously colored kites sold here. He signs each of his creations and guarantees them for three years. ✉ *4019 rue Ste-Catherine Est, Hochelaga-Maisonneuve* ☎ *514/845–7613* Ⓜ *Pie-IX.*

Jouets Choo-Choo. This shop 20 minutes from downtown sells quality European toys and educational games. ✉ *940 blvd.St-Jean,, Pointe-Claire* ☎ *514/697–7550.*

Valet d'Coeur. Game-lovers of all ages can find an impressive collection of board games, including just about every variation on the chess board imaginable. The store also stocks comic books, posters, and toys. ✉ *4408 rue St-Denis, Plateau Mont-Royal* ☎ *514/499–9970 or 888/499–5389* Ⓜ *Mont-Royal.*

MONTRÉAL ESSENTIALS

Transportation

BY AIR

Montréal–Trudeau International Airport (still commonly called Dorval), 22½ km (14 mi) west of the city, handles all passenger flights.

A taxi from Trudeau International to downtown costs about C$35. All taxi companies must charge the same rate for travel between the airport and downtown.

La Québecoise shuttles are a much cheaper alternative for getting to and from the airport. Shuttles leave from Montréal Central Bus Station and pick up and drop off passengers at the downtown train station, as well as at major hotels. Shuttles run every 20 minutes from 4 AM to 11 PM and cost C$13 one-way, C$22.75 round-trip.

ℹ **Aéroports de Montréal** ✉ 1100 René-Lévesque blvd. Ouest, Suite 2100 ☎ 514/394-7200 🌐 www.admtl.com. **Montréal–Pierre Elliott Trudeau International Airport**

✉ 975 Roméo-Vachon blvd. Nord, Dorval ☎ 514/394-7377. **La Québecoise** ☎ 514/842-2281 🌐 www.autobus.qc.ca.

BY BUS

Orléans Express provides service between Montréal and Sherbrooke. All buses arrive at and depart from the city's downtown bus terminal, the Station Centrale d'Autobus Montréal, which connects with the Berri-UQAM Métro station. The staff has schedule and fare information for all bus companies at the station.

Within the city, Société de Transport de Montréal (STM) administers municipal buses as well as the Métro; the same tickets and transfers are valid on either service.

Central Bus Station ✉ 505 blvd.de Maisonneuve Est,, Latin Quarter ☎ 514/842-2281 Ⓜ Berri-UQAM. **Greyhound** ☎ 800/231-2222, 800/661-8747 in Canada 🌐 www.greyhound.ca. **Orléans Express** ☎ 514/395-4000 🌐 www.orleansexpress.com. **Société de Transport de Montréal** (STM) ☎ 514/288-6287 or 514/786-4636 🌐 www.stcum.qc.ca.

BY CAR

Montréal is accessible from the rest of Canada via the Trans-Canada Highway, which crosses the southern part of the island as Route 20, with Route 720 leading into downtown. Route 40 parallels Route 20 to the north; exits to downtown include St-Laurent and St-Denis. From New York, take I–87 north until it becomes Route 15 at the Canadian border; continue for another 47 km (29 mi) to the outskirts of Montréal. You can also follow U.S. I–89 north until it becomes two-lane Route 133, which eventually joins Route 10, an east-west highway that leads west across the Champlain Bridge and right into downtown. From I–91 through Massachusetts via New Hampshire and Vermont, you can take Route 55 to Route 10. Again, turn west to reach Montréal. At the border you must clear Canadian Customs, so be prepared with proof of citizenship (with photo ID) and your vehicle's ownership papers. On holidays and during the peak summer season, expect to wait a half hour or more at the major crossings.

Once on the island of Montréal or its surrounding boroughs, public transportation is far and away the best and cheapest way to get around. Finding your way around Montréal by car is not difficult, since the streets are laid out in a fairly straightforward grid and one-way streets are clearly marked. Parking isn't easy, however, and the narrow cobbled streets of Vieux-Montréal can be a trial. It's much easier to park near a Métro station and use public transit.

In winter, remember that your car may not start on extra-cold mornings unless it has been kept in a heated garage.

PARKING The City of Montréal has a diligent tow-away and fine system for cars double-parked or stopped in no-stopping zones downtown during rush hours and business hours. A parking ticket costs between C$42 and C$100. If your car is towed after being illegally parked, it will cost an additional C$62 to C$88 to retrieve it. Be especially alert in winter: Montréal's street plowers are ruthless in dealing with parked cars in their way. If they don't tow them, they'll bury them. When parking in residential neighborhoods, beware of the alternate-side-of-the-street-parking rules.

RULES OF THE ROAD In Québec the road signs are in French, but the important ones have pictograms. Signs with a red circle and a slash indicate that something, such as a left or right turn, is prohibited. Those with a green circle show what is permitted. Parking signs display a green-circled *P* with either the number of hours you can park or a clock showing the hours parking is permitted. It's not unusual to have two or three road signs all together to indicate several different strictures. Keep in mind the following terms: *centre-ville* (downtown), *arrêt* (stop), *détenteurs de permis* (permit holders only), *gauche* (left), *droit* (right), *ouest* (west), and *est* (east).

The speed limit is posted in kilometers; on highways the limit is 100 kph (about 62 mph), and the use of radar-detection devices is prohibited. There are heavy penalties for driving while intoxicated, and drivers and passengers must wear seat belts. New York, Maine, and Ontario residents should take note: your traffic violations in the province of Québec are entered on driving records back home (and vice versa).

If you drive in the city, remember three things: Montréal law forbids you to turn right on a red light (though Québec allows the practice in the rest of the province), Montrealers are notorious jaywalkers, and the city has some potholes the size of craters.

BY MÉTRO

The Montréal Métro, the city's impressive subway system, is clean, quiet (it runs on rubber wheels), and comfortable (it's heated in winter and cooled in summer). It's also very safe, but as in any metropolitan area you should be alert and attentive to personal property such as purses and wallets. The Métro is connected to the more than 30 km (19 mi) of the Underground City, meaning that you can go shopping around the city and never come above ground.

Free maps are available at Métro ticket booths. Try to get the *Carte Réseau* (System Map); it's the most complete. Each Métro station connects with one or more bus routes, which cover the rest of the island. Transfers from Métro to buses are available from the dispenser just beyond the ticket booth inside the station. Bus-to-bus and bus-to-Métro transfers may be obtained from the bus driver.

FARES & SCHEDULES Métro hours on the Orange, Green, Blue, and Yellow lines are weekdays 5:30 AM to 12:30 AM and weekends 5:30 AM to 12:30, 1, or 1:30 AM (it varies by line). Trains run as often as every three minutes on the most crowded lines—Orange and Green—at rush hours.

Tickets and transfers are valid on any bus or the subway line. You should be able to get within a few blocks of anywhere in the city on one fare. Rates are C$2.50 for a single ticket, C$11.25 for six tickets, C$18.50 for a weeklong pass, and C$63 for a monthly pass. Transfers are free. You can buy a day pass for C$9 or a three-day pass for C$17.

Various bus passes can be obtained at many of the larger hotels, at the Berri-UQAM Métro station, and at some other downtown stations.

The Société de Transport de Montréal (STM) operates an automated phone line for information on bus and Métro schedules, but it's only in French. The STM Web site, however, is in French and English and is a particularly good resource, with excellent maps and route planners.

Société de Transport de Montréal (STM) ☎ 514/288-6287 or 514/786-4636 🌐 www.stcum.qc.ca.

BY TAXI

Taxis in Montréal all run on the same rate: C$2.75 minimum and C$1.40 per kilometer (½ mi). Taxis are usually easy to hail on the street, although finding one on a rainy night after the Métro has closed can be difficult. You can see if a taxi is available by checking its white or orange plastic rooftop light; if the panel is lighted, the driver is ready to take passengers. You can also call a dispatcher to send a driver to pick you up at no extra cost (you'll usually have to wait about 15 minutes).

Taxi Companies **Atlas Taxi** ☎ 514/485-8585. **Champlain Taxi** ☎ 514/273-2435. **Co-op Taxi** ☎ 514/725-9885. **Unitaxi** ☎ 514/482-3000.

BY TRAIN

Gare Centrale (Central Station), on rue de la Gauchetière between rues University and Mansfield (behind Le Reine Elizabeth), is the rail terminus for all trains from the U.S. and from other Canadian provinces. It's connected underground to the Bonaventure Métro station. The Amtrak *Adirondack* leaves New York's Penn Station every morning for the 10½-hour trip through upstate New York to Montréal. Amtrak also has bus connections with the *Vermonter* in St. Albans, Vermont. VIA Rail connects Montréal with all the major cities of Canada, including Québec City, Halifax, Ottawa, Toronto, Winnipeg, Edmonton, and Vancouver.

Train Lines **Amtrak** ☎ 800/872-7245 🌐 www.amtrak.com. **VIA Rail** ☎ 514/989-2626 or 888/842-7245 🌐 www.viarail.ca.

Contact & Resources

EMERGENCIES

The U.S. Consulate maintains a list of medical specialists in the Montréal area. There's a dental clinic on avenue Van Horne that's open 24 hours; Sunday appointments are for emergencies only.

Many pharmacies stay open until midnight, including Jean Coutu and Pharmaprix stores. Some are open around the clock, including the Pharmaprix on chemin de la Côte-des-Neiges.

Dentists **Dental clinic** ✉ 3546 av. Van Horne, Côte-des-Neiges ☎ 514/342-4444 Ⓜ Plamondon.

Emergency Services **Ambulance, fire, police** ☎ 911. **Québec Poison Control Centre** ☎ 800/463-5060. **U.S. Consulate** ☎ 514/398-9695, 514/981-5059 emergencies.

Hospital **Montréal General Hospital (McGill University Health Centre)** ✉ 1650 av. Cedar, Downtown ☎ 514/934-1934 Ⓜ Guy-Concordia.

Late-Night Pharmacies **Jean Coutu** ✉ 501 rue Mont-Royal Est, Plateau Mont-Royal ☎ 514/521-1058 Ⓜ Mont-Royal ✉ 5510 chemin de la Côte-des-Neiges, Côte-des-Neiges ☎ 514/344-8338 Ⓜ Côte-des-Neiges. **Pharmaprix** ✉ 1500 rue Ste-Catherine Ouest, Downtown ☎ 514/933-4744 Ⓜ Guy-Concordia ✉ 5038 Sherbrooke Ouest, Notre-Dame-de-Grace ☎ 514/484-3531 Ⓜ Vendôme ✉ 901 rue Ste-Catherine Est, Village ☎ 514/842-4915 Ⓜ Berri-UQAM ✉ 5122 chemin de la Côte-des-Neiges, Côte-des-Neiges ☎ 514/738-8464 Ⓜ Côte-des-Neiges.

TOURS

BOAT TOURS

From May through October, Amphi Tour sells a unique one-hour tour of Vieux-Montréal and the Vieux-Port on both land and water in an amphibious bus. Bateau-Mouche runs four harbor excursions and an evening supper cruise daily from May through October. The boats are reminiscent of the ones that cruise the canals of the Netherlands—wide-beamed and low-slung, with a glassed-in passenger deck. Boats leave from the Jacques Cartier Pier at the foot of Place Jacques-Cartier in the Vieux-Port.

Amphi Tour ☎ 514/849-5181 🌐 www.montreal-amphibus-tour.com. **Bateau-Mouche** ☎ 514/849-9952 or 800/361-9952 🌐 www.bateau-mouche.com.

BUS TOURS

Gray Line has nine different types of tours of Montréal from June through October and one tour the rest of the year. There are also day trips to Ottawa and Québec City. The company offers pickup service at the major hotels and at Info-Touriste (1001 Square Dorchester).

Imperial Tours' double-decker buses follow a nine-stop circuit of the city. You can get off and on as often as you like and stay at each stop as long as you like. There's pickup service at major hotels.

Imperial Tours ☎ 514/871-4733. **Gray Line** ☎ 514/934-1222 🌐 www.coachcanada.com.

CALÈCHE RIDES

Open horse-drawn carriages (fleece-lined in winter) leave from Place Jacques-Cartier, Square Dorchester, Place d'Armes, and rue de la Commune. A one- to two-hour ride costs about C$65, although slow days mean you have a better chance of bargaining.

WALKING TOURS

You can walk through various historic, cultural, or architecturally diverse areas of the city with a costumed guide, courtesy of Guidatour. Popular tours include Old Montréal, the red-light district, and the elite 19th-century neighborhood known as the Golden Square Mile.

From mid-April to mid-November, Circuit des Fantômes du Vieux-Montréal has walking tours through the old city where a host of spirits are said to still haunt the streets. Kaleidoscope has a wide selection of guided walking tours through Montréal's many culturally diverse neighborhoods.

Circuit des Fantômes du Vieux-Montréal (Old Montréal Ghost Trail) ✉ Vieux-Port de Montréal, Vieux-Montréal ☎ 514/868-0303 or 877/868-0303 🌐 www.phvm.qc.ca Ⓜ Champ-de-Mars. **Guidatour** ✉ 477 rue St-François-Xavier, Suite 300, Vieux-Montréal ☎ 514/844-4021 or 800/363-4021 🌐 www.guidatour.qc.ca Ⓜ Place-d'Armes. **Kaleidoscope** ✉ 6592 Châteaubriand,, Villeray ☎ 514/990-1872 📠 514/277-4630 🌐 www.tourskaleidoscope.com Ⓜ Beaubien

VISITOR INFORMATION

Centre Info-Touriste, on Square Dorchester, has extensive tourist information on Montréal and the rest of the province of Québec, as well as a currency-exchange service and Internet café. It's open June through early September, daily 8:30–7:30, and early September through May, daily 9–6. The Vieux-Montréal branch is open daily 9–7 between June and September and is often open daily 9–5 in winter, although it's sometimes closed during slow periods.

Tourist Information **Centre Info-Touriste** ✉ 1001 Square Dorchester, Downtown ☎ 514/873–2015 or 800/363–7777 🌐 www.bonjourquebec.com Ⓜ Bonaventure ✉ 174 rue Notre-Dame Est, at pl. Jacques-Cartier, Vieux-Montréal Ⓜ Champ-de-Mars. **Tourisme-Montréal** ☎ 514/844–5400 or 877/BONJOUR [877/266–5687]) 🌐 www.tourisme-montreal.org.

Montréal Side Trips

WORD OF MOUTH

"Go to Knowlton—it's a charming little town with lots of nice places. Go to the lakeside town of Georgeville on Lake Memphremagog, go to Sutton."

—pattysuericia

"I just got back from a quick trip up to the Laurentians just north of Montreal. The ride is quite pretty with pine-filled hills and rocky contours about 20 km outside of Laval or so. The houses located on the sides of mountains really were a sight to behold. I highly recommend visitors check out this gorgeous region."

—Daniel Williams

www.fodors.com/forums

TWO MAJOR RECREATIONAL AREAS attract stressed-out urban dwellers and anyone else who wants to relax: the Laurentians and the Eastern Townships. The Laurentian region, with its ski hills and lakes, is sheer paradise for those looking for a quick break from the hustle and bustle of urban life. Quaint villages, many steeped in colorful history, line the delightful countryside—all hardly a stone's throw away from the center of Montréal. The Eastern Townships are a favorite ski and sun destination for those looking to get away from it all, although not blessed with quite as many lakes as its sister recreational getaway to the north. Rich with pastoral beauty, charming bed-and-breakfasts, and excellent regional dining, the Townships offer a certain peaceful tranquillity that is uniquely Québec.

EXPLORING THE REGION

The Laurentians resort area begins 60 km (37 mi) north of Montréal. The Eastern Townships start approximately 80 km (50 mi) east of the city in a southern corner of the province. Both are an easy, picturesque drive from Montréal.

About the Restaurants & Hotels

The Eastern Townships area is one of Québec's foremost regions for good food, and chefs at the finer Laurentian inns have attracted an international following. Whether you choose a mixed-game pie such as *cipaille* or a sweet-and-salty dish like ham with maple syrup, you won't soon forget your meals here. Cooking in the province tends to be hearty: cassoulet, *tourtières* (meat pies), onion soup, and apple pie head up menus. Maple syrup, much of it produced locally, is a mainstay of Québecois dishes. Cloves, nutmeg, cinnamon, and pepper—spices used by the first settlers—haven't gone out of style. Early reservations are essential. Many restaurants are closed Monday, but Tuesday isn't too soon to book weekend tables at the best provincial restaurants.

More-casual fare, such as a croissant and an espresso, or *poutine*—a heaped plate of *frites* (french fries) smothered with gravy and melted cheese curds—is available from sidewalk cafés and fast-food restaurants.

Accommodations in the province range from resort hotels and elegant Relais & Châteaux properties to simple motels and *auberges* (inns). Many inns operate on the Modified American Plan—especially in high season (winter in the Laurentians and other ski areas, summer elsewhere), which means that two meals, usually breakfast and dinner, are included in the cost of a night's stay. Be sure to ask what's included, and expect prices to be lower off-season. Some inns require a minimum two-night stay; always ask.

2

GREAT ITINERARIES

IF YOU HAVE 2 DAYS

If you have only a couple of days for a visit, you need to concentrate on one area, and the Laurentians are a good choice. This resort area has recreational options (depending on the season) that include golf, hiking, and great skiing. Pick a resort town to stay in, whether it's St-Sauveur-des-Monts, Ste-Adèle, or Mont-Tremblant near the vast Parc du Mont-Tremblant, and use that as a base to visit some of the surrounding towns. There's good eating and shopping here.

IF YOU HAVE 5 DAYS

You can combine a taste of the Eastern Townships with a two-day visit to the Laurentians. Get a feel for the Laurentians by staying overnight in St-Sauveur-des-Monts or Ste-Adèle and exploring surrounding towns such as St-Jérôme and Morin Heights. Then head back south of Montréal to the Townships, which extend to the east along the border with New England. Overnight in Granby or Bromont: Granby has a zoo and Bromont is known for golf and its water park. The next day, you can shop in pretty Knowlton (look for signs to Lac Brome) and explore regional history in such towns as Valcourt. Spend a night or two in the appealing resort town of Magog, along Lac Memphrémagog, or the quieter North Hatley, on Lac Massawippi. You'll have good dining in either. Save a day for something outdoors, whether it's golfing, skiing, biking, or hiking.

WHAT IT COSTS In Canadian dollars

	$$$$	$$$	$$	$	¢
RESTAURANTS	over C$30	C$21–C$30	C$13–C$20	C$8–C$12	under C$8
HOTELS	over C$250	C$176–C$250	C$126–C$175	C$75–C$125	under C$75

Restaurant prices are for a main course at dinner (or at the most expensive meal served). Hotel prices are for two people in a standard double room in high season, excluding 6% GST and 7.5% provincial tax.

When to Go

The Laurentians are a big skiing destination in winter, but the other seasons all have their own charms: you can drive up from Montréal to enjoy the fall foliage; to hike, bike, or play golf; or to engage in spring skiing—and still get back to the city before dark. The only slow periods are early November, when there isn't much to do, and June, when the area has plenty to do but is also plagued by blackflies. Control programs have improved the situation somewhat.

The Eastern Townships are best in fall, when the foliage is at its peak; the region borders Vermont and has the same dramatic colors. It's possible to visit wineries at this time, but you should call ahead, since harvest is a busy time.

THE LAURENTIANS

Updated by Chris Barry

The Laurentians (les Laurentides) are divided into two major regions: the Lower Laurentians (les Basses Laurentides) and the Upper Laurentians (les Hautes Laurentides). But don't be fooled by the designations; they don't signify great driving distances. The rocky hills here are relatively low, but many are eminently skiable, with a few peaks above 2,500 feet. Mont-Tremblant, at 3,150 feet, is the highest.

The P'tit Train du Nord—the former railroad line that is now a 200-km (124-mi) "linear park" used by cyclists, hikers, skiers, and snowmobilers—made it possible to transport settlers and cargo easily to the Upper Laurentians. It also opened up the area to skiing by the early 1900s. Before long, trainloads of skiers replaced settlers and cargo as the railway's major trade. At first a winter weekend getaway for Montrealers who stayed at boardinghouses and fledgling resorts, the Upper Laurentians soon began attracting international visitors.

Ski lodges and private family cottages for wealthy city dwellers were accessible only by train until the 1930s, when Route 117 was built. Today there is an uneasy peace between the longtime cottagers, who want to restrict development, and resort entrepreneurs, who want to expand. At the moment, commercial interests seem to be prevailing. A number of large hotels have added indoor pools and spa facilities, and efficient highways have brought the country even closer to the city—45 minutes to St-Sauveur, 1½–2 hours to Mont-Tremblant.

The resort area truly begins at St-Sauveur-des-Monts (Exit 60 on Autoroute 15) and extends as far north as Mont-Tremblant. Beyond, the region turns into a wilderness of lakes and forests best visited with an outfitter. Guides who offer fishing trips are concentrated around Parc du Mont-Tremblant. To the first-time visitor, the hilly areas around St-Sauveur, Ste-Adèle, Morin Heights, Val Morin, and Val David up to Ste-Agathe-des-Monts form a pleasant hodgepodge of villages, hotels, and inns that seem to blend one into another.

Oka

 *40 km (25 mi) west of Montréal.*

Founded in 1721 by the Roman Catholic Sulpician Order, Oka is best known for the cheese produced at nearby Abbaye Cistercienne d'Oka. In the winter months an ice bridge links Oka with Hudson, its sister town just on the opposite shore of Lake of Two Mountains.

For wine lovers, so many apple orchards produce cider around St-Joseph-du-Lac, about a 10-minute drive from Oka, that there's a *Route des Vergers*. This "Orchard Route" lists 39 growers selling all types of cider: dry, sweet, white, and red. Many of the growers have tastings and tours. There's also a winery on the route: La Roche des Brises, whose whites and reds include the portlike *L'été Indien* (Indian Summer).

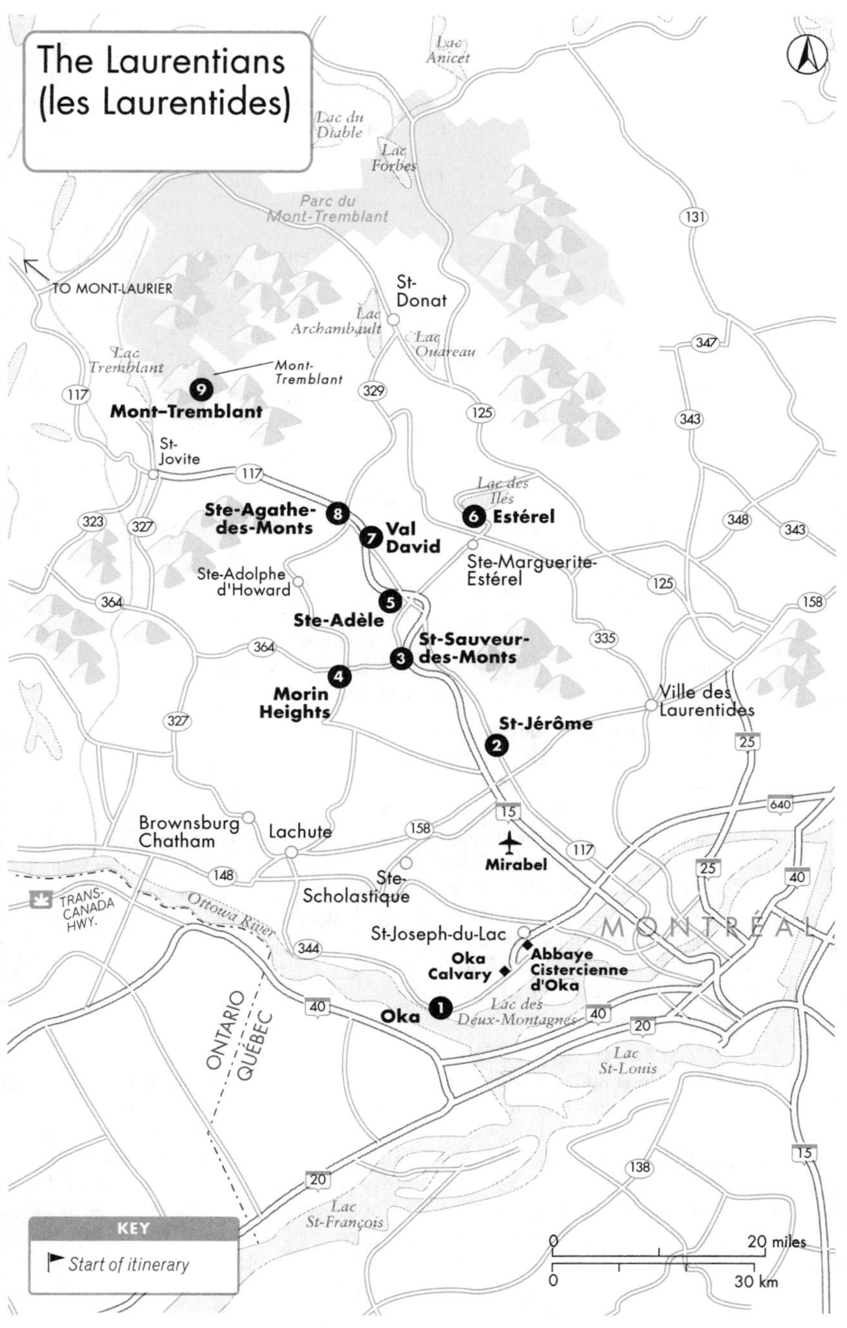
The Laurentians
(les Laurentides)
Lac Anicet
Lac du Diable
Lac Forbes
Parc du Mont-Tremblant
131
TO MONT-LAURIER
St-Donat
Lac Archambault
Lac Ouareau
347
Lac Tremblant
Mont-Tremblant
117
9 Mont-Tremblant
329
125
343
St-Jovite
117
Lac des Îles
Ste-Agathe-des-Monts
6 Estérel
323
327
7 Val David
348
343
Ste-Marguerite-Estérel
Ste-Adolphe d'Howard
125
364
5
Ste-Adèle
158
335
364
3 St-Sauveur-des-Monts
4 Morin Heights
Ville des Laurentides
327
St-Jérôme
2
25
640
15
Brownsburg Chatham
Lachute
158
117
Mirabel
148
Ste-Scholastique
25
40
TRANS-CANADA HWY.
Ottowa River
St-Joseph-du-Lac
MONTRÉAL
344
Oka Calvary
Abbaye Cistercienne d'Oka
40
1 Oka
Lac des Deux-Montagnes
40
20
ONTARIO
QUÉBEC
Lac St-Louis
138
15
20
Lac St-François
KEY
Start of itinerary
0
20 miles
0
30 km

What to See

Fodor'sChoice ★ **Abbaye Cistercienne d'Oka.** In 1887 the Sulpicians donated about 865 acres of their property near the Oka Calvary to the Trappist monks, who had arrived in 1880 from Bellefontaine Abbey in France. Within a decade the monks had built their monastery, one of the oldest North American abbeys. Trappists established the Oka School of Agriculture, which operated until 1960. The monks became famous for their creamy Oka cheese; it's now produced commercially, but the monks still oversee the operations. (The abbey store sells Oka cheese and products from other Québec monasteries, such as chocolate, cheese, and cider.) The monastery is notable for its prayer retreat. ✉ *1600 chemin Oka* ☎ *450/479–8361* 🌐 *www.abbayeoka.com* 🎫 *Free* ⏲ *Chapel Mon.–Sat. 4 AM–8 PM; gardens and shop Mon. 10–noon and 12:30–4:30, Tues.–Fri. 9:30–noon and 12:30–4:30, Sat. 9:30–4.*

Auberge Roches des Brises. You can tour the vineyard, taste the wines for C$5, and dine in the adjacent four-star restaurant serving the best in regional cuisine. Across the road overlooking some of the grape vines is a charming five-room bed-and-breakfast with a spa. It's worth the trip if only to take in the splendor of the exceptionally lovely grounds. ✉ *2007 rue Principale, St-Joseph-du-Lac* ☎ *450/472–2722* 🌐 *www.rochedesbrises.com* ⏲ *Mid-Feb.–Dec.*

Hudson. A quick detour on the ferry (C$8 one-way) across Lac des Deux-Montagnes brings you to this small town with old homes housing art galleries, boutiques, and Christmas shops. In winter, there's an ice bridge: basically a plowed path across a well-frozen lake. Taking a walk across the bridge is a singular experience.

Parc d'Oka. Surrounded by low hills, the park has a lake fringed by a sandy beach with picnic areas and hiking and biking trails. This is a good place for kayaking, canoeing, fishing, and, in winter, snowshoeing and cross-country skiing. There are nearly 900 campsites here. ✉ *2020 chemin Oka* ☎ *450/479–8365, 800/665–6527 activities* 🌐 *www.sepaq.com* 🎫 *C$3.50 plus C$5 per car* ⏲ *Daily 8 AM–10 PM.*

SIDE TRIP TIP

Clothing-optional bathing is tolerated at the beach in Parc national d'Oka. On weekends hundreds of Montrealers can be found sunning themselves "au naturel" here.

Where to Stay & Eat

$–$$$$ **Hotel du Lac Carling.** The modern but classically furnished hotel is near Lachute (about 40 km [25 mi] northwest of Oka) and on the doorstep to 5,000 acres of wilderness. In addition to a large sports center, 20 km (12 mi) of cross-country ski trails, and an excellent par-72 golf course, there's also an impressive restaurant. The menu includes salmon smoked by the chef. The hotel's rooms are furnished with oil paintings, and antiques line the corridors. The standard rooms are among the largest in the province. Loft suites, with kitchenettes and fireplaces, are entered from the upper floor. ✉ *2255 Rte. 327 Nord,*

Grenville-sur-la-Rouge J0V 1B0 ☎ 450/533–9211 or 800/661–9211 ℻ 450/533–9197 🌐 www.laccarling.com ⇆ 90 rooms, 9 suites ♨ Restaurant, room service, some fans, in-room safes, some in-room hot tubs, some kitchenettes, minibars, cable TV with movies, Wi-Fi, 18-hole golf course, 2 tennis courts, pro shop, pool, lake, gym, hot tub, sauna, spa, beach, dock, boating, fishing, mountain bikes, racquetball, squash, volleyball, cross-country skiing, ice-skating, 2 bars, babysitting, children's programs (ages 3–18), laundry service, meeting rooms, some pets allowed, no-smoking rooms ▭ AE, DC, MC, V 🍴 BP.

St-Jérôme

❷ *25 km (16 mi) north of St-Eustache, 48 km (30 mi) north of Montréal.*

Founded in 1834, St-Jérôme is a thriving economic center and cultural hub. The town first gained prominence in 1868, when Curé Antoine Labelle became a pastor of this parish. His most important legacy was the famous P'tit Train du Nord railroad line, which he persuaded the government to build in order to open St-Jérôme to travel and trade.

What to See

Linear Park (Parc Linéaire). The P'tit Train du Nord no longer exists, but in 1996 the track was transformed into the 200-km (124-mi) Linear Park. From the moment it opened, the park proved hugely popular. The well-signed trail starts at the former railway station (1 place de la Gare) in St-Jérôme and is used mostly by cyclists (walkers use it at their peril, because the bikers hurtle by quickly). The path runs all the way to Mont-Laurier in the north. It's flanked by distance markers, so that cyclists can track their progress; some of the old railway stations and historic landmarks along the route have been converted into places where *vélo-touristes* (bike tourists) can stop for a snack. In winter, the trail is taken over by cross-country skiers and snowmobilers.

Fodor'sChoice ★ **Parc Régional de la Rivière du Nord.** Created as a nature retreat, the regional park's trails lead to the spectacular **Wilson Falls.** The **Pavillon Marie-Victorin** has summer weekend displays and workshops devoted to nature, culture, and history. You can hike, bike, cross-country ski, snowshoe, or snow-slide here. ✉ *1051 International blvd., R.R. 2* ☎ *450/431–1676* 🎟 *C$5* ⏲ *Sept.–May, daily 9–5; June–Aug., daily 9–7.*

Promenade. St-Jérôme's promenade, stretching 4 km (2½ mi), follows the Rivière du Nord from the rue de Martigny bridge to the rue St-Joseph bridge. Descriptive plaques en route highlight episodes of the 1837 Rebellion, a French-Canadian uprising.

Sports & the Outdoors

Parachutisme Adrénaline. This parachuting school and flying center, 15 minutes from St-Jérôme, caters to novice and seasoned jumpers alike (C$260–C$285 per person for beginners). ✉ *881 rue Lamontagne, St-Jérôme* ☎ *450/438–0855 or 866/306–0855* ℻ *450/438–0585* 🌐 *www.paradrenaline.ca.*

St-Sauveur-des-Monts

3 *25 km (16 mi) north of St-Jérôme, 63 km (39 mi) north of Montréal.*

The town of St-Sauveur encompasses St-Sauveur-des-Monts, a focal point for area resorts. Rue Principale, the main street, has dozens of restaurants serving everything from lamb brochettes to spicy Thai fare. The narrow strip is so choked with cars and tourists in summer that it's called Crescent Street of the North, after the action-filled street in Montréal. Despite all this development, St-Sauveur-des-Monts has maintained some of its rural character.

Skiing and other snow sports are the main things to do in winter here. Mont-St-Sauveur, Mont-Avila, Mont-Gabriel, and Mont-Olympia all have special season passes and programs, and some ski-center passes can be used at more than one center in the region. Blue signs on Route 117 and Autoroute 15 indicate where the ski hills are.

What to See

Mont-St-Sauveur Water Park. Mont-St-Sauveur Water Park keeps children occupied with slides, a giant wave pool, a wading pool, and snack bars. The rafting river attracts an older, braver crowd; the nine-minute ride follows the natural contours of steep hills. On the tandem slides, plumes of water flow through figure-eight tubes. ✉ *350 rue St-Denis* ☎ *450/227–4671 or 800/363–2426* 🌐 *www.mssi.ca* *Full day C$30, after 3 PM C$25, after 5 PM C$18* ⊙ *Early June–mid-June and late Aug.–early Sept., daily 10–5; mid-June–mid-Aug., daily 10–7.*

Where to Stay & Eat

$–$$$ ✕ **Le Bifthèque.** French Canadians flock to this local institution for perfectly aged steaks and other hearty fare. This branch of the chain, in the heart of St-Sauveur, also serves lamb loin with Dijon mustard and trout stuffed with crab and shrimp. Pick up steaks to go at the meat counter if you're staying where you can grill your own. ✉ *86 rue de la Gare* ☎ *450/227–2442* ▭ *AE, MC, V* ⊙ *No lunch Mon.–Thurs.*

$–$$$$ ✕ **Relais St-Denis.** A traditional sloping Québecois roof and dormer windows cap this inn, where every guest room has a fireplace. Junior suites have whirlpool baths. La Treille de Bacchus ($$–$$$$) serves multicourse meals with an emphasis on regional cuisine. ✉ *61 rue St-Denis, J0R 1R4* ☎ *450/227–4766 or 888/997–4766* 📠 *450/227–8504* 🌐 *www.relaisstdenis.com* *22 rooms, 22 suites* *Restaurant, some in-room hot tubs, refrigerators, cable TV, in-room data ports, pool, outdoor hot tub, massage, bar, meeting rooms, some pets allowed, no-smoking floors* ▭ *AE, D, MC, V* *CP, MAP.*

Sports & the Outdoors

La Vallée de St-Sauveur. This is the collective name for the ski area north of St-Sauveur-des-Monts. The area is especially well known for its night skiing.

Mont-Avila. This mountain has 11 trails (2 rated for beginners, 3 at an intermediate level, and 6 for experts), three lifts, and a 615-foot vertical drop. ✉ *500 chemin Avila, Piedmont* ☎ *450/227–4671 or 514/871–0101* 🌐 *www.mssi.ca.*

Mont-St-Sauveur. Mont St-Sauveur has 29 trails (9 for beginning and intermediate-level skiers, 15 for experts, and 5 that are extremely difficult), eight lifts, and a vertical drop of 700 feet. ✉ *350 rue St-Denis, St-Sauveur* ☎ *450/227–4671, 514/871–0101, or 800/363–2426* 🌐 *www.mssi.ca.*

2

Station de Ski Mont-Habitant. Featuring 14 trails (3 rated beginner, 4 expert, and 7 intermediate), three lifts, and a vertical drop of 600 feet, Ski Mont-Habitant is a choice hill for both novice and intermediate level skiers. ✉ *12 blvd. des Skieurs, St-Sauveur-des-Monts* ☎ *450/227–2637 or 866/887–2637* 🌐 *www.monthabitant.com.*

Shopping

Fodor'sChoice ★ **Factoreries St-Sauveur.** Canadian, American, and European manufacturers sell goods, from designer clothing to household items, at this emporium at reduced prices. The factory-outlet mall has more than 25 stores and sells labels such as Guess, Nike, Jones New York, and Reebok. ✉ *100 rue Guindon, Autoroute 15, Exit 60* ☎ *450/227–1074.*

Rue Principale. Fashion boutiques and gift shops, adorned with bright awnings and flowers line this popular shopping street.

Morin Heights

❹ *10 km (6 mi) west of St-Sauveur-des-Monts, 73 km (45 mi) northwest of Montréal.*

The town's British architecture and population reflect its settlers' heritage; most residents here speak English. Although Morin Heights has escaped the overdevelopment of neighboring St-Sauveur, there are still many restaurants, bookstores, boutiques, and craft shops to explore.

In summer, windsurfing, swimming, and canoeing on the area's two lakes—Claude and Lafontaine—are popular. You can also head for the region's golf courses (including the 18 holes at Mont-Gabriel) and the campgrounds at Val David and the two lakes, which have beaches. In fall and winter, come for the foliage and the alpine and Nordic skiing.

SIDE TRIP TIP

Instead of taking Route 15 up through the Laurentians, relax and enjoy the old highway 117, which passes through many of the historic towns of the region.

Where to Stay & Eat

$$–$$$$ Fodor'sChoice ★ ✕ **Auberge Restaurant Clos Joli.** If you're looking for superior French cuisine and are prepared to pay top dollar for the privilege, this family-owned and -operated establishment offers an outstanding gastronomic experience. Award-winning chef Marie-Josée Roux cooks up a wide variety of dishes, including her legendary sea bass on fennel. The Sunday brunch is said to be the finest in the Laurentians. ✉ *19 chemin du Clos Joli* ☎ *450/226–5401* ▭ *AE, MC, V* ⊙ *No lunch.*

$$–$$$$ ✕ **Le Petit Prince.** Many locals adore this restaurant in a tiny blue-shingled wood house on a side road near Highway 364 that runs through

Morin Heights. Lace curtains on the windows and wood walls accent the bistro-style cuisine. Scallops in Pernod sauce and grilled rib steak are excellent choices. ✉ *139 rue Watchorn* ☎ *450/226–6887* ▭ *AE, MC, V* ⊙ *Closed Mon. and Tues. No lunch.*

$–$$ **Le Flamant et la Tortue.** This charming auberge is set in a beautifully wooded area within striking range of a small, pristine lake. Although the rooms are spartan, they are comfortable, clean, and relatively inexpensive. The outdoor terrace here is one of the most pleasant places to relax in the entire region. ✉ *796 chemin St-Adolphe, J0R 1H0* ☎ *450/226–2009 or 877/616–2009* 📠 *450/226–3670* 🌐 *www.aubergeleflamantetlatortue.ca* *10 rooms* *Dining room, bar; no a/c, no room TVs, no smoking* ▭ *AE, MC, V.*

$ **L'Ombrelle B&B.** Down comforters cover brass queen-size beds in the rooms of this stately New England–style house. A main attraction is the three-course breakfast, which sometimes includes homemade raspberry cake. You can eat in your room or at the dining table framed by windows overlooking the garden. Relax by the outdoor pool or, in winter, by the fireplace in the lounge. ✉ *160 de Christieville, JOR 1H0* ☎ *450/226–2334 or 514/592–2840* 📠 *450/226–8027* 🌐 *www.lombrelle.com* *3 rooms* *Some fans, some in-room hot tubs, cable TV, Wi-Fi, pool, hiking, lounge, babysitting; no room phones, no smoking* ▭ *MC, V* *BP.*

Sports & the Outdoors

Ski Morin Heights. The vertical drop at this ski resort is 656 feet. There are 23 trails, including 8 for beginners, 7 each for intermediate and expert levels, and 1 glade run. The 44,000-square-foot chalet houses eateries, a pub, a day-care center, and equipment rental, but the center doesn't have lodging. ✉ *231 rue Bennett, near Exit 60 of Autoroute 15 Nord* ☎ *450/227–2020* 🌐 *www.mssi.ca.*

Ste-Adèle

5 *12 km (7 mi) north of Morin Heights, 85 km (53 mi) north of Montréal.*

With a permanent population of more than 10,000, Ste-Adèle is the largest community in the lower part of the Laurentians. A number of government offices and facilities for local residents are here: cinemas, shopping malls, and summer theater (in French). Of interest to visitors are the sports shops, boutiques, restaurants, and family-oriented amusements.

What to See

Au Pays des Merveilles. Fairy-tale characters such as Snow White, Little Red Riding Hood, and Alice in Wonderland wander the grounds, playing games with children. Small fry may also enjoy the petting zoo, amusement rides, wading pool, and puppet theater. A ride called Le Petit Train des Merveilles (the Marvelous Little Train) is a nod to the historic train that launched the tourism industry in the Laurentians. There are 39 activities, enough to occupy those aged two to nine for about half a day. Check the Web site for discount coupons. The theme park is 100% accessible to wheelchairs. ✉ *3795 rue de la Savane* ☎ *450/229–3141* 📠 *450/229–4148* 🌐 *www.paysmerveilles.com* *C$15* ⊙ *Early June–mid-June, weekends 10–6; mid-June–late Aug., daily 10–6.*

Super Splash Ste-Adèle. On hot, humid weekends, Montrealers with families fill the water park, which has waterslides, a wading pool, a wave pool, and miniature golf. *1791 blvd. Ste-Adèle 450/229–2909 or 450/435–4175 800/801–7138 www.supersplash.qc.ca C$10–C$17 Mid-June–late Aug., daily 10–7.*

2

Where to Stay & Eat

$$$–$$$$ **La Clef des Champs.** The French food served at this romantic restaurant tucked amid trees is quite good. Game dishes, such as medallions of roasted ostrich in a port-infused sauce, grilled venison, or caribou in red-currant marinade, are specialties. Good dessert choices include *gâteaux aux deux chocolats* (two-chocolate cake) and crème brûlée. For C$70 there is a *menu dégustation* if you're looking to sample a little bit of everything. *875 chemin Pierre-Péladeau 450/229–2857 AE, DC, MC, V Closed Mon. No lunch.*

$$$–$$$$ Fodor'sChoice ★ **L'Eau à la Bouche.** Superb service, stunning rooms awash with color, a Nordic spa, and a terrace with a flower garden are highlights of this charming inn. Guest rooms, some with fireplaces, are decorated in styles that include Victorian, safari, and Inuit. Skiing is literally at your door, since the inn faces Le Chantecler's slopes. The restaurant here ($$$$) interprets nouvelle cuisine with regional ingredients. The menu changes with the seasons, but it has included foie gras with apple-cider sauce, breast of Barbary duck, and red-wine-marinated venison. Owner-chef Anne Desjardins is a well-known and highly regarded Québecois personality. *3003 blvd. Ste-Adèle, J8B 2N6 450/229–2991 or 888/828–2991 450/229–7573 www.leaualabouche.com 21 rooms, 1 suite Restaurant, some fans, some in-room hot tubs, cable TV with movies, in-room data ports, pool, bar, babysitting, dry cleaning, laundry service; no smoking AE, DC, MC, V EP.*

$–$$$ **Hôtel Mont-Gabriel.** Built by Josephine Hartford Bryce, whose grandfather founded the A&P grocery chain, the hotel started as a log structure with about a dozen rooms. The site has evolved into a 1,200-acre resort where you can relax in a contemporary room with a valley view or commune with nature in a rustic-style cabin with a fireplace. In winter, you can ski out from many rooms. The French cuisine ($$$$) is good, with entrées such as salmon with braised leeks, and pork with ginger and orange. *1699 chemin du Mont-Gabriel (Autoroute 15, Exit 64), J8B 1A5 450/229–3547, 800/668–5253, or 450/229–3547 450/229–7034 www.montgabriel.com 129 rooms, 1 suite, 3 chalets Restaurant, snack bar, room service, some in-room hot tubs, room TVs with movies and video games, in-room data ports, driving range, 18-hole golf course, putting green, 6 tennis courts, pro shop, 2 pools (1 indoor), gym, sauna, spa, basketball, boccie, hiking, shuffleboard, volleyball, cross-country skiing, downhill skiing, ski shop, ski storage, sports bar, babysitting, business services, meeting rooms, no-smoking rooms AE, DC, MC, V EP.*

$–$$$ **Le Chantecler.** This favorite of Montrealers is beside Lac Ste-Adèle and at the base of a mountain with 25 downhill ski runs; trails begin almost at the hotel entrance. The rooms and chalets, furnished with Canadian pine, have a rustic appeal. Given all the activities here, which include snowshoeing with a trapper as well as cycling races, Le Chantecler is for people looking for an energetic holiday. ✉ *1474 chemin Chantecler, J0B 1A2* ☎ *450/229–3555 or 888/916–1616* 🖷 *450/229–5593* 🌐 *www.lechantecler.com* ⇨ *186 rooms, 29 suites, 7 chalets* ♨ *Restaurant, room service, some in-room hot tubs, some kitchenettes, minibars, cable TV with movies, in-room data ports, Wi-Fi, 9-hole golf course, 6 tennis courts, indoor pool, lake, gym, hair salon, sauna, spa, beach, dock, boating, bicycles, boccie, hiking, horseback riding, horseshoes, shuffleboard, squash, volleyball, cross-country skiing, downhill skiing, ski shop, bar, video game room, shop, children's programs (ages 6 and older), laundry service, concierge, business services, no-smoking rooms; no a/c in some rooms* ▭ *AE, D, DC, MC, V* 🍴 *EP.*

$–$$ **Auberge & Spa Beaux Rêves.** Rooms at this rustic Québecois retreat along a riverbank give you plenty of space in which to spread out. The fieldstone building has hardwood floors; furnishings are spare, but many of the suites have fireplaces. The outdoor hot tub and Finnish sauna are used year-round. The restaurant's homey dishes include chicken in wine sauce and leg of rabbit marinated in mushroom sauce. A table d'hôte of five courses is available for dinner. ✉ *2310 blvd. Ste-Adèle, J8B 2N5* ☎ *450/229–9226 or 800/279–7679* 🖷 *450/229–2999* 🌐 *www.beauxreves.com* ⇨ *7 rooms, 6 suites* ♨ *Restaurant, some in-room hot tubs, outdoor hot tub, massage, sauna, spa, meeting rooms; no room phones, no room TVs, no smoking* ▭ *MC, V* 🍴 *CP.*

Sports & the Outdoors

GOLF **Club de Golf Chantecler.** This par-72, 18-hole (6,215 yards) course is off Exit 67 of Autoroute 15. Greens fees range from C$30 on weekdays to C$38 on weekends. ✉ *2520 chemin du Club* ☎ *450/476–1339 or 450/229–3742* 🌐 *www.golflechantecler.com.*

SKIING **Ski Chantecler.** This mountain has 25 trails, six lifts, and a vertical drop of 663 feet, in addition to 50 km (31 mi) of cross-country trails. ✉ *1474 rue Chantecler, Mont-Chantecler* ☎ *450/229–3555.*

Ski Mont-Gabriel. About 19 km (12 mi) northeast of Ste-Adèle, Mont-Gabriel has 18 superb downhill trails, which are primarily for intermediate and advanced skiers, and seven lifts. The vertical drop is 656 feet. ✉ *31501 chemin du Mont-Gabriel, Ste-Adèle* ☎ *450/227–1100 or 800/363–2426* 🌐 *www.skimontgabriel.com.*

Estérel

❻ *15 km (9 mi) north of Ste-Adèle, 100 km (62 mi) north of Montréal.*

The permanent population of Estérel is just more than 2,400, but visitors to the Estérel Resort and Convention Centre off Route 370, at Exit 69 near Ste-Marguerite Station, swell the total population throughout the year. Founded in the 1920s on the shores of Lac Dupuis, the 5,000-acre estate was named Estérel by Baron Louis Empain because it evoked memories of

SIDE TRIP TIP

Bring along a French/English dictionary. Outside Montréal one can sometimes go for miles before finding anyone who speaks English.

2

his native village in Provence. In 1959 Fridolin Simard bought the property, and Hôtel l'Estérel soon became a household word for Québecois in search of a first-class resort.

Where to Stay & Eat

$$–$$$$ Fodor'sChoice ★ ✕ **Bistro à Champlain.** Its astonishing selection of wines—some 2,000—put this bistro on the map. You can tour the cellars, housing 35,000 bottles (at last count) with prices from C$28 to C$25,000. The restaurant is in a former general store built in 1864. The C$80 *menu dégustation* (tasting menu) includes a different wine with each of several courses. Fillet of Angus beef in red wine, and roast duckling with dried figs and port are typical dishes. Next to the 150-seat dining room is a lounge for cigar smokers. ✉ *75 chemin Masson, Ste-Marguerite-Estérel* ☎ *450/228–4988 or 450/228–4949* 🌐 *www.bistroachamplain.com* 💳 *AE, DC, MC, V* ⏲ *Restaurant closed Sun. early Sept.–late June. No lunch.*

$$–$$$ 🏨 **Estérel Resort and Convention Centre.** Dogsledding and an ice-skating disco are two of the more unusual options at this resort, where buses shuttle guests to nearby downhill ski sites. In summer, comfortable air-conditioned rooms have a view of either the lake or the beautiful flower gardens. On weekdays the resort tends to attract groups and conventioneers. Following the lead of the airlines, it offers "name your price" deals on rooms, available only online. Only table d'hôte meals are available at dinner. ✉ *39 blvd. Fridolin Simard, J0T 1L0* ☎ *450/228–2571 or 888/378–3735* 📠 *450/228–4977* 🌐 *www.esterel.com* 🛏 *121 rooms, 3 suites* 👍 *Restaurant, room service, Wi-Fi, driving range, 18-hole golf course, tennis court, pro shop, indoor pool, gym, hair salon, hot tub, spa, beach, dock, windsurfing, boating, bicycles, billiards, hiking, racquetball, volleyball, cross-country skiing, ice-skating, ski shop, ski storage, sleigh rides, snowmobiling, sports bar, babysitting, dry cleaning, laundry service, meeting rooms, no-smoking rooms* 💳 *AE, DC, MC, V* 🍽 *BP.*

Val David

❼ *18 km (11 mi) west of Estérel, 82 km (51 mi) north of Montréal.*

Besides being a center for arts and crafts, Val David is a premier destination for mountain climbers, hikers, and campers. Offering several galleries and marvelous art shops, Val David is a renowned cultural village that many Québec artists and artisans call home.

What to See

Village du Père Noël (Santa Claus Village). At Santa Claus's summer residence, kids can sit on his knee and speak to him in French or English. The grounds contain bumper boats, a petting zoo (with goats, sheep, horses, and colorful birds), games, and a large outdoor pool. There is a snack bar, but visitors are encouraged to bring their own food (there are numerous picnic tables). ✉ *987 rue Morin* ☎ *819/322–2146 or 800/287–6635* 🌐 *www.noel.qc.ca* 🎫 *C$10.50* ⏲ *Early June–late Aug., daily 11–5.*

Where to Stay & Eat

¢–$$ ✕ **Au Petit Poucet.** At this beloved Laurentians institution (in business since 1945), you can savor hearty traditional fare such as meatball ragout, the restaurant's own maple-smoked ham, cipaille (a stew of game meats and chicken), pigs' knuckles with meatballs, and ham casserole. The dinner buffet served on weekends has an even wider selection of high-calorie items. Maple-syrup pie makes the perfect ending. ✉ *1030 Rte. 117* ☎ *819/322–2246 or 888/334–2246* ⊕ *www.aupetitpoucet.com* ▭ *MC, V.*

★ **$$–$$$** ✕▣ **Hôtel La Sapinière.** This homey, wood-frame hotel overlooks a lake surrounded by fir trees (*sapins* in French). Rooms have country-style furnishings and pastel floral accents and come with thick terry bathrobes. Some have romantic four-poster beds and fireplaces. The property is renowned for its French nouvelle cuisine ($$$–$$$$): salmon smoked on the premises comes with black-olive tapenade, and bison is cooked in a red-wine sauce with shiitake mushrooms. For dessert, try the mascarpone cheese mousse with berries and a spicy fruit terrine. ✉ *1244 chemin de la Sapinière, J0T 2N0* ☎ *819/322–2020 or 800/567–6635* 🖷 *819/322–6510* ⊕ *www.sapiniere.com* *44 rooms, 25 suites* *Restaurant, room service, some refrigerators, cable TV, in-room data ports, Wi-Fi, driving range, putting green, 2 tennis courts, pool, lake, gym, hair salon, outdoor hot tub, massage, dock, boating, mountain bikes, billiards, boccie, croquet, hiking, Ping-Pong, cross-country skiing, ice-skating, bar, recreation room, babysitting, dry cleaning, business services, meeting rooms, no-smoking rooms* ▭ *AE, DC, MC, V* *MAP.*

$–$$$ ✕▣ **Auberge Edelweiss.** From the outside, this small inn with a white stucco exterior and carved wood balconies resembles a Swiss chalet. Adding to the charm are two live deer in the backyard. Inside, it's cozy and romantic; each room has a balcony, and most have hot tubs. The restaurant draws nonguests to its highly rated dinners ($$$–$$$$), which include such dishes as Belgium ragout cooked in beer, and breast of duck with verbena tea sauce. ✉ *3050 chemin Doncaster, JOT 2NO* ☎ *819/322–7800 or 866/355–7800* 🖷 *819/322–1550* ⊕ *www.ar-edelweiss.com* *13 rooms, 4 suites* *Restaurant, some fans, cable TV, pool, outdoor hot tub, massage, bicycles, hiking, bar, meeting room; no room phones, no smoking* ▭ *AE, MC, V* *Restaurant closed Mon. and Tues. Jan.–June* *BP.*

Sports & the Outdoors

Centre de Ski Vallée-Bleue. Geared toward intermediate and expert skiers, Vallée-Bleue has 17 trails, three lifts, and a vertical drop of 365 feet. ✉ *1418 chemin Vallée-Bleue* ☎ *819/322–3427 or 866/322–3427* 🖷 *819/322–1025* ⊕ *www.vallee-bleue.com.*

Mont-Alta. This ski resort has 22 downhill trails—about 40% of them for advanced skiers—and one lift. The vertical drop is 600 feet. ✉ *2114 Rte. 117* ☎ *819/322–3206.*

Shopping

1001 Pots. One of the most interesting events in Val David is this boutique, which showcases the Japanese-style pottery of Kinya Ishikawa—as well as pieces by some 110 other ceramicists. The exhibition takes

2

place from mid-July through mid-August. Ishikawa's studio also displays work by his wife, Marie-Andrée Benoît, who makes fish-shape bowls with a texture derived from pressing canvas on the clay. ✉ *L'Atelier du Potier, 2435 rue de l'Église* ☎ *819/322–6868* 🌐 *www.1001pots.com* ⏲ *Daily 10–6 (summer); call for hours in other seasons.*

Atelier Bernard Chaudron, Inc. Atelier Bernard Chaudron sells hand-forged, lead-free pewter objets d'art such as oil lamps, plus hammered-silver beer mugs, pitchers, and candleholders, as well as some crystal. ✉ *2449 chemin de l'Île* ☎ *819/322–3944 or 888/322–3944.*

La Verdure. Everything from wood walking sticks to duck decoys and gold, platinum, and silver jewelry are made by the owner, Paul Simard. ✉ *1310 Dion* ☎ *819/322–7813.*

Ste-Agathe-des-Monts

8 *5 km (3 mi) north of Val David, 96 km (60 mi) northwest of Montréal.*

The wide, sandy beaches of Lac des Sables are the most surprising feature of Ste-Agathe-des-Monts, a tourist town best known for its ski hills. Water activities include canoeing, kayaking, swimming, and fishing. Ste-Agathe is also a stopover point on the Linear Park, the bike trail between St-Jérôme and Mont-Laurier.

Where to Stay

$–$$ **Auberge Watel.** A steep driveway leads up to this white-painted, distinguished hotel overlooking Lac des Sables. Inside, the lounge and restaurant are decorated in a casual country style. Some rooms have a double-size Jacuzzi, a fireplace, and a balcony with a superb view of the lake. You have a choice of either a basic motel-style room or a larger room with pine or wicker furnishings. ✉ *250 rue St-Venant, J8C 2Z7* ☎ *819/326–7016 or 800/363–6478* 🖷 *819/326–7556* 🌐 *www.watel.ca* *25 rooms* *Restaurant, fans, cable TV, some in-room data ports, pool, hot tub, sauna, beach, dock, boating, fishing, cross-country skiing, ice-skating, snowmobiling, lounge, no-smoking floors* 💳 *AE, MC, V* 🍽 *MAP.*

¢ **Au Parc des Campeurs.** In the woods near a lively resort area, this spacious campground has activities for all age groups, from sport competitions to outings for the kids. There's a sandy beach where you can rent canoes and kayaks and launch your boat from the town's marina. Reservations are recommended. *Flush toilets, pit toilets, full hookups, partial hookups, dump station, drinking water, guest laundry, showers, fire pits, picnic tables, food service, electricity, public telephone, general store, swimming (lake)* *482 tent sites, 67 RV sites* ✉ *Lac des Sables and Rte. 329, K8C 1M9* ☎ *819/324–0482 or 800/561–7360* 🖷 *819/324–2307* 🌐 *www.parcdescampeurs.com* *C$29 tent site with water,*

SIDE TRIP TIP

When traveling here winter, make certain your vehicle has winter tires—and drive slowly and carefully. Even when roads appear clear, black ice can have you spinning off the road in seconds.

C$32 tent site with water and electricity, C$38RV site ▭ *MC, V* ⏲ *Mid-May–Sept.*

Sports & the Outdoors

24 Heures de la Voile. Sailing is the favorite summer sport around here, especially during the 24 Heures de la Voile, a weekend sailing competition that takes place in mid-July.

***Alouette V* and *VI*.** These sightseeing boats offer guided 50-minute tours of Lac des Sables. They leave the dock at least four times a day from mid-May to mid-October and six times a day in July and August. ✉ *Municipal Dock, rue Principale* ☎ *819/326–3656 or 866/326–3656* 📠 *819/326–8332* 🌐 *www.croisierealouette.com.*

Mont-Tremblant

★ ❾ *25 km (16 mi) north of Ste-Agathe-des-Monts, 100 km (62 mi) north of Montréal.*

Mont-Tremblant, at more than 3,000 feet, is the highest peak in the Laurentians and a major draw for skiers. It's also the name of a nearby village. The resort area at the foot of the mountain (called simply Tremblant) is spread around 14-km-long (9-mi-long) Lac Tremblant.*Ski* magazine consistently rates it among the top ski resorts in eastern North America.

The hub of the resort is a pedestrians-only village that looks a bit like a displaced Québec City. The buildings, constructed in the style of New France, with dormer windows and steep roofs, house pubs, restaurants, boutiques, sports shops, a movie theater, self-catering condominiums, and hotels. A historical town this is not: built for the resort, it may strike you as a bit of Disney in the mountains.

What to See

Fodor'sChoice ★ **Parc National du Mont-Tremblant.** Created in 1894, the park was the home of the Algonquins, who called this area Manitonga Soutana, meaning "mountain of the spirits." Today it's a vast wildlife sanctuary of more than 400 lakes and rivers holding nearly 200 species of birds and animals, including moose, bear, and beaver. In winter its trails are used by cross-country skiers, snowshoers, and snowmobilers. Camping and canoeing are the main summer activities. Entrance to the park is C$3.50; the main entry point is through the town of St-Donat, about 45 minutes north of Mont-Tremblant, via Routes 329 and 125. ☎ *819/688–2281* 🌐 *www.sepaq.com.*

Where to Stay & Eat

$$$–$$$$ ✕ **Restaurant Le Cheval de Jade.** "The Jade Horse" specializes in French haute cuisine. The elegant dining room has lace curtains, white linens, and ivory china. The food is the real thing—local ingredients and organic produce are used to create classic French fare such as rack of lamb, bouillabaisse, and shrimp flambéed with black pepper sauce and green tea. ✉ *688 rue de St-Jovite, Mont-Tremblant* ☎ *819/425–5233* 🌐 *www.chevaldejade.com* ✍ *Reservations essential* ▭ *AE, DC, V* ⏲ *Closed Wed. No lunch.*

$$–$$$ **Auberge du Coq de Montagne.** This restaurant on Lac Moore, five minutes from the ski slopes, has garnered much praise for its Italian cuisine. Menu offerings include tried-and-true favorites such as veal marsala and veal *fiorentina* (cooked with spinach and cheese). Hosts Nino and Kay are reputed to be some of the friendliest folks you'll ever meet—and they prepare good food, too! *2151 chemin du Village 819/425–3380 or 800/895–3380 Reservations essential AE, MC, V.*

★ **$$$$** **Fairmont Tremblant.** The sporty but classy centerpiece of the Tremblant resort area takes its cues from the historic railroad "castles" scattered throughout Canada. The hotel has wood paneling, copper and wrought-iron details, stained glass, and stone fireplaces. Guests on the Gold floor receive complimentary breakfast, evening appetizers, and Internet access. Skiers can zoom off the mountain right into the ground-level deli, near the full-service spa. Elaborate themed buffets are the draw at the Windigo restaurant ($$$$). *Box 100, 3045 chemin de la Chapelle, J8E 1E1 819/681–7000 or 800/441–1414 819/681–7099 www.fairmont.com/tremblant 207 rooms, 107 suites Restaurant, café, room service, some kitchens, room TVs with movies and video games, in-room data ports, Wi-Fi, 2 pools (1 indoor), gym, outdoor hot tub, sauna, spa, steam room, downhill skiing, ski shop, ski storage, bar, lobby lounge, video game room, shops, babysitting, laundry service, concierge, business services, meeting rooms, convention center, no-smoking floors AE, DC, MC, V BP.*

$$$$ **Hotel Club Tremblant.** Built as a family house in the early 1900s, this building has been a rooming house, brothel, and private club. Now a European-owned hotel, it's just down the lakeside road from the ski station at Mont-Tremblant. The original log-cabin lodge is furnished in a colonial style, with wooden staircases and huge stone fireplaces. Rustic but comfortable, it has excellent facilities. The French restaurant ($$$–$$$$) is outstanding; the Saturday-night buffet includes a wide selection of seafood. Both the main lodge and the split-level condominium complex (with fireplaces, private balconies or patios, and kitchenettes), up the hill from the lodge, have magnificent views of Mont-Tremblant. A complimentary shuttle takes you to the ski hills. *121 rue Cuttle, J8E 1B9 819/425–2731 or 800/567–8341 819/425–5617 www.clubtremblant.com 122 suites Restaurant, café, some fans, some in-room hot tubs, kitchenettes, cable TV, in-room data ports, tennis court, indoor-outdoor pool, gym, hair salon, sauna, spa, beach, 3 docks, boating, parasailing, waterskiing, fishing, billiards, boccie, croquet, Ping-Pong, volleyball, cross-country skiing, ski shop, ski storage, bar, dance club, babysitting, children's programs (ages 4–16), 2 playgrounds, concierge, business services, meeting rooms, convention center, no-smoking rooms; no a/c in some rooms AE, DC, MC, V MAP.*

$$$–$$$$ **Westin Resort–Tremblant.** The Westin, part of the Tremblant resort town and a short walk from the ski slopes, is plush and polished. Some rooms have fireplaces, most have balconies, and all have kitchenettes. The pathway to the heated saltwater pool and hot tub is also heated, enabling you to use these facilities all winter long. At the chic U restaurant ($$$), you can sample sushi in its many forms as well as entrées such as seared filet mignon in teriyaki sauce. This is a nonsmoking resort. *100 chemin Kan-*

dahar, J8E 1E2 ☎ 819/681–8000, 866/687–9330 in U.S. 🖷 819/681–8001 🌐 www.westin.com ⇨ 55 rooms, 71 suites ◊ Restaurant, room service, kitchenettes, some microwaves, room TVs with movies and video games, in-room data ports, pool, gym, outdoor hot tub, sauna, spa, babysitting, dry cleaning, concierge, business services, meeting rooms; no smoking ▭ AE, D, DC, MC, V 🍽 EP.

★ $$$$ **Quintessence.** This stone-and-wood all-suites hotel bills itself as the first boutique property in Mont-Tremblant. The quiet, chic Quintessence is on 3 acres along the shore of Lac Tremblant and near the ski slopes. Each suite has a king-size bed, a balcony or patio with lake views, a wood-burning fireplace, a stereo, and a bathroom with a heated marble floor and Jacuzzi. Service, including a ski shuttle and a concierge who can provide firewood, is an emphasis here. ✉ *3004 chemin de la Chapelle, J8E 1E1 ☎ 819/425–3400 or 866/425–3400 🖷 819/425–3480 🌐 www.hotelquintessence.com ⇨ 30 suites, 1 cabin ◊ Restaurant, room service, in-room safes, in-room hot tubs, minibars, cable TV with movies, in-room VCRs, in-room data ports, Wi-Fi, pool, lake, gym, outdoor hot tub, sauna, spa, steam room, ice-skating, ski storage, bar, wine bar, library, babysitting, dry cleaning, laundry service, concierge, business services, meeting room, some pets allowed; no smoking ▭ AE, DC, MC, V 🍽 CP.*

$–$$$$ **Le Grand Lodge.** This Scandinavian-style log cabin hotel is on 13½ acres on Lac Ouimet. Accommodations, from studios to two-bedroom suites, are spacious, with kitchenettes, stone fireplaces, and balconies that overlook the water. The indoor-outdoor café, which serves light dishes, also looks out on the lake. The more formal Chez Borivage, which has a good wine cellar, specializes in French cuisine. Although the resort attracts a sizable number of business travelers here for conferences, it caters to families as well, with day-care facilities, a game room for teens, and activities that include making summer bonfires on the beach and taffy on the winter snow. ✉ *2396 rue Labelle, J8E 1T8 ☎ 819/425–2734 or 800/567–6763 🖷 819/425–9725 🌐 www.legrandlodge.com ⇨ 11 rooms, 101 suites ◊ Restaurant, café, kitchenettes, room TVs with video games, in-room data ports, Wi-Fi, 4 tennis courts, indoor pool, lake, gym, sauna, spa, steam room, boating, bicycles, badminton, billiards, Ping-Pong, shuffleboard, volleyball, cross-country skiing, ice-skating, ski shop, ski storage, bar, lounge, recreation room, video game room, shop, babysitting, 2 playgrounds, dry cleaning, laundry service, concierge, business services, meeting rooms, no-smoking rooms ▭ AE, D, DC, MC, V 🍽 EP.*

SIDE TRIP TIP

Relax at the **Spa Nature Le Scandinave Mont-Tremblant** (✉ 4280 Montée Ryan Mont-Tremblant ☎ 819/425-5524 or 888/537-2263 🌐 www.scandinave.com) by spending a few hours in their Finnish sauna, Norwegian steam bath, or by taking a dip in one of their several outdoor pools. Swedish massage is available, the grounds are delightful, and admission fees are refreshingly reasonable.

Sports & the Outdoors

Mont-Tremblant. With a 2,131-foot vertical drop, Mont-Tremblant has 94 downhill trails, 13 lifts, and 110 km (68 mi) of cross-country trails.

The speedy Duncan Express is a quadruple chairlift; there's also a heated, high-speed gondola. **Versant Soleil** (sunny slope), the area on the other side of the mountain, has a vertical drop of 2,132 feet and 15 trails (including glade skiing) served by a high-speed quad chair that's capable of moving 2,250 people to the summit every hour. Sixty percent of the trails are for advanced or expert skiers only. The remainder are at an intermediate level. ☎ *800/461–8711 or 819/681–3000* 🌐 *www.tremblant.ca.*

THE EASTERN TOWNSHIPS

Updated by Chris Barry

The Eastern Townships (also known as les Cantons de l'Est, and formerly as l'Estrie) refers to the area in the southeast corner of the province of Québec—bordering Vermont, New Hampshire, and Maine. By early spring, the sugar shacks are busy with the new maple syrup. In summer, boating, swimming, sailing, golfing, rollerblading, hiking, and bicycling take over. And every fall the inns are booked solid with visitors eager to take in the brilliant foliage. Fall is also a good time to visit the wineries (although most are open all year). Because of its mild microclimate, the Townships area has become one of the fastest-developing wine regions in Canada, with a dozen of the more than 30 wineries in Québec province.

The Townships were populated by Empire Loyalists fleeing first the Revolutionary War and, later, the newly created United States of America. The Loyalists were followed, around 1820, by the first wave of Irish immigrants (ironically, Catholics fleeing their country's union with Protestant England). Some 20 years later the potato famine sent more Irish pioneers to the Townships. The area became more Francophone after 1850 as French Canadians moved in to work on the railroad and in the lumber industry. During the late 19th century, English families from Montréal and Americans from the border states began summering at cottages along the lakes.

SIDE TRIP TIP

The Eastern Townships region is home to seven truly exquisite agro-tourism routes, each identified by a sign bearing the "Au grédes champs" (Follow the Fields) symbol. It's a great tour to take for anyone interested in the Townships' agro-tourism and agri-food industries. Call 819/820–2020 for more details about the various routes.

Granby

 *80 km (50 mi) east of Montréal.*

Granby, the western gateway to the Eastern Townships, is home to a notable zoo. It also hosts a number of annual festivals: among them are the Festival of Mascots and Cartoon Characters, a great favorite with youngsters and families, and the Granby International, an antique-car competition held at the Granby Autodrome. Both of these are held in July.

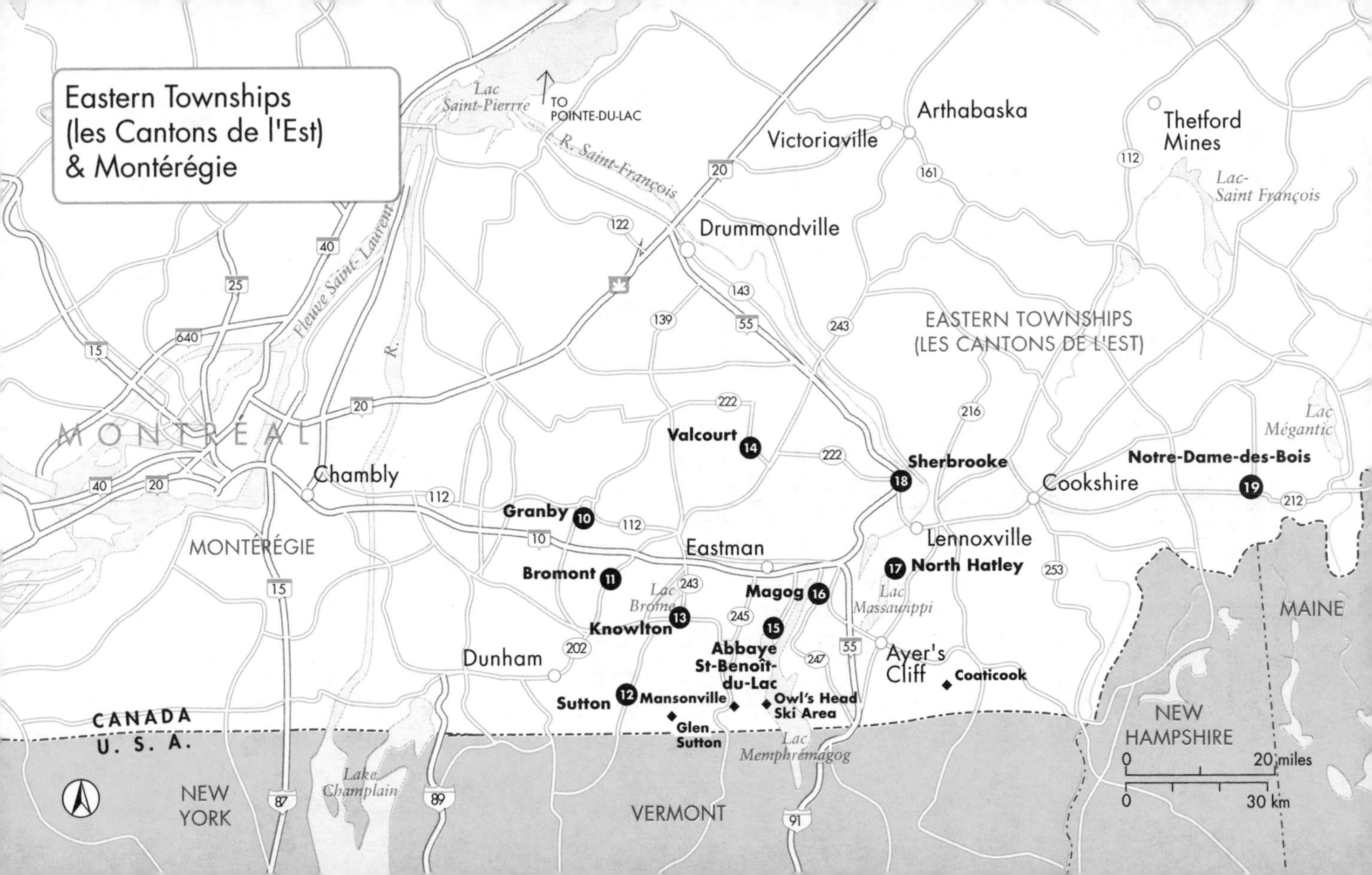
Eastern Townships
(les Cantons de l'Est)
& Montérégie
Lac Saint-Pierre
TO POINTE-DU-LAC
R. Saint-François
Fleuve Saint-Laurent
R.
Victoriaville
Arthabaska
Thetford Mines
Lac-Saint François
Drummondville
EASTERN TOWNSHIPS
(LES CANTONS DE L'EST)
MONTRÉAL
MONTÉRÉGIE
Chambly
Valcourt
14
Sherbrooke
18
Cookshire
Notre-Dame-des-Bois
19
Lac Mégantic
Granby
10
Eastman
Lennoxville
Bromont
11
North Hatley
17
Lac Brome
Knowlton
13
Magog
16
Lac Massawippi
15
Abbaye St-Benoît-du-Lac
Ayer's Cliff
Coaticook
Dunham
Sutton
12
Mansonville
Owl's Head Ski Area
Glen Sutton
Lac Memphrémagog
CANADA
U. S. A.
NEW YORK
Lake Champlain
VERMONT
NEW HAMPSHIRE
MAINE
0
20 miles
0
30 km
15
640
25
40
20
40
20
112
10
112
15
122
20
139
143
55
243
222
222
161
112
216
212
253
243
245
202
247
55
87
89
91

What to See

★ **Jardin Zoologique de Granby** (Granby Zoo). One of the biggest attractions in the area, the Granby Zoo houses some 1,000 animals representing 225 species in a naturally landscaped setting and with a focus on education. Zoo zones—from Africa to Oceania—allow you to visit Hippo's River, Gorilla's Valley, Lemur's Island, and more. Youngsters love the shark touch tanks and Amazoo, an aquatic park with turbulent wave pools and rides. At certain times of day, keepers demonstrate the acrobatic skills of the birds of prey as well as the clever tricks of the elephants, who perform for the public like old circus pros. The complex includes amusement rides and souvenir shops, as well as a playground and picnic area. *525 rue St-Hubert 450/372–9113 or 877/472–6299 www.zoogranby.ca C$24.99 Mid-May–late June, daily 10–5; late June–end Aug., daily 10–7; Sept. and Oct., weekends only 10–5.*

Sports & the Outdoors

Biking is big here. The quiet back roads lend themselves to exploring the region on two wheels, as does the 450-km-long (279-mi-long) network of bike-friendly trails. In the Townships, mountain biking is very popular.

Canada Cup. The mountain-biking season kicks off in late May with the Canada Cup, a 6-km (4-mi) race. *450/534–3333 www.cyclisme-bromont.ca.*

l'Estriade. One of the most popular bike and in-line skating trails (and also the flattest), this 21-km (13-mi) paved trail links Granby to Waterloo.

La Route Verte (The Green Route). This is a province-wide network that is being expanded by leaps and bounds. For details and a map, contact Vélo Québec *514/521–8356 or 800/567–8356 www.routeverte.com.*

Masters World Cup. Competitions for serious mountain bikers are held in summer, culminating in early September's Masters World Cup which attracts competitors from around the world. *450/534–3333 www.cyclisme-bromont.ca.*

Montérégiade. This trail runs between Granby and Farnham, and is 21 km (13 mi) long.

Bromont

11 *78 km (48 mi) east of Montréal.*

The boating, camping, golf, horseback riding, swimming, tennis, biking, canoeing, fishing, hiking, cross-country and downhill skiing, and snowshoeing available here make this a place for all seasons. Bromont has the only night skiing in the Eastern Townships—and there's even a slope-side disco, Le Bromontais. The town also has more than 100 km (62 mi) of maintained trails for mountain bikers.

What to See

Bromont Aquatic Park. This water park has more than 23 rides and games, including the Corkscrew and the Elephant's Trunk (where kids shoot out of a model of an elephant's head). Slides are divided into four degrees of difficulty, from easy to extreme (recommended for adults and older children only). Admission includes a chairlift ride to the top of the ski hill. From September through late October it's open only for mountain biking. ✉ *Autoroute 10, Exit 78* ☎ *450/534–2200* 🌐 *www.skibromont.com* 🎫 *C$40 (season pass)* ⏲ *June–late Aug., daily 10–5.*

International Bromont Equestrian Competition. Once an Olympic equestrian site, Bromont hosts this equestrian competition every July. ☎ *450/534–0787* 🌐 *www.internationalbromont.org.*

Safari Aventure Loowak. The brainchild of butterfly collector Serge Poirier, this park sprawls over 500 acres of wooded land 10 km (6 mi) northeast of Bromont. With an emphasis on team building and cooperation, Safari Loowak has more than 40 different adventure games, including an Indiana Jones–theme guided tour in which you head off into the bush to hunt for treasure and look for downed planes. It's a great hit with little ones, but parents get caught up in the fantasy, too. Reservations are essential. ✉ *475 Horizon blvd., off Autoroute 10, Exit 88, Waterloo* ☎ *450/539–0501* 🌐 *www.safariloowak.qc.ca* 🎫 *C$15 and up per person (4 people minimum)* ⏲ *Daily 10–5 by reservation.*

OFF THE BEATEN PATH

DUNHAM – Almost a dozen wineries along the Route des Vins (Wine Route) in and around the town of Dunham, about 20 km (12 mi) south of Bromont on Route 202, offer tastings and tours. Call for business hours, which can be erratic, especially in autumn, when harvesting is under way. **Vignoble Domaine Côtes d'Ardoise** was one of the first wineries to set up shop in the area, back in 1980 (✉ 879 rue Bruce, Rte. 202, Dunham ☎ 450/295–2020 🌐 www.cotesdardoise.com). **Vignoble de l'Orpailleur** (✉ 1086 Rte. 202, Dunham ☎ 450/295–2763 🌐 www.orpailleur.ca.). Before walking through the vineyard here be sure to stop by the ecomuseum to learn about the production of wine, from the growing of the grapes right up to the bottling process. There's a gift shop, patio restaurant, and daily tastings. **Vignoble Les Trois Clochers** (✉ 341 chemin Bruce, Rte. 202, Dunham ☎ 450/295–2034). This lovely winery produces a dry, fruity white from Seyval grapes as well as several other white, ice, and red wines.

Where to Stay & Eat

$$$ **Hôtel Château Bromont.** Massages, "electropuncture," algae wraps, and aromatherapy are just a few of the services at this European-style resort. It also includes a large, Turkish-style *hammam* (steam room). Rooms are large and comfortable, with contemporary furniture. Sunny Mediterranean colors dress the atrium walls, and center-facing rooms have balconies and window boxes. Greenery and patio furniture surround the swimming pool in the middle of the atrium. Restaurant Les Quatres Canards ($$$–$$$$)—with chef Mario Patry at the helm—serves regional cuisine, much of which features duck, an area specialty. The dining room has a panoramic view. For an additional fee, you may choose a meal plan that includes breakfast and dinner. ✉ *90 rue Stanstead, J2L 1K6* ☎ *450/534–3433 or 800/304–3433* 📠 *450/534–0514* 🌐 *www.chateaubromont.com* *164 rooms, 8 suites* *2 restaurants, some in-room hot tubs, cable TV with movies and video games, Wi-Fi, 2 pools*

(1 indoor), hot tub, sauna, spa, badminton, racquetball, squash, volleyball, bar, babysitting, meeting rooms, no-smoking rooms ▭ *AE, D, DC, MC, V* 🍴 *EP.*

$–$$$ **Hôtel Le Menhir.** Set among the rolling hills of the Townships and with great views of the local countryside from every room, this modern hotel is well priced, considering all the amenities available. The indoor pool, sauna, and whirlpool, along with its proximity to some of the best ski hills in the area, make this a great choice for a winter getaway. ✉ *125 Bromont blvd., J2L 2K7* ☎ *450/534–3790 or 800/461–3790* 📠 *450/534–1933* 🌐 *www.hotellemenhir.com* *41 rooms* *Some in-room hot tubs, kitchenettes, indoor pool, hot tub, bar, meeting room, no-smoking rooms* ▭ *AE, MC, V.*

2

Sports & the Outdoors

Royal Bromont. This is a superior 18-hole, par-72, bent-grass course. Greens fees are C$40–C$63 and an additional C$31 to rent a cart. ✉ *400 chemin Compton* ☎ *450/534–4653 or 888/281–0017* 📠 *450/534–4577* 🌐 *www.royalbromont.com.*

Station de Ski Bromont. With 46 trails for downhill skiing (20 of which are lighted for night skiing), Ski Bromont was the site of the 1986 World Cup Slalom. The vertical drop is 1,336 feet, and there are three lifts. Hiking and mountain biking are popular here in summer and early fall. ✉ *150 rue Champlain* ☎ *450/534–2200 or 866/276–6668* 📠 *450/534–4617* 🌐 *www.skibromont.com.*

Shopping

Shopping for bargains at yard sales and flea markets is a popular weekend activity in the Townships.

Fodor'sChoice ★ **Bromont Five-Star Flea Market.** The gigantic sign on Autoroute 10 is hard to miss. More than 1,000 vendors sell their wares here—everything from T-shirts to household gadgets—each Saturday and Sunday from May to the end of October, 10 AM–6 PM. Shoppers come from Montréal as well as Vermont, just over the border.

Sutton

⓬ *106 km (66 mi) southeast of Montréal.*

Sutton is a sporty community with craft shops, welcoming eateries, and bars (La Paimpolaise is a favorite among skiers). Surrounded by mountains, the town is best explored on foot; a circuit of 12 heritage sites makes an interesting self-guided walk past the boutiques and the houses built by Loyalists. For a route map with a description of each building and its history, go to the tourist office. It's inside the City Hall building at 11B rue Principale.

SIDE TRIP TIP

Serious snowboard enthusiasts would be well advised to check out Mont-Sutton. With a vertical drop of more than 1,500 feet, and several very challenging runs, it's the preferred hill of local snowboarders.

Where to Stay & Eat

$$–$$$ ✕ **Le Gastronome.** Offering up sumptuous first-rate French and regional dishes, former Montrealers Jessica Kinahan and chef Patrice Lobet are your hosts at this quaint little dining room set along Sutton's main drag. Sit out on their delightful terrace and sample one of Patrice's much celebrated specialties, Warm Lac Brome duck gizzards and leg confit with blue Benedictine cheese dressing and walnuts, or try his delectable Salmon Tartare with Yam Chips. Serving exquisite food at relatively moderate prices, locals will tell you this is one of the best-kept secrets in the Townships. ✉ *6 rue Principale Sud* ☎ *450/538–2121* 💳 *AE, MC, V* ⏲ *Seasonal. General hours Thurs.–Sun. from 5:30 p.m.*

$–$$ **Au Diable Vert.** This inn is in one of the most beautiful areas of the province, deep in the heart of the Appalachian Mountains and overlooking the waters of the Missisquoi River. The interior of this early-1900s farmhouse is tastefully decorated with antiques. Set on 200 acres, Au Diable Vert hosts a wide variety of outdoor activities, including hiking, guided moonlight kayak excursions along the Missisquoi, and horseback-riding lessons. It is also home to the hosts' Scottish Highland Cattle which are raised free-range for meat. Dogs are allowed at Au Diable Vert and guests are encouraged to bring them. ✉ *169 chemin Staines, J0E 2K0* ☎ *450/538–5639* 📠 *450/538–2059* 🌐 *www.audiablevert.qc.ca* *4 rooms, 1 with bath; 1 suite, 2 cabins, 30 campsites* *Hiking, pond* 💳 *AE, MC, V* *EP.*

$ **Auberge la Paimpolaise.** The alpine-style auberge on Mont-Sutton is 50 feet from the ski trails. It's nothing fancy, but the location is hard to beat. Rooms are simple and comfortable, with a woodsy appeal. Weekend ski packages are available. ✉ *615 rue Maple, J0E 2K0* ☎ *450/538–3213 or 800/263–3213* 📠 *450/538–3970* 🌐 *www.paimpolaise.com* *29 rooms, 2 suites* *Dining room, cable TV, bar, meeting rooms; no a/c, no phones in some rooms, no smoking* 💳 *AE, DC, MC, V* *BP.*

Sports & the Outdoors

GOLF **Les Rochers Bleus.** You'll need a reservation to golf at this 6,230-yard, par-72, 18-hole course. Its narrow fairways, surrounded by mountains, can be a challenge. Greens fees are C$20–C$41 plus an additional C$30 to rent a cart. ✉ *550 Rte. 139* ☎ *450/538–2324 or 800/361–2468* 🌐 *www.lesrochersbleus.com.*

HIKING **Au Diable Vert.** Au Diable Vert, which translated means the Green Devil, is a stunningly beautiful 200-acre mountainside site with challenging hiking trails that look out over spectacular scenery. (Glen Sutton, 15 minutes from the village of Sutton, is between the Appalachians and Vermont's Green Mountains; the Missisquoi River runs through the middle.) ✉ *160 chemin Staines, Glen Sutton* ☎ *450/538–5639 or 888/779–9090* 🌐 *www.audiablevert.qc.ca.*

SKIING **Mont-Sutton.** Known for some of the best snowboarding hills in Québec, Mont-Sutton has 53 downhill trails, a vertical drop of 1,518 feet, and nine lifts. This ski area, one of the region's largest, attracts a die-hard crowd of mostly Anglophone skiers and snowboarders from Québec. Trails plunge and meander through pine, maple, and birch trees. ✉ 671

Maple St. (Rte. 139 Sud) ☎ 450/538–2339, 450/538–2545, or 866/538–2545 🌐 www.montsutton.com.

Shopping

Rumeur Affamée. Carrying more than 130 kinds of cheese—60 of them produced locally—along with local and imported meats, fresh bread, and spectacular desserts, Rumeur Affamée is a must just for their famous maple-syrup pie, a tasty treat unique to the region. ✉ *15 rue Principale Nord* ☎ *450/538–1888.*

Arts Sutton. This tiny gallery, run by a local nonprofit organization, is dedicated to promoting the works of contemporary regional artists. ✉ *7 rue Academy* ☎ *450/538–2563.*

Galerie D'Art Les Imagiers. Primarily showcasing the works of 17 local painters and sculptors, Les Imagiers also exhibits work from reputable yet often lesser-known Québecois and international artists. ✉ *12 rue Principale Sud* ☎ *450/538–1771.*

Knowlton (Lac Brome)

⓭ *101 km (63 mi) southeast of Montréal.*

Knowlton is a good stop for antiques, clothes, and gifts. The village is full of high-quality boutiques, art galleries, and interesting little restaurants that have taken residence in renovated clapboard buildings painted every shade of the rainbow. The town also has several factory outlets. Along the shore of Lac Brome, Knowlton is also known for its distinctive Lake Brome ducks, which are found on local menus and celebrated in a food event over several weeks during late September and early October. You can pick up a self-guided walking-tour map at the reception area of Auberge Knowlton.

Where to Stay & Eat

$ Fodor'sChoice ★ **Auberge Knowlton.** The 12-room inn, at the main intersection in Knowlton, has been a local landmark since 1849, when it was a stagecoach stop. The inn attracts businesspeople, as well as vacationers and locals who like coming to the old, familiar hotel for special occasions. Bistro Le Relais ($$–$$$) serves local wines and cheeses and has a wide range of duck dishes, including warm duck salad served with gizzards and confit *de canard.* ✉ *286 chemin Knowlton, J0E 1V0* ☎ *450/242–6886* 📠 *450/242–1055* 🌐 *www.aubergeknowlton.ca* *12 rooms* *Restaurant, fans, cable TV, in-room data ports, Wi-Fi, meeting rooms, some pets allowed, no-smoking rooms; no a/c in some rooms* 💳 *AE, MC, V* *EP.*

Nightlife & the Arts

Fodor'sChoice ★ **Arts Knowlton.** This local theater company stages plays, musicals, and productions of classic Broadway and West End hits. It hosts professional and amateur English-language productions but has also dabbled in bilingual productions and some new Canadian works. The 175-seat, air-conditioned theater is behind the Knowlton Pub. ✉ *9 Mount Echo Rd.* ☎ *450/242–2270 or 450/242–1395* 📠 *450/242–2320* 🌐 *www.theatrelacbrome.ca.*

Sports & the Outdoors

Golf Inverness. Not far from Knowlton is this 18-hole, par-71 course (6,326 yards) with an elegant clubhouse that dates back to 1915. Greens fees are C$35–C$45 plus an additional C$30 to rent a cart. ✉ *511 chemin Bondville, Rte. 215* ☎ *450/242–1595 or 800/468–1595* 🌐 *www.golf-inverness.com.*

Shopping

Agnes & Grace. Agnes & Grace is a unique clothing line designed by Jodi Mallinson, a former Elite model. With five boutiques in the United States, Jodi Mallinson chose only two Canadian locations to showcase her creations, which have been described as "elegant" and "timeless," one in Montréal and the other in the idyllic hamlet of Knowlton. ✉ *3 Mt. Echo* ☎ *450/243–1000* 🌐 *www.agnesandgrace.com* ⏲ *Daily 10–5:30.*

Camlen. Cameron and Helen Brown (get it? Cam + len.) import gorgeous antiques from China and Eastern Europe and manufacture their own "antiques" using old wood. Their passion for and dedication to the art of furniture making is reflected in their—and their team's—workmanship. They claim to have reinvented the antiques business and, in their own way, they most certainly have. ✉ *336 Victoria St.* ☎ *450/242–4499* 📠 *450/242–2868* 🌐 *www.camlenantiques.com* ⏲ *Daily 10–5:30.*

Rococo. This boutique is owned by U.S.-born Anita Laurent, a former model. Drawing on her many contacts in the fashion world, she buys samples directly from manufacturers and sells her stylish, elegant suits and pants at a fraction of the price charged by large retail stores. ✉ *299 chemin Knowlton* ☎ *450/243–6948* ⏲ *Daily 10–5:30.*

Township Toy Trains. Big and small kids visit this delightful shop to check out its stock of trains and dollhouse miniatures. ✉ *5 chemin du Mont-Echo* ☎ *450/243–1881* 🌐 *www.townshiptoytrains.com* ⏲ *Thurs.–Sun. 10–5.*

Fodor'sChoice ★ **Station Knowlton.** Inside an old wrought-iron workshop, colorful Station Knowlton carries locally made gift items, including its own line of homemade soaps and bath salts. The comfortable café here attracts a mix of tourists and locals. ✉ *7 chemin du Mont-Echo* ☎ *450/242–5862* 🌐 *www.stationknowlton.com* ⏲ *Weekdays 11–6.*

Valcourt

14 *158 km (98 mi) east of Montréal.*

Valcourt is the birthplace of the inventor of the snowmobile, and the sport is understandably popular in the Eastern Townships with more than 2,000 km (1,240 mi) of paths cutting through the woods and meadows.

What to See

Grand Prix Ski-doo de Valcourt. Grand Prix Ski-doo is a three-day event every February with competitions, concerts, and family-oriented festivities. Ticket prices range from $12 to $120. ☎ *450/532–3443 or 866/532–7543* 🌐 *www.grandprixvalcourt.com.*

Fodor's Choice ★ **Musée Joseph-Armand Bombardier.** This museum displays innovator Bombardier's many inventions, including the snowmobile. It's partly a showcase for Bombardier's products, including the Ski-Doo snowmobiles, but it also documents the history of snow transportation, with interesting facts about winter weather, a topic of import in this corner of the world. As you walk around, you can compare yesteryear's simple modes of snow transportation—loggers working with horses in the woods, Lapps harnessing their reindeer, and so on—shown on photographic backdrops, with today's sleek vehicles. ✉ *1001 av. Joseph-Armand Bombardier* ☎ *450/532–5300* 🌐 *www.museebombardier.com* 🎫 *C$7* ⏲ *May–Labor Day, daily 10–5; closed Mon. Sept.–Jan.*

SIDE TRIP TIP

Indulge your sweet tooth by visiting a sugar shack in spring. Two of the best are Au Bec Sucre in Valcourt (450/532-3772) and La Sucrerie Haut Bois Normand in Eastman (866/297-2659).

2

Abbaye St-Benoît-du-Lac

15 *132 km (82 mi) southeast of Montréal.*

Fodor's Choice ★ The abbey's bell tower juts above the trees like a fairy-tale castle. Built by the Benedictines in 1912 on a wooded peninsula on Lac Memphrémagog, the abbey is home to some 60 monks who sell apples and sparkling apple wine from their orchards, as well as cheeses: Ermite (which means "hermit"), St-Benoît, and ricotta. Gregorian prayers are sung daily, and some masses are open to the public; call for the schedule. Dress modestly if you plan to attend vespers or other rituals, and avoid shorts. If you wish to experience a few days of retreat, reserve well in advance (a contribution of C$40 per night, which includes meals, is suggested). To get to the abbey from Magog, take Route 112 and follow the signs for the side road (Rural Route 2, or rue des Pères) to the abbey. ✉ *R.R. 2, St-Benoît-du-Lac* ☎ *819/843–4080* 📠 *819/868–1861* 🌐 *www.st-benoit-du-lac.com* ⏲ *Store Mon.–Sat. 9–10:45 and 11:45–4:30 (between services).*

Magog

16 *118 km (74 mi) east of Montréal.*

This bustling town is at the northern tip of Lac Memphrémagog, a large body of water that reaches into northern Vermont. Its sandy beaches are a draw, and it's also a good place for boating, bird-watching, sailboarding, horseback riding, dogsledding, rollerblading, golfing, and snowmobiling. You might even see Memphré, the lake's sea dragon, on one of the many lake cruises—there have been more than 100 sightings since 1816.

The streets downtown are lined with century-old homes that have been converted into boutiques, stores, and eateries—including Japanese and Vietnamese restaurants, fast-food outlets, bistros serving Italian and French dishes, and many others.

What to See

Le Cep d'Argent. The sparkling white wine is particularly good, and the dessert wine, which is similar to a port and flavored with a little maple syrup, goes well with the local cheese. The winery plays a leading role in the annual wine festival that's held in Magog (late August and early September). The guided visit and tasting of four different wines for C$7 is available only from May to December. ✉ *1257 chemin de la Rivière* ☎ *819/864–4441 or 877/864–4441* 📠 *819/864–7534* 🌐 *www.cepdargent.com* 🕒 *Daily 10–5.*

OFF THE BEATEN PATH

SUCRERIE DES NORMAND – One of the oldest, most traditional maple-syrup operations in the Eastern Townships is in Eastman, about 15 km (9 mi) west of Magog. Run by third-generation farmer Richard Normand, the farm is spread over 250 acres of wooded land and includes 10,000 maple trees. You can tour the property in a horse-drawn wagon and watch the "sugaring off" process—from the tapping of trees to the rendering down of the sweet liquid into syrup and sugar. After the tour, Richard and his wife, Marlene (she designs the menus), serve traditional Québecois food in a wood cabin, to the sounds of harmonica and spoons. ✉ *426 chemin Georges Bonnalie, Eastman* ☎ *450/297–2659 or 866/297–2659* 🌐 *www.hautboisnormand.ca* 🕒 *10 AM–3 PM, Daily, Dec.–Apr. (inclusively).*

Where to Stay & Eat

★ $$–$$$$ **Ripplecove Inn.** The accommodations, service, and food at the Ripplecove, 11 km (7 mi) south of Magog, are excellent. Bedrooms are elegant, furnished with antiques; colorful walls nicely set off the artwork. Some rooms and suites have lake views. The chef assembles Eastern Townships menus that might consist of pheasant with wild-mushroom sauce, braised leg of rabbit, panfried local trout with a white-wine-and-watercress emulsion, and crème brûlée with a crust of local maple syrup for C$80 a person. There is also a spa with a variety of treatments. ✉ *700 rue Ripplecove, Ayer's Cliff J0B 1C0* ☎ *819/838–4296 or 800/668–4296* 📠 *819/838–5541* 🌐 *www.ripplecove.com* *30 rooms, 5 suites, 3 cottages* *Restaurant, some in-room hot tubs, cable TV, Wi-Fi, pool, beach, windsurfing, boating, cross-country skiing, Internet room, meeting room, no-smoking rooms; no TV in some rooms* 💳 *AE, MC, V* *MAP.*

$ **Auberge l'Étoile Sur-le-Lac.** The rooms at this popular inn on Magog's waterfront are modern and have fresh furnishings; some have water views or whirlpools and fireplaces. Large windows overlooking mountain-ringed Lac Memphrémagog make the restaurant ($$–$$$)—which specializes in French cuisine—bright and airy. In summer you can eat outside. ✉ *1200 rue Principale Ouest, Magog J1X 2B8* ☎ *819/843–6521 or 800/567–2727* 📠 *819/843–5007* 🌐 *www.etoile-sur-le-lac.com* *51 rooms, 2 suites* *Restaurant, cable TV, in-room data ports, spa, boating, bicycles, hiking, ice-skating, meeting rooms* 💳 *AE, DC, MC, V* *CP, MAP.*

★ $$–$$$$ **Spa Eastman.** The oldest spa in Québec has evolved from a simple health center into a bucolic haven for anyone seeking rest and therapeutic treatments, including lifestyle and weight-management counseling. Surrounded by 350 acres of rolling, wooded land 15 km (9 mi) west of Magog, the spa itself is an elegant, simple structure that brings to mind the calm of a Japanese garden. Some bedrooms have fireplaces, large balconies, and views of Mont-Orford. Vegetarian dishes, prepared with organic ingredients and produce from the chef's garden, predominate in the dining room. Fish, rabbit, and chicken courses accompanied by interesting herbs and sauces are also served from time to time. For a complete head-to-toe spa experience, check out the Hair Spa, featuring a complete range of specialized treatments to revitalize and pamper your hair. ✉ *895 chemin des Diligences, Eastman J0E 1P0* ☎ *450/297–3009 or 800/665–5272* 🖷 *450/297–3370* 🌐 *www.spa-eastman.com* *44 rooms* *Dining room, pool, spa, cross-country skiing, meeting rooms; no a/c in some rooms, no room TVs, no kids* 💳 *AE, MC, V* 🍽 *MAP.*

Nightlife & the Arts

Magog is lively after dark, with many bars, cafés, bistros, and restaurants catering not only to the local population, but to the numerous tourists and weekend refugees from nearby Montréal who flock here for the exceptional beauty of the surrounding region.

In recent years this formerly depressed textile town has enjoyed something of an economic and cultural rebirth, largely thanks to the tourism industry, but also partially due to the substantial number of artists who have chosen to relocate to this welcoming, and relatively inexpensive, region of the province.

NIGHTLIFE **Auberge Orford.** A patio bar overlooks the Magog River (you can moor your boat alongside it). Sometimes there's live entertainment, but when musicians aren't around to keep them at bay, flocks of ducks line up alongside the café to beg crumbs from patrons' plates—an entertaining sight in itself. ✉ *20 rue Merry Sud* ☎ *819/843–9361.*

Café St-Michel. In a century-old building, this chic pub, outfitted in shades of charcoal and ebony, serves Tex-Mex food, pasta, and local beers. Its patio bar, which is noisy because it's at Magog's main intersection, is a great spot to watch the world go by. Chansonniers (singers) belt out popular hits for a full house on weekends—and every night but Monday in summer. ✉ *503 rue Principale Ouest* ☎ *819/868–1062.*

Microbrasserie La Memphré. A pub named after the monster said to lurk in Lake Memphrémagog, La Memphré dates back to the 1800s when it belonged to Magog's first mayor. Now a microbrewery, it serves Swiss-cheese fondue, sausages with sauerkraut, and panini (pressed sandwiches)—good accompaniments for a cold one. ✉ *12 rue Merry Sud* ☎ *819/843–3405.*

THE ARTS **Le Vieux Clocher de Magog.** One of two former churches converted into theaters by local impresario Bernard Caza (the other is in Sherbrooke), Le Vieux headlines well-known comedians and singers. Most performances are in French. ✉ *64 rue Merry Nord* ☎ *819/847–0470* 🌐 *www.vieuxclocher.com.*

Sports & the Outdoors

GOLF **Golf Owl's Head.** This course, close to the Vermont border, has some spectacular views. Laid out with undulating fairways, bent-grass greens, and 64 sand bunkers, the 6,705-yard, 18-hole course (par 72), designed by Graham Cooke, is surrounded by mountain scenery. The clubhouse, a stunning timber-and-fieldstone structure with five fireplaces and 45-foot-high ceilings, is a favorite watering hole for locals and visitors alike. Greens fees are C$40–C$50; cart rental costs C$30. ✉ *181 chemin du Mont-Owl's Head, Mansonville* ☎ *450/292–3666 or 800/363–3342* 🌐 *www.owlshead.com.*

Manoir des Sables golf course. This 6,120-yard, 18-hole, par-71 course was built on a sandy base. Lessons with Marc Viens, the resident pro, start at C$50. Greens fees start at C$32. ✉ *90 av. des Jardins, Magog-Orford* ☎ *819/847–4299 or 800/567–3514* 🌐 *www.hotelsvillegia.com.*

Orford Le Golf. This venerable course—it was laid out in 1939—is an 18-hole, par-70, 6,287-yard course that winds around forested land; from many of the greens you can see the peak of Mont-Orford. Greens fees are C$14–C$39. ✉ *3074 chemin du Parc* ☎ *819/843–5688* 🌐 *www.mt-orford.com.*

SKIING **Owl's Head Ski Area.** On the Knowlton Landing side of Lake Memphrémagog, Owl's Head is great for skiers seeking sparser crowds. It has eight lifts, a 1,782-foot vertical drop, and 43 trails, including a 4-km (2½-mi) intermediate run, the longest such run in the Eastern Townships. ✉ *40 chemin de Mont-Owl's Head, Rte. 243 Sud; Autoroute 10, Exit 106* ☎ *450/292–3342 or 800/363–3342* 🌐 *www.owlshead.com.*

North Hatley

17 *134 km (83 mi) east of Montréal.*

North Hatley, the small resort town on the tip of Lac Massawippi, has a theater and excellent inns and restaurants. Set among hills and farms, it was discovered by rich vacationers in the early 1900s and has been drawing visitors ever since.

Where to Stay & Eat

$–$$$ ✕ **Pilsen Pub.** Québec's first microbrewery no longer brews beer on-site, but Massawippi pale and brown ales and a vast selection of microbrews and imports are on tap here. Good pub food—pasta, homemade soups, burgers, and the like—is served in the upstairs restaurant and in the tavern, both of which overlook the water. It can get busy at lunch, so try to get here by noon. ✉ *55 rue Principale* ☎ *819/842–2971* 🌐 *www.pilsen.ca* ▭ *AE, MC, V.*

★ $$–$$$$ ✕🏨 **Manoir Hovey.** Overlooking Lac Massawippi, this retreat feels like a private estate, with many of the activities included in room rates. Built in 1900, the manor was modeled after George Washington's Mount Vernon. Rooms have a mix of antiques and more-modern wood furniture, richly printed fabrics, and lace trimmings; many have fireplaces and private balconies overlooking the lake. The restaurant ($$$$) serves exquisite Continen-

SIDE TRIP TIP

Watch out for moose along the highways and routes of the Eastern Townships. Moose-crossing signs are posted all along the roads but motorists often don't believe these massive beasts are as populous as they've become in recent years. They are.

tal and French cuisine; try the asparagus with purée of kalamata olives, quinoa, and white truffle oil; the roasted loin of caribou from Nunavut; or the pan-seared fillet of striped bass with Scottish sauce and lardons. There's also a light menu. Home-baked scones, clotted cream, jam, and more than 40 teas and infusions are served at the posh English-style afternoon tea. ✉ *575 chemin Hovey, J0B 2C0* ☎ *819/842–2421 or 800/661–2421* 🖷 *819/842–2248* 🌐 *www.manoirhovey.com* *40 rooms, 3 suites, 1 four-bedroom cottage* *Restaurant, cable TV, Wi-Fi, tennis court, pool, massage, beach, mountain bikes, cross-country skiing, ice-skating, 2 bars, library, Internet room, meeting rooms, no-smoking rooms* *AE, DC, MC, V* *MAP.*

$ **Auberge Le Saint-Amant.** Rooms at this B&B, a 19th-century home on a hill overlooking Lac Massawippi, are hung with plants and furnished with antiques. Jean-Claude, the chef-owner, whips up sophisticated fare ($$$–$$$$): veal kidney with Dijonnaise, rabbit terrine, fresh salmon grilled with miso damari and honey, sweetbreads in raspberry-vinegar sauce, and knuckle of lamb in spiced wine jelly. A four-course "health menu"—miso soup, salad, a tofu dish, and dessert—is C$31. ✉ *33 chemin de l'Auberge, J0B 2C0* ☎ *819/842–1211* 🌐 *www.aubergelesaintamant.com* *3 rooms* *Restaurant, pool, meeting rooms; no a/c in some rooms, no room TVs* *MC, V* *MAP.*

Nightlife & the Arts

Fodor's Choice ★ **Piggery.** A theater that was once a pig barn reigns supreme in the Townships' cultural life. The venue, which has an on-site restaurant, often presents new plays by Canadian writers and experiments with bilingual productions. The season runs July through mid-September. ✉ *215 chemin Simard, off Rte. 108* ☎ *819/842–2431* 🌐 *www.piggery.com.*

L'Association du Festival du Lac Massawippi. The association presents an annual antiques and folk-art show in July, sponsors classical-music concerts at the Église Ste-Elizabeth in North Hatley on Sunday from late April through December, and presents lively Sunday open-air concerts at Dreamland Park in summer. ☎ *819/842–2784.*

Sherbrooke

18 *130 km (81 mi) east of Montréal.*

The region's unofficial capital and largest city, Sherbrooke was founded by Loyalists in the 1790s. This town didn't get its current name, however, until 1818, when it was named for Canadian governor general Sir John Coape Sherbrooke.

On the corner of rues Dufferin and Frontenac is a realistic mural illustrating storefronts and businesses from Sherbrooke's past. Close up you notice whimsical little details—a bulldog blocking the path of a Foss-Mobile (Canada's first gas-powered automobile, designed by local inventor George Foote Foss); a woman, hair in rollers, yelling at a dog from a balcony; a policeman trying to coax the animal to move out of the way.

What to See

OFF THE BEATEN PATH

LA FERME MARTINETTE – In the heart of Québec's dairy country, this farm, which doubles as a modest B&B, hosts "sugaring off" parties with traditional menus in March and April. Lisa Nadeau and her husband, Gérald Martineau, have 2,500 maple trees as well as a herd of 50 Holsteins. You can tour the farm in a trailer pulled by the tractor that belonged to Gérald's grandfather and fill up on the C$20.95 all-you-can-eat traditional meal during the sugaring off season in March and April. There is also a gift shop on the premises. Coaticook is 32 km (20 mi) south of Sherbrooke. ✉ *1728 chemin Martineau, Coaticook* ☎ *819/849–7089 or 888/881–4561* 🌐 *www.lafermemartinette.com.*

Musée des Beaux-Arts de Sherbrooke. This fine-arts museum has a permanent exhibit on the history of art in the region from 1800 to the present. ✉ *241 rue Dufferin* ☎ *819/821–2115* 🌐 *www.mbas.qc.ca* 🎫 *C$6* ⏲ *Tues.–Sun. noon–5.*

Musée de la Nature et des Sciences. This museum is in what used to be the Julius-Kayser & Co. factory, famous for the silk stockings it made. The elegant building has granite floors and marble stairs, and makes good use of its lofty space. State-of-the-art light and sound effects (the buzzing of mosquitoes may be *too* lifelike) and hands-on displays enhance the exhibits. ✉ *225 rue Frontenac* ☎ *819/564–3200* 📠 *819/564–3200* 🌐 *www.mnes.qc.ca* 🎫 *C$7.50* ⏲ *Wed.–Sun. 10–5.*

Sherbrooke Tourist Information Center. The tourist center conducts animated tours, mainly in French, led by costumed actors representing figures from Sherbrooke's past. The history-focused tours, which run weekends from mid-July to late August, are designed for prearranged groups, but individuals can tag along ($20 per person; reservations essential). ✉ *2964 King St. Ouest* ☎ *819/821–1919* 🌐 *www.tourismesherbrooke.com.*

Where to Stay & Eat

$$–$$$$ Fodor'sChoice ★ ✕ **La Falaise St-Michel.** A warmly decorated redbrick-and-wood room takes the chill off even before you sit down. The superb French offerings at this restaurant, considered to be one of the best in town, include sautéed kidneys, veal sweetbreads, escargots, and warm duck salad. A large selection of wines complements the table d'hôte. ✉ *100 rue Webster* ☎ *819/346–6339* 💳 *AE, DC, MC, V* ⏲ *Closed Sun. No dinner Mon.*

$$–$$$ ✕ **Restaurant au P'tit Sabot.** The adventurous menus here use local ingredients such as wild boar, quail, sweetbreads, venison, and bison in classic French dishes. The serene decor and small dining area (it seats around 35 people) make it a pleasant refuge from the busy and not very attractive shopping mall that houses it. ✉ *1410 rue King Ouest* ☎ *819/563–0262* 💳 *AE, DC, MC, V.*

¢–$$ 🏨 **Bishop's University.** If you're on a budget, these students' residences are a great place to stay mid-May through August. The prices can't be beat, and the location—5 km (3 mi) south of Sherbrooke—is good for touring. The university's lovely grounds have architecture reminiscent of stately New England campuses. The 1857 Gothic-style chapel, paneled with richly carved ash, shows fine local craftsmanship. Reservations for summer are accepted as early as the previous September, and it's a good idea to book far in advance. They also offer special rates for students. ✉ *Rue College, Box 5000, Lennoxville J1M 1Z7* ☎ *819/822–9651* 📠 *819/822–9615* 🌐 *www.ubishops.ca* *438 rooms without bath, 54 apartments* *Restaurant, 9-hole golf course, tennis court, 2 pools (1 indoor), gym; no a/c, no room TVs* 💳 *MC, V* ⏲ *Closed Sept.–mid-May.*

Nightlife & the Arts

Centennial Theatre. The 600-seat Centennial Theatre is a part of Bishops University and presents a roster of jazz, classical, and rock concerts, as well as opera, dance, mime, and children's theater. ✉ *Bishop's University, Lennoxville* ☎ *819/822–9600 Ext. 2691, 819/822–9692 box office* 🌐 *www.ubishops.ca/centennial.*

Le Vieux Clocher de Sherbrooke. In a converted church, Le Vieux Clocher de Sherbrooke presents music, from classical to jazz, and a variety of theater and comedy shows. ✉ *1590 rue Galt Ouest* ☎ *819/822–2102* 🌐 *www.vieuxclocher.com.*

Notre-Dame-des-Bois

19 *204 km (127 mi) east of Montréal.*

With a population of 759 people—as of last count—Notre-Dame-des-Bois remains a sleepy little town surrounded by some of the steepest mountains in the Townships. It's a picturesque part of the world, to be sure, with the big tourist draw being the Astrolab observatory atop Mont-Megantic park.

What to See

Astrolab du Mont-Mégantic (Mont-Mégantic's Observatory). Both amateur stargazers and serious astronomers head to his observatory, located in a beautifully wild and mountainous area. The observatory is at the summit of the Townships' second-highest mountain (3,601 feet), whose northern face records annual snowfalls rivaling any in North America. A joint venture of the University of Montréal and Laval University, the observatory has a powerful telescope, the largest on the East Coast. At the welcome center at the mountain's base, you can view an exhibition and a multimedia show to learn about the night sky. ✉ *Parc Mégantic, 189 Rte. du Parc* ☎ *819/888–2941* 🌐 *www.astrolab.qc.ca* *C$11.25, summit tour C$20; additional C$3.50 to enter Parc Mégantic* ⏲ *Mid-May–mid-June, weekends noon–5; mid June–late Aug., daily noon–7:30 and 8:30 PM–11:30 PM; late Aug.–early Oct., weekends noon–5 and 7:30 PM–10:30 PM. Closed Mon. night.*

Where to Stay & Eat

$ Fodor's Choice ★ **Aux Berges de l'Aurore.** Although this tiny B&B has attractive furnishings and spectacular views (it's at the foot of Mont-Mégantic), the food is the main attraction. The restaurant ($$$$) serves a four-course meal using produce from the inn's huge garden, as well as local wild game: elk, fish, hare, and caribou. ✉ *139 Rte. du Parc, J0B 2E0* ☎ *819/888–2715* 🌐 *www.auberge-aurore.qc.ca* *5 rooms* *Restaurant, meeting rooms; no a/c in some rooms, no room TVs, no kids under 12* 💳 *MC, V* ⏲ *Closed Jan.–May* *EP.*

MONTRÉAL SIDE TRIPS ESSENTIALS

Transportation

BY AIR

Montréal is the gateway city to explore the Laurentians and the Eastern Townships—both beginning only a short drive from the Pierre Elliot Trudeau (P.E.T.) International airport.

There are no regional airports of note in either the Laurentians or Eastern Townships and passenger rail travel to the small villages of both areas is virtually nonexistent. Still, they are both easily accessible by car, with the foothills of the Laurentian mountains less than a half-hour drive north of the airport along Highway 30, and the Townships region beginning an hour's drive southeast of the airport along Highway 20 and Highway 10 (also known as the Eastern Townships autoroute).

There are several car-rental outlets operating out of P.E.T., so finding a vehicle to explore these areas shouldn't present much of a problem.

BY BIKE

Québec is in the middle of developing the Route Verte, or the Green Route, a 3,600-km (2,230-mi) network of bike trails covering the southern half of the province, which will eventually link with trails in New England and New York. More than half of the marked trails are already open and when the project is completed, it will comprise 4,300 km (over 2,600 mi) of bikeways. For information and a map, contact Vélo Québec.

Vélo Québec ☎ 514/521-8356 or 800/567-8356 🌐 www.routeverte.com

BY BUS

Daily service to Granby, Lac-Mégantic, Magog, and Sherbrooke in the Eastern Townships leaves from the Montréal central bus station. Greyhound's Canada Coach Pass Plus gives you access to Québec as well as the Maritime Provinces. Passes must be purchased in Canada at a Greyhound terminal or online before leaving home. They are an excellent value for travelers who want to wander the highways and byways of the country, packing a lot of miles into a relatively short period of time. However, for occasional day trips (from Montréal to Québec City, for example) they're hardly worth it.

Voyageur is a province-wide bus line. Several smaller private companies also serve the regions and connect with Voyageur.

Limocar service in the area covers the Laurentians: stops include Mont-Laurier, Ste-Adèle, Ste-Agathe-des-Monts, and St-Jovite. Limocar has a service to the Lower Laurentians region (including St-Jérôme), departing from the Laval Bus Terminal at the Henri-Bourassa Métro stop in north Montréal; Limocar also services Lanaudière, Montérégie, and the Eastern Townships.

Gare du Palais (Québec bus terminal) ✉ 320 rue Abraham-Martin, Québec City ☎ 418/525-3000. **Greyhound Lines** ☎ 800/661-8747 in Canada, 800/231-2222 in the U.S. 🌐 www.greyhound.ca. **Limocar** ☎ 450/435-8899 🌐 www.limocar.ca. **Station Centrale**

d'Autobus Montréal ✉ 505 blvd. de Maisonneuve Est, Montréal ☎ 514/842-2281. **Voyageur** ☎ 514/842-2281 🌐 www.greyhound.cas

2

BY CAR

Major entry points are Ottawa/Hull; U.S. 87 from New York State south of Montréal; U.S. 91 and U.S. 89 from Vermont into the Eastern Townships area; and the Trans-Canada Highway (Highway 40 to the west of Montréal, Highway 20 to the east).

Québec has fine roads—and speedy drivers. The major highways are Autoroute des Laurentides 15 Nord, a six-lane highway from Montréal to the Laurentians; Autoroute 10 Est from Montréal to the Eastern Townships; U.S. 91 from New England, which becomes Autoroute 55 as it crosses the border to the Eastern Townships; Autoroutes Jean-Lesage 20 and Félix-LeClerc 40 between Montréal and Québec; and the scenic Route 138 (called the chemin du Roy between St-Barthélémy and Québec City), which runs from Montréal along the north shore of the St. Lawrence River. Road maps are available at Québec tourist offices.

Autoroute des Laurentides 15 North and Route 117—a slower but more scenic secondary road at its northern end—lead to the Laurentians. Exit numbers on Autoroute 15 are the distance in kilometers from the U.S. border. Try to avoid traveling to and from the region Friday evening or Sunday afternoon, because you're likely to sit in traffic for hours.

Autoroute 10 Est heads from Montréal through the Eastern Townships; from New England, U.S. 91 becomes Autoroute 55, a major road.

Contacts & Resources

EMERGENCIES

Hospitals **Centre Hospitalier Universitaire de Sherbrooke (CHUS)** (CUSE) ✉ 580 rue Bowen Sud, Sherbrooke ☎ 819/346-1110. **CSSS des Sommets** ✉ 234 rue St-Vincent, Ste-Agathe-des-Monts ☎ 819/324-4000.

LODGING

CAMPING For information about Québec's national parks contact Parks Canada. Contact the individual park administration about camping in provincial parks. For information on camping in the province's private trailer parks and campgrounds, request the free publication "Québec Camping," from Tourisme Québec.

Parks Canada Box 6060, Passage du Chien d'Or, Québec City G1R 4V7 ☎ 418/648-4177 or 800/463-6769 🌐 www.pc.gc.ca. **Tourisme Québec** Box 979, Montréal H3C 2W3 ☎ 514/873-2015, 800/363-7777, or 877/266-5687 🌐 www.bonjourquebec.com.

GUEST FARMS Agricotours, the Québec farm-vacation association, can provide lists of guest farms in the province.

Agricotours ✉ 4545 av. Pierre-de-Coubertin, C.P. 1000, Succursale M, Montréal H1V 3R2 ☎ 514/252-3138 🌐 www.agricotours.qc.ca.

TOURS

The Zoological Society of Montréal is a nature-oriented group that runs lectures, field trips, and weekend excursions. Tours include whale-watch-

ing in the St. Lawrence estuary and hiking and bird-watching in national parks throughout Québec, Canada, and the northern United States.
Zoological Society of Montréal ☎ 514/845-8317 🌐 www.zoologicalsocietymtl.org.

VISITOR INFORMATION

Tourisme Québec can provide information on specific towns' tourist bureaus.

In the Laurentians, the major tourist office is the Association Touristique des Laurentides, just off Autoroute des Laurentides 15 Nord at Exit 39. The office is open mid-June–August, daily 9–8:30; September–mid-June it's open Saturday–Thursday 9–5 and Friday 9–7. Mont-Tremblant, Piedmont/St-Sauveur, Ste-Adèle, St-Adolphe-d'Howard, Ste-Agathe-des-Monts, St-Eustache, St-Jovite, and Val-David have regional tourist offices that are open year-round. Seasonal tourist offices (open mid-June–early September) are in Ferme Neuve, Grenville, Labelle, Lac-du-Cerf, Lachute, Nominique, Notre-Dame-du-Laus, Oka, St-Jérôme, Ste-Marguerite-Estérel, and St-Sauveur.

In the Eastern Townships, year-round regional provincial tourist offices are in Bromont, Coaticook, Granby, Lac-Mégantic, Magog-Orford, Sherbrooke, and Sutton. Seasonal tourist offices (open June–early September) are in Birchton, Danville, Dudswell, Dunham, Eastman, Frelighsburg, Lac-Brome (Foster), Lambton, Masonsville, Pike River, Ulverton, and Waterloo. The schedules of seasonal bureaus are irregular, so it's a good idea to contact the Association Touristique des Cantons de l'Est before visiting. This association also provides lodging information.

Tourist Information **Association Touristique des Cantons de l'Est** ✉ 20 rue Don Bosco Sud, Sherbrooke J1L 1W4 ☎ 819/820-2020 or 800/355-5755 📠 819/566-4445 🌐 www.easterntownships.cc. **Association Touristique des Laurentides** ✉ 14142 rue de la Chapelle, Mirabel J7J 2C8 ☎ 450/224-7007, 450/436-8532, 800/561-6673, 514/990-5625 in Montréal 📠 450/436-5309 🌐 www.laurentides.com. **Tourisme Québec** ✉ 1001 rue du Square-Dorchester, No. 100, C.P. 979, Montréal H3C 2W3 ☎ 800/363-7777 🌐 www.bonjourquebec.com.

Québec City

WORD OF MOUTH

"Montréal is lively and exciting . . . but Québec City wins hands-down for me . . . Seeing it is like traveling to any beautiful old European city, right here in the heart of North America. The city is very walkable. I saw it all by foot myself, and loved discovering all the hidden treasures . . . And oh my, the food!"

–westcoasthoney8

"You should try to visit La Citadelle, the historic fort that dominates the Upper Town. There are guided tours, and in summer, the Royal 22e Régiment performs the changing of the guard every morning, and on weekends, the beating of retreat ceremony in the evening. The views from the ramparts are outstanding."

–laverendrye

www.fodors.com/forums

Updated by Michèle Thibeau

NO TRIP TO FRENCH-SPEAKING CANADA is complete without a visit to romantic Québec City. There's a definite European sensibility here and you'll feel farther from home then you are, walking down cobblestone streets and stopping in small shops selling everything from pastries and artisanal cheese to antiques and art. In 2008, the city will celebrate its 400th anniversary, and preparations are well under way for what's sure to be the biggest party the city's seen in decades.

The heart of the city is Vieux-Québec (Old Québec), which is divided between the Haute-Ville (Upper Town) and the Basse-Ville (Lower Town). Surrounded by walkable stone ramparts that once protected the city, Old Québec is today a small, dense, well-maintained neighborhood steeped in four centuries of French, English, and Canadian history and tradition. The city's finest 17th- and 18th-century buildings are here, as are its best parks and monuments. Because of the fortified city's immaculate preservation, Old Québec was designated a UNESCO World Heritage Site in 1985But the Old City is just a part of the Québec City experience. Outside the city walls, there are plenty of interesting areas a short walk or bus ride away. One of the newly hip places to hang out is St-Roch, just west of the Old City, with its grand square, artsy galleries, and funky shops. Or, walk down avenue Cartier in the area known as Montcalm, southwest of the Old City, for high-end shopping of all kinds, as well as the Halles Petit Cartier market.

SAVVY IN THE CITY

Québec City is hilly, so plan accordingly. Use the funicular, off Dufferin Terrace, or the elevator between Upper and Lower Town to avoid the climb. There are cabs to take you back and forth as well.

Although summer here is the most popular time to visit, when there's a general relaxed vibe as its residents soak up the warmth and festivals galore, seeing the city in winter shows its true colors. The thing to know about the people who live in Québec City is that they don't hole up once the weather gets cold—they revel it in, all bundled in their parkas, ready to go out on the town.

By far the best way—and in some places the only way—to explore Québec City is on foot. Top sights, restaurants, and hotels are within or near Old Québec, which takes up only 11 square km (4 square mi). The area is not flat, so walking takes a bit of effort, especially if you decide to walk to the Upper Town from the Lower Town. Helpful city maps are available at visitor-information offices, the best of which is on the public square in front of the Château Frontenac.

UPPER TOWN

Home to many of the city's most famous sites, Upper Town also offers a dramatic view of the St. Lawrence River and the surrounding coun-

GREAT ITINERARIES

IF YOU HAVE 2 DAYS

With only a couple of days, you should devote one day to Lower Town, which is the earliest site of French civilization in North America, and the second day to Upper Town. On Day 1, stroll the narrow streets of the Quartier Petit-Champlain, visiting the Maison Chevalier and browsing at the many handicraft stores. Moving on to Place Royale, head for the Église Notre-Dame-des-Victoires; in summer there's almost always entertainment in the square. On Day 2, view the St. Lawrence River from Terrasse Dufferin and visit the impressive buildings of Upper Town, where 17th- and 18th-century religious and educational institutions predominate.

IF YOU HAVE 4 DAYS

Four days will give you some time to explore outside the walls of the old city as well as the countryside. Follow the itinerary above for a two-day trip. On Day 3, plan a picnic on the Plains of Abraham, site of the battle that ended France's colonial dreams in North America and marked the beginning of British rule in Canada. In the afternoon check out the Musée National des Beaux-Arts du Québec or the Musée de la Civilisation. On Day 4, head out of town to explore the Côte de Beaupré, including the colossal Basilique Ste-Anne-de-Beaupré, or see Montmorency Falls and Île d'Orléans.

tryside. It's where you'll find historic institutions and, of course, rue St-Jean's bars, cafés, and shops, along with hotels and bed-and-breakfasts.

Like the Citadel, most of the many elegant homes that line the narrow streets in Upper Town are made of granite cut from nearby quarries in the 1800s. The stone walls, copper r oofs, and heavy wooden doors on the government buildings and high-steepled churches in the area also reflect the Upper Town's place as the political, educational, and religious nerve center of both the province and the country during much of the past four centuries.

No other place in Canada has so much history squeezed into such a small spot. The Upper Town was a barren, windswept cape when Champlain built a fort here almost 400 years ago. Now, of course, it's a major tourist destination surrounded by cannon-studded stone ramparts.

Main Attractions

13 **Basilique Notre-Dame-de-Québec** (Our Lady of Québec Basilica). This basilica has the oldest parish in North America, dating from 1647. Its somber, ornate interior includes a canopy dais over the episcopal throne, a ceiling of painted clouds decorated with gold leaf, richly colored stained-glass windows, and a chancel lamp that was a gift from Louis XIV. The large and famous crypt was Québec City's first cemetery; more than 900 bodies are interred here, including 20 bishops and four governors of New France. Samuel de Champlain may be buried near the basilica: archaeologists have been searching for his tomb since 1950. There are infor-

QUÉBEC CITY HISTORY

Québec City was founded by French explorer Samuel de Champlain in 1608 and is the oldest municipality in the province of Québec. In the 17th century the first French explorers, fur trappers, and missionaries came here to establish the colony of New France.

French explorer Jacques Cartier arrived 1535, but it was Champlain who founded "New France" some 70 years later, and built a fort on the banks of the St. Lawrence on a spot that is today called Place Royale.

The British were persistent in their efforts to dislodge the French from North America, but the colonists of New France built forts and other military structures, such as a wooden palisade (defensive fence) that reinforced their position on top of the cliff. It was Britain's naval supremacy that ultimately led to New France's demise. After capturing all French forts east of Québec, General James Wolfe led a British army to Québec City in the summer of 1759.

After a months-long siege, thousands of British soldiers scaled the heights along a narrow cow path on a moonless night. Surprised to see British soldiers massed on a farmer's field so near the city, French General Louis-Joseph Montcalm rushed out to meet the British in what became known as the Battle of the Plains of Abraham. The French were routed in the violent 20-minute conflict, which claimed the lives of both Wolfe and Montcalm. The battle marked the death of New France and the birth of British Canada.

British rule was a boon for Québec City. Thanks to more robust trade and large capital investments, the fishing, fur-trading, shipbuilding, and timber industries expanded rapidly. As the city's economic, social, religious, and political sectors developed and diversified, the quality of people's lives also greatly improved.

Wary of new invasions from its former American colonies, the British also expanded the city's fortifications. They replaced the wooden palisades with a massive cut-stone wall and built a star-shape fortress. Both works are still prominent in the city's urban landscape.

The constitution of 1791 established Québec City as the capital of Lower Canada, a position it held until 1840, when the Act of Union united Upper and Lower Canada and made Montréal the capital. When Canada was created in 1867 by the Act of Confederation, which united four colonial provinces (Québec, Ontario, New Brunswick, and Nova Scotia), Québec City was named the province's capital city, a role it continues to play. Many Québecois also call the city *"la capitale Nationale,"* a reflection of the nationalist sentiments that have marked Québec society and politics for the past 40 years.

mation panels that allow you to read about the history of this church. Or, if you prefer, there are guided tours available. ✉ *16 rue de Buade, Upper Town* ☎ *418/692–2533 church* 🌐 *www.patrimoine-religieux.com* 🎫 *Basilica free, C$2 for a guided tour; crypt C$2* ⏲ *Mid-Oct.–Apr., daily 7:30–4; May–mid-Oct., weekdays 7:30–4, weekends 7:30–5.*

5 **Couvent des Ursulines** (Ursuline Convent). North America's oldest teaching institution for girls, still a private school, was founded in 1639 by French nun Marie de l'Incarnation and laywoman Madame de la Peltrie. The convent has many of its original walls intact and houses a little chapel and a museum. The **Chapelle des Ursulines** (Ursuline Chapel; ✉ 10 rue Donnacona, Upper Town ☎ No phone ⏲ The chapel is open May–Oct., Tues.–Sat. 10–11:30 and 1:30–4:30; Sun. 1:30–4:30. Admission is free.) is where French general Louis-Joseph Montcalm was buried after he died in the 1759 battle that decided the fate of New France. In September 2001, Montcalm's remains were transferred to rest with those of his soldiers at the Hôpital Général de Québec's cemetery, at 260 boulevard Langelier. The exterior of the Ursuline Chapel was rebuilt in 1902, but the interior contains the original chapel, which took sculptor Pierre-Noël Levasseur from 1726 to 1736 to complete. The votive lamp was lighted in 1717 and has never been extinguished.

The **Musée des Ursulines** (✉ 12 rue Donnacona, Upper Town ☎ 418/694–0694 🎫 Admission is C$6. ⏲ The museum is open May–Sept., Tues.–Sat. 10–noon and 1–5, Sun. 1–5; Oct., Nov., and Feb.–Apr., Tues.–Sun. 1–4:30.) was once the residence of one Madame de la Peltrie. The museum provides an informative perspective on 120 years of the Ursulines' life under the French regime, from 1639 to 1759. It took an Ursuline nun nine years of training to attain the level of a professional embroiderer; the museum contains magnificent pieces of ornate embroidery, such as altar frontals with gold and silver threads intertwined with semiprecious jewels. In the lobby of the museum is the **Centre Marie-de-l'Incarnation** (✉ 10 rue Donnacona, Upper Town ☎ 418/694–0413

QUÉBEC CITY'S TOP 5

- **Admire the St. Lawrence.** Stand on Dufferin Terrace or the Plains of Abraham and and look out at the mighty river that gave the city its name—the Algonquins called this place Kebec, meaning "where the river narrows."
- **Buff Up on History.** Don't miss the Musée de la Civilisation in Lower Town or La Citadelle in Upper Town.
- **Gaze Upward.** With no fewer than 11 architectural styles of buildings here—from classic revival to art deco—there's a lot to learn about how Québec City came to look as it does today. See the Château Frontenac, Hôtel-Dieu, and Place Royale.
- **Laze at a Café.** Take a break from sightseeing to do as the locals do—grab a chair and chat over a café au lait and a crêpe. Try Tatum on rue St-Jean or Café Krieghoff on avenue Cartier.
- **Parler Français.** If you love listening to French—or speaking it, if you're so inclined—then Québec City will win your heart, as more than 90% of residents claim it as their first language.

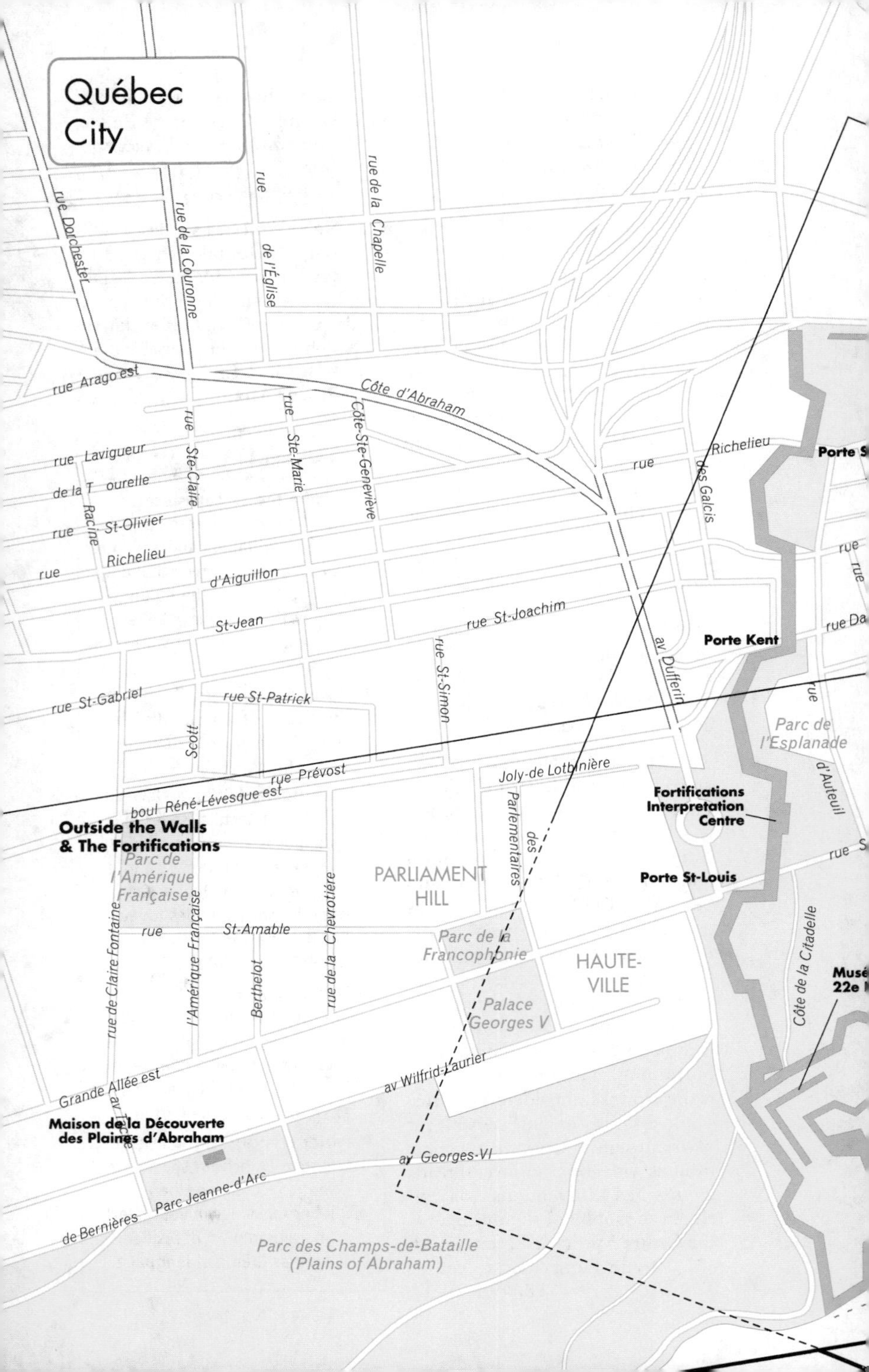
Québec City
rue Dorchester
rue de la Couronne
rue de l'Église
rue de la Chapelle
rue Arago est
Côte d'Abraham
rue Ste-Claire
rue Ste-Marie
Côte-Ste-Geneviève
rue Lavigueur
de la Tourelle
Racine
rue St-Olivier
rue Richelieu
d'Aiguillon
St-Jean
rue St-Joachim
rue St-Simon
rue St-Gabriel
rue St-Patrick
Scott
rue Prévost
boul René-Lévesque est
Joly-de Lotbinière
des Parlementaires
rue Richelieu
des Galcis
av Dufferin
Porte Kent
Parc de l'Esplanade
d'Auteuil
Fortifications Interpretation Centre
Porte St-Louis
Outside the Walls & The Fortifications
Parc de l'Amérique Française
PARLIAMENT HILL
rue St-Amable
rue de Claire Fontaine
l'Amérique Française
Berthelot
rue de la Chevrotière
Parc de la Francophonie
HAUTE-VILLE
Palace Georges V
Côte de la Citadelle
Grande Allée est
av Wilfrid-Laurier
av Taché
Maison de la Découverte des Plaines d'Abraham
av Georges-VI
Parc Jeanne-d'Arc
de Bernières
Parc des Champs-de-Bataille (Plains of Abraham)

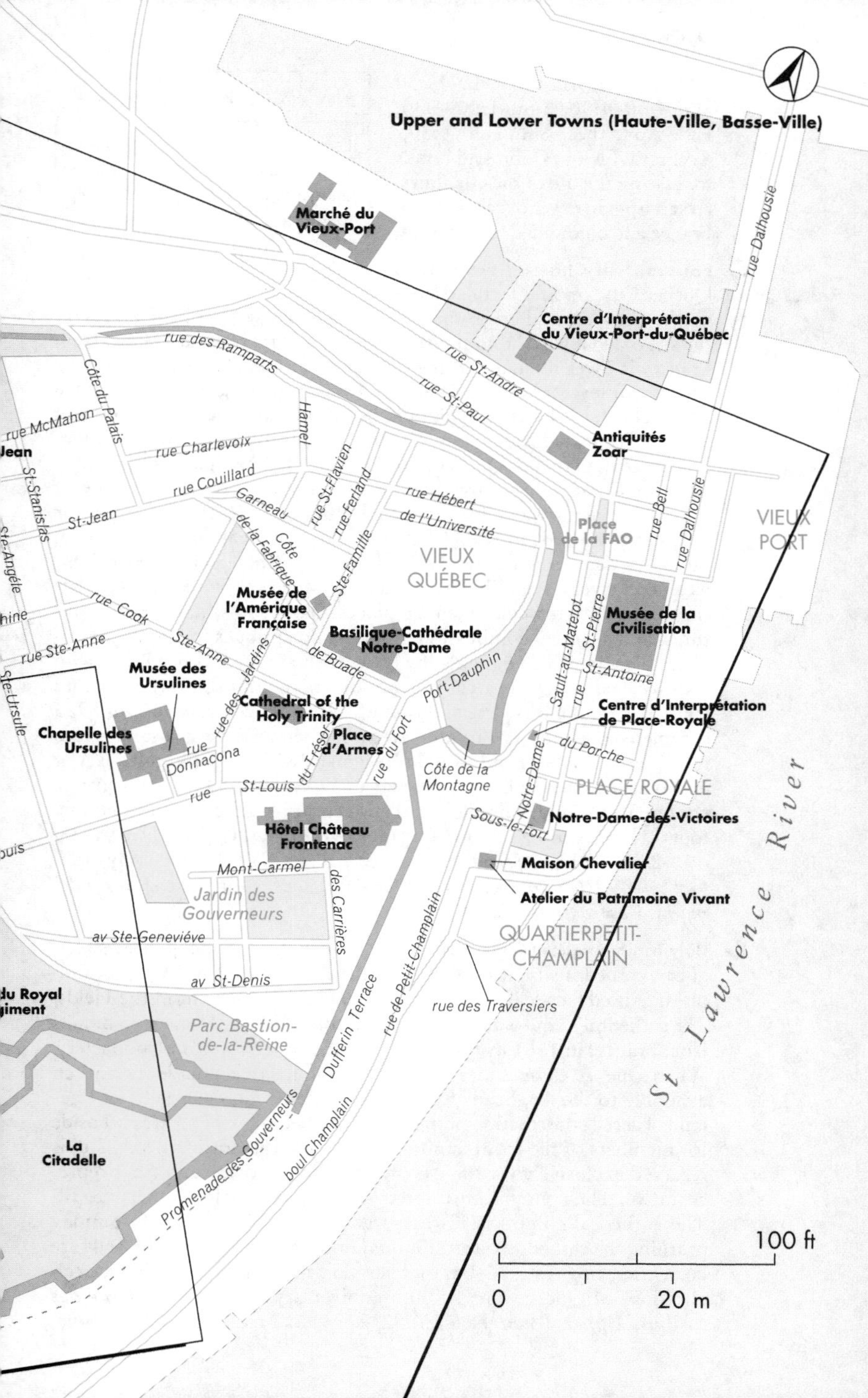
Upper and Lower Towns (Haute-Ville, Basse-Ville)
Marché du Vieux-Port
Centre d'Interprétation du Vieux-Port-du-Québec
rue Dalhousie
rue des Remparts
rue St-André
rue St-Paul
Antiquités Zoar
Côte du Palais
rue McMahon
Jean
Hamel
rue Charlevoix
rue Couillard
St-Stanislas
St-Jean
Garneau
rue St-Flavien
rue Ferland
rue Hébert
de l'Université
rue Bell
rue Dalhousie
Place de la FAO
VIEUX PORT
Ste-Angèle
Côte de la Fabrique
Ste-Famille
VIEUX QUÉBEC
Musée de l'Amérique Française
rue Cook
Basilique-Cathédrale Notre-Dame
Musée de la Civilisation
rue Ste-Anne
Ste-Anne
de Buade
Sault-au-Matelot
rue St-Pierre
St-Antoine
Musée des Ursulines
Ste-Ursule
rue des Jardins
Cathedral of the Holy Trinity
Port-Dauphin
Centre d'Interprétation de Place-Royale
Chapelle des Ursulines
rue Donnacona
du Trésor
Place d'Armes
rue du Fort
Notre-Dame
du Porche
Côte de la Montagne
PLACE ROYALE
rue St-Louis
Notre-Dame-des-Victoires
Sous-le-Fort
Hôtel Château Frontenac
Maison Chevalier
Mont-Carmel
Atelier du Patrimoine Vivant
Jardin des Gouverneurs
des Carrières
rue de Petit-Champlain
St Lawrence River
av Ste-Geneviéve
QUARTIERPETIT-CHAMPLAIN
av St-Denis
du Royal
rue des Traversiers
Dufferin Terrace
Parc Bastion-de-la-Reine
La Citadelle
Promenade des Gouverneurs
boul Champlain
0
100 ft
0
20 m

⏲ May–Oct., Tues.–Sat. 10–11:30 and 1:30–4:30, Sun. 1:30–4:30; Feb.–Apr., Tues.–Sun. 1:30–4:30), a center with an exhibit and books for sale on the life of the Ursulines' first superior, who came from France and cofounded the convent.

SAVVY IN THE CITY

It's often cooler by the river, so remember to bring a sweater, light rain gear, and walking shoes with good grips for those slippery cobblestone streets.

Fodor's Choice ★ ❷ **Fairmont Le Château Frontenac.** Québec City's most celebrated landmark, this imposing green-turreted castle with a copper roof stands on the site of what was the administrative and military headquarters of New France. It owes its name to the Comte de Frontenac, governor of the French colony between 1672 and 1698. Considering the magnificence of the château's location overlooking the St. Lawrence River, you can see why Frontenac said, "For me, there is no site more beautiful nor more grandiose than that of Québec City." Samuel de Champlain was responsible for Château St-Louis, the first structure to appear on the site of the Frontenac; it was built between 1620 and 1624 as a residence for colonial governors. In 1784 Château Haldimand was constructed here, but it was demolished in 1892 to make way for Château Frontenac, built as a hotel a year later. The Frontenac was remarkably luxurious at that time: guest rooms contained fireplaces, bathrooms, and marble fixtures, and a special commissioner purchased antiques for the establishment. The hotel was designed by New York architect Bruce Price, who also worked on Québec City's Gare du Palais (rail station) and other Canadian landmarks. The addition of a 20-story central tower in 1925 completed the hotel. It's accumulated a star-studded guest roster, including Queen Elizabeth and Ronald Reagan as well as Franklin Roosevelt and Winston Churchill, who met here in 1943 and 1944 for two wartime conferences. Guides dressed in 19th-century-style costumes conduct tours of the luxurious interior. ✉ *1 rue des Carrières, Upper Town* ☎ *418/691–2166* 🌐 *www.fairmont.com* 🎟 *Tours C$8* ⏲ *Tours May–mid-Oct., daily 10–6 on the hr; mid-Oct.–Apr., weekends noon–5 or on demand. Reservations essential.*

★ ❻ **Holy Trinity Anglican Cathedral.** This stone church was one of the first Anglican cathedrals built outside the British Isles. Built in 1804, its simple, dignified facade is reminiscent of London's St. Martin-in-the-Fields. The cathedral's land was given to the Recollet fathers (Franciscan monks from France) in 1681 by the king of France for a church and monastery. When Québec came under British rule, the Recollets made the church available to the Anglicans for services. Later, King George III of England ordered construction of the present cathedral, with an area set aside for members of the royal family. A portion of the north balcony still is reserved exclusively for the use of the reigning sovereign or her representative. The church houses precious objects donated by George III. The cathedral's impressive rear organ has 3,058 pipes. On Sunday morning the cathedral has traditional English bell ringing. The bells are currently being restored, but they should be back in time to sing the celebrations of Québec City's 400th anniversary in 2008. ✉ *31 rue des Jardins, Upper Town* ☎ *418/692–2193* 🎟 *Free* ⏲ *Mid-May–June,* *daily 9–6; July and Aug., daily 9–8; Sept.–mid-Oct., weekdays 10–4; mid Oct.–mid-May, services only; morning services year-round in English daily at 8:30, and Sun. also at 11 AM, in French at 9:30 AM.*

4 Fodor'sChoice ★ **Jardin des Gouverneurs** (Governors' Park). In this small park just south of the Château Frontenac stands the **Wolfe-Montcalm Monument,** a 50-foot-tall obelisk that is unique because it pays tribute to both a winning (English) and a losing (French) general. The monument recalls the 1759 battle on the Plains of Abraham, which ended French rule here. British general James Wolfe lived only long enough to hear of his victory; French general Louis-Joseph Montcalm died shortly after Wolfe with the knowledge that the city was lost. On the south side of the park is **avenue Ste-Geneviève,** lined with well-preserved Victorian houses dating from 1850 to 1900. Several have been converted to inns.

3

★ 9 **Parc de l'Artillerie** (Artillery Park). This national historic park includes four buildings—all that remains of several structures situated to guard the St. Charles River and the Old Port. The oldest buildings, dating to the early 1700s, served as headquarters for the French garrison. When they were overtaken by the British in 1759, they were used as barracks for British troops—30 years earlier than the first barracks used in England. In 1765, the Royal Artillery Regiment was stationed here, giving the fortress its name. From 1882 until 1964 the area served as an industrial complex, providing ammunition for the Canadian army. The **Dauphin Redoubt,** was constructed from 1712 to 1748. It served as a barracks for the French and then the English garrisons until 1784–85, when it became an officers' mess for the Royal Artillery Regiment. The **Officers' Quarters,** a dwelling for Royal Artillery officers until the British army's departure in 1871, illustrates military family life during the British regime. In July and August you may be able to sample bread baked in the outdoor oven and, in the afternoon, watch a French soldier reenactor demonstrate shooting with a flintlock musket. **Les Dames de Soie** (The Ladies of Silk; ☎ 418/692–1516 ⏲ Mon.–Sat. 11–5 and Sun. noon–4 except from Jan. 1–15.), in a former cannon warehouse, allows you to watch porcelain dolls being made and view an exhibit on the history of dolls. You can bring your favorite doll or teddy bear to the doll hospital or take a workshop by appointment. ✉ *2 rue d'Auteuil, Upper Town* ☎ *418/648–4205* 🌐 *www.parkscanada.gc.ca* 🎫 *C$4* ⏲ *Apr., Wed.–Sun. 10–5; May–mid-Oct., daily 10–5.*

1 **Place d'Armes.** For centuries, this square atop a cliff has been used for parades and military events. Upper Town's most central location, the plaza is bordered by government buildings; at its west side stands the majestic **Ancien Palais de Justice** (Old Courthouse), a Renaissance-style building from 1887. The plaza is on land that was occupied by a church and convent of the Recollet missionaries (Franciscan monks), who in 1615 were the first order of priests to arrive in New

SAVVY IN THE CITY

Rue St-Jean becomes a pedestrian street for the summer at Place d'Youville—that means you'll have to leave your car behind at the public parking lot and walk.

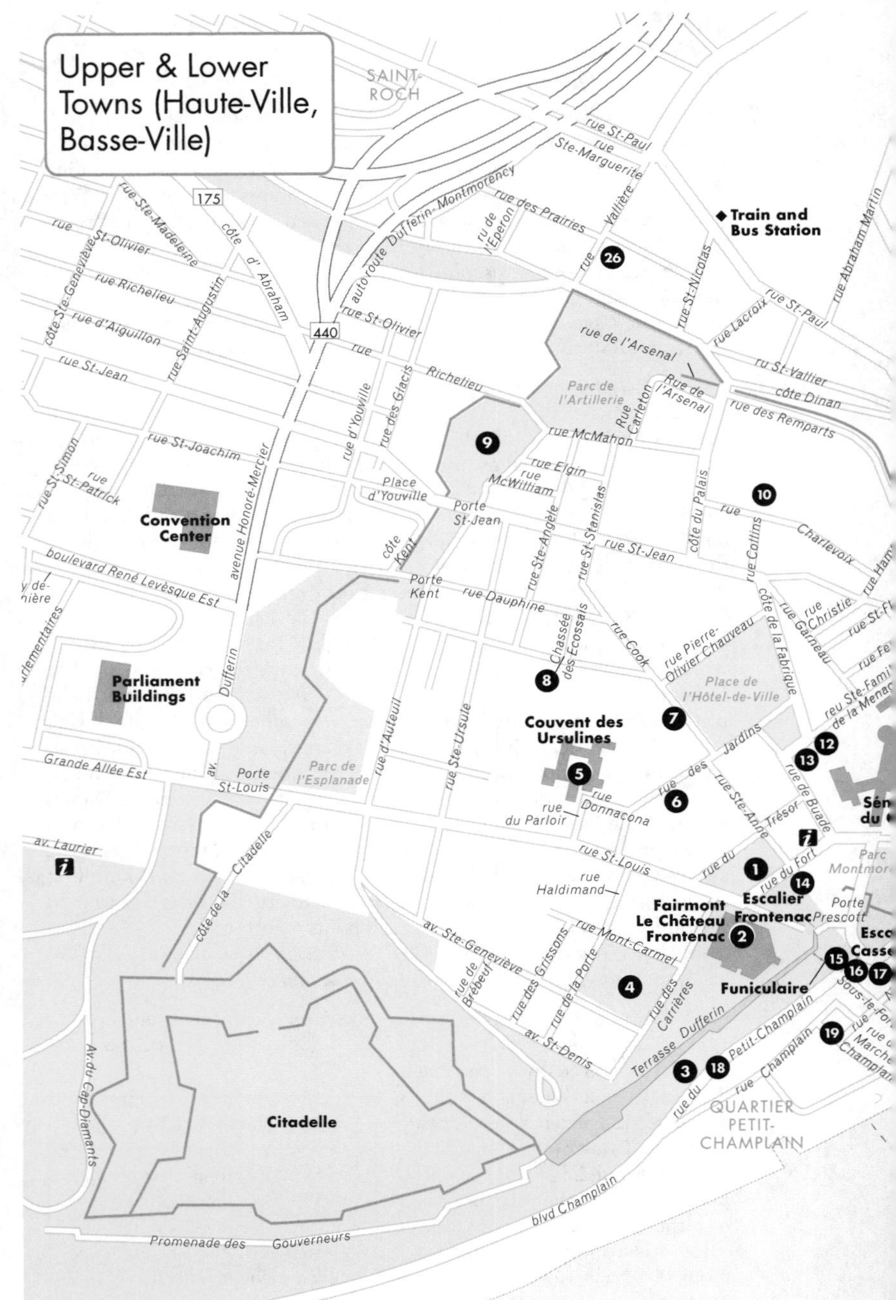
Upper & Lower Towns (Haute-Ville, Basse-Ville)
SAINT-ROCH
Train and Bus Station
Convention Center
Parliament Buildings
Couvent des Ursulines
Fairmont Le Château Frontenac
Escalier Frontenac
Funiculaire
Citadelle
QUARTIER PETIT-CHAMPLAIN
Parc de l'Artillerie
Place de l'Hôtel-de-Ville
Parc de l'Esplanade
Porte St-Louis
Porte St-Jean
Porte Kent
Porte Prescott
Place d'Youville
rue St-Paul
rue Ste-Marguerite
autoroute Dufferin-Montmorency
rue des Prairies
rue St-Jean
rue St-Louis
Grande Allée Est
boulevard René Levèsque Est
avenue Honoré-Mercier
Terrasse Dufferin
Promenade des Gouverneurs
blvd Champlain
Av. du Cap-Diamants
rue St-Olivier
rue Richelieu
rue d'Aiguillon
côte d'Abraham
rue de l'Arsenal
rue McMahon
rue Dauphine
rue Donnacona
rue du Parloir
rue du Trésor
rue Ste-Anne
rue des Jardins
côte de la Fabrique
rue de Buade
rue du Fort
rue Mont-Carmel
av. Ste-Geneviève
av. St-Denis
rue du Petit-Champlain
rue Champlain
côte de la Citadelle
rue d'Auteuil
rue Ste-Ursule
côte du Palais
rue Charlevoix
rue Collins
rue Cook
175
440
1
2
3
4
5
6
7
8
9
10
12
13
14
15
16
17
18
19
26

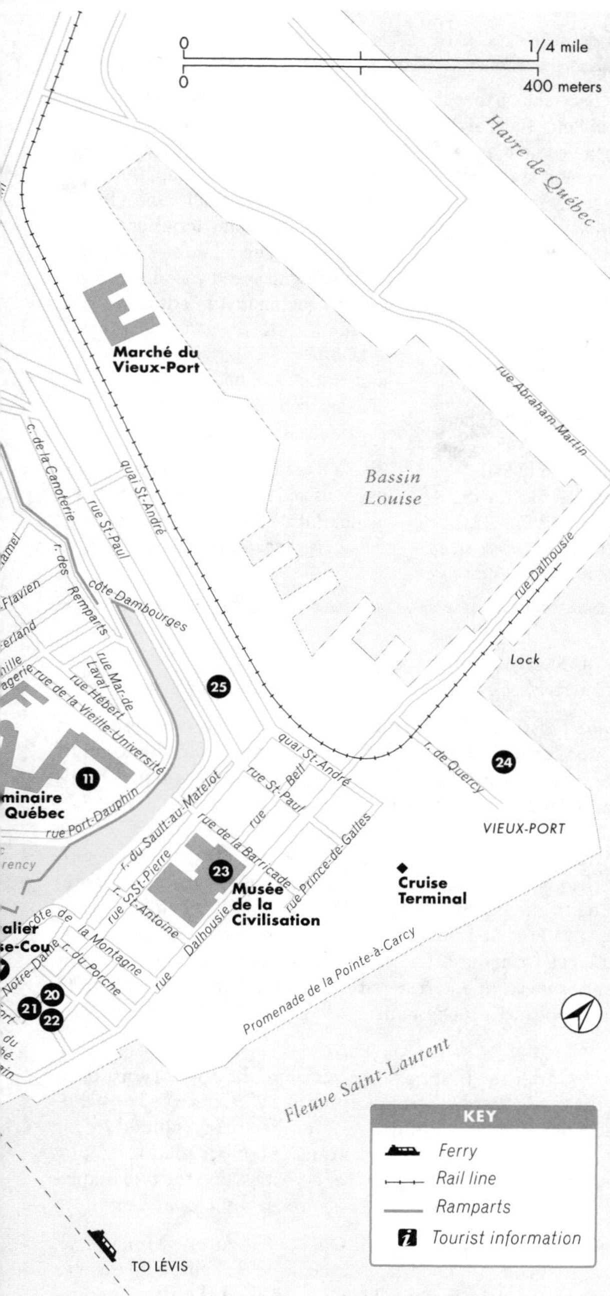

0
1/4 mile
0
400 meters
Havre de Québec
Marché du Vieux-Port
Bassin Louise
rue Abraham-Martin
quai St-André
rue St-Paul
c. de la Canoterie
r. des Remparts
côte Dambourges
rue Dalhousie
Lock
rue Mar-de Laval
rue Hébert
rue de la Vieille-Université
rue Port-Dauphin
r. de Quercy
VIEUX-PORT
rue Bell
rue St-Paul
r. du Sault-au-Matelot
rue de la Barricade
rue Prince-de-Galles
r. St-Pierre
r. St-Antoine
Musée de la Civilisation
Cruise Terminal
côte de la Montagne
r. du Porche
Notre-Dame
rue Dalhousie
Promenade de la Pointe-à-Carcy
Fleuve Saint-Laurent
TO LÉVIS
KEY
Ferry
Rail line
Ramparts
Tourist information

CLOSE UP

Crêpes: A Moveable Feast

CRÊPES—those delectable, paper-thin pancakes made of flour, eggs, and milk or cream—can be found on menus everywhere. But in Québec City, you can order a crêpe in French and know that what you're holding has been part of French gastronomy for centuries.

You'll want to plan your crêpe tour carefully. These little folded up packages of sweet or savory goodness are quite rich, and so it's not advisable to mix crêpes in the same meal. Your first crêpe of the day can be from the commercial but still yummy **Chez Cora** (✉ 545 rue de l'Église, St-Roch ☎ 418/524-3232), which stays open until 3 PM, so sleep in late and make it brunch. After three hours or so, you'll be ready for a salad and a decadent fruit or ice cream-filled crêpe for dessert at **Casse-Crêpe Breton** (✉ 1136 rue St-Jean, Upper Town ☎ 418/692-0438). Expect to wait in line—even the locals do! Skip the funicular and hit those steps while sightseeing to speed your digestions before heading to **Au Petit Coin Breton** (✉ 1029 St-Jean, Upper Town ☎ 418/694-0758). Here, you'll find more traditional gourmet crêpes, filled with seafood, wild boar, ham, or asparagus with béchamel sauce.

Take a deep breath—but not too deep—as you reminisce about all the wonderful crêpes you encountered today. Hemingway would be proud.

France. The Gothic-style **fountain** at the center of Place d'Armes pays tribute to their arrival. ✉ *Rues St-Louis and du Fort, Upper Town.*

3 **Terrasse Dufferin.** This wide boardwalk with an intricate wrought-iron guardrail has a panoramic view of the St. Lawrence River, the town of Lévis on the opposite shore, Île d'Orléans, and the Laurentian Mountains. It was named for Lord Dufferin, governor of Canada between 1872 and 1878, who had this walkway constructed in 1878. Dufferin Terrace is currently a dig site, scheduled to be completed by 2008, as archaeologists from Parks Canada work to uncover the remains of the château, which was home to the governors from 1626 to 1834, when it was destroyed by fire, and Fort St-Louis. There are 90-minute tours of the fortifications that leave from here. The **Promenade des Gouverneurs** begins at the boardwalk's western end; the path skirts the cliff and leads up to Québec's highest point, Cap Diamant, and also to the Citadelle.

Also Worth Seeing

7 **Edifice Price.** Styled after the Empire State Building, the 15-story, art deco structure was the city's first skyscraper. Built in 1929, it served as headquarters of the Price Brothers Company, a lumber firm founded by Sir William Price. Don't miss the interior: exquisite copper plaques depict scenes of the company's early pulp and paper activities, and the two maplewood elevators are '30s classics. ✉ *65 rue Ste-Anne, Upper Town.*

10 **Monastère des Augustines de l'Hôtel-Dieu de Québec** (Augustine Monastery). Augustine nuns arrived from Dieppe, France, in 1639 with a mission to care for the sick in the new colony. They established the first hospital

north of Mexico, the **Hôtel-Dieu,** the large building west of the monastery. Upon request the Augustines offer free guided tours of the 1800 **chapel** and the cellars used by the nuns as a shelter, beginning in 1695, during bombardments by the British. During World War II, the cellars hid national treasures that had been smuggled out of Poland for safekeeping. The monastery will likely begin long-awaited renovations in 2008. ✉ *32 rue Charlevoix, Upper Town* ☎ *418/692–2492 tours* 🎫 *Free* ⏲ *Tues.–Sat. 9:30–noon and 1:30–5, Sun. 1:30–5.*

8 **Morrin College.** This stately gray-stone building was Québec City's first prison under British rule, built between 1802 and 1813. Roughly 16 criminals were hanged publicly outside the building. Two cell blocks, with a half dozen cells in each, are still intact. Some are part of the new Morrin Centre, an English-language cultural center that opened in summer 2006.

When the jail closed in 1868, the building was converted into Morrin College, one of the city's first private schools, and the **Literary and Historical Society of Québec** moved in. Founded in 1824, this forerunner of Canada's National Archives still operates a public lending library and has a superb collection that includes some of the first books printed in North America. There are historical and cultural talks held in English, as well as tours of the building. ✉ *44 rue Chaussée des Ecossais, Upper Town* ☎ *418/694–9147* 🌐 *www.morrin.org* 🎫 *Free; fee for building tours* ⏲ *Tues. noon–9, Wed.–Fri. noon–4, Sat. 10–4, Sun. 1–4.*

12 **Musée de l'Amérique Française.** A former student residence of the Québec Seminary at Laval University houses this museum that focuses on the history of the French in North America. You can view about 20 of the museum's 400 landscape and still-life paintings, some from as early as the 15th century, along with French colonial money and scientific instruments. The attached former chapel is used for exhibits, conferences, and cultural activities. Don't miss the 26-minute film (English subtitles) about Francophones and the accompanying exhibit that details their journey across North America. ✉ *2 côte de la Fabrique, Upper Town* ☎ *418/692–2843* 🌐 *www.mcq.org* 🎫 *C$5, free Tues. Nov.–May* ⏲ *June 24–early Sept., daily 9:30–5; early Sept.–June 23, Tues.–Sun. 10–5.*

14 **Musée du Fort.** A sound-and-light show reenacts the area's important battles, including the Battle of the Plains of Abraham and the 1775 attack by American generals Arnold and Montgomery. Three permanent expositions on the history of New France—including weapons, uniforms, and military insignia—were recently added. In 2006, the model of the city—complete with ships, cannons, and soldiers lined up for battle—was cleaned and repainted to celebrate its 40th anniversary. A tribute to the museum's founder, Anthony Price, provides insight into this labor of love. ✉ *10 rue Ste-Anne, Upper Town* ☎ *418/692–1759* 🌐 *www.museedufort.com* 🎫 *C$7.50* ⏲ *Feb. and Mar., Thurs.–Sun. 11–4; Apr.–Oct., daily 10–5; Nov.–Jan., by appointment.*

11 **Séminaire du Québec.** Behind these gates lies a tranquil courtyard surrounded by austere stone buildings with rising steeples; these structures have housed classrooms and student residences since 1663. François de

Montmorency Laval, the first bishop of New France, founded Québec Seminary to train priests in the new colony. In 1852 the seminary became Université Laval, the first Catholic university in North America. In 1946 the university moved to a larger campus in suburban Ste-Foy. Today, priests live on the premises, and Laval's architecture school occupies part of the building. The on-site **Musée de l'Amérique Française** gives tours of the seminary grounds and the interior in summer. Tours start from the museum, located at 2 côte de la Fabrique. The small Second Empire–style **Chapelle Extérieure,** at the west entrance of the seminary, was built in 1888 after fire destroyed the 1750 original. Joseph-Ferdinand Peachy designed the chapel; its interior is patterned after that of the Église de la Trinité in Paris. ✉ *1 côte de la Fabrique, Upper Town* ☎ *418/692–3981* 🎫 *C$5* ⏲ *Tours weekends mid-June–early Sept.; call for tour times.*

LOWER TOWN

Lower Town is the new hot spot, its once-dilapidated warehouses now boutique hotels, trendy shops, chic art galleries, and popular restaurants and bars. It's home to a great diversity of cultural communities, from businessmen and women to hip youngsters sipping coffee or beer at cafés. After exploring Place Royale and its cobblestone streets, you can walk along the edge of the St. Lawrence River and watch the sailboats and ships go by, shop at the market, or kick back on a terrace with a Kir Royal. Rue Petit-Champlain also has charming places to stop and listen to street musicians. Take note, Lower Town can feel a bit more touristy at times than Upper Town.

In 1608 Champlain chose this narrow, U-shape spit of land as the site for his settlement. Champlain later abandoned the fortified *abitation* (residence) at the foot of Cap Diamant and relocated to the more easily defendable Upper Town.

Main Attractions

21 **Église Notre-Dame-des-Victoires** (Our Lady of Victory Church). The oldest church in Québec stands on the site of Samuel de Champlain's first residence, which also served as a fort and trading post. The church was built in 1688 and has been restored twice. Its name comes from two French victories against the British: one in 1690 against Admiral William Phipps and another in 1711 against Sir Hovendon Walker. The interior contains copies of paintings by European masters such as Van Dyck, Rubens, and Boyermans; its altar is shaped like a fort. A scale model suspended from the ceiling represents *Le Brezé,* the boat that transported French soldiers to New France in 1664. The side chapel is dedicated to Ste. Geneviève, the patron saint of Paris. ✉ *Pl. Royale, Lower Town* ☎ *418/692–1650* 🎫 *Free, C$2 for guided tours* ⏲ *Early May–late Oct., daily 9–5; late Oct.–early May, daily 10–4; closed to visitors during mass (Sun. at 10:30 and noon), marriages, and funerals.*

16 **Escalier Casse-Cou.** The steepness of the city's first iron stairway, an ambitious 1893 design by city architect and engineer Charles Baillairgé, is ample evidence of how it got its name: Breakneck Steps. The 170 steps

were built on the site of the original 17th-century stairway that linked the Upper Town and Lower Town. There are shops and restaurants at various levels.

19 **Maison Chevalier.** This old stone house was built in 1752 for shipowner Jean-Baptiste Chevalier. The house's classic French style is one rich aspect of the urban architecture of New France. The fire walls, chimneys, vaulted cellars, and original wood beams and stone fireplaces are noteworthy. ✉ *50 rue du Marché-Champlain, Lower Town* ☎ *418/643–2158* *Free* ⏲ *May–June 23, Tues.–Sun. 10–5; June 24–Oct. 21, daily 9:30–5; Oct. 22–Apr., weekends 10–5.*

15 **Maison Louis-Jolliet.** The first settlers of New France used this 1683 house as a base for further westward explorations. Today it's the lower station of the funicular. A monument commemorating French explorer Louis Jolliet's 1672 discovery of the Mississippi River stands in the park next to the house. The ⇨ **Escalier Casse-Cou** is at the north side of the house. ✉ *16 rue du Petit-Champlain, Lower Town.*

NEED A BREAK?

Beer has been brewed in Québec since the early 1600s, and L'Inox (✉ 37 quai St-André, Lower Town ☎ 418/692–2877) carries on the tradition with a combination brewpub and museum. Cherry-red columns and a stainless-steel bar contrast with exposed stone and brick walls, blending the old with the new. A large, sunny terrace is open in summer. L'Inox serves many of its own beers, as well as other beverages, alcoholic and not. Food is limited to plates of Québec cheeses or European-style hot dogs served in baguettes. Tours of the brewery are available for groups of eight or more.

★ 23 **Musée de la Civilisation** (Museum of Civilization). Wedged between narrow streets at the foot of the cliff, this spacious museum with a striking limestone-and-glass facade was artfully designed by architect Moshe Safdie to blend into the landscape. Its campanile echoes the shape of the city's church steeples. Two excellent permanent exhibits at the museum examine Québec's history. People of Québec, Now and Then engagingly synthesizes 400 years of social and political history—including the role of the Catholic church and the rise of the separatist movement—with artifacts, time lines, original films and interviews, and news clips. It's a great introduction to the issues that face the province today. The Nous, les Premières Nations (Encounter with the First Nations) exhibit looks at the 11 aboriginal nations that inhabit Québec. Several of the shows, with their imaginative use of artwork, video screens, computers, and sound, appeal to both adults and children. ✉ *85 rue Dalhousie, Lower Town* ☎ *418/643–2158* 🌐 *www.mcq.org* *C$8, free Tues. Nov.–May* ⏲ *Late June–early Sept., daily 9:30–6:30; early Sept.–mid-June, Tues.–Sun. 10–5.*

OFF THE BEATEN PATH

QUÉBEC–LÉVIS FERRY – En route to the opposite shore of the St. Lawrence River on this ferry, you get a striking view of the Québec City skyline, with the Château Frontenac and the Québec Seminary high atop the cliff. The view is even more impressive at night. Ferries generally run every half hour from 6 AM until 6 PM, and then hourly until 2:20 AM; there are additional ferries from April through November. From late June to August you can combine a Québec–Lévis ferry ride with a bus tour of Lévis, getting off at such sights as the star-shape Fort No. 1, one of three built by the British between 1865 and 1872 to defend Québec. ✉ *Rue Dalhousie, 1 block south of pl. de Paris, Lower Town* ☎ *418/644–3704 or 877/787–7483* 🌐 *www.traversiers.gouv.qc.ca* 🎟 *June–Sept. C$2.50, Oct.–May C$2.60.*

20 **Place Royale.** Once the homes of wealthy merchants, houses with steep
Fodor's Choice ★ Normandy-style roofs, dormer windows, and chimneys encircle this cobblestone square. Until 1686 the area was called Place du Marché, but its name changed when a bust of Louis XIV was placed at its center. During the late 1600s and early 1700s, when Place Royale was continually under threat of British attack, the colonists moved progressively higher to safer quarters atop the cliff in Upper Town. After the French colony fell to British rule in 1759, Place Royale flourished again with shipbuilding, logging, fishing, and fur trading. The *Fresque des Québecois,* a 4,665-square-foot trompe-l'oeil mural depicting 400 years of Québec's history, is to the east of the square, at the corner of rue Notre-Dame and côte de la Montagne. An information center, the **Centre d'Interprétation de Place Royale** (✉ 27 rue Notre-Dame, Lower Town ☎ 418/646–3167) includes exhibits and a Discovery Hall with a replica of a 19th-century home, where children can try on period costumes. A clever multimedia presentation, good for kids, offers a brief history of Québec. Admission is C$4, but it's free on Tuesday from November to May. It's open daily 9:30–5 from June 24 to early September; the rest of the year it's open Tuesday–Sunday 10–5.

18 **Rue du Petit-Champlain.** The oldest street in the city was once the main street of a harbor village, with trading posts and the homes of rich merchants. Today it has pleasant boutiques and cafés, although on summer days the street is packed with tourists. Natural-fiber weaving, Inuit carvings, hand-painted silks, and enameled copper crafts are some of the local specialties that are good buys here.

NEED A BREAK?

For a respite from the shoppers on rue du Petit-Champlain, take a table outdoors at Bistrot Le Pape Georges (✉ 8 rue du Cul-de-Sac, Lower Town ☎ 418/692–1320 🌐 www.papegeorges.com) and cool off with a drink and creamy, tangy local cheeses and fruit. This stone-and-wood wine bar is also nice indoors; there's folk and chanson music from Thursday to Sunday nights.

17 **Verrerie La Mailloche.** The glassblowing techniques used in this workshop, boutique, and museum are as old as ancient Egypt, but the results are contemporary. In the workshop, master glassblower Jean Vallières and his assistants can answer your questions as they turn 1,092°C (2,000°F) molten glass into works of art. Examples of Vallières's work have been presented by the Canadian government to visiting dignitaries such as Queen Elizabeth and Ronald Reagan. ✉ *58 rue Sous-le-Fort, Lower Town* ☎ *418/694–0445* 🌐 *www.lamailloche.com* 🎟 *Free* ⏲ *Mid-June–mid-Oct., daily 9–10; Mid Oct.–mid-June daily 9:30–5:30.*

CLOSE UP

Don't Move My Cheese!

IT USED TO BE THAT ALL GOOD CHEESE in Québec City was imported from France—but not anymore. During the last several years, there's been a cheese movement, and regional cheese makers have begun producing award-winning aged cheddar and *lait cru* (unpasteurized) cheeses that you won't want to go home without sampling.

Luckily, there are enough cheese shops to keep you cheese-shop-hopping all afternoon. Stop by the **Épicerie Européenne** (✉ 560 rue St-Jean ☎ 418/529-4847) in the St-Jean-Baptiste quarter to try some of the lait cru that everyone is raving about. Along the same street, wander through **Épicerie J. A. Moisan** (✉ 699 rue St-Jean ☎ 418/522-0685), another well-known, well-stocked market, or visit **Aux Petits Délices** (✉ 1191 av. Cartier ☎ 418/522-5154) in the market at Les Halles du Petit Quartier for a large selection of specialty cheeses, along with fruit, breads, crackers, and wine for a picnic on the Plains.

Some good cheeses to watch out for at these shops and others include Bleu Bénédictin from the St-Benoît Abbey, the Île aux-Grues four-year-old cheddar, Portneuf Camembert or the same region's La Sauvagine, a 2006 top prize winner. There's also a chèvre noire, a raw, semifirm goat cheese by Fromagerie Tournevant—wrapped in black wax—that's not to be missed, and the fresh goat by La Biquetteriand. If Gouda is your thing, try a piece from Fromagerie Bergeron.

24 **Vieux-Port de Québec** (Old Port of Québec). If you're looking for nightlife, this is where to find it. But during the day, you can stroll along the riverside promenade, where merchant and cruise ships dock. The old harbor dates from the 17th century, when ships brought supplies and settlers to the new colony. At one time this port was among the busiest on the continent: between 1797 and 1897, Québec shipyards turned out more than 2,500 ships, many of which passed the 1,000-ton mark. At the port's northern end, where the St. Charles meets the St. Lawrence, a lock protects the marina in the Louise Basin from the generous Atlantic tides that reach even this far up the St. Lawrence. In the northwest section of the port, the **Old Port of Québec Interpretation Center** (✉ 100 quai St-André, Lower Town ☎ 418/648–3300) presents the history of the port in relation to the lumber trade and shipbuilding. The center is closed until 2008 to prep for special exhibits during Québec City's 400th anniversary celebrations. At the **Marché du Vieux-Port** (Old Port Market), at the port's northwestern tip, farmers sell fresh produce and cheese, as well as handicrafts. The market, near quai St-André, is open daily 9–5 in summer. Some stalls stay open daily in winter and the market is all dressed up for the Christmas season. Take a stroll through and taste some refreshing local produce, such as apples and berries.

Also Worth Seeing

25 **Antiques district.** Antiques shops cluster around rues St-Pierre and St-Paul. Rue St-Paul was once part of a business district packed with ware-

houses, stores, and businesses. After World War I, shipping and commercial activities plummeted; low rents attracted antiques dealers. Today numerous cafés, restaurants, and art galleries have made this area one of the town's more fashionable sections.

SAVVY IN THE CITY

Watch for the three-dimensional murals painted on walls in Lower Town. There are two spectacular ones in Place Royale. Stroll down Côte de la Montagne and look to your right as you round the final corner. The other one is at the end of Petit-Champlain. There are benches nearby if this is the end of a long walk.

26 **L'Îlot des Palais** (The Palace Block). More than 300 years of history are laid bare at this archaeological museum on the site of the first two palaces of New France's colonial administrative officials. The first palace, built as a brewery by Jean Talon in 1669, was turned into a residence in 1685 and destroyed by fire in 1713. In 1716 a second palace was built facing the first. It was later turned into a modern brewery, but the basement vaults that remain house an archaeology exhibit and a multimedia display. ✉ *8 rue Vallière, Lower Town* ☎ *418/691–6092* *C$3* *June 24–early Sept., daily 10–5.*

22 **Place de Paris.** An often-ridiculed black-and-white geometric sculpture, *Dialogue avec l'Histoire* (*Dialogue with History*) dominates this square. A 1987 gift from France, the sculpture is on the site where the first French settlers landed. ✉ *Rue Dalhousie, Lower Town.*

THE FORTIFICATIONS

Declared a Canadian historical monument in 1957, the 4½-km-long (3-mi-long) wall is the heart of a defensive belt that circles the Old City. The wall began as a series of earthworks and wooden palisades built by French military engineers to protect the Upper Town from an inland attack following the siege of the city by Admiral Phipps in 1690. Two of the city's three sides have the natural protection of the 295-foot-high facade of Cap Diamant, so the cape itself was studded with cannon batteries overlooking the river.

Over the next century, the French expended much time, energy, and money to shore up and strengthen the city's fortifications. Dauphine Redoubt, built in 1712, it is the only one of 11 such buildings that remain, and is fully restored and open to the public. After the fall of New France, the British were equally concerned about strengthening the city's defenses. They built an earth-and-wood citadel atop Cap Diamant. During the Napoleonic Wars, they added four medieval-looking martello towers to the fortifications. Of the three that remain, two are open to the public. The British also slowly replaced the wooden palisades that surrounded the city with a massive cut-stone wall. Other buildings, added later, include the Officers' Quarters (1818) and an iron foundry. Both have been restored and are open to the public.

The crowning touch came after the War of 1812, with the construction of the cut-stone, star-shape citadel. An irregular pentagon with two cannon-lined sides facing the river below, the structure earned Québec City its 19th-century nickname "North America's Gibraltar." When the citadel was finished, the city's fortifications took up one-quarter of the entire city's surface. American naturalist Henry David Thoreau was so struck with the fortress atmosphere of Québec City during a visit in 1850 that he wrote, "A fortified town is like a man cased in the heavy armor of antiquity with a horse-load of broadswords and small arms slung to him, endeavouring to go about his business."

Main Attractions

2 **La Citadelle** (The Citadel). Built at the city's highest point, on Cap Diamant, the Citadel is the largest fortified base in North America still occupied by troops. The 25-building fortress was intended to protect the port, prevent the enemy from taking up a position on the Plains of Abraham, and provide a refuge in case of an attack. Having inherited incomplete fortifications, the British completed the Citadel to protect themselves against French retaliations. By the time the Citadel was finished in 1832, the attacks against Québec City had ended.

Fodor's Choice ★

Since 1920 the Citadel has served as a base for the Royal 22nd Regiment. Firearms, uniforms, and decorations from the 17th century are displayed in the **Royal 22nd Regiment Museum,** in the former powder magazine, built in 1750. If weather permits, you can watch the changing of the guard, a ceremony in which troops parade before the Citadel in red coats and black fur hats, and a band plays. The regiment's mascot, a well-behaved goat, also watches the activity. At times in summer, the governor general of Canada's home and workplace in the Citadel can be toured. ✉ *1 côte de la Citadelle, Upper Town* ☎ *418/694–2815* 🌐 *www.lacitadelle.qc.ca* 🎫 *C$8* ⏲ *Apr.–mid-May, daily 10–4; mid-May–June, daily 9–5; July–Labor Day, daily 9–6; early Sept.–end Sept., daily 9–4; Oct., daily 10–3; Nov.–Mar., groups only (reservations required). Changing of the guard June 24–Labor Day, daily at 10* AM. *Retreat ceremony July and Aug., Fri.–Sun. at 7* PM.

1 **Fortifications of Québec National Historic Site.** In the early 19th century, this was a clear space surrounded by a picket fence and poplar trees. What's here now is the **Poudrière de l'Esplanade** (✉ 100 rue St-Louis, Upper Town ☎ 418/648–7016 🌐 www.parkscanada.gc.ca 🎫 There's a C$3.50 charge to enter the site, which is open 10–5 daily from early May to early Oct.), the powder magazine (used to store gunpowder) that the British constructed in 1820, and an interpretation center with a multimedia video and a model depicting the evolution of the wall surrounding Vieux-Québec. The French began building ramparts along the city's cliffs as early as 1690 to protect themselves from British invaders. However, the colonists had trouble convincing the French government to take the threat of invasion seriously, and when the British invaded in 1759 the walls were still incomplete. The British, despite attacks by the Americans during the American Revolution and the War of 1812, took a century to finish them. From June 1 to early October, the park can also be the starting point for walking the city's 4½ km (3 mi) of walls. There are two guided tours (C$10 each); one starts at the interpretation center and the other begins at Terrasse Dufferin.

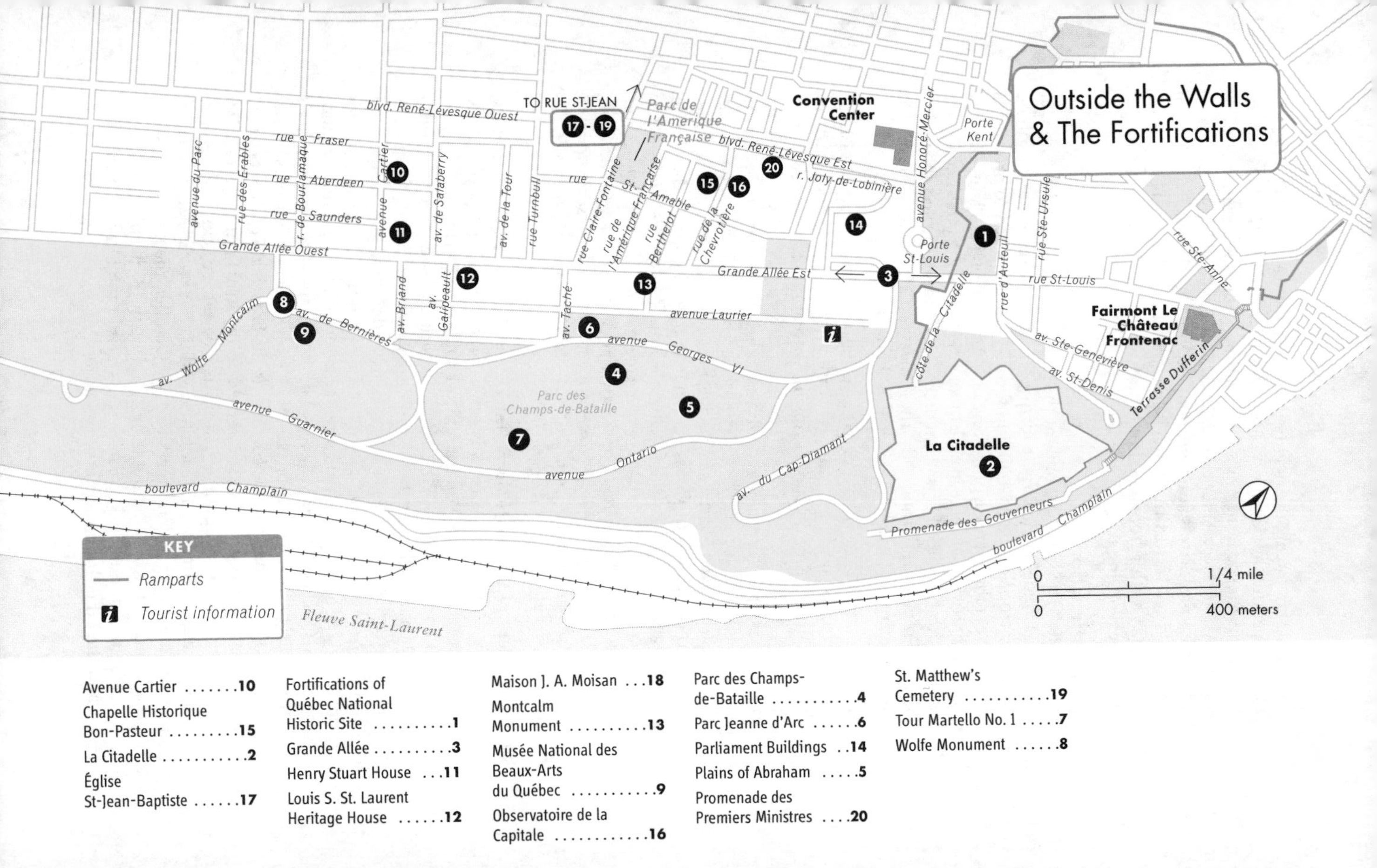
Outside the Walls
& The Fortifications
TO RUE ST-JEAN
17 - 19
Convention Center
Parc de l'Amerique Française
blvd. René-Lévesque Ouest
blvd. René-Lévesque Est
Porte Kent
Porte St-Louis
avenue Honoré-Mercier
r. Joly-de-Lobinière
rue Fraser
rue Aberdeen
rue Saunders
avenue du Parc
rue des Erables
r. de Bourlamaque
avenue Cartier
av. de Salaberry
av. de la Tour
rue Turnbull
rue Claire-Fontaine
rue de l'Amerique Française
rue St-Amable
rue Berthelot
rue de la Chevrotière
Grande Allée Ouest
Grande Allée Est
avenue Laurier
av. Briand
av. Galipeault
av. Taché
av. de Bernières
av. Wolfe Montcalm
avenue Georges VI
avenue Guarnier
avenue Ontario
av. du Cap-Diamant
Parc des Champs-de-Bataille
La Citadelle
côte de la Citadelle
rue d'Auteuil
rue Ste-Ursule
rue St-Louis
rue Ste-Anne
Fairmont Le Château Frontenac
av. Ste-Geneviève
av. St-Denis
Terrasse Dufferin
Promenade des Gouverneurs
boulevard Champlain
Fleuve Saint-Laurent
KEY
Ramparts
Tourist information
0
1/4 mile
0
400 meters
Avenue Cartier 10
Chapelle Historique Bon-Pasteur 15
La Citadelle 2
Église St-Jean-Baptiste 17
Fortifications of Québec National Historic Site 1
Grande Allée 3
Henry Stuart House ...11
Louis S. St. Laurent Heritage House 12
Maison J. A. Moisan ...18
Montcalm Monument 13
Musée National des Beaux-Arts du Québec 9
Observatoire de la Capitale 16
Parc des Champs-de-Bataille 4
Parc Jeanne d'Arc 6
Parliament Buildings ..14
Plains of Abraham 5
Promenade des Premiers Ministres 20
St. Matthew's Cemetery 19
Tour Martello No. 1 7
Wolfe Monument 8

12 **Louis S. St. Laurent Heritage House.** A costumed maid or chauffeur greets you when you visit this elegant Grande Allée house, the former home of Louis S. St. Laurent, prime minister of Canada from 1948 to 1957. Within the house, which is now part of the federally owned Plains of Abraham properties, period furnishings and multimedia touches tell St. Laurent's story and illustrate the lifestyle of upper-crust families in 1950s Québec City. ✉ *201 Grande Allée Est, Montcalm* ☎ *418/648–4071* 🎫 *C$10, including house, nearby martello tower, and minibus tour of Plains of Abraham* ⏲ *June 24–Labor Day, daily 1–5; early Sept.–June 23, group visits by reservation only.*

13 **Montcalm Monument.** France and Canada jointly erected this monument honoring Louis-Joseph Montcalm, the French general who gained his fame by winning four major battles in North America. His most famous battle, however, was the one he lost, when the British conquered New France on September 13, 1759. Montcalm was north of Québec City at Beauport when he learned that the British attack was imminent. He quickly assembled his troops to meet the enemy and was wounded in battle in the leg and stomach. Montcalm was carried into the walled city, where he died the next morning. The monument depicts the standing figure of Montcalm, with an angel over his shoulder. ✉ *Pl. Montcalm, Montcalm.*

★ 9 **Musée National des Beaux-Arts du Québec** (National Museum of Fine Arts of Québec). A neoclassical beaux arts showcase, the museum has more than 22,000 traditional and contemporary pieces of Québec art. The museum unveiled a major permanent exhibit, the Brousseau Inuit Art Collection, containing 150 objects from the past three centuries, in fall of 2006. That's only a small part of the 5,635 objects collected by Brousseau now in the collection. Portraits by Jean-Paul Riopelle (1923–2002), Jean-Paul Lemieux (1904–90), and Horatio Walker (1858–1938) are particularly notable as well. The museum's dignified building in Parc des Champs-de-Bataille was designed by Wilfrid Lacroix and erected in 1933 to commemorate the 300th anniversary of the founding of Québec. Incorporated within is part of an abandoned prison dating from 1867. A hallway of cells, with the iron bars and courtyard, has been preserved as part of a permanent exhibition on the prison's history. ✉ *1 av. Wolfe-Montcalm, Montcalm* ☎ *418/643–2150* 🌐 *www.mnba.qc.ca* 🎫 *Free, special exhibits C$12* ⏲ *Sept.–May, Tues. and Thurs.–Sun. 10–5, Wed. 10–9; June–Aug., Thurs.–Tues. 10–6, Wed. 10–9.*

4 **Parc des Champs-de-Bataille** (Battlefields Park). These 250 acres of gently rolling slopes have unparalleled views of the St. Lawrence River. Within the park and west of the Citadel are the Plains of Abraham.

Fodor'sChoice ★ 6 **Parc Jeanne d'Arc.** An equestrian statue of Joan of Arc is the focus of this park, which is bright with colorful flowers in summer. A symbol of military courage and of France itself, the statue stands in tribute to

WORD OF MOUTH

"I loved Québec City; very old world European feel." –AuntAnnie the heroes of 1759 near the place where New France was lost to the British. The park also commemorates the Canadian national anthem, "O Canada"; it was played here for the first time on June 24, 1880. ✉ *Avs. Laurier and Taché, Montcalm.*

5 Fodor's Choice ★ **Plains of Abraham.** This park, named after the river pilot Abraham Martin, is the site of the famous 1759 battle that decided New France's fate. People cross-country ski here in winter and in-line skate in summer. In summer a bus driven by a guide portraying Abraham Martin provides an entertaining tour—with commentary in French and English—around the park. At the **Discovery Pavilion of the Plains of Abraham** you can take in the multimedia display, Odyssey: A Journey Through History on the Plains of Abraham, which depicts 400 years of Canada's history. ✉ *Discovery Pavilion of the Plains of Abraham, 835 av. Wilfrid-Laurier, level 0 (next to Drill Hall), Montcalm* ☎ *418/648–4071 for Discovery Pavilion and bus-tour information* 🌐 *www.ccbn-nbc.gc.ca* *Discovery Pavilion C$8 for 1-day pass, bus tour included* ⏲ *Discovery Pavilion June 24–Labor Day, daily 8:30–5:30; Labor Day–June 23, weekdays 8:30–5, Sat. 9–5, Sun. 10–5.*

8 **Wolfe Monument.** This tall monument marks the place where the British general James Wolfe died in 1759. Wolfe landed his troops about 3 km (2 mi) from the city's walls; 4,500 English soldiers scaled the cliff and began fighting on the Plains of Abraham. Wolfe was mortally wounded in battle and was carried behind the lines to this spot. ✉ *Rue de Bernières and av. Wolfe-Montcalm, Montcalm.*

Also Worth Seeing

OFF THE BEATEN PATH

GROSSE ÎLE NATIONAL PARK – For thousands of immigrants from Europe in the 1800s, the first glimpse of North America was the hastily erected quarantine station at Grosse Île—Canada's equivalent of Ellis Island. During the time Grosse Île operated (1832–1937), 4.3 million immigrants passed through the port of Québec. For far too many passengers on plague-racked ships, particularly the Irish fleeing the potato famine, Grosse Île became a final resting place. Several buildings have been restored to tell the story of the tragic period of Irish immigration. It's necessary to take a boat tour or ferry to visit the park, and you should reserve in advance. **Croisières Le Coudrier** (☎ 888/600–5554 🌐 www.croisierescoudrier.qc.ca) has tours that depart from Québec City's Old Port, Lévis, Île d'Orléans, and Ste-Anne-de-Beaupré for Grosse Île. Tours cost C$59.99, which includes admission to the island. **Croisières Lachance** (☎ 888/476–7734 🌐 www.croisiereslachance.ca) runs a ferry that departs from Berthier-sur-Mer to Grosse Île for C$41, which includes admission to the island. From Québec City, head south on the Pont Pierre-Laporte (Pierre Laporte Bridge) and follow Autoroute 20 east for about an hour to Berthier-sur-Mer. Follow the signs to the marina. ☎ *418/234–8841 Parks Canada, 888/773–8888* 🌐 *www.pc.gc.ca* *C$41–C$59.99, including boat tour or ferry* ⏲ *May 15–Oct. 15, daily 9–6.*

11 **Henry Stuart House.** If you want to get a firsthand look at how the well-to-do English residents of Québec City lived in a bygone era, this is the place. Built in 1849 by the wife of wealthy businessman William Henry, the Regency-style cottage was bought in 1918 by the sisters Adèle and

Mary Stuart. Active in such philanthropic organizations as the Red Cross and the Historical and Literary Society, the sisters were pillars of Québec City's English-speaking community. They also maintained an English-style garden behind the house. Soon after Adèle's death in 1987 at the age of 98, the home was classified a historic site for its immaculate physical condition and the museum-like quality of its furnishings, almost all of them Victorian. Guided tours of the house and garden start on the hour and include a cup of tea. ✉ *82 Grande Allée Ouest, Montcalm* ☎ *418/647–4347* 🎫 *C$5* ⏲ *June 24–Labor Day, daily 11–4; day after Labor Day–June 23, Sun. 1–5.*

3

NEED A BREAK?

Halles Petit-Cartier (✉ 1191 av. Cartier, Montcalm ☎ 418/688–1635), a small but busy food and shopping mall just a few steps north of the Henry Stuart House on avenue Cartier, has restaurants and shops that sell flowers, cheeses, pastries, breads, vegetables, and candies. You'll find some excellent local cheeses, as well as a few Italian and other European specialties. Bite into a delicious submarine sandwich or sit and relax over coffee or tea and watch the world go by. Pick up a newspaper at one of the shops along the street and enjoy a long espresso. If you're looking for picnic snacks for a day trip the Plains of Abraham, plan to fill your basket here and then head up to the park.

7 **Tour Martello No. 1** (Martello Tower No. 1). Of the 16 martello towers in Canada, 4 were built in Québec City, because the British government feared an invasion after the American Revolution. Tour Martello No. 1, which exhibits the history of the four structures, was built between 1802 and 1810. **Tour Martello No. 2,** at avenues Taché and Laurier, hosts Council of War, a three-hour weekend mystery dinner show with a theme that draws on the War of 1812. Tour No. 3, which guarded westward entry to the city, was demolished in 1904. Tour No. 4, on rue Lavigueur overlooking the St. Charles River, is not open to the public. ✉ *South end of Parc Jeanne d'Arc, Montcalm* ☎ *418/648–4071 for information on towers or for Tour No. 2 mystery dinner show* 🎫 *C$10 for a day pass to tower and the Discovery Pavilion on the Plains of Abraham* ⏲ *Daily 10–5 PM.*

OUTSIDE THE WALLS

One of the city's trendiest neighborhoods is down the hill on rue St-Jean, with unique boutiques, snazzy restaurants, and historic churches to tour. St. Matthew's Cemetery is a fine place to sit under a beautiful old tree and enjoy a treat from one of the street's artisanal bakeries. There's also the newly trendy St-Roch, now the urban heart of Québec City. High-tech businesses share blocks with artists' studios, galleries, cafés, and boutiques. Avenue Cartier is the place to experience Québec City's nightlife; after dark, the bars, clubs, and pubs here are filled to the brim year-round.

But Québec City extends much farther than these neighborhoods. If you follow it, St-Jean turns into chemin Ste-Foy, which runs all the way out to Ste-Foy and Cap Rouge. Here, there are restaurants, leafy streets, and the Cinéma Le Clap, a great place to see a flick. Much farther out, you'll head down a steep hill, with a view, to Cap Rouge's landmarks—its trellis bridge and yacht club. Other major streets include René-Lévesque and boulevard Laurier, which takes you past the Université Laval campus and the three major shopping centers in Ste-Foy.

Boulevard Champlain runs from Lower Town all around the southern edge of Québec City, following the St. Lawrence River. It's a beautiful drive, day or night. Above are the cliffs that lead to the Plains of Abraham and farther on, you'll see the Sillery Coves. Any one of the steep hills will take you back toward the main roads that run east–west or the highways that cross north–south: Duplessis, the farthest west; Henri IV; Du Vallon; and Dufferin-Montmorency.

Main Attractions

⑩ **Avenue Cartier.** A mix of reasonably priced restaurants and bars, groceries and specialty food shops, hair salons, and similar stores, Cartier is a favorite lunchtime and after-work stop for many downtown office workers. After business hours, the street hums with locals running errands or soaking in sun (and beer) on patios. When darkness falls, the avenue's patrons get noticeably younger. The attraction? A half dozen nightclubs and pubs that offer everything from cigars and quiet conversation to Latin music and ear-splitting dance tunes.

⑮ **Chapelle Historique Bon-Pasteur** (Historic Chapel of the Good Shepherd). Charles Baillairgé designed this slender church with a steep sloping roof in 1868. Within the ornate baroque-style interior are carved-wood designs elaborately highlighted in gold leaf. The chapel houses 32 religious paintings created by the nuns of the community from 1868 to 1910. In addition to the regular weekday hours below, the chapel is also open Sunday between 10 and 1, before and after a musical artists' mass, which begins at 10:45; call ahead on weekdays if you want to visit during this time. ✉ *1080 rue de la Chevrotière, Montcalm* ☎ *418/522–6221* 🎟 *C$2 for a tour of the chapel; $C15 for classical, choral concerts* ⏲ *Weekdays 9–5; weekends by reservation only.*

★ ⑰ **Église St-Jean-Baptiste** (St. John the Baptist Church). Architect Joseph-Ferdinand Peachy's crowning glory, this church was inspired by the facade of the Église de la Trinité in Paris and rivals the Our Lady of Québec Basilica in beauty and size. The first church on the site, built in 1847, burned in the 1881 fire that destroyed much of the neighborhood. Seven varieties of Italian marble were used in the soaring columns, statues, and pulpit of the present church, which dates from 1884. Its 36 stained-glass windows consist of 30 sections each, and the organ, like the church, is classified as a historic monument. From October 1 to June 23 and outside regular opening hours, knock at the **presbytery** at 490 rue St-Jean to see the church. ✉ *410 rue St-Jean, St-Jean-Baptiste* ☎ *418/525–7188* ⏲ *June 24–Sept., weekdays 10–4:30, Sun. 9–4.*

③ **Grande Allée.** One of the city's oldest streets, Grande Allée was the route people took from outlying areas to sell their furs in town. In the 19th century, the wealthy built neo-Gothic and Queen Anne–style mansions here; they now house trendy cafés, clubs, and restaurants. The street actually has four names: inside the city walls it's rue St-Louis; outside

CLOSE UP

St-Roch: It's Only Just Begun

IF YOU WANT TO BE where it's at in Québec City, take a trip to the funky, former industrial area, St-Roch, bordered by the St-Charles River and the cliff, where artists first flocked about a decade ago and cafés, boutiques, galleries, restaurants, lofts, and condos followed.

St-Roch's epicenter is Parc St-Roch, with its elongated flower beds and benches around a modern square. Rue St-Joseph is a shopping hot spot with places to savor a pot of imported tea, and pick up a little something for the house at **Villa** (✉ 600 St-Joseph Est ☎ 418/524-2666) or **Baltazar** (✉ 461 rue St-Joseph ☎ 418/524-1991). For high-end shopping, there's **Hugo Boss** (✉ 505 rue St-Joseph Est ☎ 418/522-5444) as well as a flurry of smaller boutiques with the latest urban wear.

On boulevard Charest, there is a unique overpass, left over from the 1970s, that runs into the cliff. At its feet lives a modern sculpture garden, Îlot Fleurie, with stunning murals. Complexe Méduse is an avant-garde arts cooperative that houses multimedia artists, a community radio station, a café, galleries, artists-in-residence, and performance spaces.

St-Roch is also becoming known for its exquisite dining experiences, such as the luxurious **L'Utopie** (✉ 226½ rue St-Joseph Est ☎ 418/523-7878) within walking distance of a night on the town. After dinner, you can boogie down to a live DJ's picks at **Le Boudoir** (✉ 441 rue du Parvis ☎ 418/524-2777).

Any way you slice it, St-Roch is cutting edge.

3

the walls, Grande Allée; farther west, chemin St-Louis; and farther still, boulevard Laurier.

18 **Maison J. A. Moisan.** Founded in 1871 by Jean-Alfred Moisan, this store claims the title of the oldest grocery store in North America. The original display cases, woodwork, and tin ceilings preserve the old-time feel. The store's many products include difficult-to-find delicacies from other regions of Québec. You might want to try the maple syrup ale. ✉ *699 rue St-Jean, St-Jean-Baptiste* ☎ *418/522–0685* ⊕ *www.jamoisan.com* ⊙ *Daily 8:30 AM–9 PM.*

NEED A BREAK?

La Piazzeta (✉ 707 rue St-Jean, St-Jean-Baptiste ☎ 418/529-7489), with its delicious thin-crust square pizzas, is just one of the many good and affordable restaurants along the stretch of rue St-Jean near Maison J. A. Moisan.

16 **Observatoire de la Capitale.** This observation gallery is atop Edifice Marie-Guyart, Québec City's tallest office building. The gray, modern concrete tower, 31 stories tall, has by far the best view of the city and the surrounding area. ✉ *1037 rue de la Chevrotière, Montcalm* ☎ *418/644–9841* 🎫 *C$5* ⊙ *Late June–mid-Oct., daily 10–5; mid-Oct.–late June, Tues.–Sun. 10–5.*

★ 14 **Parliament Buildings.** Erected between 1877 and 1884, these structures are the seat of the Assemblée Nationale (National Assembly) of 125 provincial representatives. Québec architect Eugène-Étienne Taché designed the stately buildings in the late-17th-century Renaissance style of Louis XIV, with four wings set in a square around an interior court. On the front of the Parliament, statues pay tribute to important figures of Québec history: Cartier, Champlain, Frontenac, Wolfe, and Montcalm. A 30-minute tour (in English, French, or Spanish) takes in the President's Gallery, the Parlementaire restaurant, the Legislative Council Chamber, and the National Assembly Chamber. Tours may be restricted during legislative sessions. ✉ *Av. Honoré-Mercier and Grande Allée, Door 3, Montcalm* ☎ *418/643–7239* 🌐 *www.assnat.qc.ca* 🎫 *Free* ⏲ *Guided tours weekdays 9–4:30; late June–early Sept. also open for tours weekends 10–4:30.*

SAVVY IN THE CITY

Nothing is ever very far in Québec City. But a day pass for the city bus might come in handy for the return trip to the hotel. Avenue Cartier, with its shops and tempting restaurants, is a great walk from inside the walls, but you might want to be able to grab the Métrobus for $C2.50 if the weather turns.

20 **Promenade des Premiers Ministres.** This walk has a series of panels that tell the story (in French) of the premiers who have led the province and their contributions to its development. Because of strong winds, the panels are taken down (usually November–February) in winter. ✉ *Parallel to blvd. René-Lévesque Est between rue de la Chevrotière and the Parliament Buildings, Montcalm.*

19 **St. Matthew's Cemetery.** The burial place of many of the earliest English settlers in Canada was established in 1771 and is the oldest cemetery remaining in Québec City. Also buried here is Robert Wood, the disavowed half brother of Queen Victoria. Closed in 1860, the cemetery has been turned into a park. Next door is **St. Matthew's Anglican Church,** now a public library. It has a book listing most of the original tombstone inscriptions, including those on tombstones removed to make way for the city's modern convention center. ✉ *755 rue St-Jean, St-Jean-Baptiste* ☎ *No phone.*

Also Worth Seeing

OFF THE BEATEN PATH

ICE HOTEL – At this hotel—the first of its kind in North America—constructed completely of ice and snow, you can tour the art galleries of ice sculptures, get married in the chapel, lounge in the hot tub, have a drink at the bar made of ice, dance in the ice club, then nestle into a bed lined with deerskin. The hotel is open from mid-January to March 31. A night's stay, a four-course supper, breakfast, and a welcome cocktail cost around C$250 per person. ✉ *Duchesnay Ecotourism Station, 143 Rte. Duchesnay, Ste-Catherine-de-Jacques-Cartier, about 20 mins west of Québec City* ☎ *418/875–4522 or 877/505–0423* 🌐 *www.icehotel-canada.com.*

Parc Aquarium du Québec. Like the zoo, which has since closed its doors, Québec City's aquarium reopened in 2003 after a great deal of work. Next to the Québec Bridge on the heights that overlook the St. Lawrence River and about 10 km (6 mi) from the city center, the 16-acre site contains 3,500 specimens drawn from as near as the river's estuary and as far as the Arctic. The aquarium's centerpiece is a massive three-level aquatic gallery of fresh- and saltwater animals and plants. It is the only aquarium in North America with examples of all five species of cold-water seals. Other mammals on display include polar bears and a walrus. ✉ *1675 av. des Hôtels, Ste-Foy* ☎ *418/659–5264* 🌐 *www.parcaquarium.ca* *C$15.50* ⏲ *Daily 10–5.*

WHERE TO EAT

Most restaurants here have a selection of dishes available à la carte, but more creative specialties are often found on the table d'hôte, a two- to four-course meal chosen daily by the chef. This can also be an economical way to order a full meal. At dinner many restaurants will offer a *menu dégustation* (tasting menu), a five- to seven-course dinner of the chef's finest creations. In French-speaking Québec City, an *entrée,* as the name suggests, is an entry into a meal, or an appetizer. It is followed by a *plat principal,* the main dish. Lunch generally costs about 30% less than dinner, and many of the same dishes are available. Lunch is usually served 11:30 to 2:30, dinner 6:30 until about 11. Tip at least 15% of the bill.

Reservations are necessary for most restaurants during peak season, May through September, as well as on holidays and during Winter Carnival, in January and/or February. In summer, do as the locals do and dine outdoors. Every café and restaurant on the Grande Allée or elsewhere sets up tables outside if it can.

Québec City restaurants and bars, along with any public buildings, became smoke-free in June 2006. Some may have protected smoking sections, but chances are that folks looking to light up may have to do so outdoors.

WHAT IT COSTS In Canadian dollars

	$$$$	$$$	$$	$	¢
AT DINNER	over C$30	C$21–C$30	C$13–C$20	C$8–C$12	under C$8

Prices are per person for a main course.

Upper Town

Cafés

¢–$ ✕ **Brulerie Tatum.** Piles of coffee beans and an old coffee grinder in the window signal this lively café's specialty, and the smell of coffee roasting permeates the brightly colored main floor and mezzanine. The Brulerie is a favorite with students and shoppers, who come for their daily fix as well as for soup, sandwiches, salads, and desserts. It's also popular at breakfast for its omelets, crêpes, and such dishes as egg in phyllo pastry with hollandaise sauce and potatoes and fruit. About 40 different types each of coffee and tea are sold here. ✉ *1084 rue St-Jean, Upper Town* ☎ *418/692–3900* 💳 *AE, D, MC, V.*

¢–$ ✕ **Café-Boulangerie Paillard.** Owned by Yves Simard and his partner Rebecca, originally from Michigan, Wisconsin, this bakery beckons you inside with its selection of Viennese pastries and gelato. For a quick, inexpensive bite, there's soup, sandwiches, and pizza. The decor is simple and comfortable. There might be a line while the locals buy their lunch, but it's well worth the wait. ✉ *1097 rue St-Jean, Upper Town* ☎ *418/692–1221* 🌐 *www.paillard.ca* 💳 *MC, V.*

★ ¢–$ ✕ **Casse-Crêpe Breton.** Crêpes in generous proportions are served in this busy café-style restaurant. From a menu of more than 20 fillings, pick your own chocolate or fruit combinations; design a larger meal with cheese, ham, and vegetables; or sip a bowl of Viennese coffee topped with whipped cream. Many tables surround four round griddles at which you watch your creations being made. Crêpes made with two to five fillings cost less than C$8. This place is popular with tourists and locals alike, and there can be lines to get in at peak hours and seasons. ✉ *1136 rue St-Jean, Upper Town* ☎ *418/692–0438* ✍ *Reservations not accepted* 💳 *MC, V.*

¢ ✕ **Le Temporel.** At this small, crowded, once-upon-a-time smoky café, city dwellers of all sorts—struggling writers, marginal musicians, street-smart bohemians, bureaucrats, businessmen, and busy moms and dads—enjoy the city's best coffee, not to mention its best *croque monsieurs* (open-face French-bread sandwiches with ham, tomato, and broiled cheese), chili, and soups. Good, modestly priced beer and wine are also served. Some patrons start their day here with croissants and coffee at 7 AM and are still here when the place closes at 1:30 AM (an hour later on Friday and Saturday). ✉ *25 rue Couillard, Upper Town* ☎ *418/694–1813* ✍ *Reservations not accepted* 💳 *V.*

Canadian

$$–$$$$ ✕ **Aux Anciens Canadiens.** This establishment is named for a 19th-century book by Philippe-Aubert de Gaspé, who once resided here. The house, dating from 1675, has servers in period costume and five dining rooms with different themes. For example, the *vaisselier* (dish room) is bright and cheerful, with colorful antique dishes and a fireplace. People come for the authentic French-Canadian cooking; hearty specialties include duck in a maple glaze, Lac St-Jean meat pie, and maple-syrup pie with fresh cream. Enjoy a triple treat of filet mignon—caribou, bison, and deer—served with a cognac pink pepper sauce, or wapiti with a mustard sauce. One of the best deals is a three-course meal for C$14.75, served from noon until 5:45. ✉ *34 rue St-Louis, Upper Town* ☎ *418/692–1627* ✍ *Reservations essential* 💳 *AE, DC, MC, V.*

Chinese

★ $–$$ ✕ **L'Elysée Mandarin.** A 19th-century home has been transformed into an elegant Chinese mandarin's garden where you can sip jasmine tea to the strains of soothing Asian music. Owner David Tsui uses rosewood and imported stones from China to emulate his native Yanchao, a city near Shanghai known for training great chefs. Among the restaurant's Szechuan specialties are beef fillets with orange flavoring and crispy chicken in ginger sauce. The crispy duck with five spices is delicious. ✉ *65 rue d'Auteuil, Upper Town* ☎ *418/692–0909* 💳 *AE, DC, MC, V.*

Continental

$$–$$$$ ✕ **Le Continental.** If Québec City had a dining hall of fame, Le Continental would be there among the best. Since 1956, the Sgobba family has been serving very good traditional dishes. House specialties include orange duckling and filet mignon, flambéed right at your table. Try the appetizer with foie gras, sweetbreads, scampi, and snow crab delicately served on a square glass plate. A staple for this place is the tender, velvety filet mignon "en boîte," flambéed in a cognac sauce at the table and then luxuriously covered in a gravy seasoned with mustard and sage. ✉ *26 rue St-Louis, Upper Town* ☎ *418/694–9995* ▭ *AE, D, DC, MC, V.*

French

$$$–$$$$ ✕ **Le Saint-Amour.** Light spills in through an airy atrium at one of the city's most romantic restaurants. The acclaimed chef and co-owner Jean-Luc Boulay entices diners with such creations as caribou steak grilled with a wild-berry and peppercorn sauce, and filet mignon with port wine and local blue cheese. Sauces are generally light, with no flour or butter. Desserts are inspired; try the white-chocolate flower bud accompanied by a maple cream cup, white-wine ice cream, and vanilla sauce. The C$95 menu has nine courses; the C$48 table d'hôte has five. More than 800 wines are available. ✉ *48 rue Ste-Ursule, Upper Town* ☎ *418/694–0667* 🌐 *www.saint-amour.com* ✍ *Reservations essential* ▭ *AE, DC, MC, V.*

$–$$$ ✕ **Les Frères de la Côte.** With its central location, Mediterranean influence, and reasonable prices, this busy bistro is a favorite among politicians and the journalists who cover them. The menu, inspired by the south of France, changes constantly, but osso buco and a tender leg of lamb are among the regular choices. If you sit near the back, you can watch the chefs at work. This kitchen is often among those open the latest. ✉ *1190 rue St-Jean, Upper Town* ☎ *418/692–5445* ▭ *AE, D, MC, V.*

Italian

$–$$$ ✕ **Portofino Bistro Italiano.** By joining two 18th-century houses, owner James Monti has created an Italian restaurant with a bistro flavor. The room is distinctive: burnt-sienna walls, soccer flags hanging from the ceiling, a wood pizza oven set behind a semicircular bar, and deep-blue tablecloths and chairs. Don't miss the thin-crust pizza and its accompaniment of oils flavored with pepper and oregano. The *pennini all'arrabbiata*—tubular pasta with a spicy tomato sauce—is also good. Save room for the homemade tiramisu. From 3 PM to 7 PM the restaurant serves a beer-and-pizza meal for less than C$11. Guillermo Saldana performs music to eat to each weeknight. ✉ *54 rue Couillard, Upper Town* ☎ *418/692–8888* 🌐 *www.portofino.qc.ca* ▭ *AE, D, DC, MC, V.*

Lower Town

Café

$–$$ ✕ **Le Cochon Dingue.** The café fare at this cheerful chain, whose name translates into the Crazy Pig, includes delicious mussels, *steak-frites* (steak with french fries), thick soups, and apple pie with maple cream. At the boulevard Champlain location, sidewalk tables and indoor dining rooms

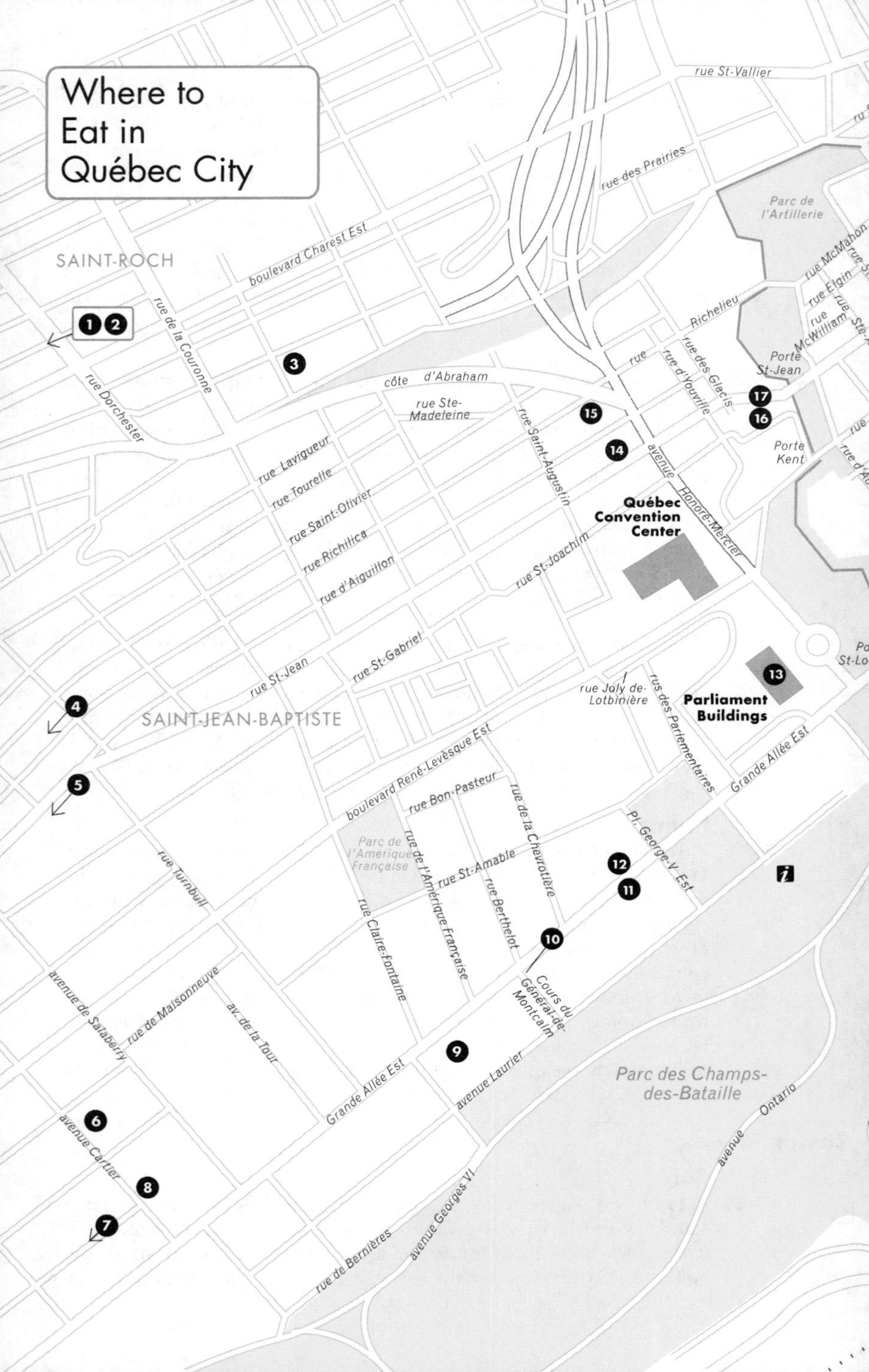
Where to Eat in Québec City
SAINT-ROCH
SAINT-JEAN-BAPTISTE
rue St-Vallier
rue des Prairies
Parc de l'Artillerie
boulevard Charest Est
rue de la Couronne
rue Dorchester
côte d'Abraham
rue Ste-Madeleine
rue Saint-Augustin
rue Lavigueur
rue Tourelle
rue Saint-Olivier
rue Richilica
rue d'Aiguillon
rue St-Joachim
rue St-Jean
rue St-Gabriel
Richelieu
rue
rue d'Youville
rue des Glacis
rue McMahon
rue Elgin
rue McWilliam
Porte St-Jean
Porte Kent
avenue Honoré-Mercier
Québec Convention Center
rue Joly de-Lotbinière
rus des Parlementaires
Parliament Buildings
Grande Allée Est
boulevard René-Levèsque Est
rue Bon-Pasteur
rue de la Chevrotière
Parc de l'Amérique Française
rue de l'Amérique-Française
rue St-Amable
rue Berthelot
rue Claire-Fontaine
Pl. George-V Est
Cours du Général-de-Montcalm
rue Turnbull
avenue de Salaberry
rue de Maisonneuve
av. de la Tour
avenue Laurier
Parc des Champs-des-Bataille
avenue Ontario
avenue Cartier
avenue Georges VI
rue de Bernières
1 2 3 4 5 6 7 8 9 10 11 12 13 14 15 16 17

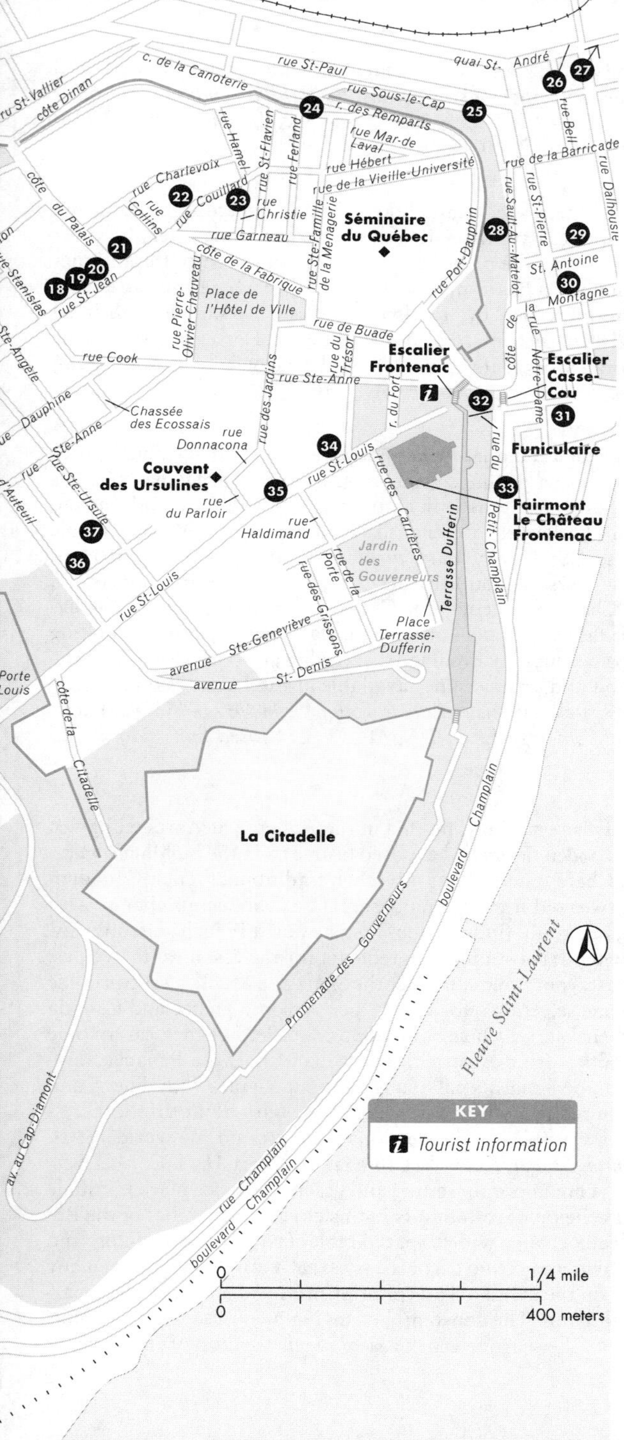

L'Astral . . . .
Aux Anciens Canadie
Brulerie Tatum . . . .
Le Buffet de L'Antiquaire . 25
Café Boulangerie Paillard 19
Le Café du Monde 27
Le Café Krieghoff 6
Casse-Crêpe Breton 20
Chez Cora 3
Chez Victor 5
La Closerie 11
Le Cochon Dingue 31, 33
Le Commensal 14
Le Continental 37
L'Échaudé 28
L'Elysée Mandarin 36
La Fenouillère 7
Les Frères de la Côte 21
Le Graffiti 8
L'Initiale 30
Largo 2
Laurie Raphaël 26
Louis Hébert 12
Le Marie Clarisse 32
Panache 29
Le Parlementaire 13
La Pointe des Amériques . . . 4, 16
Portofino Bistro Italiano 22
Ristorante Michelangelo 9
Le Saint-Amour 34
Il Teatro 17
Le Temporal 23
Le Toast! 24
Thang Long 15
L'Utopie .1

artfully blend the chic and the antique; black-and-white checkerboard floors contrast with ancient stone walls. ✉ *46 blvd. Champlain, Lower Town* ☎ *418/692–2013* ✉ *6 rue Cul-de-Sac, Lower Town* ☎ *418/694–0303* ▭ *AE, DC, MC, V.*

Canadian

¢–$ ✕ **Le Buffet de L'Antiquaire.** Hearty home cooking, generous portions, and rock-bottom prices have made this no-frills, diner-style eatery a Lower Town institution. As the name suggests, it's in the heart of the antiques district. In summer it has a small sidewalk terrace where you can sit and watch the shoppers stroll by. It's also a good place to sample traditional Québecois dishes such as *tourtière* (meat pie). Desserts, such as the triple-layer orange cake, are homemade and delicious. ✉ *95 rue St-Paul, Lower Town* ☎ *418/692–2661* ▭ *AE, MC, V.*

Contemporary

$$$–$$$$ Fodor'sChoice ★ ✕ **Laurie Raphaël Restaurant-Atelier-Boutique.** Local and regional products are at the heart of fine cuisine here. Among chef Daniel Vézina's creations are duck foie gras with cranberry juice and port, and smoked salmon from Charlevoix with English cucumbers, curry oil, and a maple glaze. There's a C$89 seven-course *menu dégustation,* with wines to complement each course available by the glass. If you're seeking adventure, opt for the Chef Chef menu—for C$56 a surprise meal will be delivered to your table. If that's not enough, sign up for a private cooking class, offered Wednesday evening or Saturday at noon. Don't miss the exclusive food and product lines available at the Laurie Raphaël boutique. ✉ *117 rue Dalhousie, Lower Town* ☎ *418/692–4555* 🌐 *www.laurieraphael.com* ▭ *AE, D, DC, MC, V* ⏲ *Closed Sun., Mon., and Jan. 1–15.*

French

$$$$ ✕ **Panache.** This restaurant, nestled in the Auberge St-Antoine, has an enchanting wooden floors and exposed beams from the building's warehouse days. Chef François Blais has taken traditional French-Canadian cuisine and tweaked it for the modern palate. The menus change with the seasons, but you'll find the duck, roasted on a French spit, any day. A family-owned farm supplies ingredients for the restaurant's recipes. For a true feast, your table can order the Signature Menu, a seven-course meal with wine selections, for C$149 per person. Québec and Canada wines top their list, which start at C$35 a bottle, but they carry some exclusive imports from Australia, France, and Italy. Le Panache sommelier Guillaume Simard's passion is discussing wines with diners, and he'll help you make a wise choice. For those who don't drink, there's an impressive water list with selections from around the world. ✉ *10 rue St-Antoine, Lower Town* ☎ *418/692–1022* ▭ *AE, DC, MC, V.*

$$$–$$$$ Fodor'sChoice ★ ✕ **L'Initiale.** A contemporary setting and gracious service place L'Initiale in the upper echelon of restaurants in this city; it's a member of the Relais & Châteaux group. Widely spaced tables favor intimate dining, and the warm brown-and-cream decor is cozy. Chef Yvan Lebrun roasts many of the meats on the menu over a spit: this produces a unique taste, particularly with lamb. The constantly changing menu follows the whims of the chef and the season. Try the *escalope de* (scallop of) foie gras or

the lamb. There's also a C$89 eight-course *menu dégustation*. For dessert, many small treats are arranged attractively on a single plate. ✉ *54 rue St-Pierre, Lower Town* ☎ *418/694–1818* ▭ *AE, DC, MC, V* ⊗ *Closed Sun. and early Jan.*

$$$–$$$$ ✕ **Le Toast!** Le Toast! is the talk of the town. This very chic, very intimate restaurant is in Le Priori hotel on Sault-au-Matelot. It's where time stands still. Visit the Web site for a peek at the inside, the menus, and the extensive wine list. Taste vegetable and red curry imperial rolls, and poached eggs with Sir Laurier cheese and ham, or goat cheese and salmon, on Sunday's brunch menu (available 10 AM–2 PM). Note that e-mail reservations take 48 hours to be processed. ✉ *17 rue Sault-au-Matelot, Lower Town* ☎ *418/692–1334* ⊕ *www.restauranttoast.com* ▭ *AE, DC, MC, V* ⊗ *No lunch weekends; no dinner Mon.*

3

$$–$$$$ ✕ **L'Echaudé.** A chic beige-and-green bistro, L'Echaudé attracts a mix of businesspeople and tourists because of its location between the financial and antiques districts. Lunch offerings include duck confit with french fries and fresh salad. Highlights of the three-course brunch are eggs Benedict and tantalizing desserts. The decor is modern, with hardwood floors, a mirrored wall, and a stainless-steel bar where you can dine atop a high stool. ✉ *73 Sault-au-Matelot, Lower Town* ☎ *418/692–1299* ▭ *AE, DC, MC, V* ⊗ *No Sun. brunch mid-Oct.–mid-May.*

$$$ ✕ **L'Utopie.** L'Utopie is a spacious spot for a meal. Sixteen-foot ceilings, a solid orange wall, beige and grey chairs, and tall, slim potted trees used as table dividers create a calm, modern atmosphere. Fine wines, with expert service, and highly creative cuisine complete the picture. There is an accent on all things French, with a Mediterranean influence, and owners Bruno Bernier and chef Stéphane Modat are not afraid to aim high. The creative master is famous for his popular "menu architecture," inspired by architect Pierre Bouvier, designer of this utopian space. This architectural meal, wines included, runs C$109. The specially mounted plates include an appetizer of coho smoked salmon, main dishes of lamb, foie gras, Roquefort panna cotta, and a parfait perfumed with maple syrup for dessert. L'Utopie serves lunch, 11 to 2 PM, and supper, 6 to 10 PM. ✉ *226½ rue St-Joseph Est, St-Roch* ☎ *418/523–7878* 🖷 *418/523–2349* ▭ *AE, DC, MC, V* ⊗ *Closed Mon. No lunch weekends.*

★ $$ ✕ **Le Café du Monde.** Next to the cruise terminal in the Old Port, this restaurant has a view to equal its food. The outdoor terrace in front overlooks the St. Lawrence River, while the side *verrière* (glass atrium) looks onto l'Agora amphitheater and the old stone Customs House. Etched-glass dividers, wicker chairs, and palm trees complement the Parisian-bistro-style menu, which includes such classics as duck confit accompanied by garlic-fried potatoes and appetizers such as artichoke pudding with smoked salmon. ✉ *84 rue Dalhousie, Lower Town* ☎ *418/692–4455* ✍ *Reservations essential* ▭ *AE, DC, MC, V.*

$$ ✕ **Largo.** Jazz is what you'll hear and jazzed is what you'll feel at this St-Roch restaurant. Owners Gino Ste-Marie and Paolo Putignaro, art connoisseurs, have combined passions to create a dynamic, evolving gallery and restaurant space that attracts a faithful local clientele. The art on the walls is for sale and the proceeds help to fund young local artists

through the Fondation Largo pour les Arts. The food is Mediterranean, Moroccan, Spanish. You'll find light, textured meals, omelets, salads, lamb, veal, and fresh sea fare. Specialties include a bouillabaisse Marseillaise "et sa rouille," and tartares. Once you take your seat in the evening, there's no rush to leave. Plan to shell out C$25 for the show, and get there an hour before it starts. Weekend brunch is hopping as well, and the place to see and be seen is on the custom-made red sofa. ✉ *643 rue St-Joseph Est, St-Roch* ☎ *418/529–3111* 🌐 *www.largorestoclub.com* ✍ *Reservations essential* 💳 *AE, MC, V.*

Seafood

$$–$$$$ ✕ **Le Marie Clarisse.** This restaurant at the bottom of Escalier Casse-Cou is known for unique seafood dishes, such as halibut with nuts and honey and scallops with port and paprika. A good game dish is usually on the menu—try the deer and beef duo with berries and sweet garlic. The menu du jour has a choice of about seven main courses; dinner includes soup, salad, dessert, and coffee. Wood-beam ceilings, stone walls, and a fireplace make this one of the coziest spots in town. ✉ *12 rue du Petit-Champlain, Lower Town* ☎ *418/692–0857* ✍ *Reservations essential* 💳 *AE, DC, MC, V* ⊗ *No lunch weekends Oct.–Apr.*

Outside the Walls

Café

¢–$ ✕ **Le Café Krieghoff.** Modeled after a typical Paris bistro café and named for a Canadian painter who lived just up the street (and whose prints hang on the walls), this busy, noisy restaurant with patios in front and back is a popular place with the locals. Open every day from 7 AM to midnight, Krieghoff serves specialties that include croissants, "la Toulouse" (big French sausage with sauerkraut), steak with french fries, spinach pie, *boudin* (pig-blood sausage), and "la Bavette" (a French-style minute steak). This place is a big local literary hangout, with great coffee, tea, and desserts. ✉ *1089 rue Cartier, Montcalm* ☎ *418/522–3711* 💳 *DC, MC, V.*

Contemporary

$$–$$$$ ✕ **L'Astral.** A spectacular view of Québec City is the chief attraction at this revolving restaurant atop the Hôtel Loews Le Concorde. Chef Jean-Claude Crouzet makes use of local products—fillet of pork from the Beauce region, in soy and orange sauce with pearl barley, braised-celeriac stew, and fried leeks, for example, or Barbarie duck with honey and Szechuan pepper, turnip confit, and red cabbage with apples. L'Astral offers a three-course table d'hôte and a C$40 nightly buffet but no à la carte menu. ✉ *1225 Cours du Général-de Montcalm, Montcalm* ☎ *418/647–2222* 💳 *AE, D, DC, MC, V.*

★ $–$$ ✕ **Le Parlementaire.** Despite its magnificent beaux arts interior and its reasonable prices, the National Assembly's restaurant remains one of the best-kept secrets in town. Chef Réal Therrien prepares contemporary cuisine with products from Québec's various regions. In summer, for example, the three-course lunch menu includes everything from mini-fondues made with Charlevoix cheese to ravioli made from lobster caught in the Gaspé. Other dishes might include pork from the Beauce region, trout from the Magdalen Islands, and candied-duck salad. The restaurant's typical hours are 8–11 for breakfast and 11:30–2 for lunch. Opening hours may change when the National Assembly is in session in fall and spring, and the restaurant sometimes opens for supper during late-evening debates. Call ahead. ✉ *Av. Honoré-Mercier and Grande Allée Est, Door 3, Montcalm* ☎ *418/643–6640* ▭ *AE, MC, V* ⊙ *Closed weekends June 24–Labor Day; closed Sat.–Mon. Labor Day–June 23. Usually no dinner.*

3

Eclectic

¢–$ ✕ **Chez Cora.** Spectacular breakfasts with mounds of fresh fruit are the specialty at this sunny chain restaurant. Whimsy is everywhere, from the plastic chicken decorations to the inventive dishes, often named after customers and family members who inspired them. Try the Eggs Ben et Dictine, which has smoked salmon, or the Gargantua—two eggs, sausage, ham, pancakes, *cretons* (pâtés), and baked beans. Kids love the Banana Surprise, a banana wrapped in a pancake with chocolate or peanut butter and honey. The restaurant also serves light lunch fare, such as salads and sandwiches. ✉ *545 rue de l'Église, St-Roch* ☎ *418/524–3232* ▭ *AE, DC, MC, V* ⊙ *No dinner.*

Fast Food

¢–$ ✕ **Chez Victor.** It's no ordinary burger joint: this cozy café with brick and stone walls attracts an arty crowd to rue St-Jean. Lettuce, tomatoes, onions, mushrooms, pickles, hot mustard, mayonnaise, and a choice of cheeses (mozzarella, Swiss, blue, goat, and cream) top the hearty burgers. French fries are served with a dollop of mayonnaise and poppy seeds. Salads, sandwiches, and a daily dessert are also available. ✉ *145 rue St-Jean, St-Jean-Baptiste* ☎ *418/529–7702* ▭ *MC, V.*

French

$$$ ✕ **Louis Hébert.** With its fine French cuisine and convenient location on the bustling Grande Allée, this restaurant has long been popular with many of Québec's top decision makers. Dining areas range from the very public summer terrace to discreet second-floor meeting rooms, a solarium with bamboo chairs, and a cozy dining room with exposed stone walls and warm wood accents. In winter, chef Hervé Toussaint's roast lamb in a nut crust with Stilton and port is a favorite. In summer, seafood dishes such as lobster and fresh pasta with a lobster sauce and asparagus are popular. ✉ *668 Grande Allée Est, Montcalm* ☎ *418/525–7812* ▭ *AE, D, DC, MC, V* ⊙ *No lunch weekends Oct.–Apr.*

$$–$$$ ✕ **La Closerie.** In 2003 acclaimed chef-owner Jacques LePluart returned from France to relaunch two restaurants, both named La Closerie, in the Hôtel Château Laurier. In the spacious, more elegant Grande Table dining room, rich sauces enhance such dishes as *magret de canard aux cerises séchées* (duck breast with dried-cherry sauce). A casserole of scallops and lobster roe comes with crunchy vegetables in rice vinegar. For dessert, try the delicious white-chocolate mille-feuille with fresh cherries. The kitchen also supplies the slightly less-expensive French bistro, serving dishes such as artichoke heart pizza and salmon filet. ✉ *1220 pl. Georges V Ouest, Montcalm* ☎ *418/523–9975* ▭ *AE, DC, MC, V.*

$$–$$$ ✕ **La Fenouillère.** Although this restaurant is connected to a standard chain hotel, inside there's an elegant, spacious dining room with a view of the Pierre Laporte Bridge. Chefs Yvon Godbout and Bernard St. Pierre serve a constantly rotating table d'hôte, going out of their way to use seasonal products. The house specialty is salmon, but veal and other fresh fish are staples, along with the occasional lamb dish. ✉ *Hotel Best Western Aristocrate, 3100 chemin St-Louis, Ste-Foy* ☎ *418/653–3886* ▭ *AE, DC, MC, V.*

$$–$$$ ✕ **Le Graffiti.** Housed in an upscale food mall, this French restaurant with tiny lights roped around the ceiling is a good alternative to Vieux-Québec dining. Large windows look out onto avenue Cartier. The seasonal menu lists such dishes as deer flank with oyster mushrooms in red wine sauce, and veal medallions with apples in a calvados sauce. The table d'hôte is priced between C$22.50 and C$35.50 per person. ✉ *1191 av. Cartier, Montcalm* ☎ *418/529–4949* ▭ *AE, DC, MC, V* ⏲ *No lunch Sat.*

Italian

★ **$$$–$$$$** ✕ **Ristorante Michelangelo.** Don't be put off by the funeral-home appearance of this first-class restaurant. One of only a handful of eateries outside Italy recognized as genuine Italian restaurants by the Italian government, Michelangelo's has a menu with many succulent meat, pasta, and seafood dishes. Among the house's specialties are *côte de veau* (veal cutlets), *escalopes de veau* (veal scallops), and homemade pasta. The restaurant also has the city's largest wine cellar, with some 18,000 bottles. There's also an impressive dessert table. ✉ *3111 chemin St-Louis, Ste-Foy* ☎ *418/651–6262* ▭ *AE, DC, MC, V* ⏲ *Closed Sun. No lunch Sat.*

$–$$$$ ✕ **Il Teatro.** Celebrities show up regularly at this upscale Italian restaurant just outside the St-Jean Gate. The person sitting at the next table may be singing on stage at the adjacent Capitole theater after dinner, or may be in town to promote his or her latest record, film, or play. The drama is enhanced by royal-blue curtains and cherry-red chairs. Pastas are made on-site. Try the spaghetti with scampi or the osso buco *d'agnello alle erbe* (braised lamb shanks with herbs). ✉ *972 rue St-Jean, Carré d'Youville* ☎ *418/694–9996* ✍ *Reservations essential* ▭ *AE, DC, MC, V.*

Pan-Asian

$–$$ ✕ **Thang Long.** Low prices and some of the best Asian food in the city ensure this restaurant's popularity. The simple menu of Vietnamese, Chinese, Thai, and Japanese dishes has a few surprises. *Chakis,* for example, is a tasty fried appetizer of four wrappers filled with shrimp, onions, and sugared potatoes. Thang Long doesn't serve any alcohol, but you can bring your own (SAQ, the government liquor store, is two blocks up the hill on rue St-Jean). Chinese lanterns and dark-blue walls and tablecloths decorate this tiny spot. ✉ *869 Côte d'Abraham, St-Jean-Baptiste* ☎ *418/524–0572* ✍ *Reservations essential* ▭ *MC, V* 🍷 *BYOB* ⏲ *No lunch weekends.*

Pizza

$–$$$ ✕ **La Pointe des Amériques.** Adventurous pizza lovers should explore the fare at this bistro. Some pizza combos (like alligator, smoked Gouda, Cajun sauce, and hot peppers) are strange. But don't worry—there are more than 27 different pizzas as well as meat and pasta dishes, soups, salads, and Southwestern cuisine. The original brick walls of the century-old building just outside the St-Jean Gate contrast boldly with modern mirrors and artsy wrought-iron lighting. Connected to the downtown restaurant is the Biloxi Bar, which has the same menu. ✉ *964 rue St-Jean, Carré d'Youville* ☎ *418/694–1199* ✉ *2815 blvd. Laurier, Ste-Foy* ☎ *418/658–2583* ▭ *AE, DC, MC, V.*

Vegetarian

$–$$ ✕ **Le Commensal.** At this upscale cafeteria, you serve yourself from an outstanding informal vegetarian buffet and then grab a table in the vast dining room, where brick walls and green plants add a touch of class. Plates are weighed to determine the price. Hot and cold dishes, all health conscious in some way, include stir-fry tofu and ratatouille with couscous. ✉ *860 rue St-Jean, St-Jean-Baptiste* ☎ *418/647–3733* ▭ *AE, DC, MC, V* *BYOB.*

3

WHERE TO STAY

More than 35 hotels are within Québec City's walls, and there is also an abundance of family-run bed-and-breakfasts. Landmark hotels are as prominent as the city's most historic sights; modern high-rises outside the ramparts have spectacular views of the Old City. Another choice is to immerse yourself in the city's historic charm by staying in an old-fashioned inn, where no two rooms are alike.

Be sure to make a reservation if you visit during peak season (May through September) or during the Winter Carnival, in January and/or February.

During especially busy times, hotel rates usually rise 30%. From November through April, many lodgings offer weekend discounts and other promotions.

Everyone is bidding to hold a conference in Québec City in 2008 during its 400th anniversary celebrations, so book as soon as possible. The 400th anniversary celebrations officially run from December 31, 2007, through to the end of October 2008.

WHAT IT COSTS In Canadian dollars

	$$$$	$$$	$$	$	¢
FOR 2 PEOPLE	over C$250	C$176–C$250	C$126–C$175	C$75–C$125	under C$75

Prices are for a standard double room in high season; they exclude 7.5% provincial sales tax, 6% goods-and-services tax (GST), and a C$2.30 city tax.

Upper Town

$$$$ **Fairmont Le Château Frontenac.** Towering above the St. Lawrence River, the Château Frontenac is a Québec City landmark. Its public rooms—from the intimate piano bar to the 700-seat ballroom reminiscent of the Hall of Mirrors at Versailles—are all opulent. Rooms are el-

Fodor's Choice ★

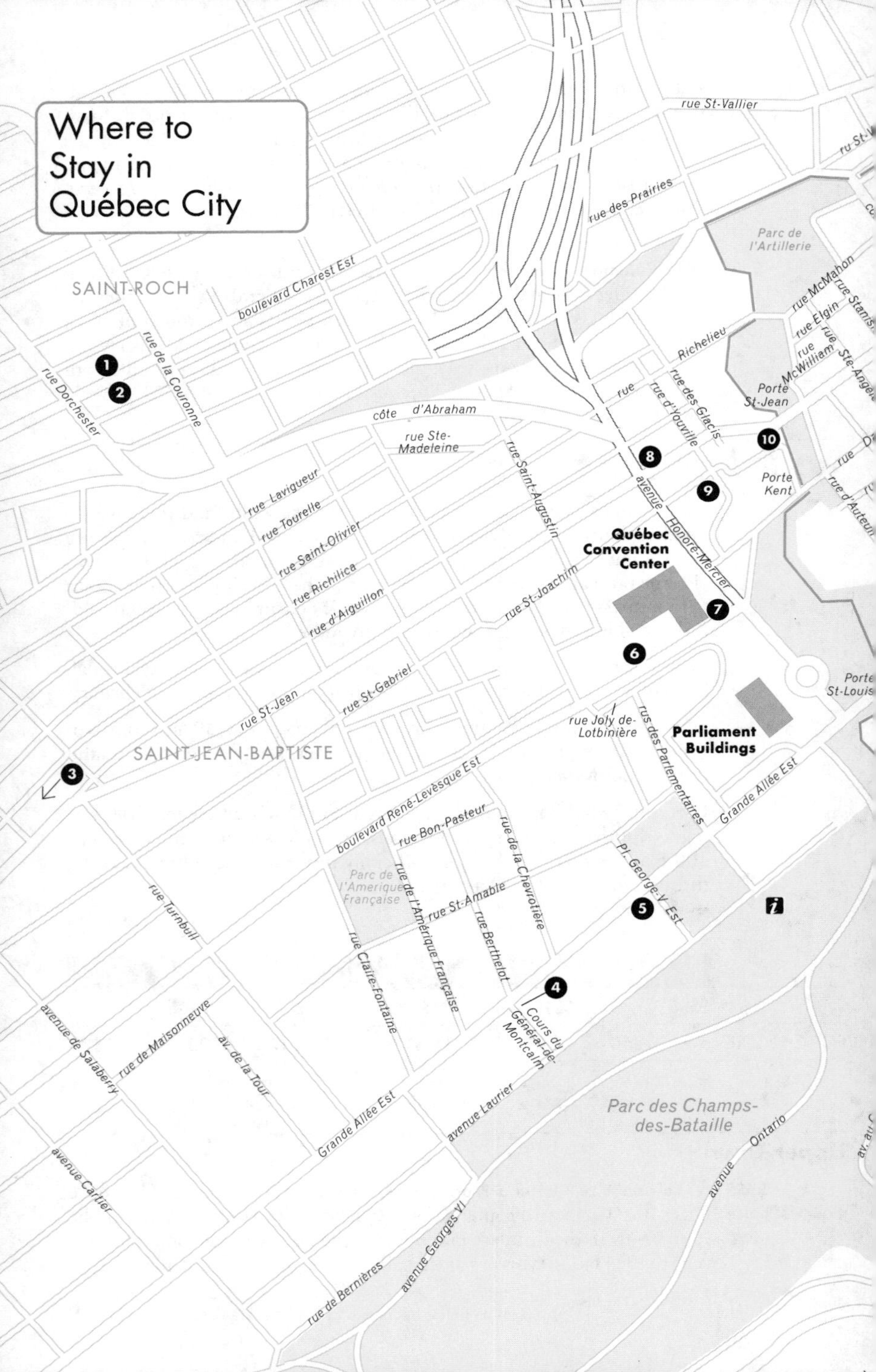

Where to Stay in Québec City
SAINT-ROCH
SAINT-JEAN-BAPTISTE
rue St-Vallier
rue des Prairies
boulevard Charest Est
rue de la Couronne
rue Dorchester
côte d'Abraham
rue Ste-Madeleine
rue Saint-Augustin
rue Lavigueur
rue Tourelle
rue Saint-Olivier
rue Richilica
rue d'Aiguillon
rue St-Joachim
rue St-Jean
rue St-Gabriel
rue Richelieu
rue des Glacis
rue d'Youville
avenue Honoré-Mercier
Québec Convention Center
Parliament Buildings
Parc de l'Artillerie
rue McMahon
rue Elgin
rue McWilliam
rue Ste-Angele
rue Stanislas
Porte St-Jean
Porte Kent
Porte St-Louis
rue d'Auteuil
rue Joly de-Lotbinière
rus des Parlementaires
boulevard René-Levesque Est
Grande Allée Est
rue Bon-Pasteur
rue de la Chevrotière
Pl. George-V Est
Parc de l'Amerique Française
rue de l'Amérique Française
rue St-Amable
rue Berthelot
rue Claire-Fontaine
rue Turnbull
Cours du Général-de-Montcalm
avenue de Salaberry
rue de Maisonneuve
av. de la Tour
avenue Laurier
Parc des Champs-des-Bataille
avenue Ontario
avenue Cartier
avenue Georges VI
rue de Bernières
1
2
3
4
5
6
7
8
9
10

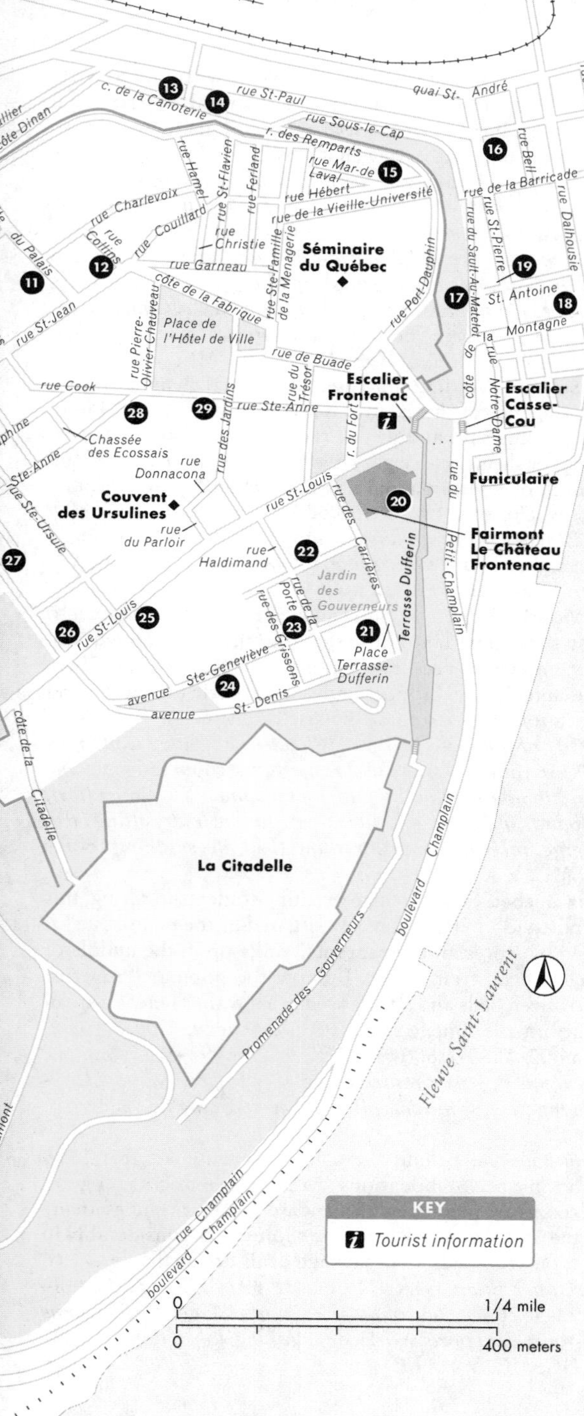

- Au Jardin du Gouverneur **22**
- Auberge St-Antoine **18**
- L'Autre Jardin Auberge **2**
- Château Bonne Entente **3**
- Courtyard by Marriot Québec **9**
- Fairmont Le Château Frontenac **20**
- Hilton Québec **7**
- Hôtel Belley **14**
- Hôtel Cap Diamant **24**
- Hôtel Château Bellevue **23**
- Hôtel Château Laurier **5**
- Hôtel Clarendon **29**
- Hôtel Delta Québec **6**
- Hôtel Dominion 1912 . . . .**16**
- L'Hôtel du Capitole **10**
- Hôtel Le Clos St-Louis **25**
- Hôtel Le Priori **17**
- Hôtel Le St-Paul **13**
- Hôtel Loews Le Concorde **4**
- Hôtel Manoir de l'Esplanade . . .**26**
- Hôtel Manoir des Remparts **15**
- Hôtel Manoir Victoria **11**
- Hôtel Marie Rollet **28**
- Hôtel Palace Royal **8**
- Hôtel 71 . . . .**19**
- Hôtel Royal William **1**
- Hôtel du Vieux Québec **12**
- Manoir d'Auteuil **27**
- Manoir Sur le Cap **21**

egantly furnished, but some are small; some have views of the river. At Le Champlain, classic French cuisine is served by waitstaff in traditional French costumes. This hotel is a tourist attraction in its own right, so the lobby can be quite busy. Reserve well in advance, especially for late June to mid-October. ✉ *1 rue des Carrières, Upper Town, G1R 4P5* ☎ *418/692–3861 or 800/441–1414* 🖷 *418/692–1751* 🌐 *www.fairmont.com* *585 rooms, 33 suites* *2 restaurants, snack bar, room service, some in-room hot tubs, minibars, cable TV with movies and video games, in-room broadband, indoor pool, wading pool, health club, hair salon, massage, piano bar, shops, babysitting, dry cleaning, laundry service, concierge, concierge floors, business services, convention center, parking (fee), some pets allowed* 💳 *AE, D, DC, MC, V* *EP.*

★ **$$$–$$$$** **Hôtel Le Clos St-Louis.** Winding staircases and crystal chandeliers add to the Victorian elegance of this central inn made up of two 1845-era houses. All of the rooms have antiques or reproductions; some have romantic four-poster or sleigh beds; eight have decorative fireplaces. If you stay on the main floor you can avoid having to climb the steep stairs. ✉ *69 rue St-Louis, Upper Town, G1R 3Z2* ☎ *418/694–1311 or 800/461–1311* 🖷 *418/694–9411* 🌐 *www.clossaintlouis.com* *16 rooms, 2 suites* *Some in-room hot tubs, cable TV, in-room data ports, Wi-Fi, parking (fee); no smoking* 💳 *AE, MC, V* *CP.*

$$–$$$$ **Hôtel Manoir Victoria.** A discreet, old-fashioned entrance leads you into this European-style hotel with in-house spa. Rooms are decorated simply but elegantly with wood-accented standard hotel furnishings. Three rooms and three suites have whirlpool baths and electric fireplaces. You can't beat its location. ✉ *44 côte du Palais, Upper Town, G1R 4H8* ☎ *418/692–1030 or 800/463–6283* 🖷 *418/692–3822* 🌐 *www.manoir-victoria.com* *156 rooms, 3 suites* *2 restaurants, room service, some in-room hot tubs, minibars, cable TV with movies and video games (fee), in-room broadband, indoor pool, spa, gym, sauna, babysitting, dry cleaning, concierge, meeting rooms, parking (fee), no-smoking rooms* 💳 *AE, D, DC, MC, V* *EP.*

$$–$$$$ **Hôtel du Vieux Québec.** Home to many visiting students in spring, this hotel, newly renovated in 2006, is nicely situated at the end of rue St-Jean, surrounded by stores and restaurants. Wake up in the middle of the action along a pedestrian street. Reserve the popular "Superior room" with two queen beds and an exposed brick wall. There is a small but lovely library in the lounge. ✉ *1190 rue St-Jean, Upper Town, G1R 1S6* ☎ *418/692–1850 or 800/361–7787* 🖷 *418/692–5637* 🌐 *www.hvq.com* *44 rooms* *Restaurant, massage, Wi-Fi, library, shop, laundry service, parking (fee), some pets allowed, no smoking floors* 💳 *AE, DC, MC, V* *EP.*

$$–$$$ **Hôtel Château Bellevue.** Behind the Château Frontenac, this 1898 hotel has comfortable accommodations at reasonable prices in a good location. Guest rooms are modern, with standard hotel furnishings; many have a view of the St. Lawrence River. The rooms vary considerably in size (many are a bit cramped), and package deals are available. ✉ *16 rue de la Porte, Upper Town, G1R 4M9* ☎ *418/692–2573 or 800/463–2617* 🖷 *418/692–4876* 🌐 *www.oldquebec.com/bellevue* *58 rooms* *Cable TV, in-room data ports, Wi-Fi, dry cleaning, lobby lounge, parking* 💳 *AE, D, DC, MC, V* *EP.*

$$–$$$ **Hôtel Clarendon.** Built in 1866, the Clarendon is the oldest operating hotel in Québec City, and now it's been refurbished in art deco and art nouveau styles, most notably in the public areas. Some guest rooms have period touches, and some are more modern. Half the rooms have excellent views of Old Québec; the others overlook a courtyard. *57 rue Ste-Anne, Upper Town, G1R 3X4 418/692–2480 or 888/554–6001 418/692–4652 www.hotelclarendon.com 138 rooms, 5 suites Restaurant, café, room service, some in-room hot tubs, cable TV with movies and video games, in-room data ports, Wi-Fi, massage, bar, business services, meeting rooms, parking (fee) AE, D, DC, MC, V EP.*

$–$$$ **Manoir d'Auteuil.** One of the more lavish manors in town, this lodging was originally a private house. A major renovation in the 1950s reinstated many of its art deco and art nouveau details. An ornate sculpted iron banister wraps up through four floors (note that there is no elevator), and guest rooms blend modern design with the art deco structure. Each room is different; one was once a chapel, and two have a tiny staircase leading to their bathrooms. Two rooms have showers with seven showerheads. Rooms on the fourth floor are smaller but are less expensive and come with great views of the Parliament Buildings. The manoir now has an airy lobby with a computer for guests. The Édith Piaf room, named for the French singer who used to frequent the hotel, is still a popular hit with some who stay here. *49 rue d'Auteuil, Upper Town, G1R 4C2 418/694–1173 418/694–0081 www.manoirdauteuil.com 13 rooms, 3 suites Cable TV, in-room data ports, Wi-Fi, babysitting, dry cleaning, laundry service, parking (fee); no smoking AE, D, MC, V CP.*

★ **$–$$** **Hôtel Cap Diamant.** An eclectic collection of vintage furniture and ecclesiastical accents—stained glass from a church, a confessional door, even the odd angel—complement the decorative marble fireplaces, stone walls, and hardwood floors at this hotel made up of two adjacent 1826 houses. In the morning you can bring coffee, orange juice, and muffins to your room or dine in a sunroom that overlooks one of the Old City's few gardens. Stairs to third-floor rooms are a bit steep, but there is a baggage lift. *39 av. Ste-Geneviève, Upper Town, G1R 4B3 418/694–0313 418/692–1375 www.hcapdiamant.qc.ca 12 rooms Refrigerators, cable TV, in-room data ports, dry cleaning, laundry service; no room phones, no smoking MC, V CP.*

★ **$–$$** **Hôtel Marie Rollet.** In the heart of Vieux-Québec, this intimate little inn built in 1876 by the Ursuline Order has warm woodwork and antique charm to match its surroundings. It's one of the few hotels in the Old City to have two rooms with working fireplaces. Some bathrooms are so tiny, the sink is in the bedroom. Steep stairs lead to a rooftop terrace with a garden view. *81 rue Ste-Anne, Upper Town, G1R 3X4 418/694–9271 or 800/275–0338 www.hotelmarierollet.com 10 rooms Cable TV, parking (fee); no room phones, no smoking AE, MC, V EP.*

$–$$ **Manoir Sur le Cap.** No two rooms are alike in this elegant 19th-century inn with beautiful views of Governors' Park and the St. Lawrence River. Built in 1837 as a private home, it was severely damaged in 1849 by a major fire in the neighborhood. It was rebuilt the same year by

George Mellis Douglas, the medical superintendent at Grosse Île. Rooms are light and airy, with antiques and hardwood floors. Some have brass beds, brick walls, or small balconies. Note that some bathrooms have only showers and no tubs and that one room is in the basement. There's no elevator. ✉ *9 av. Ste-Geneviève, Upper Town, G1R 4A7* ☎ *418/694–1987 or 866/694–1987* 📠 *418/627–7405* 🌐 *www.manoir-sur-le-cap.com* *11 rooms, 3 suites, 1 apartment* *Fans, some microwaves, some refrigerators, cable TV, some in-room data ports, Wi-Fi, babysitting; no a/c in some rooms, no phones in some rooms, no smoking* 💳 *AE, MC, V* *EP.*

$ **Au Jardin du Gouverneur.** This cream-color stone house with windows trimmed in dark blue is an inexpensive, unpretentious hotel behind the Château Frontenac. Light-wood furnishings and two double beds fill most of the rooms. The stairs are steep leading up to the fourth floor, where many rooms have sinks in the corner and only a shower. ✉ *16 rue Mont-Carmel, Upper Town, G1R 4A3* ☎ *418/692–1704 or 877/692–1704* 📠 *418/692–1713* 🌐 *www.quebecweb.com/hjg* *16 rooms, 1 suite* *Cable TV; no room phones, no smoking* 💳 *AE, MC, V* *CP.*

$ **Hôtel Manoir de L'Esplanade.** Four 1845 stone houses at the corner of rues d'Auteuil and St-Louis conceal one of the city's best deals: a charming, inexpensive hotel with well-appointed rooms. Rooms have either rich dark-wood furniture or more modern light-wood furniture, and colors and fabrics vary as well. Some rooms have exposed brick walls, a fireplace, and a glass chandelier. The front rooms, facing St-Louis Gate, are the most spacious. Those on the fourth floor (no elevator) are right under the eaves. ✉ *83 rue d'Auteuil, Upper Town, G1R 4C3* ☎ *418/694–0834* 📠 *418/692–0456* *36 rooms* *Some refrigerators, cable TV, Wi-Fi, dry cleaning, laundry service; no smoking* 💳 *AE, MC, V* *EP.*

$ **Hôtel Manoir des Remparts.** A home away from home every May for Mississippi State University students studying French, this hotel has homey furnishings, basic but cheery rooms, and inexpensive rates that also attract many Europeans. The two 1830 houses forming this hotel are opposite the wall enclosing Upper Town, only a short walk from Lower Town. Rooms at the front have a view of the port. On the fourth floor, 10 rooms contain sinks and share bathrooms and a TV. ✉ *3½ rue des Remparts, Upper Town, G1R 3R4* ☎ *418/692–2056, 866/692–2056 in Canada* 📠 *418/692–1125* 🌐 *www.manoirdesremparts.com* *34 rooms, 24 with bath* *Some fans, some kitchenettes, some refrigerators, cable TV, in-room data ports, Wi-Fi, no-smoking rooms; no a/c in some rooms, no room phones, no TV in some rooms* 💳 *AE, DC, MC, V* *CP.*

Lower Town

$$$$ Fodor'sChoice ★ **Auberge St-Antoine.** Once again, in 2005 the Auberge was listed on Condé Nast Traveler's Gold List, and has joined the prestigious Relais & Châteaux chain. On the site of a 19th-century maritime warehouse, this charming hotel incorporates the historic stone walls of the old building along with artifacts dating to the 1600s, many of which are encased in glass displays in the public areas and guest rooms. Antiques and contemporary pieces fill the bedrooms, some with fireplaces, hot tubs, large terraces, or river views. A few rooms have themes, such as the Capitaine, decorated as a ship captain's quarters, the Victorian, or the Garden. Guests can enjoy movie screenings at Cinéma St-Antoine. Two classic movies are shown each night, one in English and one in French, both subtitled, at 6 and 8 PM. Panache, the hotel's restaurant, serves fine, updated French-Canadian fare in a rustic setting. ✉ *8 rue St-Antoine, Lower Town, G1K 4C9* ☎ *418/692–2211 or 888/692–2211* 📠 *418/692–1177* 🌐 *www.saint-antoine.com* *82 rooms, 12 suites* *Restaurant, café, room service, some in-room hot tubs, cable TV, in-room data ports, in-room broadband, Wi-Fi in lobby and the café, massage, bar, lounge, cinema, babysitting, dry cleaning, laundry service, concierge, meeting rooms, business center, parking (fee), no-smoking rooms* 💳 *AE, DC, MC, V* *EP, BP.*

$$$–$$$$ **Hôtel 71.** This new four-star luxury hotel is located in the founding building of the National Bank of Canada. Owners Patrick and Sonia Gilbert also own the neighboring Auberge Saint-Pierre. Lots of natural light has been worked into the decor in rooms with 12-foot-high ceilings, functional yet contemporary design by local artists, and stunning views of Old Québec and its river, or both settings from a corner suite. Rainforest showers and surround-sound systems are in every room. ✉ *71 rue St-Pierre, Lower Town, G1K 4A4* ☎ *418/692–1171 or 888/692–1171* 📠 *418/692–0669* 🌐 *www.hotel71.ca* *31 rooms, 6 suites* *Café, in-room safes, cable TV, Wi-Fi, gym, massage, bar, babysitting, dry cleaning, concierge, meeting rooms, parking (fee), no-smoking rooms* 💳 *AE, MC, V* *CP.*

$$$–$$$$ Fodor's Choice ★ **Hotel Dominion 1912.** Sophistication and attention to the smallest detail prevail in the modern rooms of this boutique hotel—from the custom-designed swing-out night tables to the white goose-down duvets and custom umbrellas. The hotel, which was built in 1912 as a warehouse, has rooms on higher floors with views of either the St. Lawrence River or the Old City. ✉ *126 rue St-Pierre, Lower Town, G1K 4A8* ☎ *418/692–2224 or 888/833–5253* 📠 *418/692–4403* 🌐 *www.hoteldominion.com* *60 rooms* *Minibars, cable TV, in-room broadband, Wi-Fi, babysitting, dry cleaning, dogs allowed, concierge, business services, meeting rooms, parking (fee)* 💳 *AE, DC, MC, V* *CP.*

$$–$$$$ **Hôtel Le Priori.** A modern, four-star boutique hotel, Le Priori is nestled in the Lower Town. Suites have fabulous names such as Roméo and Juliette, Diva, and Rolf Benz and are over 1,000 square feet. Some have kitchens and working fireplaces. Le Priori is a member of Epoque hotels. ✉ *15 rue Sault-au-Matelot, Lower Town, G1K 3YZ* ☎ *418/692–3992 or 800/351–3992* 📠 *418/692–0883* 🌐 *www.hotellepriori.com* *20 rooms, 6 suites* *Restaurant, some refrigerators, cable TV, massage, dry cleaning, laundry services, babysitting, parking (fee), meeting room, no-smoking rooms* 💳 *AE, D, DC, MC, V* *BP.*

$$ **Hôtel Le Saint-Paul.** Perched at the edge of the antiques district, this basic hotel converted from a 19th-century office building is near art galleries and the train station. Rooms have hunter-green carpeting and bedspreads with a Renaissance motif of characters in period dress. Some rooms have exposed brick walls. ✉ *229 rue St-Paul, Lower Town, G1K 3W3* ☎ *418/694–4414 or 888/794–4414* 📠 *418/694–0889* *www.lesaintpaul.qc.ca* *23 rooms, 3 suites* *Restaurant, 1 in-room hot tub, some refrigerators, cable TV with movies, in-room data ports, Wi-Fi, dry cleaning, laundry service, meeting room, no-smoking rooms* *AE, DC, MC, V* *BP.*

$–$$ **Hôtel Belley.** Modern artwork by local artists is everywhere in this modest little hotel up the stairs above Belley Tavern, a stone's throw from the train station and the antiques district. Built as a private home around 1842, the building has housed various taverns since 1868. The current hotel opened in 1987. Rooms are simple, with exposed brick walls and beamed ceilings. Bathrooms have showers but no tubs. Downstairs, the old-fashioned tin ceilings and modern furniture attract a café crowd. Five apartments are also available in a separate building. *249 rue St-Paul, Lower Town, G1K 3W5* *418/692–1694 or 888/692–1694* *418/692–1696* *www.oricom.ca/belley* *8 rooms, 5 apartments* *Restaurant, cable TV, in-room data ports, dry cleaning, laundry service, parking (fee)* *AE, D, MC, V* *EP.*

Outside the Walls

★ $$$–$$$$ **Hôtel Palace Royal.** A soaring indoor atrium with balconies overlooking a tropical garden, swimming pool, and hot tub lends a sense of drama to this luxury hotel. Its eclectic design makes use of everything from Asian styles to art deco. Elegant rooms with antique gold accents have views of either the Old City or the atrium. Views of the river can be had from rooms on the seventh floor and up. *775 av. Honoré-Mercier, Carré d'Youville, G1R 6A5* *418/694–2000 or 800/567–5276* *418/380–2553* *www.jaro.qc.ca* *67 rooms, 167 suites* *Restaurant, room service, shop, concierge, refrigerators, cable TV with movies, in-room data ports, indoor pool, health club, bar, babysitting, meeting rooms, parking (fee)* *AE, D, DC, MC, V* *EP.*

$$–$$$$ Fodor'sChoice ★ **Château Bonne Entente.** Now a member of Leading Hotels of the World, the Château Bonne Entente offers modern simplicity at its finest. Its classic rooms have been redone in 2006 with white duvets, marble bathrooms, and refinished wood furniture. Urbania—a boutique hotel within the château—offers guests tall ceilings, leather headboards, and satinlike bedding, as well as plasma-screen TVs and bathrooms right out of a design magazine. Urbania has a Zen-like lounge called the Living Rouge, with white couches, chairs, and a red ceiling, where breakfast, coffee, and cocktails are served. Fine dining is assured. Watch the chefs prepare your dish and savor the experience of the outside grill or lounge. Golf and spa-going are favored pastimes; guests can tee off at nearby La Tempête, and Amerispa runs the luxurious spa. The hotel is 20 minutes from downtown, with free shuttle service June through mid-September. *3400 chemin Ste-Foy, Ste-Foy, G1X 1S6* *418/653–5221 or 800/463–4390* *418/653–3098* *www.chateaubonneentente.com* *120 rooms, 45 suites* *2 restaurants, in-room safes, cable TV with movies, in-room broadband, Wi-Fi, golf privileges, pool, gym, health club, outdoor hot tub, sauna, spa, ice-skating, bar, recreation room, babysitting, playground, dry cleaning, laundry service, concierge, business services, meeting rooms, convention center, airport shuttle (summer), free parking, no-smoking rooms* *AE, DC, MC, V* *EP.*

★ **$$–$$$$** **Hilton Québec.** Just opposite the National Assembly, the spacious Hilton rises from the shadow of Parliament Hill. The lobby, which can be busy at times, has a bar and an open-air restaurant. The standard, modern rooms have tall windows; those on upper floors have fine views of Vieux-Québec. The hotel is connected to the convention center and a mall, Place Québec, which has 10 shops and a food court. If you stay on an executive floor, you get a free Continental breakfast and an open bar from 5 PM to 10:30 PM. ✉ *1100 blvd. René-Lévesque Est, Montcalm, G1K 7K7* ☎ *418/647–2411, 800/447–2411 in Canada* 🖷 *418/647–3737* 🌐 *www.hiltonquebec.com* *531 rooms, 42 suites* *Restaurant, room service, minibars, cable TV with movies and video games, in-room data ports, Wi-Fi, indoor-outdoor pool, health club, massage, sauna, bar, shops, babysitting, dry cleaning, laundry service, concierge, business services, meeting rooms, parking (fee), some pets allowed, no-smoking floors* 💳 *AE, D, DC, MC, V* 🍽 *EP.*

$$–$$$$ **Hôtel Château Laurier.** Brown leather sofas and easy chairs and wrought-iron and wood chandeliers fill the spacious lobby of this former private house. All rooms have sleigh beds with bedspreads in green, beige, or blue. Rooms in the newer section are a bit larger; deluxe rooms have fireplaces and double whirlpool baths. Some rooms look out on the Plains of Abraham, but most have a view of the National Assembly and the Upper Town. Nearby, the busy Grande Allée is crowded with popular restaurants and trendy bars. ✉ *1220 pl. Georges V Ouest, Montcalm, G1R 5B8* ☎ *418/522–8108 or 800/463–4453* 🖷 *418/524–8768* 🌐 *www.oldquebec.com/laurier* *165 rooms, 3 suites* *Restaurant, room service, some in-room hot tubs, cable TV, in-room data ports, Wi-Fi, massage, bar, babysitting, dry cleaning, business services, meeting rooms, parking (fee), no-smoking floors* 💳 *AE, D, DC, MC, V* 🍽 *EP.*

$$–$$$$ **Hôtel Delta Québec.** This establishment opposite the Parliament Buildings, part of a Canadian chain, has standard and business-class rooms (the latter come with Continental breakfast and nightly appetizers and drinks). Concrete hallways and a rather dreary lobby are less than appealing, but the rooms are large. The hotel occupies the first 12 floors of a tall office complex next to the convention center; views of Vieux-Québec are limited to the higher floors. The heated outdoor pool is open year-round. ✉ *690 blvd. René-Lévesque Est, Montcalm, G1R 5A8* ☎ *418/647–1717 or 800/268–1133* 🖷 *418/647–2146* 🌐 *www.deltahotels.com* *371 rooms, 6 suites* *Restaurant, room service, minibars, cable TV with movies, in-room broadband, Wi-Fi, pool, health club, sauna, bar, dry cleaning, laundry service, meeting rooms, parking (fee), some pets allowed (fee)* 💳 *AE, D, DC, MC, V* 🍽 *EP.*

★ **$$–$$$$** **Hôtel Loews Le Concorde.** When Le Concorde was built in 1974, the 29-story concrete structure aroused controversy because it supplanted 19th-century Victorian homes. But the hotel's excellent location—on Grande Allée, dotted with cafés, restaurants, and bars—has ensured its longevity. Celebrity guests have ranged from the Rolling Stones to President George W. Bush. Rooms are larger than average, with good views of Battlefields Park and the St. Lawrence River. Nearly all rooms combine modern and traditional furnishings. ✉ *1225 Cours du Général-de Montcalm, Montcalm, G1R 4W6* ☎ *418/647–2222 or 800/463–5256*

418/647–4710 www.loewshotels.com 388 rooms, 16 suites 2 restaurants, room service, minibars, cable TV with movies, in-room data ports, Wi-Fi, pool, health club, sauna, bar, babysitting, laundry service, concierge, business services, convention center, parking (fee), some pets allowed AE, D, DC, MC, V EP.

$$$ **L'Hôtel du Capitole.** This turn-of-the-20th-century structure just outside the St-Jean Gate is a fancy hotel, an Italian bistro, and a 1920s cabaret-style dinner theater (the Théâtre Capitole) all rolled into one. The showbiz theme, with stars on the doors, has attracted Québec celebrities, including Céline Dion. Art deco furnishings fill the small, simple rooms. Painted ceilings have a blue-and-white sky motif, and white down-filled comforters dress the beds. *972 rue St-Jean, Carré d'Youville, G1R 1R5 418/694–4040 or 800/363–4040 418/694–1916 www.lecapitole.com 39 rooms, 1 suite Restaurant, room service, some in-room hot tubs, minibars, cable TV, in-room VCRs, in-room data ports, Wi-Fi, bar, 2 theaters, babysitting, dry cleaning, laundry service, business services, meeting room, parking (fee) AE, DC, D, MC, V EP.*

$$–$$$ **Courtyard by Marriott Québec.** This former office building exudes a quiet elegance with stained-glass windows, two fireplaces, and a tiny wood-lined corner bar in the lobby. At the restaurant in back, you can dine around the open kitchen or on the mezzanine. Free Danish and croissants are set out in the lobby in the morning; they're replaced by cookies in the afternoon. Wood furniture fills the modern rooms, most of which are decorated in blue and beige. The least expensive standard rooms face an office building. The best views are from rooms at the front, overlooking place d'Youville. The washing machine and dryer are a rarity in downtown Québec hotels. *850 pl. d'Youville, Carré d'Youville, G1R 3P6 418/694–4004 or 866/694–4004 418/694–4007 www.marriott-quebec.com 102 rooms, 9 suites Restaurant, room service, cable TV with movies, in-room data ports, Wi-Fi in lobby, tub, piano bar, dry cleaning, laundry facilities, business services, meeting rooms, parking (fee), no-smoking floors AE, DC, MC, V EP.*

$$ **Hôtel Royal William.** Like its namesake, the first Canadian steamship to cross the Atlantic (in 1833), the Royal William brings the spirit of technology and innovation to this hotel, designed with the business traveler in mind. Rooms have two phone lines, a fax connection, plus a high-speed Internet port. The meeting rooms on each floor have Internet connections, and several are equipped for video conferencing. Throughout, the style is art deco with a modern twist. Five minutes from Vieux-Québec, the hotel is in the St-Roch district, popular with young artists, academics, and techies. *360 blvd. Charest Est, St-Roch, G1K 3H4 418/521–4488 or 888/541–0405 418/521–6868 www.royalwilliam.com 36 rooms, 8 suites Restaurant, in-room safes, some in-room hot tubs, minibars, in-room broadband, gym, library, babysitting, dry cleaning, meeting rooms, parking (fee), no-smoking AE, D, DC, MC, V EP.*

$–$$ Fodor's Choice ★ **L'Autre Jardin Auberge.** Across the street from the Royal William, this modern, pleasant inn is owned and operated by a nonprofit organization. In the heart of the burgeoning St-Roch district in downtown Québec, the inn is geared toward the academics, high-tech entrepreneurs, and others who visit the many new office and administrative buildings that surround it. The inn, which has a friendly, helpful staff, has three floors of comfortable rooms and suites with cable TV and Internet access. Some rooms have therapeutic baths. There's also a meeting room. The breakfast buffet, which includes a variety of breads, fresh croissants, and local cheeses, is served in a dining room in the basement. In keeping with its owner's aims, there's also a "fair-trade" shop selling artisanal foods and other items from developing countries. ✉ *365 blvd. Charest Est, St-Roch, G1K 3H4* ☎ *418/523–1790 or 877/747–0447* 📠 *418/523–9735* 🌐 *www.autrejardin.com* *24 rooms, 3 suites* *Some in-room hot tubs, cable TV, in-room broadband, Wi-Fi, shop, meeting room, parking (fee), no-smoking floors* 💳 *AE, D, DC, MC, V* 🍽 *BP.*

3

NIGHTLIFE & THE ARTS

Québec City has a good variety of cultural institutions for a town of its size, from its renowned symphony orchestra to several small theater companies. The arts scene changes with the seasons. From September through May, a steady repertory of concerts, plays, and performances is presented in theaters and halls. In summer, indoor theaters close, making room for outdoor stages. Tickets for most shows are sold at **Billetech** (✉ Bibliothèque Gabrielle-Roy, 350 rue St-Joseph Est, St-Roch ☎ 418/691–7400 ✉ Colisée Pepsi, Parc de l'Expocité, 250 blvd. Wilfrid-Hamel, Limoilou ☎ 418/691–7211 ✉ Grand Théâtre de Québec, 269 blvd. René-Lévesque Est, Montcalm ☎ 418/643–8131 or 877/643–8131 ✉ Salle Albert-Rousseau, 2410 chemin Ste-Foy, Ste-Foy ☎ 418/659–6710 ✉ Théâtre Capitole, 972 rue St-Jean, Carré d'Youville ☎ 418/694–4444 🌐 www.billetech.com). Hours vary.

The Arts

Fodor's Choice ★ **Grande Théâtre de Québec.** This is Québec City's main theater, with two stages for concerts, plays, dance performances, and touring companies of all sorts. A three-wall mural by Québec sculptor Jordi Bonet depicts Death, Life, and Liberty. Bonet wrote "La Liberté" on one wall to bring attention to the Québecois struggle for freedom and cultural distinction. ✉ *269 blvd. René-Lévesque Est, Montcalm* ☎ *418/643–8111* 🌐 *www.grandtheatre.qc.ca.*

Dance

Grand Théâtre de Québec. Dancers appear at the Bibliothèque Gabrielle-Roy, Salle Albert-Rousseau, and Complexe Méduse. The Grand Théâtre presents a dance series with Canadian and international companies. ✉ *269 blvd. René-Lévesque Est, Montcalm* ☎ *418/643–8131* 🌐 *www.grandtheatre.qc.ca.*

Film

There are several multiplexes in town, and the two in Ste-Foy usually have English films. The Cartier is a cozy little space located upstairs from the Brunet drugstore on the corner of Cartier and René-Lévesque. Many films here are in English or subtitled in English. The Imax theater has extra-large movie screens—educational fare on scientific, historical, and adventure topics—and translation headsets.

Cinéma Cartier. This theater offers foreign and offbeat films. ✉ *1019 av. Cartier, Montcalm* ☎ *418/522–1011* 🌐 *www.cinemacartier.com.*

Cinéma Star Cité. If your film is sold out at the Star Cité, this is your plan B. ✉ *1150 blvd. Duplessis, Ste-Foy* ☎ *418/874–0255.*

Cineplex Odeon Ste-Foy. This multiplex offers all the new releases. ✉ *1200 blvd. Duplessis, Ste-Foy* ☎ *418/871–1550* 🌐 *www.cineplex.com.*

IMAX theater. If the weather turns, this is a great place to bring the kids. ✉ *Galeries de la Capitale, 5401 blvd. des Galeries, Lebourgneuf* ☎ *418/624–4629.*

Music

Bibliothèque Gabrielle-Roy. This branch of the Québec City library network hosts plenty of concerts in its **Joseph Lavergne Auditorium** and art exhibits in a space beside it. Tickets may be bought in advance, but are also sold at the door. ✉ *350 rue St-Joseph Est, St-Roch* ☎ *418/691–7400.*

Colisée Pepsi. Popular music concerts are often booked here. ✉ *Parc de l'Expocité, 250 blvd. Wilfrid-Hamel, Limoilou* ☎ *418/691–7211.*

Maison de la Chanson. A charming intimate theater, this is a fine spot to hear contemporary Francophone music during the year and take in a play in summer. ✉ *Théâtre Petit Champlain, 68 rue du Petit-Champlain, Lower Town* ☎ *418/692–4744.*

Fodor'sChoice ★ **Orchestre Symphonique de Québec** (Québec Symphony Orchestra). Canada's oldest symphony orchestra, renowned for its musicians and conductor Yoav Talmi, performs at Louis-Frechette Hall in the Grand Théâtre de Québec. ✉ *269 blvd. René-Lévesque Est, Montcalm* ☎ *418/643–8131.*

Theater

Most theater productions are in French. The theaters listed below schedule shows from September to April.

In summer, open-air concerts are presented at Place d'Youville (just outside St-Jean Gate) and on the Plains of Abraham.

Carrefour international de théâtre de Québec. This international theatrical adventure takes over several spaces during the month of May: Salle Albert-Rousseau, Grand Théâtre de Québec, Théâtre Périscope (near avenue Cartier), and Complexe Méduse. There are usually at least one or two productions in English or with English subtitles. ☎ *418/692–3131 or 888/529–1996* 🌐 *www.carrefourtheatre.qc.ca.*

Complexe Méduse. This multidisciplinary arts center is the hub for local artists. Have coffee or a light meal at Café-Bistrot l'Abraham-Martin. ✉ *541 St-Vallier Est, St-Roch* ☎ *418/640–9218* 🌐 *www.meduse.org.*

Grand Théâtre de Québec. Classic and contemporary plays are staged here by the leading local company, le Théâtre du Trident. ✉ *269 blvd. René-Lévesque Est, Montcalm* ☎ *418/643–8131.*

Salle Albert-Rousseau. A diverse repertoire, from classic to comedy, is staged here. ✉ *2410 chemin Ste-Foy, Ste-Foy* ☎ *418/659–6710.*

Théâtre Le Capitole. This restored cabaret-style theater schedules pop music and musical comedy shows. It has been home to Elvis Story and to Night Fever, a musical presentation, complete with dance floors, of music from the disco generation. ✉ *972 rue St-Jean, Carré d'Youville* ☎ *418/694–4444.*

Théâtre Périscope. The Periscope is a multipurpose theater that hosts about 125 shows a year, staged by several different theater companies. ✉ *2 rue Crémazie Est, Montcalm* ☎ *418/529–2183.*

3

Festivals

★ **Festival d'Été International de Québec** (Québec City Summer Festival). An annual highlight in mid-July is Québec City's Summer Festival—an exuberant, 11-day music festival with rock, folk, hip-hop, and more—but also presents classical and world sounds. The main concerts take place each evening on three outdoor stages in or near the Old City, including one on the Plains of Abraham. A button (C$25; C$15 if purchased in advance) admits you to all events throughout the festival; the Web site has a detailed program. Don't worry if you don't know the performers; this is a chance to expand your musical horizons. Some concerts at indoor theaters cost extra, but free music and activities are also plentiful, such as family concerts and street performers during the day. At night, rue St-Jean near the city gate turns into a free street theater, with drummers, dancers, and skits. Book lodging several months in advance if you plan to attend this popular event. ☎ *418/523–4540 or 888/992–5200* 🌐 *www.infofestival.com.*

Festival OFF. This is a sidekick of the Festival d'Été. Most of the shows are free and take place in offbeat spaces—in front of Église St-Jean-Baptiste, Bar Le Sacrilèe, Musée de l'Amérique Française, Bibliothèque Gabrielle-Roy, just to name a few. People of all ages check out this more-alternative scene. Folk, alternative, experimental, and everything in between is what you'll find. The Festival OFF, now in its fourth year, takes to the stage in July at the same time as its big brother. ☎ *418/692–1008* 🌐 *www.quebecoff.org.*

Fêtes de la Nouvelle France (New France Festival). The streets of the Lower Town are transported back in time during this five-day festival in early August. Events, ranging from an old-time farmers' market to games, music, demonstrations, and spontaneous skits, are held throughout the Old City, and you'll see people in period costume everywhere you look. ☎ *418/694–3311* 🌐 *www.nouvellefrance.qc.ca.*

Québec City International Festival of Military Bands. During the festival held in mid-August, the streets of Old Québec resound with military airs. Bands from several countries participate in the four-day festival, which includes a gala parade. Shows—most of them free—are held in Vieux-Québec or just outside the walls. ☎ *418/694–5757.*

Nightlife

Québec City nightlife centers on the clubs and cafés of rue St-Jean, avenue Cartier, and Grande Allée. In winter, evening activity grows livelier as the week nears its end, beginning on Wednesday. As warmer temperatures set in, the café-terrace crowd emerges, and bars are active seven days a week. Most bars and clubs stay open until 3 AM.

Bars & Lounges

Bar St-Laurent. One of the city's most romantic spots is in the Château Frontenac's bar, with its soft lights, a panoramic view of the St. Lawrence, and a fireplace. ✉ *1 rue des Carrières, Upper Town* ☎ *418/692–3861.*

Bar Les Voûtes Napoléon. The brick walls and wine cellar–like atmosphere help make Les Voûtes a popular place to listen to Québecois music and sample beer from local microbreweries. ✉ *680 Grande Allée Est, Montcalm* ☎ *418/640–9388.*

Le Boudoir. Some say this is Québec's best and classiest bar for singles and younger couples. Wednesday is rock night, Saturday is Latin hot—with someone to teach you a few steps, and Sunday is just jazz. The lower level dance floor is DJ-powered from Thursday to Sunday and you'll find all the latest beats. ✉ *441 rue du Parvis, St-Roch* ☎ *418/524-2777.*

Chez Maurice. This is a bar complex named after the former prime minister, Maurice Duplessis. The crowd is young, the atmosphere racy, provocative, and sexually charged. ✉ *575 Grande Allée Est, 2nd fl., Montcalm* ☎ *418/647–2000.*

Cosmos Café. This trendy restaurant and lively club is located on the ground floor under Chez Maurice. Great chandeliers, art, and loud music await you here. ✉ *575 Grande Allée Est, Montcalm* ☎ *418/640–0606.*

L'Inox. A popular Lower Town brewpub, L'Inox serves beers that have been brewed on-site. Some of them, like Transat and Viking, were developed to mark special events. Inside are billiard tables and excellent European-style hot dogs; outside there's a summer terrace. ✉ *37 quai St-André, Lower Town* ☎ *418/692–2877.*

Le Pub Saint-Alexandre. The Saint-Alexandre is a popular English-style pub that serves 40 kinds of single-malt scotch and 200 kinds of beer, 25 of which are on tap. ✉ *1087 rue St-Jean, Upper Town* ☎ *418/694–0015.*

Les Salons d'Edgar. Perched on the cliff just above the St-Roch district, Les Salons d'Edgar attracts those in their thirties with its eclectic music—everything from salsa beats and tango to jazz and techno. It's closed in July and August. ✉ *263 rue St-Vallier Est, St- Roch* ☎ *418/523–7811.*

Clubs

Beaugarte. Named for Humphrey Bogart, this restaurant–bar–discothèque is for dancing, being seen, drinking, and eating. There's a different theme each night—Wednesday you'll find Latino music, Friday night is disco fever. Supper is served from 4 to 11 PM. There's free indoor parking. ✉ *2600 blvd. Laurier, Ste-Foy* ☎ *418/659–2442.*

Chez Dagobert. There's a little bit of everything—from rock bands to loud disco—here in this large, popular club. Local bands also perform downstairs some nights. ✉ *600 Grande Allée Est, Montcalm* ☎ *418/522–0393.*

Le Sonar. Electronic music and a trendy vibe have made Le Sonar one of the hottest dance clubs in town. ✉ *1147 av. Cartier, Montcalm* ☎ *418/640–7333.*

Vogue. Patrons at this second-story dance floor move to techno and pop beats. ✉ *1170 rue d'Artigny, Montcalm* ☎ *418/529–9973.*

3

Folk, Jazz & Blues

Bar Le Sacrilèe. Le Sacrilèe has folk music on Thursday and some Friday nights. This place bears its name well with a couple of church pews and religious icons; it's also located across the street from Église St-Jean-Baptiste. Le Sacrilèe has McAuslin and Boréale products in bottles and on tap, and the special changes daily. ✉ *447 rue St-Jean, Montcalm* ☎ *418/649–1985.*

Le Chantauteuil. Established in 1968, this restaurant–pub is a hit with the locals. The kitchen sometimes closes early, but people stay late into the evening for drinking and discussion. ✉ *1001 rue St-Jean, Upper Town* ☎ *418/692–2030.*

Chez Son Père. French-Canadian and Québécois folk songs fill a once-smoky pub on the second floor of an old building in the Latin Quarter. Singers perform nightly. ✉ *24 rue St-Stanislas, Upper Town* ☎ *418/692–5308.*

L'Emprise at Hôtel Clarendon. It was the first jazz bar in Québec City when it opened in the mid-1980s and is the preferred spot for the music's many fans. The art deco style sets the mood for Jazz Age rhythms. ✉ *57 rue Ste-Anne, Upper Town* ☎ *418/692–2480.*

SPORTS & THE OUTDOORS

Scenic rivers and nearby mountains (no more than 30 minutes away by car) make Québec City a great place for the sporting life. For information about sports and fitness, contact **Québec City Tourist Information** (✉ 835 av. Wilfrid-Laurier, Montcalm, G1R 2L3 ☎ 418/641–6290 🌐 www.quebecregion.com/e). The **Québec City Bureau of Recreation and Community Life** (✉ 160, 76th rue E, 4e, St-Roch, G1K 6G7 ☎ 418/641–6224 🌐 www.ville.quebec.qc.ca) has information about municipal facilities.

Tickets for events can be bought at **Colisée Pepsi** (✉ Parc de l'Expocité, 250 blvd. Wilfrid-Hamel, Limoilou ☎ 418/691–7211). You can order tickets for many events through **Billetech** (🌐 www.billetech.com).

Biking

There are 64 km (40 mi) of fairly flat, well-maintained bike paths on Québec City's side of the St. Lawrence River and an equal amount on the south shore. Detailed route maps are available through tourism offices. The best and most scenic of the bike paths is the one that follows the old railway bed in Lévis. Take the Québec–Lévis ferry to reach the marvelous views along this 10-km-long (6-mi-long) trail. It is now part of the province-wide Route Verte, a government-funded, 4,000-km-long (2,500-mi-long) circuit of long-distance bicycle paths and road routes.

Corridor des Cheminots. Ambitious cyclists appreciate the 22-km-long (14-mi-long) trail which runs from Limoilou near Vieux-Québec to the town of Shannon.

Côte de Beaupré. Paths along the beginning of this coast, at the confluence of the St. Charles and St. Lawrence rivers, are especially scenic. They begin northeast of the city at rue de la Verandrye and boulevard Montmorency or rue Abraham-Martin and Pont Samson (Samson Bridge) and continue 10 km (6 mi) along the coast to Montmorency Falls.

Mont-Ste-Anne. The site of the 1998 world mountain-biking championship and races for the annual World Cup has 150 km (93 mi) of mountain-bike trails and an extreme-mountain-biking park.

Boating

Parc Nautique de Cap-Rouge. Located at the western tip of Québec City, on the St. Lawrence River, here you can rent canoes and pedal boats. ✉ *4155 chemin de la Plage Jacques Cartier, Cap-Rouge* ☎ *418/641–6148.*

Dogsledding

Aventures Nord-Bec. Located 30 minutes from the bridges south of the city, Aventures will teach you how to mush in the forest. A half day spent here, which includes initiation, dogsledding, and a snack, costs C$85 per person. Overnight camping trips, snowmobiling, and snowshoeing are also available. Transportation to and from St-Lambert de Lévis from your hotel can be provided for C$30. ✉ *665 rue St-Aimé, St-Lambert de Lévis* ☎ *418/889–8001* 🌐 *www.aventures-nord-bec.com.*

Fishing

Permits are needed for fishing in Québec. Most sporting-goods stores and all Wal-Mart and Canadian Tire stores sell permits. A one-day fishing permit for a nonresident is C$10.25, three-day permit is C$22.75, seven-day permit is C$35, season is C$52 (includes all sport fish except Atlantic salmon).

Gesti-faune. A corporate fishing outfitter, Gesti-faune has two properties within easy driving distance of Québec City. From May to September, the company's nature guides organize trout-fishing trips that include food and lodging in private wilderness retreats. Trips, organized from May to September, cost from C$300 to C$500 per day. Reservations are required. The Manoir Brulé's award-winning cookbook is a must-see. It combines succulent recipes with stunning photos of both plates and landscapes for a uniquely practical souvenir of Qué. ☎ *418/848–5424* 🌐 *www.gestifaune.com.*

Latulippe. This store sells permits and also stocks a large amount of fishing equipment. ✉ *637 rue St-Vallier Ouest, St-Roch* ☎ *418/529–0024.*

Réserve Faunique des Laurentides. A wildlife reserve with good lakes for fishing, it is approximately 48 km (30 mi) north of Québec City via Route 73. Reserve a boat 48 hours in advance by phone. ☎ *418/528–6868, 800/665–6527 fishing reservations* 🌐 *www.sepaq.com.*

Golf

The Québec City region has 18 golf courses, and most are open to the public. Reservations are essential in summer.

Club de Golf de Cap-Rouge. The 18-hole, par-72 course is 25 minutes by car from Vieux-Québec, and is one of the closest courses to Québec City. Eighteen holes are C$70. The women's course is 5,508 yards, the men's (blue) 6,297 yards and the advanced course is 6,756 yards. ✉ *4600 rue St-Felix, Cap-Rouge* ☎ *418/653–9381.*

Club de Golf de Mont Tourbillon. A par-70, 18-hole course that covers 6,600 yards, the Mont Tourbillon is 20 minutes from the city by car via Route 73 North (Lac Beauport exit). Eighteen holes are C$45. ✉ *55 montée du Golf, Lac Beauport* ☎ *418/849–4418.*

Le Saint-Ferréol. This course is a half-hour drive north of Québec City and has one of the best and best-priced 18-hole, par-72 courses (C$39) in the region. The course covers 6,470 yards. ✉ *1700 blvd. les Neiges, St-Ferréol-les-Neiges* ☎ *418/827–3778.*

Hiking & Jogging

Bois-de-Coulonge Park. Along with Battlefields Park, Bois-de-Coulonge is one of the most popular places for jogging. ✉ *1215 chemin St-Louis, Sillery* ☎ *418/528–0773.*

Cartier-Brébeuf National Historic Site. North of the Old City, along the banks of the St. Charles River, you'll be able to keep going along about 13 km (8 mi) of hiking and biking trails. This historic site also has a small museum and a reconstruction of a Native American longhouse. ✉ *175 rue de l'Espinay, Limoilou* ☎ *418/648–4038.*

Ice-Skating

The ice-skating season is usually December through March.

Patinoire de la Terrasse. Try the terrace ice rink, adjacent to the Château Frontenac and open November–April, daily 11–11; it costs C$5 to skate with skate rental included, and C$2 to skate if you have your own. ☎ *418/828–9898.*

Place d'Youville. This well-known outdoor rink just outside St-Jean Gate is open daily November through the end of March, from 8 AM to 10 PM. Skate rental is C$5, and skating itself is free. A locker will run you C$1. ☎ *418/641–6256.*

Village Vacances Valcartier. Nighttime skating is an option here, although closing times vary. The price for skating is C$5. ✉ *1860 blvd. Valcartier, St-Gabriel-de-Valcartier* ☎ *418/844–2200.*

Rafting

Excursions et Mechoui Jacques Cartier. The Jacques Cartier River, about 48 km (30 mi) northwest of Québec City, has good rafting. The outfitter runs rafting trips on the river from May through October. Tours originate from Tewkesbury, a half-hour drive from Québec City. A half-day tour costs less than C$45; wet suits are C$18. In winter, you can slide on inner tubes for about C$22 a day. ✉ *978 av. Jacques-Cartier Nord, Tewkesbury* ☎ *418/848–7238.*

Village Vacances Valcartier. This center runs rafting excursions on the Jacques Cartier River from May through September. A three-hour excursion costs C$44, plus C$20 to rent a wet suit. Also available are hydrospeeding—running the rapids on surfboards—and quieter family river tours. ✉ *1860 blvd. Valcartier, St-Gabriel-de-Valcartier* ☎ *418/844–2200.*

Skiing

Brochures offering general information about ski centers in Québec are available from the **Québec Tourism and Convention Bureau** (☎ 877/266–5687 🌐 www.bonjourquebec.com). Thirty-seven cross country ski centers in the Québec area have 2,000 km (1,240 mi) of groomed trails and heated shelters between them; for information, contact the **Regroupement des Stations de Ski de Fond** (☎ 418/653–5875 🌐 www.rssfrq.qc.ca). The **Hiver Express** (☎ 418/525–5191) winter shuttle runs between major hotels in Vieux-Québec and ski centers. It leaves hotels in Vieux-Québec at 8 and 10 AM for the ski hills and returns at 2:30 and 4:30 PM. The cost is C$23; reserve and pay in advance at hotels.

CROSS-COUNTRY

Le Centre de Randonnée à Skis de Duchesnay. Located north of Québec City, this center has 150 km (93 mi) of marked trails. ✉ *143 Rte. de Duchesnay, St-Catherine-de-Jacques-Cartier* ☎ *418/875–2711.*

Mont-Ste-Anne. About 40 km (25 mi) northeast of Québec City, you might just find the best cross-country ski center in Canada, if not North America. The training ground for Olympic-level athletes from across the continent, Mont-Ste-Anne has 27 trails: 224 km (139 mi) for classic skiing and 135 km (84 mi) for skating stride. ✉ *2000 blvd. du Beauré, Beaupré* ☎ *418/827–4561.*

Parc des Champs-de-Bataille (Battlefields Park). You can reach the park from Place Montcalm. It has more than 10 km (6 mi) of scenic, marked, cross-country skiing trails.

Les Sentiers du Moulin. This center is 19 km (12 mi) north of the city, and it has more than 20 marked trails covering 150 km (93 mi). ✉ *99 chemin du Moulin, Lac Beauport* ☎ *418/849–9652.*

DOWNHILL

Three downhill ski resorts, all with night skiing, are within a 30-minute drive of Québec City.

Le Massif. This resort, just 20 minutes east of Mont-Ste-Anne in Charlevoix and owned by Cirque du Soleil cofounder Michel Gauthier, is the highest skiing mountain in eastern Canada. Le Massif has a vertical drop of 770 meters (2,526 feet) and has 43 trails. ☎ *877/536–2774* 🌐 *www.lemassif.com.*

Mont-Ste-Anne. This is one of the two biggest, most challenging hills in the region, just 40 minutes east of Québec City on the Côte de Beaupré. It has a vertical drop of 2,050 feet, 56 downhill trails, a half-pipe for snowboarders, a terrain park, and 13 lifts. It also has the longest system of brightly lighted night-ski runs in Canada. ✉ *2000 blvd. du Beaupré, Beaupré* ☎ *418/827–4561, 800/463–1568 lodging.*

Le Relais. There are 25 trails and a vertical drop of 734 feet at this relatively small ski center, where you can buy lift tickets by the hour. Le

Relais is about 20 minutes from downtown Québec City. ✉ *1084 blvd. du Lac, Lac Beauport* ☎ *418/849–1851.*

Station Touristique Stoneham. Stoneham is just 20 minutes north of Old Québec. The hill has a vertical drop of 1,380 feet and is known for its long, easy slopes. It has 32 downhill runs and 10 lifts, plus three terrain parks and one super-half-pipe. ✉ *1420 av. du Hibou, Stoneham* ☎ *418/848–2411.*

Snow Slides

Glissades de la Terrasse. A wooden toboggan takes you down a 700-foot snow slide that's adjacent to the Château Frontenac. The cost is C$2 per ride per adult and C$1.25 for children under six. ☎ *418/829–9898.*

Village Vacances Valcartier. Use inner tubes or carpets on any of 42 snow slides here. Or join 6 to 12 others for a snow-raft ride down one of three groomed trails. You can also take a dizzying ride on the Tornado, a giant inner tube that seats eight and spins down the slopes. Rafting and sliding cost C$23 per day, C$25 with skating. Trails open daily at 10 AM; closing times vary. ✉ *1860 blvd. Valcartier, St-Gabriel-de-Valcartier* ☎ *418/844–2200* 🌐 *www.valcartier.com.*

Snowmobiling

Québec is the birthplace of the snowmobile, and with 32,000 km (19,840 mi) of trails, it's one of the best places in the world for the sport. Two major trails, the 2,000-km (1,250-mi) Trans-Québec Snowmobile Trail and the 1,300-km (806-mi) Fur Traders Tour, run just north of Québec City. Trail maps are available at tourist offices.

Centre de Location de Motoneiges du Québec. Snowmobiles can be rented here near Mont-Ste-Anne, a half-hour drive north of the city, starting at C$40 an hour or C$110 a day, plus taxes, insurance, and gas. ✉ *15 blvd. du Beaupré, Beaupré* ☎ *418/827–8478.*

SM Sport. These folks will pick you up from several downtown hotels at prices starting at C$20 per person. Snowmobile rentals begin at C$45 per hour, or C$135 per day, plus tax, C$15 insurance, and the cost of gas. ✉ *113 blvd. Valcartier, Loretteville, Québec City* ☎ *418/842–2703.*

Water Parks

Village Vacances Valcartier. This is the largest water park in Canada, with 25 waterslides, a wave pool, a 1-km (½-mi) tropical-river adventure called the Amazon, and a 100-foot accelerating water slide, on which bathers reach a speed of up to 80 kph (50 mph). The park's newest attraction is a winding indoor river in a medieval setting. Admission is C$25 a day for those at least 52 inches tall, C$17 for those under 52 inches. ✉ *1860 blvd. Valcartier, St-Gabriel-de-Valcartier* ☎ *418/844–2200.*

Winter Carnival

Fodor's Choice ★ **Carnaval de Québec.** The whirl of activities over three weekends in January and/or February includes night parades, a snow-sculpture competition, and a canoe race across the St. Lawrence River. You can participate in or watch just about every snow activity imaginable, from dogsledding to ice climbing. 📫 *290 rue Joly, Québec City GIL 1N8* ☎ *418/626–3716* 🌐 *www.carnaval.qc.ca.*

SHOPPING

On the fashionable streets of Old Québec, shopping has a European tinge. The boutiques and specialty shops clustered along narrow streets such as rue du Petit-Champlain, and rues de Buade and St-Jean in the Latin Quarter, are like trips back in time.

Prices in Québec City tend to be on a par with those in Montréal and other North American cities. The city's main attractions for shoppers have been antiques, furs, and works by local artisans rather than good prices, but the exchange rate for the U.S. dollar and sales-tax rebates available to international visitors make shopping particularly tempting. Sales are usually advertised in both of Québec City's daily French-language newspapers, *Le Soleil* and *Le Journal de Québec.*

Stores are generally open Monday–Wednesday 9:30–5:30, Thursday and Friday until 9, Saturday until 5, and Sunday noon–5. In summer, most shops have later evening hours.

Department Stores

Large department stores can be found in the malls of suburban Ste-Foy.

La Baie. The Bay is Québec's version of the Canadian Hudson's Bay Company conglomerate, founded in 1670 by Montréal trappers Pierre Radisson and Médard Chouart des Groseilliers. La Baie carries clothing for the entire family, as well as household wares. ✉ *Pl. Laurier, Ste-Foy* ☎ *418/627–5959.*

Holt Renfrew. One of the country's more expensive stores, Holt Renfrew carries furs in winter, perfume, and tailored designer collections for men and women. ✉ *Pl. Ste-Foy, Ste-Foy* ☎ *418/656–6783.*

Simons. An old Québec City store, Simons used to be the city's only source for fine British woolens and tweeds. Now the store also carries designer clothing, linens, and other household items. ✉ *20 côte de la Fabrique, Upper Town* ☎ *418/692–3630* ✉ *Pl. Ste-Foy, Ste-Foy* ☎ *418/692–3630.*

Shopping Malls

Galeries de la Capitale. An indoor amusement park with a roller coaster and an IMAX theater attracts families to this 250-store mall. It's about a 20-minute drive from Vieux-Québec. ✉ *5401 blvd. des Galeries, Lebourgneuf* ☎ *418/627–5800.*

Place de la Cité. There are more than 150 boutiques, services, and restaurants at this shopping center. ✉ *2600 blvd. Laurier, Ste-Foy* ☎ *418/657–6920.*

Place Laurier. With 350 stores, this massive mall is your best bet for one-stop shopping. ✉ *2700 blvd. Laurier, Ste-Foy* ☎ *418/651–5000.*

Place Ste-Foy. Designer labels and upscale clothing are easy to find at the 190 stores here. ✉ *2450 blvd. Laurier, Ste-Foy* ☎ *418/653–4184* ⏲ *Mon. to Wed. 9:30 AM–5:30 PM; Thurs., Fri. 9:30–9 PM; Sat. 9:30–5 PM; Sun. (most stores) 10 AM–5 PM.*

Les Promenades du Vieux-Québec. You'll find high-end items—clothing, perfume, and art—great for packaging as gifts or tucking away as souvenirs of this unique little shopping corner's boutiques. There's also a restaurant and a change bureau. ✉ *43 rue Buade, Upper Town* ☎ *418/692–6000.*

Fodor's Choice ★ **Quartier Petit-Champlain.** A pedestrian mall in Lower Town, surrounded by rues Champlain and du Marché-Champlain, Quartier Petit-Champlain has some 50 boutiques, local businesses, and restaurants. This popular district is the best area for native Québec wood sculptures, weavings, ceramics, and jewelry. ☎ *418/692–2613.*

3

Specialty Stores

Antiques

Québec City's antiques district centers on rues St-Paul and St-Pierre, across from the Old Port. French-Canadian, Victorian, and art deco furniture, along with clocks, silverware, and porcelain, are some of the rare collectibles found here. Authentic Québec pine furniture, characterized by simple forms and lines, is rare—and costly.

Antiquités Marcel Bolduc. This is the largest antiques store on rue St-Paul. Wares include furniture, household items, old paintings, and knickknacks. ✉ *74 rue St-Paul, Lower Town* ☎ *418/694–9558* 🌐 *www.marcelbolduc.com.*

Argus Livres Anciens. Antique books, most of them in French, are what draw people to this store. ✉ *160 rue St-Paul, Lower Town* ☎ *418/694–2122.*

Boutique Aux Mémoires Antiquités. Here you'll find a good selection of Victorian and Edwardian pieces, plus silver, porcelain, curiosities, paintings, and bronzes. ✉ *105 rue St-Paul, Lower Town* ☎ *418/692–2180.*

Gérard Bourguet Antiquaire. You're not likely to find any bargains here, but this shop has a very good selection of authentic 18th- and 19th-century Québec pine furniture. ✉ *97 rue St-Paul, Lower Town* ☎ *418/694–0896* 🌐 *www.gerardbourguet.com.*

L'Héritage Antiquité. This is probably the best place in the antiques district to find good Québécois furniture, clocks, oil lamps, porcelain, and ceramics. ✉ *109 rue St-Paul, Lower Town* ☎ *418/692–1681.*

Art

Aux Multiples Collections. Inuit art and antique wood collectibles are sold here. ✉ *69 rue Ste-Anne, Upper Town* ☎ *418/692–1230.*

★ **Galerie Brousseau et Brousseau.** High-quality Inuit art is the specialty of this large, well-known gallery, which has magnificent displays of pieces large and small. It's worth a stop just to see the variety of work. If you want to make a purchase, the sales staff is very helpful. ✉ *35 rue St-Louis, Upper Town* ☎ *418/694–1828* 🌐 *www.sculpture.artinuit.ca.*

Galerie Madeleine Lacerte. Head to this gallery in an old car-repair garage for contemporary art and sculpture. ✉ *1 côte Dinan, Lower Town* ☎ *418/692–1566* 🌐 *www.galerielacerte.com.*

Rue du Trésor. On this street in the Upper Town, off rue Ste-Anne, local artists display their sketches, paintings, and etchings outdoors. It's a good source for less-expensive artwork as well as pieces by promising young artists. Good portrayals of Québec City and the region are plentiful.

Beauty

Lush. If you've got a great bathtub in your hotel room, treat yourself to one of their bath bombs available in a dizzying number of scents with names such as "All the Jasmine" and "The Happy Pill." ✉ *102 rue du Petit-Champlain, Lower Town* ☎ *418/694–9559.*

Books

English-language books can be harder to find in Québec City than in Montréal.

Librairie du Nouveau Monde. This bookshop stocks titles in French and some in English. ✉ *103 rue St-Pierre, Lower Town* ☎ *418/694–9475.*
Librairie Pantoute. This bookstore has a fairly extensive English-language collection, and many arts, culture, and classic books, as well as best sellers. It's well situated for those walking rue St-Jean. ✉ *1100 rue St-Jean, Upper Town* ☎ *418/694–9748* 🌐 *www.librairiepantoute.com.*
La Maison Anglaise et Internationale. The English and International House, in the Place de la Cité mall, carries English and Spanish titles in its 1,700 square-foot store. Find everything from light reading to recipes, classics to Canadian titles. ✉ *2600 blvd. Laurier, Ste-Foy* ☎ *418/654–9523* 🌐 *www.lamaisonanglaise.com.*

Ceramics

Pauline Pelletier. Ms. Pelletier specializes in porcelain, with an emphasis on comical golden porcelain cats. ✉ *38 rue du Petit-Champlain, Lower Town* ☎ *418/692–4871.*
Pot-en-Ciel. An eclectic assortment of unique ceramics and tablewares is sold here. ✉ *27 rue du Petit-Champlain, Lower Town* ☎ *418/692–1743.*

Clothing

Bedo. A popular chain with trendy, well-priced contemporary items to round out your work wardrobe, Bedo also has great sales racks to sort through at the end of seasons. ✉ *1161, rue St-Jean, Upper Town* ☎ *418/692–0761.*
Le Blanc Mouton. The White Sheep, in Quartier Petit-Champlain, specializes in unique, locally designed creations for women, including accessories and handcrafted jewelry. ✉ *51 Sous le Fort, Lower Town* ☎ *418/692–2880.*
Boutique Flirt. The name of the game is pleasure at this brightly colored boutique where lingerie for men and women cohabit, and fun meets femme fatale. Trained professionals are ready to help with fittings. Flirt specializes in hard-to-find sizes. They carry Cristina, Iaia, Parah, Argento Vivo, Simone Perèle, Le Jaby, Prima Donna, and Empreinte. ✉ *525 rue St-Joseph Est, St-Roch* ☎ *418/529–5221.*
François Côté Collection. This chic boutique sells fashions for men. ✉ *1200 Germain des Prés, Ste-Foy* ☎ *418/657–1760.*
Hugo Boss. Marc Julien appreciates Québec City's quality of life. That's in part why he brought Canada's only full-fledged Hugo Boss collection here in 2005. You'll find children's clothing and a wide range of accessories (shoes and perfume), in addition to the six men's and three women's lines. Everything is smart, sporty, and high fashion. ✉ *505 rue St-Joseph Est, St-Roch* ☎ *418/522–5444.*

Jacob. A popular chain, this Montréal-based store sells tops and bottoms that are going-out and work appropriate. ✉ *1160-1170, rue St-Jean, Upper Town* ☎ *418/ 694–0580.*

Louis Laflamme. A large selection of stylish men's clothes is available here. ✉ *1192 rue St-Jean, Upper Town* ☎ *418/692–3774.*

La Maison Darlington. Head here for well-made woolens, dresses, and other items for men, women, and children by fine names in couture. ✉ *7 rue de Buade, Upper Town* ☎ *418/692–2268.*

Oclan. One of the few truly trendy boutiques in Lower Town, Oclan has the latest from brands including Michael Kors, Splendid, and Le Tigre. ✉ *52 blvd. Champlain, Lower Town* ☎ *418/692–1214.*

3

CHILDREN'S CLOTHING AND TOYS

Benjo. This 28,000-square-foot game and toy store is heaven for children of all ages—including grown-up ones. There's children's clothing (up to 12 years), dolls, teddy bears, crafts, candy, model trains and cars, and more. Benjo, a great big green frog, greets you at the door. More importantly, little people have their own special entrance. ✉ *543 rue St-Joseph Est /550 blvd. Charest Est, St-Roch* ☎ *418/640–0001.*

Crafts

Les Trois Colombes Inc. Handmade items, including clothing made from handwoven fabric, native and Inuit carvings, furs, and ceramics, are available. ✉ *46 rue St-Louis, Upper Town* ☎ *418/694–1114.*

Food

de Blanchet Pâtisserie, Épicerie Fine. This bakery and European grocery store offers authentic, quality products. Breads, meats, pastries, and a few shelves stocked with hard-to-find specialty items fill the spacious and bright shop. Take the time to taste something new. ✉ *435 St-Joseph Est, St-Roch* ☎ *418/525–9779* 📠 *418/525–7337.*

La Boîte à Pain. Artisanal baker Patrick Nisot offers you an amazing selection of baguettes, multigrain breads (pumpernickel, rye), special flavors (olive, tomato and pesto, Sicilian), and dessert breads. Tantalizing pizzas, pies, croissants, and brioches are also available. It opens at 6:30 AM six days a week. Closed Monday. No credit cards are accepted. ✉ *289 St-Joseph Est, St-Roch* ☎ *418/647–3666.*

Camellia Sinensis Maison de thé. Established in 1998 in Montréal, this teahouse is for connoisseurs. The modest space holds 150 different imported varieties from China, Taiwan, Japan, Africa, and beyond, many of which are new to North America. Sign up for a tea tasting session on Saturday at 11 AM when you'll taste 10 different teas with an expert at your side. ✉ *624 St-Joseph Est, St-Roch* ⏲ *Open Tues.–Sun.* ☎ *418/ 525–0247* 📠 *418/525–8290* 🌐 *www.camellia-sinensis.com.*

Choco-Musée Érico. Food becomes a work of art at this store, where chocolatier Éric Normand crafts whatever you like out of chocolate within a few days. ✉ *634 rue St-Jean, St-Jean-Baptiste* ☎ *418/524–2122.*

Fur

The fur trade has been an important industry here for centuries. Québec City is a good place to purchase high-quality furs at fairly reasonable prices.

Fourrures Richard Robitaille. This top-notch fur shop has an on-site workshop that produces custom designs. ✉ *329 rue St-Paul, Lower Town* ☎ *418/692–9699.*

Fourrures Sola. A stone's throw away from the Château Frontenac, this high-end fur store specializes in Canadian fur products. ✉ *43 rue Buade, Upper Town* ☎ *418/692–4275.*

J. B. Laliberté. This furrier, founded in 1867, is still doing business in the heart of St-Roch. Laliberté carries men's and women's furs and accessories, and delivers its "Made in Canada" fur products around the world. ✉ *595 rue St-Joseph Est, St-Roch* ☎ *418/525–4841.*

Gifts

Atelier Toutou. Making a teddy bear is serious business. It could take some time to get just the right amount of stuffing, choose a name, and maybe an outfit. Before you can leave, there's one more very important step. With your hand on your heart, you must promise to forever look after your new friend. ✉ *28 Côte de la Fabrique, Upper Town* ☎ *418/692–2599* 🌐 *www.ateliertoutou.com.*

Collection Lazuli. This store carries unusual art objects and jewelry from around the world. ✉ *Place de la Cité, 2600 blvd. Laurier, Ste-Foy* ☎ *418/652–3732.*

Point d'Exclamation! When jeweler Diane Bergeron couldn't find a good place selling objects fashioned by local artists, she decided to open up shop. The work of 140 Québecois creators fills the two rue St-Jean shops. Pick up one-of-a-kind handcrafted bags, jewelry, hair accessories, paper, notebooks, cards, paintings, and other unique pieces. ✉ *387 rue St-Jean, St-Jean-Baptiste* ☎ *418/523–9091* ✉ *762 rue St-Jean, St-Jean-Baptiste* ☎ *418/525–8053.*

Housewares

Baltazar. This is an urban shopper's mecca. With so much to see, plan to spend some time browsing two floors filled with porcelain sinks, bed frames, bedding, household goods, and everything imaginable for the kitchen and for setting a stunning table. ✉ *461 rue St-Joseph, St-Roch* ☎ *418/524–1991.*

Villa. This spacious, two-floor shop carries imported contemporary designer furniture, accessories for the home, and other objects from India and the Philippines. ✉ *600 St-Joseph Est, St-Roch* ☎ *418/524–2666.*

Jewelry

Joaillier Louis Perrier. Louis Perrier sells Québec-made gold and silver jewelry. ✉ *48 rue du Petit-Champlain, Lower Town* ☎ *418/692–4633.*

Mademoiselle B. Marie-Pierre Fournier's slim costume jewelry shop carries fun pieces to spice up a night on the town. Half the collection comes from France, Isabelle de Millery, and the south of Italy. The remainder is locally produced, from Momento and Noc. ✉ *541 rue St-Joseph Est, St-Roch* ☎ *418/522–0455.*

Zimmermann. Exclusive handmade jewelry can be found at this Upper Town shop. ✉ *46 côte de la Fabrique, Upper Town* ☎ *418/692–2672.*

QUÉBEC CITY ESSENTIALS

Transportation

BY AIR

Canada's national airline, Air Canada, offers direct flights daily to Québec City from Toronto, Halifax, and Ottawa. Discount carriers Jazz (an Air Canada subsidiary) and Québecair have, respectively, 15 and 3 daily flights to Québec City from Montréal. Two U.S. carriers also offer direct flights to Québec City: Continental has one from Newark; Northwest has two from Detroit.

Jean Lesage International Airport is about 19 km (12 mi) northwest of downtown.

If you're driving from the airport into town, take Route 540 (Autoroute Duplessis) to Route 175 (boulevard Laurier), which becomes Grande Allée and leads right to Vieux-Québec. The ride takes about 30 minutes and may be slightly longer (45 minutes or so) during rush hours (7:30–8:30 AM into town and 4–5:30 PM leaving town).

Private limo service is expensive, starting at C$65 for the ride from the airport into Québec City. Taxis are available immediately outside the airport exit near the baggage-claim area. A ride into the city costs about C$30. Two local taxi firms are Taxi Coop de Québec, the largest company in the city, and Taxi Québec.

Jean Lesage International Airport ✉ 500 rue Principale, Ste-Foy ☎ 418/640-2600 🌐 www.aeroportdequebec.com. **Groupe Limousine A-1** ✉ 361 rue des Commissaires Est, St-Roch ☎ 418/523-5059. **Taxi Coop de Québec** ✉ 496 2e av., Limoilou ☎ 418/525-5191. **Taxi Québec** ✉ 975 8e av., Limoilou ☎ 418/522-2001.

BY BOAT & FERRY

The Québec–Lévis ferry crosses the St. Lawrence River to the town of Lévis and gives you a magnificent panorama of Old Québec. Although the crossing takes 15 minutes, waiting time can increase the trip to an hour. The cost is C$2.60. The first ferry from Québec City leaves daily at 6:30 AM from the pier at rue Dalhousie, opposite Place Royale. Crossings run every half hour from 7:30 AM until 6:30 PM, then hourly until 2:30 AM. From April through November, the ferry adds extra service every 10 to 20 minutes during rush hours (7–10 AM and 3–6:45 PM). Schedules can change, so be sure to check the ferry Web site or call ahead.

Boat & Ferry Information **Québec-Lévis ferry** ☎ 418/644-3704 Québec City, 418/837-2408 Lévis, 418/837-2408 [bilingual service 8:30-4:30 daily] 🌐 www.traversiers.gouv.qc.ca.

BY BUS

Orléans Express provides daily service between Montréal and Québec City. The trip takes three hours.

Buses from Montréal to Québec City depart daily on the half hour from 5:30 AM to 10:30 PM. Buses run from 6:30 AM to 10 PM on Sunday. A one-way ticket costs about C$48.31, round-trip costs C$73.62. Tickets can be purchased only at terminals.

Within Quebec City, the city's transit system, the Réseau de Transport de la Capitale, runs buses approximately every 10 minutes on up to once an hour, stopping at major points around town. The cost is C$2.50, and you must have exact change. For a discount on your fare, buy bus tickets at magazine shops and some grocery stores for C$2.25 (C$5.80 for a day pass, which can be used by two people on the weekend). The terminals are in Lower Town at Place Jacques-Cartier and outside St-Jean Gate at Place d'Youville in Upper Town. Timetables are available at some visitor information offices and at Place Jacques-Cartier.

Bus Line **Orléans Express** ☎ 418/525-3000. Terminals **Québec City Terminal** ✉ 3020 rue Abraham Martin, Lower Town ☎ 418/525-3000. **Ste-Foy Terminal** ✉ 3001 chemin Quatre Bourgeois, Ste-Foy ☎ 418/650-0087. **Voyageur Terminal** ✉ 505 blvd. de Maisonneuve Est, Downtown, Montréal ☎ 514/842-2281. **Réseau de Transport de la Capitale** ☎ 418/627-2511 🌐 www.stcuq.qc.ca.

BY CAR

Walking is the best way to see the city, and a car is necessary only if you plan to visit outlying areas.

Montréal and Québec City are linked by Autoroute 20 on the south shore of the St. Lawrence River and by Autoroute 40 on the north shore. On both highways, the ride between the two cities is about 240 km (149 mi) and takes about three hours. U.S. I–87 in New York, U.S. I–89 in Vermont, and U.S. I–91 in New Hampshire connect with Autoroute 20, as does Highway 401 from Toronto.

Driving northeast from Montréal on Autoroute 20, follow signs for Pont Pierre-Laporte (Pierre Laporte Bridge) as you approach Québec City. After you've crossed the bridge, turn right onto boulevard Laurier (Route 175), which becomes the Grande Allée.

Keep in mind that street signs are in French. It's useful to know the following terms: *droit* (right), *gauche* (left), *nord* (north), *sud* (south), *est* (east), and *ouest* (west).

The narrow streets of the Old City leave few two-hour metered parking spaces available. However, several parking garages at central locations charge about C$12 a day on weekdays or C$7 for 12 hours on weekends. Main garages are at Hôtel de Ville (City Hall), Place d'Youville, Edifice Marie-Guyart, Place Québec, Château Frontenac, rue St-Paul, and the Old Port.

BY TAXI

Taxis are stationed in front of major hotels and the Hôtel de Ville (City Hall), along rue des Jardins, and at Place d'Youville outside St-Jean Gate. You're charged an initial C$3.15, plus C$1.45 for each kilometer (½ mi). For radio-dispatched cars, try Taxi Coop de Québec or Taxi Québec.

Groupe Limousine A-1 has 24-hour limousine service.

Groupe Limousine A-1 ✉ 361 rue des Commissaires Est, St-Roch ☎ 418/523-5059. **Taxi Coop de Québec** ☎ 418/525-5191. **Taxi Québec** ☎ 418/522-2001.

BY TRAIN

VIA Rail, Canada's passenger rail service, has service between Montréal and Québec City. The train arrives at the 19th-century Gare du Palais in Lower Town. Trains from Montréal to Québec City and from Québec City to Montréal run four times daily on weekdays, three times daily on weekends. The trip takes less than three hours, with a stop in Ste-Foy. Tickets can be purchased in advance at VIA Rail offices, at the station prior to departure, through a travel agent, or online. The basic one-way fare, including taxes, is C$74.77.

3

First-class service costs C$139.18 each way and includes early boarding, seat selection, and a three-course meal with wine. One of the best deals, subject to availability, is the round-trip ticket bought 10 days in advance for C$94.32.

Train Information **Gare du Palais** ✉ 450 rue de la Gare du Palais, Lower Town ☎ No phone. **VIA Rail** ☎ 888/842-7245 in the U.S and in Canada 🌐 www.viarail.ca.

Contacts & Resources

BANKS & EXCHANGE SERVICES

ATMs, or *guichets automatiques,* are widely available throughout Québec City. ATMs accept many types of bank cards and are generally linked to international banking networks such as Cirrus.

BANKS From May through September, Caisse Populaire Desjardins de Québec is open weekends 9–6 in addition to weekday hours.

Caisse Populaire Desjardins de Québec ✉ 19 rue des Jardins, Upper Town ☎ 418/522-6806.

CURRENCY EXCHANGE Exchange de Devises Montréal is open September–mid-June, daily 9–5, and mid-June–early September, daily 8:30–7:30.

Exchange Service **Echange de Devises Montréal** ✉ 12 rue Ste-Anne, Upper Town ☎ 418/694-1014.

EMERGENCIES

Centre Hospitalier Universitaire de Québec is the city's largest institution and incorporates the teaching hospitals Pavillon CHUL in Ste-Foy and Pavillon Hôtel-Dieu, the main hospital in Vieux-Québec.

If you don't have a major emergency but require medical assistance, you can walk into the Centre Hospitalier Jeffery Hale. The city's only English-speaking hospital and mainly a long-term-care facility, it's open 24 hours. For an English-speaking doctor or dentist, call the Holland Centre referral service weekdays 8:30–4:30.

Dr. Pierre Auger operates his dental practice on weekdays; both he and his receptionist speak English. Call for an appointment.

Pharmacie Brunet, north of Québec City in the Charlesbourg district, is open daily 8 AM–10:30 PM. Most outlets of the big pharmacy chains in the region (including Jean Coutu, Racine, Brunet, and Uniprix) are open every day and offer free delivery.

Doctors & Dentists **Centre Hospitalier Jeffery Hale** ✉ 1250 chemin Ste-Foy, St-Sacrement ☎ 418/684-2252. **Dr. Pierre Auger** ✉ 1330 av. Maguire, Room 204, Sillery ☎ 418/527-2516. **Holland Centre** ☎ 418/683-9274.

Emergency Services **Distress Center** ☎ 418/688-4240. **Fire** ☎ 911. **Police** ☎ 911. **Poison Center** ☎ 418/656-8090. **Provincial police** ☎ 418/310-4141. **Suicide Prevention Line** ☎ 418/683-4588.

Hospitals **Centre Hospitalier Universitaire de Québec, Pavillon CHUL** ✉ 2705 blvd. Laurier, Ste-Foy ☎ 418/656-4141, 418/654-2114 emergencies. **Centre Hospitalier Universitaire de Québec, Pavillon Hôtel-Dieu** ✉ 11 côte du Palais, Upper Town ☎ 418/691-5151, 418/691-5042 emergencies.

Late-Night Pharmacy (until 10:30 PM every night) **Pharmacie Brunet** ✉ Les Galeries Charlesbourg, 4250 1re av., Charlesbourg ☎ 418/623-1571.

MEDIA

Québec Scope is a free bilingual magazine (easy-to-carry format) that you'll find in kiosks around town. There's also the *Quebec Chronicle-Telegraph*, which is an English language weekly.

CBC Radio One is located at 104.7 on the FM dial. This is Canada's public broadcasting corporation, and you can listen to national news briefs every hour on the hour.

TOUR OPTIONS

Tours can include Montmorency Falls, whale-watching, and Ste-Anne-de-Beaupré in addition to sights in Québec City. Combination city and harbor-cruise tours are also available. Québec City tours operate year-round; excursions to outlying areas may operate only in summer.

BOAT TOURS Croisières AML has day and evening cruises, some of which include dinner, on the St. Lawrence River aboard the MV *Louis-Jolliet*. The 1½- to 3-hour cruises run from May through mid-October and start at C$26.95 plus tax. Groupe Dufour Croisières runs 1½-hour sightseeing cruises from late May to September for C$26.95.

Croisières AML ✉ Pier Chouinard, 10 rue Dalhousie, beside the Québec-Lévis ferry terminal, Lower Town ☎ 418/692-1159 or 800/563-4643 🌐 www.croisieresaml.com. **Groupe Dufour Croisières** ✉ Bassin Louise, Wharf 19, at rues Dalhousie and St-André, Lower Town ☎ 418/692-0222 or 800/463-5250 🌐 www.cruises.dufour.ca.

BUS TOURS Autocar Dupont-Gray Line bus tours of Québec City depart across the square from the Hôtel Château Laurier (1230 place Georges V); you can purchase tickets at most major hotels. The company also runs guided tours in a minibus or trolley, as well as tours of Côte de Beaupré and Île d'Orléans, and for whale-watching. Tours run year-round and cost C$26–C$85. Call for a reservation and the company will pick you up at your hotel.

Autocar Dupont-Gray Line ☎ 418/649-9226 or 888/558-7668.

CALÈCHE TOURS You can hire a calèche, a horse-drawn carriage, at Place d'Armes near the Château Frontenac, at the St-Louis Gate, or on rue d'Auteuil between the St-Louis and Kent gates. Balades en Les Calèches de la Nouvelle-France, Les Calèches Royales du Vieux-Québec, and Les Calèches du Vieux-Québec are three calèche companies. If you call ahead, some companies can also pick you up at your hotel. Some drivers talk about

Québec's history and others don't; if you want a storyteller, ask for one in advance. The cost is about C$75 including all taxes for a 40-minute tour of Vieux-Québec.

Balades en Calèche et Diligence. Les Calèches de La Nouvelle-France ☎ 418/692-0068. **Les Calèches Royales du Vieux-Québec** ☎ 418/687-6653. **Les Calèches du Vieux-Québec** ☎ 418/683-9222.

WALKING TOURS Les Tours Voir Québec leads English-language walking tours of the Old City through the narrow streets that buses cannot enter. A two-hour tour costs C$18.35; meet at 12 rue Ste-Anne to begin your walk.

Ghost Tours of Québec gives ghoulish 90-minute evening tours of Québec City murders, executions, and ghost sightings. Costumed actors lead the C$17.50 tours, in English or French, from May through October. Ghost Tours now offers Witchcraft on Tour as well.

Le Promenade des Écrivains (Writers' Walk) takes you through the Old City, where guide Marc Rochette, a local writer, stops to read passages about Québec City from the works of famous writers that include Melville, Thoreau, Camus, Ferron, and others. The two-hour tours cost C$15 and are given Wednesday and Saturday.

La Compagnie des Six-Associés gives several historical theme-driven walking tours year-round, starting at C$12. A tour-ending drink is included. The themes cover such timeless topics as "Killers and Beggars," "The Lily and the Lion," and "Lust and Drunkenness."

La Compagnie des Six-Associés ✉ 381 des Franciscains, Upper Town ☎ 418/692-3033 🌐 www.sixassocies.com. **Ghost Tours of Québec** ✉ 85 rue St-Louis, Upper Town ☎ 418/692-9770 🌐 www.ghosttoursofquebec.com. **Le Promenade des Écrivains** ✉ 1588 av. Bergemont, Upper Town ☎ 418/264-2772. **Les Tours Voir Québec** ✉ 12 rue St-Anne, Upper Town ☎ 418/694-2001 🌐 www.toursvoirquebec.com.

VISITOR INFORMATION

The Québec City Region Tourism and Convention Bureau's visitor information centers in Montcalm and Ste-Foy are open June 24–early September, daily 8:30–7:30; early September–mid-October, daily 8:30–6:30; and mid-October–June 23, Monday–Thursday and Saturday 9–5, Friday 9–6, and Sunday 10–4. A mobile information service operates between mid-June and September 7 (look for the mopeds marked with a big question mark).

The Québec government tourism department, Tourisme Québec, has a center open September 3–March, daily 9–6; and April–September 2, daily 8:30–7:30.

Tourist Information **Québec City Tourist Information** ✉ 835 av. Laurier, Montcalm, G1R 2L3 ☎ 418/641-6290 🌐 www.quebecregion.com. **Ste-Foy information center** ✉ 3300 av. des Hôtels, Ste-Foy G1W 5A8 ☎ 418/651-2891. **Tourisme Québec** ✉ 12 rue Ste-Anne, Place d'Armes, Upper Town ☎ 877/266-5687 🌐 www.bonjourquebec.com.

Québec City Side Trips

4

WORD OF MOUTH

"In the Charlevoix region [go to] the town of La Malbaie. The views of the St. Lawrence River are terrific, there are several activities such as whale-watching, visiting art galleries, or playing golf. The food in the region is terrific."

–MF

"We did Montmorency Falls, Île d'Orléans, and Ste-Anne-de-Beaupré all in one day. We had the whole night to dine and party back in Québec City."

–supaflyfella

www.fodors.com/forums

Updated by Michèle Thibeau

SEVERAL EASY EXCURSIONS from Québec City can give you a deeper understanding of this region's history and culture. In addition to the natural beauty of Montmorency Falls and its Manoir Montmorency, experience the calm of rural life on the charming Île d'Orléans, known as "the garden of Québec," and the historic Beaupré coast. The Charlevoix region's stunning, picturesque landscape is lovely year-round, and in winter visitors flock to the area for a host of outdoor activities.

It's more than well worth crossing the Taschereau Bridge to include Île d'Orléans, but if you have your heart set on only seeing Montmorency Falls it can easily be done in less than a day. A leisurely drive around Île d'Orléans with stops at farms, markets, churches, and craft and antiques shops can be toured in an energetic day, though rural inns make it tempting to extend a visit.

While driving along Québec's Côte de Beaupré, you can make several stops to taste maple syrup and honey, and admire local crafts. You'll eventually come to Ste-Anne-de-Beaupré, an immense neo-Roman church that's been the site of pilgrimages for centuries.

The Charlevoix region is about 113 km (70 mi) northeast of Île d'Orléans and Côte de Beaupré, so consider spending the night.

EXPLORING THE REGIONS

Montmorency Falls is a short drive from downtown Québec City. Take de la Capitale (Highway 40) and then take the Dufferin–Montmorency highway (Route 440). The exit for the falls is on the right. Park the car and stretch your legs. Glide above the falls in the cable car, walk over the canopy bridge and then down the stairs to the bottom of the falls.

Pass the falls and continue along boulevard Ste-Anne (Route 138 east) to explore the Côte de Beaupré. For the more adventurous, a trip up above the cliff gives a magnificent view.

Take the Félix-Leclerc highway (Highway 40) from Québec City and then the Dufferin–Montmorency (Highway 440 east) to the bridge to Île d'Orléans. Head in the direction of Ste-Anne-de-Beaupré. This island, divided into six villages, is bigger than it may appear. At 35 km (22 mi) long and 8 km (5 mi) wide, it's comparable to the island of Manhattan.

Charlevoix is often called the Switzerland of Québec due to its terrain of mountains, valleys, streams, and waterfalls. Charming villages line the north shore of the St. Lawrence River for about 200 km (124 mi)—from Ste-Anne-de-Beaupré, east of Québec City, to the Saguenay River.

The main road through the Charlevoix region is Route 138. Though a half hour longer, Route 362 between Baie-St-Paul and La Malbaie is a scenic route that's 10 times the thrills.

About the Restaurants & Hotels

Eating on Île d'Orléans is a treat. Surrounded by farms, winding roads, and the St. Lawrence River, it's a place where you can spend hours stopping at small shops, or eating at the local diner or in one of the fine restaurants. Make sure to try locally produced black-currant wine, bread, chocolate, jams, and maple syrup.

Charlevoix is a vast territory with hidden gems—farms where the table d'hôte comes from a stone's throw away, with locally produced meats and cheeses as the stars of many menus.

Most of the island's restaurants are open during the high season, May to October, so check schedules before planning a trip.

Reservations are necessary at Île d'Orléans' 30 bed-and-breakfasts, which charge about C$58–C$175 per night for a double-occupancy room. The Chamber of Commerce runs a referral service. In Charlevoix, reservations are recommended as well, especially at the pricier lodging options.

WHAT IT COSTS In Canadian dollars

	$$$$	$$$	$$	$	¢
RESTAURANTS	over C$30	C$21–C$30	C$13–C$20	C$8–C$12	under C$8
HOTELS	over C$250	C$176–C$250	C$126–C$175	C$75–C$125	under C$75

Restaurant prices are for a main course at dinner (or at the most expensive meal served). Hotel prices are for two people in a standard double room in high season, excluding 6% GST and 7.5% provincial tax.

When to Go

The Côte de Beaupré and Île d'Orléans are spectacular in fall, when you can see the colorful changing leaves and go apple picking. Summer is pleasant for the drive and the chance to picnic along the way. In winter, the narrow and more scenic roads can be a bit tougher to maneuver, so you might prefer taking a bus tour with an experienced winter driver.

Charlevoix is full of artists, crafters, and painters in action in summer months, and it's also the perfect time to see the baby beluga whales. Fall is a great time to leaf-peep from the road, the river, or the trail. Sports change with the seasons and are practiced year-round. In winter, there's cross-country skiing, snowshoeing, and ice fishing, among other cold-weather activities.

CÔTE DE BEAUPRÉ

As legend has it, when explorer Jacques Cartier first caught sight of the north shore of the St. Lawrence River in 1535, he exclaimed, "*Quel beau pré!*" ("What a lovely meadow!"), because the area was the first inviting piece of land he had spotted since leaving France. Today the Côte de Beaupré (Beaupré Coast), first settled by French farmers, stretches 40 km (25 mi) east from Québec City to the famous pilgrimage site of Ste-Anne-de-Beaupré. Historic Route 360, or avenue Royale, winds its way from Beauport to St-Joachim, east of Ste-Anne-de-Beaupré. The impressive Montmorency Falls lie midway between Québec City and Ste-Anne-de-Beaupré.

GREAT ITINERARIES

Even with just a few days, it's possible to get a good sense of what the countryside surrounding Québec City has to offer. Île d'Orléans and Côte de Beaupré are easy day trips. Visitors with a bit more time can head north to Charlevoix and Tadoussac.

IF YOU HAVE 2 DAYS

Aim to cover the Côte de Beaupré and the island. Visit Montmorency Falls, then take avenue Royale along the coast. Stop at the Beaupré Coast Interpretation Center in the parish of Château Richer to get a feel for the coastline. Try Auberge Baker for traditional dishes with a contemporary touch.

From there, stop at the bee museum. A trip up above the cliff gives a magnificent view of the St. Lawrence and a visual understanding of the old seigneurial system. Continue along to Ste-Anne-de-Beaupré to visit the shrine. Head back along boulevard Ste-Anne back to Île d'Orléans for the night in a B&B on the river's edge. In the morning, begin exploring the island's farms, boutiques, galleries, and restaurants where you can taste local produce.

IF YOU HAVE 4 TO 6 DAYS

Spend the first two days following the above itinerary. On the third day, head to Charlevoix. See Baie-St-Paul's local crafts and galleries, and spend the night in an inn or B&B. Spend the morning of the fourth day seeing more of Baie-St-Paul, or take a drive to St-Joseph-de-la-Rive for a tour of the Maritime Museum (Exposition Maritime). In winter, you can see dogsled races here. Stop for a hearty country lunch at one of the inns before heading back to Québec City.

With more time, you can drive farther north in Charlevoix, all the way up to Tadoussac, which sits on the Saguenay River. There, you can spend a day whale-watching, as small, white beluga whales breed in the lower part of the river in summer. After a night at the impressive, white Victorian Hôtel Tadoussac, stop in the town of La Malbaie for lunch or for some time at the casino or the Musée de Charlevoix before returning to Québec City.

What to See

❶ **Basilique Ste-Anne-de-Beaupré.** On Route 138, east of Québec City, is the tiny town Ste-Anne-de-Beaupré, named for Québec's patron saint, and each year more than a million pilgrims visit the region's most famous religious site here, dedicated to the mother of the Virgin Mary.

Fodor'sChoice ★

The French brought their devotion to St. Anne (the patron saint of shipwrecked sailors) when they sailed across the Atlantic to New France. According to local legend, St. Anne was responsible over the years for saving voyagers from shipwrecks in the harsh waters of the St. Lawrence. In 1650 Breton sailors caught in a storm vowed to erect a chapel in honor of this patron saint at the exact spot where they landed.

The present neo-Roman basilica, constructed in 1923, is the fifth to be built on the site where the sailors first touched ground. The original 17th-

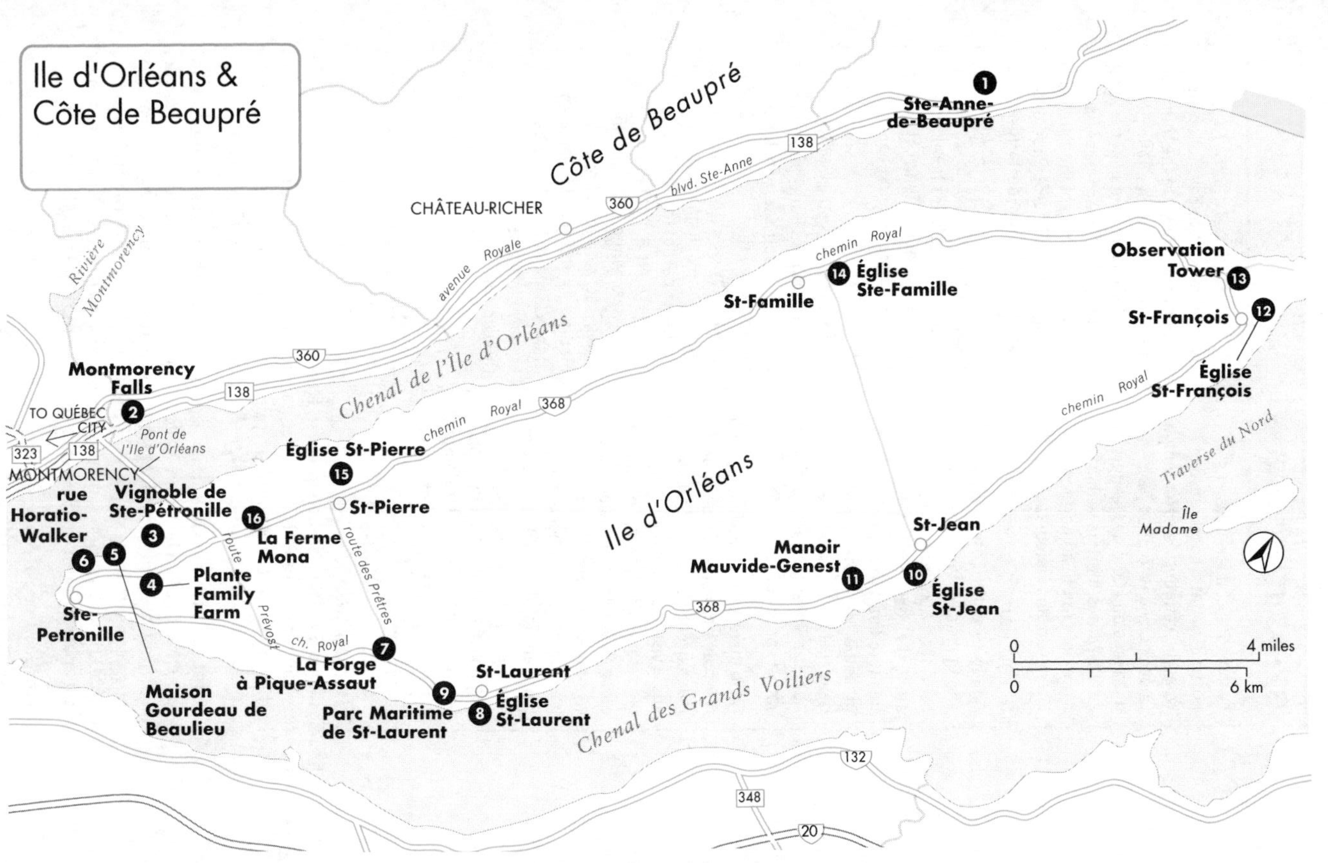
Ile d'Orléans &
Côte de Beaupré
Côte de Beaupré
Ste-Anne-de-Beaupré
CHÂTEAU-RICHER
blvd. Ste-Anne
avenue Royale
Rivière Montmorency
chemin Royal
Église Ste-Famille
St-Famille
Observation Tower
St-François
Église St-François
Montmorency Falls
TO QUÉBEC CITY
Pont de l'Ile d'Orléans
MONTMORENCY
Chenal de l'Île d'Orléans
Église St-Pierre
St-Pierre
Traverse du Nord
Île Madame
Ile d'Orléans
rue Horatio-Walker
Vignoble de Ste-Pétronille
La Ferme Mona
route Prévost
route des Prêtres
St-Jean
Manoir Mauvide-Genest
Église St-Jean
Plante Family Farm
Ste-Petronille
ch. Royal
La Forge à Pique-Assaut
St-Laurent
Église St-Laurent
Maison Gourdeau de Beaulieu
Parc Maritime de St-Laurent
Chenal des Grands Voiliers
138
360
368
323
132
348
20
0 4 miles
0 6 km

century wood chapel was built too close to the St. Lawrence and was swept away by river flooding.

The gigantic structure is in the shape of a Latin cross and has two imposing granite steeples. The interior has 22 chapels and 18 altars, as well as rounded arches and numerous ornaments in the Romanesque style. The 214 stained-glass windows, completed in 1949 are by Frenchmen Auguste Labouret and Pierre Chaudière.

Tributes to St. Anne can be seen in the shrine's mosaics, murals, altars, and ceilings. A bas-relief at the entrance depicts St. Anne welcoming her pilgrims, and ceiling mosaics represent her life. Numerous crutches and braces posted on the back pillars have been left by those who have felt the saint's healing powers.

The **Musée de Sainte Anne** (☎ 418/827–6873 🎟 C$4), in the basilica parking lot, exhibits church treasures as well as donations made by pilgrims. The museum is open 9–5 daily from early June through August. *✉ 10018 av. Royale ☎ 418/827–3781 🎟 Free ⏲ Reception booth daily 8:30–5. Guided tours early June–Labor Day., daily at 1; day after Labor Day–early June, by appointment.*

Commemorative Chapel. Across from Basilique Ste-Anne-de-Beaupré, this chapel was designed by Claude Bailiff and built in 1878. It was constructed on the transept of a church built in 1676, and Bailiff made use of the old stones and foundation. Among the remnants is a white-and-gold-trimmed pulpit designed by François Baillargé in 1807 and adorned with a sculpture depicting Moses and the Ten Commandments. **Scala Santa.** This small chapel, adjacent to the Commemorative Chapel, resembles a wedding cake. On bended knees, pilgrims climb its replica of the Holy Stairs, representing the steps Jesus climbed to meet Pontius Pilate. *✉ Av. Royale ☎ No phone ⏲ Early May–mid-Oct., daily 8–4:30.*

❷ **Montmorency Falls.** The Montmorency River was named for Charles de Montmorency, viceroy of New France in the 1620s and explorer Samuel de Champlain's immediate commander. The river cascading over a cliff into the St. Lawrence River is one of the most beautiful sights in the province—and at 27 stories high, the falls are double the height of Niagara Falls. A cable car runs to the top of the falls in **Parc de la Chute-Montmorency** (Montmorency Falls Park) from late April to early November. During very cold weather, the falls' heavy spray freezes and forms a giant loaf-shape ice cone known to Québecois as the Pain du Sucre (Sugarloaf); this phenomenon attracts sledders and sliders from Québec City. Mid-July to early August, the skies above the falls light up with **Les Grands Feux Loto-Québec** (☎418/523–3389 or 888/934–3473 🌐 www.lesgrandsfeux.com), an international competition of fireworks performances set to music.

The park also has a historic side. The British general James Wolfe, on his way to conquer New France, camped here in 1759. In 1780 Sir Frederick Haldimand, then the gov-

SIDE TRIP TIP

There's always the cable car, but those who want a workout can climb the 487 steps to the top of the falls. Bring on those extra crêpes!

ernor of Canada, built a summer home—now a good restaurant called Manoir Montmorency—atop the cliff. The structure burned down, however, and what stands today is a re-creation. The Manoir, open year-round, has a terrace in summertime that offers a stunning view of the falls and river below. ✉ *2490 av. Royale, Beauport* ☎ *418/663–3330, 418/647–4422 ice-climbing school* 🌐 *www.sepaq.com/ct/pcm/en* 🎫 *Cable car C$8 round-trip, parking C$8.75* ⏲ *Cable car daily 8:30–7* PM.

Musée de L'Abeille. Things are buzzing at this economuseum (part of an organization of museums focusing on traditional trades) devoted to bees and honey. A giant glassed-in hive with a tube leading outdoors allows you to take a close look at life inside a beehive. On the bee safari, guides take a hive apart, explaining how it works and how bees behave. You can taste honey made by bees that have fed on different kinds of flowers, from clover to blueberry. The museum is a 10-minute drive east of Montmorency Falls. ✉ *8862 blvd. Ste-Anne, Château-Richer* ☎ *418/824–4411* 🎫 *Museum free, bee safari C$3.50* ⏲ *Museum June 24–Oct., daily 9–6; Nov.–June 23, daily 9–5. Bee safari June 24–Labor Day.*

Atelier Paré (Economuseum of Legends). This economuseum represents the work of two centuries of wood carving tradition. ✉ *9269 av. Royale, Ste-Anne-de-Beaupré* ☎ *418/827–3992* 🌐 *www.clicnet/~legends* 🎫 *free; guided tour C$1* ⏲ *May 15–Oct. 15, daily 9–5; Oct. 15–May 14, weekdays 1–4, weekends 10–6.*

Réserve Faunique du Cap Tourmente (Cap Tourmente Wildlife Reserve). About 8 km (5 mi) northeast of Ste-Anne-de-Beaupré, more than 800,000 greater snow geese gather here every October and May, with an average of 100,000 birds coming per day. The park harbors hundreds of kinds of birds and mammals and more than 700 plant species. This enclave on the north shore of the St. Lawrence River also has 18 km (11 mi) of hiking trails; naturalists give guided tours. ✉ *570 chemin du Cap Tourmente, St-Joachim* ☎ *418/827–4591 Apr.–Oct., 418/827–3776 Nov.–Mar.* 🎫 *C$5* ⏲ *Jan.–Oct., daily 8:30–5.*

SIDE TRIP TIP

Check the tides when you plan your trip to the Cap Tourmente. In early May and mid-October, the snow geese fly up in a flock at high tide, so be sure to get there early.

OFF THE BEATEN PATH

RÉSERVE FAUNIQUE DES LAURENTIDES – The wildlife reserve, approximately 48 km (30 mi) north of Québec City via Route 175, which leads to the Saguenay region, has good lakes for fishing. It's advisable to reserve a time slot 48 hours ahead by phone or fax. ☎ *418/528–6868, 418/890–6527 fishing reservations* 📠 *418/528–8833.*

Where to Eat

★ **$$–$$$$** ✕ **Auberge Baker.** The best of old and new blend at this restaurant in an 1840 French-Canadian farmhouse built by the owners' ancestors. Antiques and old-fashioned woodstoves decorate the dining rooms, where you can sample traditional Québec fare, from tourtière and pork hocks to maple-sugar pie. Or opt for contemporary dishes such as the excellent herbed-and-breaded grilled lamb loin and exotic choices such as minced wapiti (elk) with pesto sauce. The lower-priced lunch menu is served until 6. Upstairs is a five-room B&B, also decorated in Canadiana; two exterior buildings hold two additional rooms. Château-Richer is 4 km (2½ mi) west of St. Anne's Basilica. ✉ *8790 av. Royale, Château-Richer* ☎ *418/824–4478 or 866/824–4478* ▭ *AE, DC, MC, V.*

Sports & the Outdoors

Le Massif. This three-peak ski resort has the longest vertical drop in Canada east of the Rockies—2,526 feet. Owned by Daniel Gauthier, cofounder of Le Cirque du Soleil, the resort has two multiservice chalets at the top and bottom. Four lifts service the 36 trails, which are divided into runs for different levels; the longest run is 3.8 km (2.4 mi). Equipment can be rented on-site. ✉ *1350 rue Principale, Petite-Rivière-St-François* ☎ *418/632–5876 or 877/536–2774* 🌐 *www.lemassif.com.*

4

Mont-Ste-Anne. Part of the World Cup downhill circuit, Mont-Ste-Anne is one of the largest resorts in eastern Canada, with a vertical drop of 2,050 feet, 56 downhill trails, two half-pipes for snowboarders, a terrain park, and 13 lifts, including a gondola. Cross-country skiing is also a draw here, with 21 trails totaling 224 km (139 mi). When the weather warms, mountain biking becomes the sport of choice. Enthusiasts can choose from 150 km (93 mi) of mountain-bike trails, and 14 downhill runs (and a gondola up to the top). Three bike runs are designated "extreme zones." ✉ *2000 blvd. Beaupré, Beaupré* ☎ *418/827–4561 or 800/463–1568* 🌐 *www.mont-sainte-anne.com.*

Centre de Location de Motoneiges du Québec. Snowmobiles can be rented at near Mont Ste-Anne, starting at C$40 per person (two to a snowmobile) for an hour or C$100 per person for the day, including equipment. ✉ *15 blvd. Beaupré, Beaupré* ☎ *418/827–8478* 🌐 *www.locationmotoneiges.com.*

ÎLE D'ORLÉANS

The Algonquins called it Minigo, the "Bewitched Place," and over the years the island's tranquil rural beauty has inspired poets and painters. Île d'Orléans is only 15 minutes by car from downtown Québec City, but a visit here is one of the best ways to get a feel for traditional life in rural Québec. Centuries-old homes and some of the oldest churches in the region dot the road that rings the island. Île d'Orléans is at its best in summer, when the boughs of trees in lush orchards bend under the weight of apples, plums, or pears, and the fields burst with strawberries and raspberries. Roadside stands sell woven articles, maple syrup, baked goods, jams, fruits, and vegetables. You can also pick your own produce at about two dozen farms. The island, immortalized by one of its most famous residents, the poet and songwriter Félix Leclerc (1914–88), is still fertile ground for artists and artisans.

The island was discovered at about the same time as the future site of Québec City, in 1535. Explorer Jacques Cartier noticed an abundance of vines and called it the Island of Bacchus, after the Greek god of wine.

(Today, native vines are being crossbred with European varieties at Ste-Pétronille's fledgling vineyard.) In 1536 Cartier renamed the island in honor of the duke of Orléans, son of the French king François I. Its fertile soil and abundant fishing made it so attractive to settlers that at one time there were more people living here than in Québec City.

About 8 km (5 mi) wide and 35 km (22 mi) long, Île d'Orléans is made up of six small villages that have sought over the years to retain their identities. The bridge to the mainland was built in 1935, and in 1970 the island was declared a historic area to protect it from most sorts of development.

Ste-Pétronille

17 km (10½ mi) northeast of Québec City.

The lovely village of Ste-Pétronille, the first to be settled on Île d'Orléans, is west of the bridge to the island. Founded in 1648, the community was chosen in 1759 by British general James Wolfe for his headquarters. With 40,000 soldiers and a hundred ships, the English bombarded French-occupied Québec City and Côte de Beaupré.

In the late 19th century, the English population of Québec developed Ste-Pétronille into a resort village. This area is considered to be the island's most beautiful, not only because of its spectacular views of Montmorency Falls and Québec City but also for its Regency-style English villas and exquisitely tended gardens.

What to See

3 **Vignoble de Ste-Pétronille.** Hardy native Québec vines have been crossbred with three types of European grapes to produce a surprisingly good dry white wine as well as a red and a rosé. A guided tour of the vineyard includes a tasting. ✉ *1A chemin du Bout de l'Île* ☎ *418/828–9554* *Guided tour C$2.50* ⏲ *Late Apr.–May and mid-Oct.–mid-Nov., weekends 11–5; June–mid-Oct., daily 10–6.*

4 **Plante family farm.** Pick apples and strawberries (in season) or buy fresh fruits, vegetables, and apple cider at this family farm. In winter, enjoy maple sugar treats from the roadside sugar shack. ✉ *20 chemin du Bout de l'Île* ☎ *418/828–9603.*

SIDE TRIP TIP

The style of houses you'll see in Ste-Petronille are known as "Regency style," and are marked by their wraparound balconies, four-sided sloped roofs, and colorful shutters.

5 **Maison Gourdeau de Beaulieu.** The island's first home was built in 1648 for Jacques Gourdeau de Beaulieu, the first seigneur (a landholder who distributed lots to tenant farmers) of Ste-Pétronille. Remodeled over the years, this white house with blue shutters now incorporates both French and Québec styles. Its thick walls and dormer windows are characteristic of Breton architecture, but its sloping, bell-shape roof, designed to protect buildings from large amounts of snow, is typical Québec style. The house is not open to the public. ✉ *137 chemin du Bout de l'Île.*

6 **Rue Horatio-Walker.** This tiny street off chemin Royal was named after the early-19th-century painter known for his landscapes of the island. Walker lived on this street from 1904 until his death in 1938. At Nos. 11 and 13 rue Horatio-Walker are his home and workshop, but they are both closed to the public.

Where to Stay & Eat

$$–$$$ **La Goéliche.** This English-style country manor, rebuilt in 1996–97 following a fire, is steps away from the St. Lawrence River. Antiques decorate the small but elegant rooms, which all have river views. Classic French cuisine ($$$–$$$$, table d'hôte only in the evening, reservations essential) includes Chef Frédéric Cassadei's specialties—fish soup with scallops and shrimp, and duck with local wine. The romantic dining room overlooks the river; an enclosed terrace is open year-round. ✉ *22 chemin du Quai, G0A 4C0* ☎ *418/828–2248 or 888/511–2248* 🖷 *418/828–2745* 🌐 *www.goeliche.ca* *12 rooms, 1 suite, 2 apartments* *Restaurant, fans, some in-room hot tubs, some minibars, cable TV, in-room data ports, Wi-Fi, pool, babysitting, dry cleaning, meeting rooms, free parking, no-smoking rooms; no a/c* 💳 *AE, DC, MC, V* *BP.*

Shopping

Chocolaterie de l'Île d'Orléans (✉ 150 chemin du Bout de l'Île ☎ 418/828–2250) combines Belgian chocolate with local ingredients to create handmade treats—chocolates filled with maple butter, for example, or *framboisette,* made from raspberries. In summer try the homemade ice creams and sherbets.

St-Laurent de l'Île d'Orléans

9 km (5½ mi) east of Ste-Pétronille.

Founded in 1679, St-Laurent is one of the island's maritime villages. Until as late as 1935, residents here used boats as their main means of transportation. St-Laurent has a rich history in farming and fishing. Work is under way to help bring back to the island some of the species of fish that were once abundant here.

What to See

7 **La Forge à Pique-Assaut.** This forge belongs to the talented and local artisan Guy Bel, who has done ironwork restoration for Québec City. He was born in Lyon, France, and studied there at the École des Beaux Arts. You can watch him and his team at work; his stylish candlesticks, chandeliers, fireplace tools, and other ironwork are for sale. ✉ *2200 chemin Royal* ☎ *418/828–9300* 🌐 *www.forge-pique-assaut.com* ⏲ *June–mid-Oct., daily 9–5; mid-Oct.–May, weekdays 9–noon and 1:30–5.*

8 **Église St-Laurent.** The tall, inspiring church that stands next to the village marina on chemin Royal was built in 1860 on the site of an 18th-century church that had to be torn down. One of the church's procession chapels is a miniature stone reproduction of the original. ✉ *1532 chemin Royal* ☎ *418/828–2551* *Free, guided tour of religious art C$1* ⏲ *Mid-June–Oct., daily 9–5.*

9 **Parc Maritime de St-Laurent.** This is a former boatyard where craftspeople specializing in boatbuilding practiced their trade. Now you can picnic here and visit the Chalouperie Godbout (Godbout Longboat), which holds a collection of tools used during the golden era of boatbuilding. See fishermen at work trapping eel in tall nets at low tide. ✉ *120 chemin de la Chalouperie* ☎ *418/828–9672* *C$3.50* ⏲ *June 24–Labor Day, daily 10–5; day after Labor Day–early Oct., weekends 10–5 and by reservation; mid-May–mid-June by reservation.*

Where to Stay & Eat

$$–$$$ **Moulin de St-Laurent.** You can dine inside or outside at the foot of the waterfall at this restaurant, converted from an early-18th-century stone mill. Scrumptious snacks, such as quiche and salads, are available on the terrace. Evening dishes include regional products salmon and sweetbreads. Stay overnight at one of the Moulin de St-Laurent's chalets, on the edge of the St. Lawrence. There is a supper, room, and breakfast package beginning at C$100–C$115 per person, per night or C$315 for two people per night. Four chalets are available in winter and seven in summer. Note: there is no supper package available when the restaurant is closed. ✉ *754 chemin Royal* ☎ *418/829–3888 or 888/629–3888* *AE, DC, MC, V* ⏲ *Restaurant closed mid-Oct.–May.*

★ **$$** **Le Canard Huppé.** As the inn's name—The Crested Duck—suggests, its contemporary cuisine ($$–$$$$) usually includes at least one dish with duck, perhaps the rendition with clover honey, fresh thyme, and wild garlic. Chef Philip Rae uses locally raised meat, fish, and fowl. Upstairs, each of the inn's rooms has unusual antiques and original paintings. ✉ *2198 chemin Royal, G0A 3Z0* ☎ *418/828–2292 or 800/838–2292* *418/828–0966* *www.canard-huppe.com* *10 rooms, 1 suite* *Restaurant, fans, refrigerators, cable TV in 1 room, meeting room, free parking, no-smoking rooms; no a/c in some rooms* *MC, V* ⏲ *No dinner Nov.–Apr.* *BP.*

St-Jean

12 km (7 mi) northeast of St-Laurent.

The village of St-Jean used to be occupied by river pilots and navigators. At sea most of the time, the sailors didn't need the large homes and plots of land that the farmers did. Often richer than farmers, they displayed their affluence by building their houses with bricks brought back from Scotland as ballast. Most of St-Jean's small, homogeneous row houses were built between 1840 and 1860.

What to See

10 **Église St-Jean.** At the eastern end of the village sits a massive granite structure built in 1749, with large red doors and a towering steeple. The church resembles a ship; it's big and round and appears to be sitting right on the river. Paintings of the patron saints of seamen line the in-

SIDE TRIP TIP

It may not look far when you have a map in hand, but it will take longer than you think to cross the island on one of the three roads—especially in winter—so plan accordingly.

terior walls. The church's cemetery is also intriguing, especially if you can read French. Back in the 1700s, piloting the St. Lawrence was a dangerous profession; the cemetery tombstones recall the many lives lost in these harsh waters. ✉ *2001 chemin Royal* ☎ *418/828–2551* 🎫 *Free* ⏲ *Late May–early Oct., daily 10–5.*

11 **Manoir Mauvide-Genest.** St-Jean's beautiful Normandy-style manor was built in 1734 for Jean Mauvide, surgeon to Louis XV, and his wife, Marie-Anne Genest. The most notable thing about this house, which still has its original thick walls, ceiling beams, and fireplaces, is the degree to which it has held up over the years. The house serves as an interpretation center of New France's seigneurial regime, with 18th-century furniture, a multimedia presentation, and tours with guides dressed in 18th-century costumes. ✉ *1451 chemin Royal* ☎ *418/829–2630* 🎫 *C$6* ⏲ *May–Nov., daily 10–5.*

4

St-François

12 km (7 mi) northeast of St-Jean.

Sprawling open fields separate 17th-century farmhouses in St-François, the island's least toured and most rustic village. This community at the eastern tip of the island was settled mainly by farmers. St-François is the perfect place to visit one of the island's *cabanes à sucre* (maple-sugaring shacks), found along chemin Royal. Stop at a hut for a tasting tour; sap is gathered from the maple groves and boiled until it turns to syrup. When it's poured on ice, it tastes like toffee. The maple syrup season is from late March through April.

What to See

12 **Église St-François.** Built in 1734, is one of eight extant provincial churches dating from the French regime. At the time the English seized Québec City in 1759, General James Wolfe knew St-François to be a strategic point along the St. Lawrence. Consequently, he stationed British troops here and used the church as a military hospital. In 1988 a car crash set the church on fire, and most of the interior treasures were lost. A separate children's cemetery stands as a silent witness to the difficult life of early residents. ✉ *341 chemin Royal* ☎ *419/828–2551* 🎫 *Free* ⏲ *June 24–Sept. 24, daily noon–5.*

13 **Observation tower.** This picnic area with a wooden tower is well situated for viewing the majestic St. Lawrence. In spring and fall, wild Canada geese can be seen here. The area is about 2 km (1 mi) north of Église St-François on chemin Royal.

Ste-Famille

14 km (9 mi) west of St-François.

The village of Ste-Famille, founded in 1661, has exquisite scenery, including abundant apple orchards and strawberry fields with views of Côte de Beaupré and Mont-Ste-Anne in the distance. But it also has plenty of historic charm, with the area's highest concentration of stone houses dating from the French regime.

What to See

14 **Église Ste-Famille.** This impressive church, constructed in 1749, is the only one in Québec province to have three bell towers at its front. The ceiling was redone in the mid-19th century with elaborate designs in wood and gold. The church also holds a famous painting, *L'Enfant Jésus Voyant la Croix* (*Baby Jesus Looking at the Cross*). It was done in 1670 by Frère Luc (Father Luc), sent from France to decorate churches in the area. ✉ *3915 chemin Royal* ☎ *418/828–2656* 🎫 *Free* 🕒 *Late June–early Sept., daily 11–5.*

St-Pierre

14 km (9 mi) southwest of Ste-Famille.

St-Pierre, established in 1679, is set on a plateau that has the island's most fertile land. The town has long been the center of traditional farming industries. The best products grown here are potatoes, asparagus, and corn. In 2002 the Espace Félix Leclerc—an exhibit by day and a *boîte à chansons* (combination coffeehouse and bar with live performances) by night—was opened to honor the late singer and songwriter who made St-Pierre his home. If you continue west on chemin Royal, just ahead is the bridge to the mainland and Route 440.

What to See

15 **Église St-Pierre.** The oldest church on the island dates from 1717. It's no longer used for worship, but it was restored during the 1960s and is open to visitors. Many original components are still intact, such as benches with compartments below where hot bricks and stones were placed to keep people warm in winter. Félix Leclerc, the first Québecois singer to make a mark in Europe, is buried in the cemetery nearby. ✉ *1249 chemin Royal* ☎ *418/828–9824* 🎫 *Free* 🕒 *May, June, and Aug.–Oct., daily 10–5; July, daily 9–6.*

16 **La Ferme Monna.** This family farm has won international awards for its *crème de cassis de l'Île d'Orléans,* a liqueur made from black currants. The farm offers free samples of the strong, sweet cassis or one of its black-currant wines; the tour explains how they are made. In summer you can sample foods made with cassis on a terrace overlooking the river at La Monnaguette. Try the salmon bagel or a salad with confit de canard, with a black-currant sauce. La Monnaguette is open mid-June–September, daily10–10. ✉ *723 chemin Royal* ☎ *418/828–1057* 🎫 *Free, guided tours C$5* 🕒 *Mid-June–Oct., daily 10–6; Mar.–mid-June, Nov., and Dec., weekends 10–5.*

Shopping

Poissonnerie Jos Paquet. The only remaining commercial fisherman on the island smokes his fish and sells it from a tiny shack. You can sample surprisingly tasty smoked eel as well as smoked trout and salmon. Also on sale are fresh and smoked walleye pike and sturgeon, all from the St. Lawrence River. New products include a sturgeon mousse and, a most rare treat—sturgeon *méchoui*: the fish is marinated in salt the traditional way, then roasted on a spit. ✉ *2705 chemin Royal* ☎ *418/828–2670* ⏲ *Apr.–Jan., daily 8:30–6.*

CHARLEVOIX

Updated by Michèle Thibeau

Bordered by the Laurentian Mountains to the north, the Saguenay River to the east, and the St. Lawrence River to the south, the Charlevoix region is famous for awe-inspiring vistas and kaleidoscopes of color that change throughout the day. The region also has rich historical significance for both French Canadians and English Canadians. The "discoverer" of Canada, Jacques Cartier, is believed to have set foot in the area in 1535. More certain is a visit 73 years later by Samuel de Champlain.New France's first historian, the Jesuit priest François-Xavier de Charlevoix (pronounced sharle-*vwah*), is the region's namesake. The area's first white inhabitants arrived in the early 1700s. Among other things, they developed a small shipbuilding industry that specialized in sturdy schooners called *goélettes,* which were used to haul everything from logs to lobsters up and down the coast in the days before rail and paved roads. In the 19th century, as steamships plied the St. Lawrence, Charlevoix became a popular tourist destination for well-to-do English Canadians and British colonial administrators from Montréal and Québec City. Since then, tourism—and hospitality—has become Charlevoix's trademark.

The region has attracted and inspired generations of painters, poets, writers, and musicians from across Québec and Canada and became a UNESCO World Biosphere Reserve in 1989. In summer, hiking, fishing, picnicking, sightseeing, and whale-watching are the area's main attractions. Winter activities include downhill and cross-country skiing, skidooing (or snowmobiling), ice fishing, dogsledding, and snowshoeing.

Baie-St-Paul

17 *120 km (72 mi) northeast of Québec City.*

Baie-St-Paul, one of the oldest towns in the province, is popular with craftspeople and artists. With its centuries-old mansard-roof houses, the village is situated on the banks of a winding river on a wide plain encircled by high hills. Boutiques and a handful of commercial galleries line the historic narrow streets in the town center; most have original artwork and crafts for sale. In addition, each August, more than a dozen artists from across Canada take part in the "Symposium of Modern Art." The artists work together to create a giant canvas about the year's theme.

What to See

Centre d'Art Baie-St-Paul. Adjacent to the city's main church, this center displays a diverse collection of works by more than 20 Charlevoix artists. In the tapestry atelier, weavers create traditional and contemporary pieces and demonstrate techniques. ✉ *4 rue Ambroise-Fafard* ☎ *418/435–3681* 🎟 *Free* ⏲ *Apr.–mid-June, Tues.–Sun. 10–5; late*

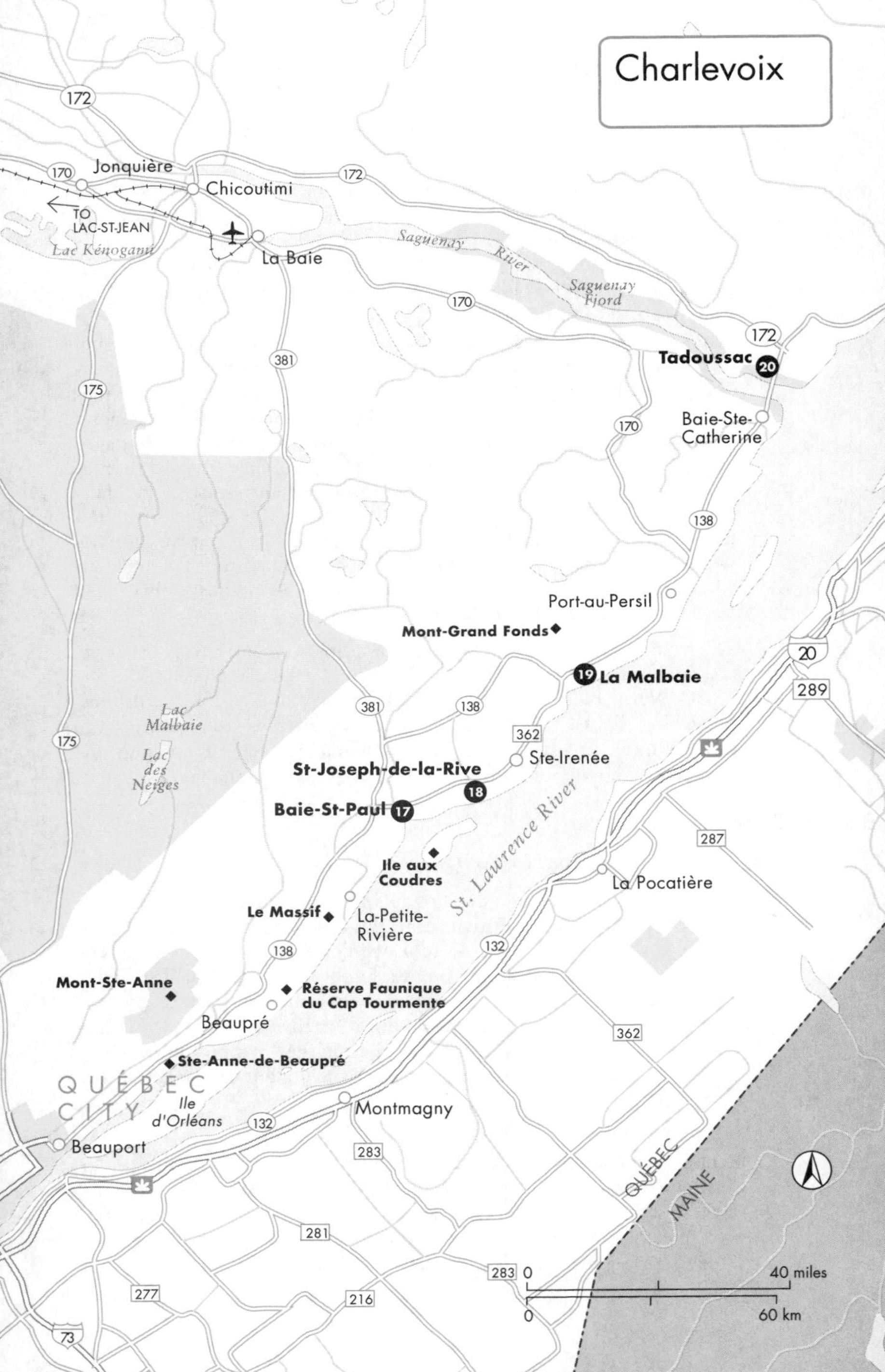
Charlevoix
172
170
Jonquière
Chicoutimi
TO
LAC-ST-JEAN
Lac Kénogami
La Baie
Saguenay River
Saguenay Fjord
170
172
Tadoussac
20
381
175
Baie-Ste-Catherine
170
138
Port-au-Persil
Mont-Grand Fonds
20
19
La Malbaie
289
Lac Malbaie
381
138
175
362
Ste-Irenée
Lac des Neiges
St-Joseph-de-la-Rive
18
Baie-St-Paul
17
St. Lawrence River
287
Ile aux Coudres
La Pocatière
Le Massif
La-Petite-Rivière
138
132
Mont-Ste-Anne
Réserve Faunique du Cap Tourmente
Beaupré
362
Ste-Anne-de-Beaupré
QUÉBEC CITY
Ile d'Orléans
Montmagny
132
Beauport
283
QUÉBEC
MAINE
281
283
0
40 miles
277
216
0
60 km
73

June–early Sept., Tues.–Sun. 10–6; early Sept.–mid-Nov., Tues.–Sun. 10–5; mid-Nov.–Mar., Fri.–Sun. 10–5.

SIDE TRIP TIP

Baie-St-Paul and Charlevoix are superb places for inspiration–no matter the season. If you've not packed your art supplies, be sure to take lots of pictures so you or someone else can bring this region to life on canvas or in a scrap book!

Centre d'Exposition de Baie-St-Paul. The mandate of the exhibition center is to promote modern and contemporary art created by Charlevoix artists from 1920 to 1970. The center is in a modern building that was awarded a provincial architectural prize in 1992. ✉ *23 rue Ambroise-Fafard* ☎ *418/435–3681* 🎫 *C$3* ⏲ *Tues.–Sun 10–5 (until 6 late June–early Sept.*

4

Maison René Richard. Jean-Paul Lemieux, Clarence Gagnon, and many more of Québec's greatest landscape artists have depicted the area. Some of these works are for sale at this gallery that also houses Gagnon's old studio. There is a modest fee for the studio tour. ✉ *58 rue St-Jean-Baptiste* ☎ *418/435–5571* ⏲ *Daily 10–6.*

Where to Stay & Eat

★ $$$–$$$$ **Auberge la Maison Otis.** Three buildings in the village center house the calm, romantic accommodations of this inn. Some guest rooms, decorated in traditional or country styles, have whirlpools, fireplaces, and antique furnishings. There are also four apartments. The restaurant ($$$$), in an elegant, Norman-style house that dates to the mid-1850s, serves creative, regionally oriented French cuisine, such as *pintade,* a local fowl, lamb, or Angus beef. Dinner is a five-course, fixed-price affair, but you can also order à la carte. Rates for Monday and Tuesday stays can be based on a breakfast-only plan. In 2006, the inn added the Café des Artistes, the only spot in town where you'll find espresso coffee and Guinness on tap. Food includes European-style pizzas, pasta, and soup. It's a very popular spot! ✉ *23 rue St-Jean-Baptiste, G3Z 1M2* ☎ *418/435–2255 or 800/267–2254* 📠 *418/435–2464* 🌐 *www.maisonotis.com* *26 rooms, 4 suites, 4 apartments* *Restaurant, café (with Internet), cable TV, some in-room VCRs, in-room data ports, indoor pool, sauna, spa, bar, lounge, meeting rooms, some pets allowed (fee); no a/c in some rooms* 💳 *MC, V* *MAP.*

EN ROUTE

From Baie-St-Paul, instead of the faster Route 138 to La Malbaie, drivers can choose the open, scenic coastal drive on **Route 362.** This section of road has memorable views of rolling hills—green, white, or ablaze with fiery hues, depending on the season—meeting the broad expanse of the "sea," as the locals like to call the St. Lawrence estuary.

St-Joseph-de-la-Rive

18 *19 km (12 mi) northeast of Baie-St-Paul.*

A secondary road descends sharply into St-Joseph-de-la-Rive, with its line of old houses hugging the mountain base on a narrow shore route.

The town has a number of peaceful inns and inviting restaurants. Drive through and see the traces of early town life and the beginning of local industry: an old firehouse and a hydroelectric building that houses a generator dating back to 1928.

What to See

Exposition Maritime (Maritime Museum). This small exhibit, housed in an old, still-active shipyard, commemorates the days of the St. Lawrence goélettes, the feisty little schooners that, until the 1950s, were the lifeblood of the region. In the mid-20th century, the roads through Charlevoix were little more than rugged tracks. (Indeed, they are still narrow and winding.) Very large families lived in cramped conditions aboard the boats. To modern eyes, it doesn't look like it was a comfortable existence, but the folklore of the goélettes, celebrated in poetry, paintings, and song, is part of the region's strong cultural identity. ✉ *305 pl. de l'Église* ☎ *418/635–1131* 🎫 *C$3* ⏲ *Mid-May–mid-June and early Sept.–mid-Oct., weekdays 9–4, weekends 11–4; mid-June–early Sept., daily 9–5.*

Île-aux-Coudres. A free, government-run ferry from the wharf in St-Joseph-de-la-Rive takes you on the 15-minute trip to the island where Jacques Cartier's men gathered *coudres* (hazelnuts) in 1535. Since then, the island has produced many a goélette, and the families of former captains now run several small inns. You can bike around the island (26 km [16 mi]) and see windmills and water mills, or stop at boutiques selling paintings and crafts such as traditional handwoven household linens. ☎ *418/438–2743 ferry information.*

Where to Stay

$–$$ 🏨 **Hôtel Cap-aux-Pierres.** One of several properties originally established by the entrepreneurial Dufour family in the 1930s to support their 17 children, the traditional Canadian main building of this hotel has a long veranda with river views. Comfortable accommodations are also available in a motel section, open only in summer. About a third of the rooms have river views. The restaurant serves a mix of Québec standards and French cuisine; summer entertainment includes folk dancing on Saturday evening. ✉ *246 chemin la Baleine, Île-aux-Coudres, La Baleine G0A 2A0* ☎ *418/438–2711 or 800/463–5250* 📠 *418/438–2127* 🌐 *www.hotelcapauxpierres.com* 🛏 *98 rooms* ♿ *Restaurant, snack bar, cable TV with movies, in-room data ports, driving range, miniature golf, tennis court, indoor-outdoor pool, hot tub, sauna, spa, badminton, croquet, lawn bowling, shuffleboard, softball, volleyball, bar, lounge, recreation room, shop, babysitting, playground, meeting rooms, some pets allowed (fee), no-smoking floors; no a/c in some rooms* 💳 *AE, D, DC, MC, V* ⏲ *Closed mid-Oct.–Apr.* 🍽 *EP.*

Shopping

Papeterie St-Gilles (✉ 354 rue F. A. Savard ☎ 418/635–2430 or 866/635–2430) produces handcrafted stationery using a 17th-century process. The paper factory, which is also a small museum, explains through photographs and demonstrations how paper is manufactured the old-fashioned way. Slivers of wood and flower petals are pressed into the paper sheets, which are as thick as the covers of a paperback book. The finished products—made into writing paper, greeting cards, and one-page poems or quotations—make beautiful, if pricey, gifts.

La Malbaie

19 *35 km (22 mi) northeast of St-Joseph-de-la-Rive.*

La Malbaie, one of the province's most elegant and historically interesting resort towns, was known as Murray Bay when wealthy Anglophones summered here. The area became popular with American and Canadian politicians in the late 1800s when Ottawa Liberals and Washington Republicans partied decorously all summer with members of the Québec judiciary. William Howard Taft built the "summer White House," the first of three summer residences, in 1894, when he was the American civil governor of the Philippines. He became the 27th president of the United States in 1908.

Many Taft-era homes now serve as handsome inns, offering old-fashioned coddling with such extras as breakfast in bed, whirlpool baths, and free shuttles to the ski areas in winter. Many serve lunch and dinner to nonresidents, so you can tour the area going from one gourmet delight to the next. The cuisine, as elsewhere in Québec, is genuine French or regional fare.

What to See

Casino de Charlevoix. The casino is one of three gaming halls in Québec (the others are in Montréal and Hull) owned and operated by Loto-Québec. The smallest of the three, it still draws more than 1 million visitors a year—some of whom stay at the Fairmont Le Manoir Richelieu, which is connected to the casino by a tunnel. There are 20 gaming tables and more than 800 slot machines. The minimum gambling age is 18. Photo I.D. is required to enter the casino. ✉ *183 rue Richelieu, Pointe-au-Pic* ☎ *418/665–5300 or 800/665–2274* 🌐 *www.casino-de-charlevoix.com* ⏲ *Mid-June–Aug., Sun.–Thurs. 10 AM–2 AM, Fri. and Sat. 10 AM–3 AM; Sept.–mid-June, Sun.–Thurs. 11 AM–midnight, Fri. and Sat. 11 AM–3 AM.*

Musée de Charlevoix. The museum traces the region's history through a major permanent exhibit called Appartenances (Belonging), installed in 2003. Folk art, paintings, and artifacts recount the past, starting with the French, then the Scottish settlers, and the area's evolution into a vacation spot and artists' haven. ✉ *10 chemin du Havre, Pointe-au-Pic* ☎ *418/665–4411* 🎟 *C$4* ⏲ *Late June–early Sept., daily 10–6; early Sept.–late June, Tues.–Fri. 10–5, weekends 1–5.*

OFF THE BEATEN PATH

POTERIE DE PORT-AU-PERSIL – Visiting potters, many from France, study Canadian ceramic techniques at this pottery studio, about 25 km (15½ mi) east of La Malbaie. Classes for amateurs are available from late June through August (by the hour or longer starting at C$12). Half of the bright yellow barn housing the studio is a store, with ceramics and other crafts made by Québec artists. ✉ *1001 rue St-Laurent (Rte. 138), St-Siméon* ☎ *418/638–2349* 🌐 *www.poteriedeportaupersil.com* ⏲ *Mid-May–Sept., daily 9–6.*

Where to Stay & Eat

★ $$–$$$$ **Auberge la Pinsonnière.** An atmosphere of country luxury prevails at this Relais & Châteaux inn, which has an impressive art collection. Every guest room is different—some have fireplaces, whirlpools, and king-size four-poster beds—and half overlook Murray Bay on the St. Lawrence River. The restaurant ($$$$) is excellent, and the auberge has one of the largest wine cellars in North America, housing 12,000 bottles. The haute cuisine doesn't come cheap; the appetizers, including foie gras with pear confit, duck ravioli, and braised sweetbreads, cost as much as the entrées in other area establishments, but the dining experience is worth the money. *124 rue St-Raphaël, Cap-à-l'Aigle, G5A 1X9 418/665–4431 or 800/387–4431 418/665–7156 www.lapinsonniere.com 25 rooms, 1 suite Restaurant, fans, some in-room hot tubs, cable TV, in-room data ports, tennis court, indoor pool, spa, beach, bar, 2 lounges, meeting rooms, no-smoking rooms; no a/c in some rooms AE, MC, V BP.*

$$–$$$ **Auberge des Peupliers.** About half the guest rooms at this hilltop inn overlook the St. Lawrence River. Accommodations, outfitted in country-style furnishings, are spread among three buildings, including a farmhouse more than two centuries old. A former barn holds more-luxurious rooms, some with terraces; a stone house has rooms with fireplaces and balconies. At the restaurant ($$$), chef Dominique Truchon earns high marks for dishes such as arctic trout in pastis-and-raspberry sauce. For an extra C$60, your lodging can include the evening five-course table d'hôte for two. *381 rue St-Raphaël, Cap-à-l'Aigle, G5A 2N8 418/665–4423 or 888/282–3743 418/665–3179 www.aubergedespeupliers.com 22 rooms Restaurant, fans, cable TV, tennis court, hot tub, massage, sauna, badminton, croquet, lounge, piano bar, recreation room, babysitting, meeting room, no-smoking rooms; no a/c in some rooms AE, DC, MC, V No lunch BP.*

★ $$–$$$$ **Fairmont Le Manoir Richelieu.** Constructed in 1929, this castlelike building and its sweeping grounds underwent a C$100 million restoration in the late 1990s. The restaurants offer a wide range of food, from family fare to haute cuisine. At the clubby after-dinner lounge, you can smoke a cigar and sip a single malt or vintage port. The full-service spa has 22 treatment rooms, and the links-style golf course overlooks the St. Lawrence. A tunnel connects the hotel with the Casino de Charlevoix. A sports facility—including two heated pools and a Jacuzzi outside, and a pool, hot tub, and steam bath indoors—is great for all ages. *181 rue Richelieu, Pointe-au-Pic, G5A 1X7 418/665–3703 or 800/463–2613 418/665–3093 www.fairmont.com 390 rooms, 15 suites 3 restaurants, room service, in-room safes, some in-room hot tubs, minibars, cable TV with movies and video games, in-room data ports, driving range, 18-hole golf course, 9-hole golf course, miniature golf, 3 tennis courts, indoor pool, saltwater pool, outdoor Jacuzzi and heated pool, health club, spa, mountain bikes, croquet, hiking, horseback riding, Ping-Pong, shuffleboard, volleyball, cross-country skiing, ice-skating, sleigh rides, snowmobiling, tobogganing, 2 bars, lounge, casino, piano, recreation room, babysitting, children's programs (ages 4–12), dry cleaning, laundry service, concierge,*

concierge floor, convention center, some pets allowed (fee), no-smoking floors 💳 *AE, DC, MC, V* 🍴 *BP.*

The Arts

Domaine Forget is a (✉ 5 St-Antoine, Ste-Irenée ☎ 418/452–3535 or 888/336–7438 ⊕ www.domaineforget.com) music and dance academy that has a 600-seat hall in Ste-Irenée, 15 km (9 mi) south of La Malbaie. Fine musicians from around the world, many of whom teach or study at the school, perform during its International Festival. The festival, which runs from mid-June to late August, includes Sunday musical brunches. Despite a fire in 2005 that ravaged the cafeteria and services pavilion, the Domaine has continued its mandate and is working to rebuild.

Sports & the Outdoors

Club de Golf de Manoir Richelieu (✉ 595 côte Bellevue, Pointe-au-Pic ☎ 418/665–2526 or 800/463–2613 ⊕ www.fairmont.com) is a par-71, 6,225-yard, links-style course with 18 holes. Greens fees start at C$125. The resort also has a 9-hole course.

Mont-Grand Fonds (✉ 1000 chemin des Loisirs ☎ 418/665–0095 or 877/665–0095 ⊕ www.montgrandfonds.com), a winter-sports center 10 km (6 mi) north of La Malbaie, has 16 downhill slopes, a 1,105-foot vertical drop, and two lifts. It also has 160 km (99 mi) of cross-country trails. Two trails meet International Ski Federation standards, and the ski center occasionally hosts major competitions. You may also go dogsledding, sleigh riding, ice-skating, and tobogganing here.

Tadoussac

 *71 km (44 mi) north of La Malbaie.*

The small town of Tadoussac shares the view up the magnificent Saguenay Fjord with Baie-Ste-Catherine, across the Saguenay River. The drive here from La Malbaie, along Route 138, leads past lovely villages and views along the St. Lawrence. Jacques Cartier made a stop at this point in 1535, and from 1600 to the mid-19th century it was an important meeting site for fur traders. Whale-watching excursions and fjord cruises now depart from Tadoussac, as well as from Chicoutimi, farther up the deep fjord.

As the Saguenay River flows from Lac St-Jean south toward the St. Lawrence, it has a dual character: between Alma and Chicoutimi, the once rapidly flowing river has been harnessed for hydroelectric power; in its lower section, it becomes wider and deeper and flows by steep mountains and cliffs en route to the St. Lawrence. Small, white beluga whales, which live here year-round, breed in the lower portion of the Saguenay in summer. The many marine species that live in the confluence of the fjord and the seaway attract other whales, too, such as pilots, finbacks, and humpbacks.

Sadly, the beluga is an endangered species; the whales, with 35 other species of mammals and birds and 21 species of fish, are threatened by pollution in the St. Lawrence River. This has spurred a C$100 million project (funded by the federal and provincial governments) aimed at removing or capping sediment in the most polluted areas, stopping industrial and residential emissions into the river, and restoring natural habitat.

What to See

Centre d'Interprétation des Mammifères Marins. You can learn more about the whales and their habitat at this interpretation center run by members of a locally based research team. They're only too glad to answer questions. In addition, explanatory videos and exhibits (including a collection of whale skeletons) tell you everything there is to know about the mighty cetaceans. ✉ *108 rue de la Cale-Sèche* ☎ *418/235–4701* 🌐 *www.whales-online.net* *C$6.25* ⏲ *Mid-May–mid-June and mid-Sept.–mid-Oct., daily noon–5; mid-June–mid-Sept., daily 9–8.*

Parc Marine du Saguenay–St-Laurent. The 800-square-km (309-square-mi) marine park, at the confluence of the Saguenay and St. Lawrence rivers, has been created to protect the latter's fragile ecosystem. ✉ *Park office: 182 rue de l'Église* ☎ *418/235–4703 or 800/463–6769.*

Where to Stay

$$–$$$$ **Hôtel Tadoussac.** The rambling white Victorian-style hotel with a red mansard roof is as much a symbol of Tadoussac as the Château Frontenac is of Québec City. The 1942 wood building has retained its gracefulness over the years. The spacious lobby has a stone fireplace and sofas for relaxing. Long corridors lead to country-furnished rooms; half of them overlook the bay, the starting point for whale-watching and fjord tours. Hand-painted murals and wood paneling from the 1852 hotel that originally stood on this site encircle the oldest dining room. ✉ *165 rue Bord d'Eau, G0T 4A0* ☎ *418/235–4421 or 800/561–0718* *418/235–4607* 🌐 *www.hoteltadoussac.com* *149 rooms* *3 restaurants, cable TV, miniature golf, tennis court, pool, spa, horseshoes, bar, recreation room, convention center, no-smoking floor; no a/c* *AE, D, DC, MC, V* ⏲ *Closed late Oct.–late May* *EP.*

Sports & the Outdoors

The best months for seeing whales are August and September, although some operators extend the season at either end if whales are around.

Croisières AML (☎ 418/692–1159 or 800/463–1292 🌐 www.croisieresaml.com) offers two- to three-hour whale-watching tours for C$45–C$55. The tours, in Zodiacs or larger boats, depart from Baie-Ste-Catherine and Tadoussac. Fjord tours are also available.

> **SIDE TRIP TIP**
>
> The zodiacs get you close to the whales, but the ride can be jarring and tough for that sore back.

Croisières Dufour (☎ 800/463–5250 🌐 www.dufour.ca) offers daylong cruises combined with whale-watching from Québec City as well as 2¼- and 3-hour whale-watching cruises (C$55) from Baie-Ste-Catherine and Tadoussac. Tours, some of which cruise up the Saguenay Fjord, use Zodiacs or larger boats.

QUÉBEC CITY SIDE TRIP ESSENTIALS

Transportation

Autocar Dupont-Gray Line ☎ 418/649-9226 🌐 www.tourdupont.com

BY CAR

To reach Montmorency Falls, take Route 440 (Autoroute Dufferin–Montmorency) east from Québec City approximately 9½ km (6 mi) to the exit for Montmorency Falls. For Ste-Anne-de-Beaupré take Route 440 (Autoroute Dufferin–Montmorency) east from Québec City approximately 23 km (14 mi).

To get to Île d'Orléans, take Route 440 (Autoroute Dufferin–Montmorency) northeast. After a drive of about 10 km (6 mi) take the Pont de l'Île d'Orléans (a bridge) to the island. The main road, chemin Royal (Route 368), circles the island, extending 67 km (42 mi) through the island's six villages; the route turns into chemin du Bout de l'Île in Ste-Pétronille.

Parking can sometimes be a problem, but you can leave your car in each town's church parking lot and explore each village on foot. Many people enjoy biking around the island's curvy roads. Bikes can also be rented in St-Laurent at Ecolocyclo.

To get to Charlevoix from Québec City, take Route 440 (Autoroute Dufferin–Montmorency) northeast and then continue past the Côte de Beaupré on Route 138. From there you'll be able to branch out for destinations such as Petit-Rivière-St-François or Baie-St-Paul.

Contact & Resources

BANKS & EXCHANGE SERVICES

Bank cards are widely accepted in Québec and Canada. There are many branches of Québec's financial cooperative, La Caisse populaire Desjardins, as well as bank machines (ATMs), throughout the region. A "Caisse Pop" as it's locally referred to, is located in St-Pierre on Île d'Orléans, and there are several scattered throughout the Côte de Beaupré on avenue Royale and in Ste-Anne-de-Beaupré itself on the boulevard.

In Charlevoix there are services from Baie-St-Paul and Petit-Rivière St-François to Île-aux-Coudres and La Malbaie.

Funds from ATMs will be in Canadian currency. Most have money exchange services, although personnel at the counter will likely speak more French than English.

Château-Richer ✉ 7973 av. Royale ☎ 418/822-1818. **Baie St-Paul** ✉ 74 rue Ambroise-Fafard. **Petite-Rivière-St-François** ✉ 1065 rue Principale. **Île-aux-Coudres** ✉ 29 chemin de la Traverse. **La Malbaie** ✉ 130 rue John-Nairne.

EMERGENCIES

Centre Médical Prévost is the principal medical clinic on Île d'Orléans. Centre Hospitalier de Charlevoix is the hospital in Charlevoix.

Centre Médical Prévost ✉ 1015 Rte. Prévost, St-Pierre ☎ 418/828–2213. **Centre Hospitalier de Charlevoix** ✉ 74 blvd. Ambroise-Fafard, Baie-St-Paul ☎ 418/435–5150.

TOUR OPTIONS

A 4½-hour bus tour of Côte de Beaupré, with a 15-minute stop at Montmorency Falls, is available from Autocar Dupont-Gray Line. Hop on a shuttle from some downtown hotels or begin the tour at Québec City's train station, La Gare du Palais, at 1:30 pm. for C$42.95.

From Québec City, take a bus-and-boat adventure with Autocar Dupont-Gray Line to discover Charlevoix. The bus lets you off at Baie Ste-Catherine, where you'll board a boat for the second half of the adventure. Tours leave from La Gare du Palais at 9:15 AM from June 1 to October 9 with a 7:30 PM return. It includes three hours of whale-watching. Prices range from C$99.95 in a boat to C$104.95 in a Zodiac.

Autocar Dupont-Gray Line ☎ 418/649–9226 ⊕ www.tourdupont.com.

VISITOR INFORMATION

At the Beaupré Coast Interpretation Center, in a former convent, guides in costume explain displays on the history of the region. Admission is C$5. The center is open mid-May–mid-October, daily 10–5. The rest of the year, the center is open by reservation only. Québec City Tourist Information has a bureau in Beauport, in Montmorency Falls Park. It's open June 3–mid-October, daily 9–5.

Any of the offices of the Québec City Region Tourism and Convention Bureau can provide information on island tours and accommodations. The island's Chamber of Commerce operates a tourist-information kiosk just over the bridge at the first stoplight, at the western corner of côte du Pont and chemin Royal in St-Pierre. Look for the question mark on signs as you approach.

Association Touristique Régionale de Charlevoix ✉ 495 blvd. de Comporté, C.P. 275, La Malbaie G5A 3G3 ☎ 418/665–4454 or 800/667–2276 🖷 418/665–3811 ⊕ www.tourisme-charlevoix.com. **Beaupré Coast Interpretation Center** ✉ 7976 av. Royale, C. P. 40, Château-Richer ☎ 418/824–3677 🖷 418/824–5907. **Chamber of Commerce** ✉ 490 côte du Pont, St-Pierre ☎ 418/828–9411 or 866/941–9411 ⊕ www.iledorleans.com. **Québec City Tourist Information** ✉ Montmorency Falls Park, Beauport ☎ 418/641–6649 ✉ 4300 blvd. Ste-Anne [Rte. 138], Québec City ☎ No phone.

UNDERSTANDING QUÉBEC

QUÉBEC AT A GLANCE

FRENCH VOCABULARY

MENU GUIDE

QUÉBEC AT A GLANCE

Fast Facts

Nickname: La Belle Province (The Beautiful Province)
Capital: Québec City
Motto: Je me souviens (I remember)
Province bird: Snowy owl
Province flower: Blue flag iris
Province tree: Yellow birch
Administrative divisions: 17
Entered the Confederation: July 1, 1867
Population: 7.5 million
Population density: 5 people per square kilometer (13 people per square mile)
Median age: 38.8
Infant mortality rate: 4.9 deaths per 1,000 live births
Ethnic groups: White 93%; black 2%; South Asian 1%; Chinese 1%; Southeast Asian 1%; Arab/West Asian 1%; Latin American 1%
Religion: Roman Catholic 83%; unaffiliated 6%; Protestant 5%; other 3%; Muslim 2%; Jewish 1%

Some say that no one ever leaves Montréal, for that city, like Canada itself, is designed to preserve the past, a past that happened somewhere else.
–Leonard Cohen

Why should Canada, wild and unsettled as it is, impress us as an older country than the States, unless because her institutions are old? All things appeared to contend there with a certain rust of antiquity, such as forms on old armor and iron guns—the rust of conventions and formalities. It is said that the metallic roofs of Montréal and Québec keep sound and bright for 40 years in some cases. But if the rust was not on the tinned roofs and spires, it was on the inhabitants and their institutions.
–Henry David Thoreau

Geography & Environment

Land area: 1.6 million square km (594,860 square mi); Canada's largest province
Terrain: Rocky, forested hills, including the Laurentian Mountains, with many rivers and lakes to the north and the population centered in the south, along the northern bank of the St. Lawrence River
Natural resources: Aluminum, asbestos, copper, gold, iron, silver, wood, zinc
Natural hazards: Earthquakes, forest fires, ice storms, landslides, tornados

Environmental issues: Effluent from textiles, pulp and paper, and wastewater treatment are a problem in Québec's rivers; volatile organic compounds such as benzene and sulfur oxide are closely monitored in the air on the east end of Montréal; 10 of Canada's 11 aluminum smelters are located in Québec, and the province is working to reduce the output of industry pollutants; wood burning in Montréal and other big cities is affecting air quality and is discouraged.

Economy

GSP: C$221.8 billion (US$162.1 billion)
Per capita income: C$34,275 (US$27,920)
Unemployment: 8.4%
Workforce: 3.7 million (manufacturing 17%; trade 16%; health care and social assistance 13%; other 8%; finance, insurance, real estate and leasing 6%; professional, scientific and technical services 6%; educational services 6%; accommodation and food services 6%; public administration 6%; transportation and warehousing 5%; construction 4%; information, culture, and recreation 4%; business, building, and other support services 3%)
Major industries: Aircraft, beverages, chemicals, clothing, fishing, food products, fur, furniture, iron, motor vehicles, paper, refined petroleum, steel, tourism
Agricultural products: Dairy products, maple syrup, sugar beets, tobacco
Exports: C$5.2 billion (US$4.2 billion)
Major export products: Aircraft, machinery, paper products

Did You Know?

- Québec's vast water resources generate much of Canada's electricity. Using the La Grande River and other waterways, Hydro-Québec has created an underground set of spillways three times the height of Niagara Falls. This and other massive projects make it the largest generator in the country.

- Québec is three times the size of France, but at 6 million has just one-tenth the number of French speakers.

- The world's largest edible fungi was found in Québec in 1987. The giant puffball (Calvatia gigantea) was more than 8 feet in circumference and weighed 48 pounds.

- According to Canada's 2001 census, the majority of immigrants to Montréal are from Italy. Haitian immigrants are the second-largest group.

- There are 380 islands inside the borders of metropolitan Montréal.

- Although the rest of Canada uses English common law, Québec's civil law is based on old French laws. All of Canada has one criminal code.

- How much cheese does 540,000 pounds of milk make? Québec's Agropur turned exactly that much milk into a cheddar weighing 57,508 pounds in 1995.

- Eighty-four percent of Québec is covered by the Canadian Shield, a geographical area believed to be the nucleus of North America. Geologic evidence shows rock in Québec was the first in North America to be permanently elevated above sea level, leaving formations millions of years old unaltered since ice sheets drifted across the continent.

- Québec was the sports capital of North America in the 19th century. Here the rules for ice hockey were invented, and lacrosse, football, and curling were all altered here. Snowshoes, canoes, and toboggans were adapted from versions the Native Americans used here.

- Michael Barski made Québec the sit-up capital of the world in 2003 when he completed 7,203 abdominal crunches in an hour. That's two sit-ups every second.

- Québec City is the only city in North America to have preserved its surrounding ramparts, bastions, gates, and defenses. For that, it was named a World Heritage Site by UNESCO.

FRENCH VOCABULARY

One of the trickiest French sounds to pronounce is the nasal final *n* sound (whether or not the *n* is actually the last letter of the word). You should try to pronounce it as a sort of nasal grunt—as in "huh." The vowel that precedes the *n* will govern the vowel sound of the word, and in this list we precede the final *n* with an *h* to remind you to be nasal.

Another problem sound is the ubiquitous but untransliterable *eu,* as in *bleu* (blue) or *deux* (two), and the very similar sound in *je* (I), *ce* (this), and *de* (of). The closest equivalent might be the vowel sound in "put," but rounded. The famous rolled *r* is a glottal sound. Consonants at the ends of words are usually silent; when the following word begins with a vowel, however, the two are run together by sounding the consonant. There are two forms of "you" in French: *vous* (formal and plural) and *tu* (a singular, personal form). When addressing an adult you don't know, *vous* is always best.

Basics

English	French	Pronunciation
Yes/no	Oui/non	wee/nohn
Please	S'il vous plaît	seel voo play
Thank you	Merci	mair-**see**
You're welcome	De rien	deh ree-**ehn**
Excuse me, sorry	Pardon	pahr-**don**
Good morning/ afternoon	Bonjour	bohn-**zhoor**
Good evening	Bonsoir	bohn-**swahr**
Goodbye	Au revoir	o ruh-**vwahr**
Mr. (Sir)	Monsieur	muh-**syuh**
Mrs. (Ma'am)	Madame	ma-**dam**
Miss	Mademoiselle	mad-mwa-**zel**
Pleased to meet you	Enchanté(e)	ohn-shahn-**tay**
How are you?	Comment allez-vous?	kuh-mahn-tahl-ay **voo**
Very well, thanks	Très bien, merci	tray bee-ehn, mair-**see**
And you?	Et vous?	ay voo?

Numbers

English	French	Pronunciation
one	un	uhn
two	deux	deuh
three	trois	twah
four	quatre	**kaht**-ruh

five	cinq	sank
six	six	seess
seven	sept	set
eight	huit	wheat
nine	neuf	nuf
ten	dix	deess
eleven	onze	ohnz
twelve	douze	dooz
thirteen	treize	trehz
fourteen	quatorze	kah-torz
fifteen	quinze	kanz
sixteen	seize	sez
seventeen	dix-sept	deez-**set**
eighteen	dix-huit	deez-**wheat**
nineteen	dix-neuf	deez-**nuf**
twenty	vingt	vehn
twenty-one	vingt-et-un	vehnt-ay-**uhn**
thirty	trente	trahnt
forty	quarante	ka-**rahnt**
fifty	cinquante	sang-**kahnt**
sixty	soixante	swa-**sahnt**
seventy	soixante-dix	swa-sahnt-**deess**
eighty	quatre-vingts	kaht-ruh-**vehn**
ninety	quatre-vingt-dix	kaht-ruh-vehn-**deess**
one hundred	cent	sahn
one thousand	mille	meel

Colors

black	noir	nwahr
blue	bleu	bleuh
brown	brun/marron	bruhn/mar-**rohn**
green	vert	vair
orange	orange	o-**rahnj**
pink	rose	rose
red	rouge	rouge
violet	violette	vee-o-**let**
white	blanc	blahnk
yellow	jaune	zhone

Days of the Week

Sunday	dimanche	dee-**mahnsh**
Monday	lundi	luhn-**dee**
Tuesday	mardi	mahr-**dee**
Wednesday	mercredi	mair-kruh-**dee**
Thursday	jeudi	zhuh-**dee**
Friday	vendredi	vawn-druh-**dee**
Saturday	samedi	sahm-**dee**

Months

January	janvier	zhahn-vee-**ay**
February	février	feh-vree-**ay**
March	mars	marce
April	avril	a-**vreel**
May	mai	meh
June	juin	zhwehn
July	juillet	zhwee-**ay**
August	août	ah-**oo**
September	septembre	sep-**tahm**-bruh
October	octobre	awk-**to**-bruh
November	novembre	no-**vahm**-bruh
December	décembre	day-**sahm**-bruh

Useful Phrases

Do you speak English?	Parlez-vous anglais?	par-lay **voo** **ahn**-glay
I don't speak . . . French	Je ne parle pas . . . français	zhuh nuh parl pah frahn-**say**
I don't understand	Je ne comprends pas	zhuh nuh kohm-**prahn** pah
I understand	Je comprends	zhuh kohm-**prahn**
I don't know	Je ne sais pas	zhuh nuh say **pah**
I'm American/ British	Je suis américain/ anglais	zhuh sweez a-may-ree-**kehn**/ ahn-**glay**
What's your name?	Comment vous ap-pelez-vous?	ko-mahn voo za-pell-ay-**voo**
My name is . . .	Je m'appelle . . .	zhuh ma-**pell** . . .
What time is it?	Quelle heure est-il?	kel air eh-**teel**

How?	Comment?	ko-**mahn**
When?	Quand?	kahn
Yesterday	Hier	yair
Today	Aujourd'hui	o-zhoor-**dwee**
Tomorrow	Demain	duh-**mehn**
Tonight	Ce soir	suh **swahr**
What?	Quoi?	kwah
What is it?	Qu'est-ce que c'est?	kess-kuh-**say**
Why?	Pourquoi?	**poor**-kwa
Who?	Qui?	kee
Where is . . . the train station? the subway station? the bus stop? the post office? the bank? the . . . hotel? the store? the cashier? the . . . museum? the hospital? the elevator? the telephone?	Où est . . . la gare? la station de métro? l'arrêt de bus? la poste? la banque? l'hôtel . . .? le magasin? la caisse? le musée . . .? l'hôpital? l'ascenseur? le téléphone?	oo ay la gar la sta-**syon** duh may-**tro** la-**ray** duh **booss** la post la bahnk lo-**tel** luh ma-ga-**zehn** la **kess** luh mew-**zay** lo-pee-**tahl** la-sahn-**seuhr** luh tay-lay-**phone**
Where are the restrooms? (men/women)	Où sont les toilettes? (hommes/femmes)	oo sohn lay twah-**let** (**oh**-mm/**fah**-mm)
Here/there	Ici/là	ee-**see**/la
Left/right	A gauche/à droite	a goash/a dwaht
Straight ahead	Tout droit	too dwah
Is it near/far?	C'est près/loin?	say pray/lwehn
I'd like . . . a room the key a newspaper a stamp	Je voudrais . . . une chambre la clé un journal un timbre	zhuh voo-**dray** ewn **shahm**-bruh la clay uhn zhoor-**nahl** uhn **tam**-bruh
I'd like to buy . . . cigarettes matches soap city map road map	Je voudrais acheter . . . des cigarettes des allumettes du savon un plan de ville une carte routière	zhuh voo-**dray** **ahsh**-tay day see-ga-**ret** days a-loo-**met** dew sah-**vohn** uhn plahn de **veel** ewn cart roo-tee-**air**

magazine	une revue	ewn reh-**vu**
envelopes	des enveloppes	dayz ahn-veh-**lope**
writing paper	du papier à lettres	dew pa-pee-**ay** a **let**-ruh
postcard	une carte postale	ewn cart pos-**tal**
How much is it?	C'est combien?	say comb-bee-**ehn**
A little/a lot	Un peu/beaucoup	uhn peuh/bo-**koo**
More/less	Plus/moins	plu/mwehn
Enough/too (much)	Assez/trop	a-say/tro
I am ill/sick	Je suis malade	zhuh swee ma-**lahd**
Call a . . . doctor	Appelez un . . . docteur	a-play uhn dohk-**tehr**
Help!	Au secours!	o suh-**koor**
Stop!	Arrêtez!	a-reh-**tay**
Fire!	Au feu!	o fuh
Caution!/Look out!	Attention!	a-tahn-see-**ohn**

Dining Out

A bottle of . . .	une bouteille de . . .	ewn boo-**tay** duh
A cup of . . .	une tasse de . . .	ewn tass duh
A glass of . . .	un verre de . . .	uhn vair duh
Bill/check	l'addition	la-dee-see-**ohn**
Bread	du pain	dew pan
Breakfast	le petit-déjeuner	luh puh-**tee** day-zhuh-**nay**
Butter	du beurre	dew burr
Cheers!	A votre santé!	ah vo-truh sahn-**tay**
Cocktail/aperitif	un apéritif	uhn ah-pay-ree-**teef**
Dinner	le dîner	luh dee-**nay**
Dish of the day	le plat du jour	luh plah dew **zhoor**
Enjoy!	Bon appétit!	bohn a-pay-**tee**
Fixed-price menu	le menu	luh may-**new**
Fork	une fourchette	ewn four-**shet**
I am diabetic	Je suis diabétique	zhuh swee dee-ah-bay-**teek**
I am on a diet	Je suis au régime	zhuh sweez oray-**jeem**
I am vegetarian	Je suis végé-tarien(ne)	zhuh swee vay-zhay-ta-ree-**en**
I cannot eat . . .	Je ne peux pas manger de . . .	zhuh nuh **puh** pah mahn-**jay** deh

I'd like to order	Je voudrais commander	zhuh voo-**dray** ko-mahn-**day**
Is service/the tip included?	Est-ce que le service est compris?	ess kuh luh sair-**veess** ay comb-**pree**
It's good/bad	C'est bon/mauvais	say bohn/ mo-**vay**
It's hot/cold	C'est chaud/froid	say sho/frwah
Knife	un couteau	uhn koo-**toe**
Lunch	le déjeuner	luh day-zhuh-**nay**
Menu	la carte	la cart
Napkin	une serviette	ewn sair-vee-**et**
Pepper	du poivre	dew **pwah**-vruh
Plate	une assiette	ewn a-see-**et**
Please give me . . .	Donnez-moi . . .	doe-nay-**mwah**
Salt	du sel	dew sell
Spoon	une cuillère	ewn kwee-**air**
Sugar	du sucre	dew **sook**-ruh
Waiter!/Waitress!	Monsieur!/ Mademoiselle!	muh-**syuh**/ mad-mwa-**zel**
Wine list	la carte des vins	la cart day vehn

MENU GUIDE

French	English

General Dining

Entrée	Appetizer/Starter
Garniture au choix	Choice of vegetable side
Plat du jour	Dish of the day
Selon arrivage	When available
Supplément/En sus	Extra charge
Sur commande	Made to order

Petit Déjeuner (Breakfast)

Confiture	Jam
Miel	Honey
Oeuf à la coque	Boiled egg
Oeufs sur le plat	Fried eggs
Oeufs brouillés	Scrambled eggs
Tartine	Bread with butter

Poissons/Fruits de Mer (Fish/Seafood)

Anchois	Anchovies
Bar	Bass
Brandade de morue	Creamed salt cod
Brochet	Pike
Cabillaud/Morue	Fresh cod
Calmar	Squid
Coquilles St-Jacques	Scallops
Crevettes	Shrimp
Daurade	Sea bream
Ecrevisses	Prawns/Crayfish
Harengs	Herring
Homard	Lobster
Huîtres	Oysters
Langoustine	Prawn/Lobster
Lotte	Monkfish
Maquereau	Mackerel
Moules	Mussels
Palourdes	Clams
Saumon	Salmon
Thon	Tuna
Truite	Trout

Viande (Meat)

Agneau	Lamb
Boeuf	Beef
Boudin	Sausage

Boulettes de viande	Meatballs
Brochettes	Kabobs
Cassoulet	Casserole of white beans, meat
Cervelle	Brains
Chateaubriand	Double fillet steak
Choucroute garnie	Sausages with sauerkraut
Côtelettes	Chops
Côte/Côte de boeuf	Rib/T-bone steak
Cuisses de grenouilles	Frogs' legs
Entrecôte	Rib or rib-eye steak
Épaule	Shoulder
Escalope	Cutlet
Foie	Liver
Gigot	Leg
Porc	Pork
Ris de veau	Veal sweetbreads
Rognons	Kidneys
Saucisses	Sausages
Selle	Saddle
Tournedos	Tenderloin of T-bone steak
Veau	Veal

Methods of Preparation

A point	Medium
A l'étouffée	Stewed
Au four	Baked
Ballotine	Boned, stuffed, and rolled
Bien cuit	Well-done
Bleu	Very rare
Frit	Fried
Grillé	Grilled
Rôti	Roast
Saignant	Rare
Sauté/Poêlée	Sautéed

Volailles/Gibier (Poultry/Game)

Blanc de volaille	Chicken breast
Canard/Caneton	Duck/Duckling
Cerf/Chevreuil	Venison (red/roe)
Coq au vin	Chicken stewed in red wine
Dinde/Dindonneau	Turkey/Young turkey
Faisan	Pheasant
Lapin/Lièvre	Rabbit/Wild hare
Oie	Goose
Pintade/Pintadeau	Guinea fowl/Young guinea fowl
Poulet/Poussin	Chicken/Spring chicken

Légumes (Vegetables)

Artichaut	Artichoke
Asperge	Asparagus
Aubergine	Eggplant
Carottes	Carrots
Champignons	Mushrooms
Chou-fleur	Cauliflower
Chou (rouge)	Cabbage (red)
Laitue	Lettuce
Oignons	Onions
Petits pois	Peas
Pomme de terre	Potato
Tomates	Tomatoes

Fruits/Noix (Fruits/Nuts)

Abricot	Apricot
Amandes	Almonds
Ananas	Pineapple
Cassis	Blackcurrants
Cerises	Cherries
Citron/Citron vert	Lemon/Lime
Fraises	Strawberries
Framboises	Raspberries
Pamplemousse	Grapefruit
Pêche	Peach
Poire	Pear
Pomme	Apple
Prunes/Pruneaux	Plums/Prunes
Raisins/Raisins secs	Grapes/Raisins

Desserts

Coupe (glacée)	Sundae
Crème Chantilly	Whipped cream
Gâteau au chocolat	Chocolate cake
Glace	Ice cream
Tarte tatin	Caramelized apple tart
Tourte	Layer cake

Drinks

A l'eau	With water
Avec des glaçons	On the rocks
Bière	Beer
Blonde/brune	Light/dark
Café noir/crème	Black coffee/with steamed milk
Chocolat chaud	Hot chocolate
Eau-de-vie	Brandy

Eau minérale	Mineral water
gazeuse/non gazeuse	*carbonated/still*
Jus de . . .	. . . juice
Lait	Milk
Sec	Straight or dry
Thé	Tea
au lait/au citron	*with milk/lemon*
Vin	Wine
blanc	*white*
doux	*sweet*
léger	*light*
brut	*very dry*
rouge	*red*

SMART TRAVEL TIPS

There are planners and there are those who, excuse the pun, fly by the seat of their pants. We happily place ourselves among the planners. Our writers and editors try to anticipate all the issues you may face before and during any journey, and then they do their research. This section is the product of their efforts. Use it to get excited about your trip to Montréal and Québec City, to inform your travel planning, or to guide you on the road should the seat of your pants start to feel threadbare.

AIR TRAVEL

For service to Montréal, Montréal–Trudeau International Airport (also known by its previous name, Dorval International Airport, airport code YUL) is 22½ km (14 mi) west of the city. Québec City's Jean Lesage International Airport (YQB) is about 19 km (12 mi) northwest of downtown. Both airports handle domestic and international flights.

Flying time (gate-to-gate) to Montréal is about 1½ hours from New York, 2½ hours from Chicago, 4 hours from Dallas, and 6 hours from Los Angeles. Flying time to Québec City is about 2 hours from New York, 3 hours from Chicago, 5 hours from Dallas, and 7 hours from Los Angeles.

Long layovers don't have to be only about sitting around or shopping. These days they can be about burning off vacation calories. Check out www.airportgyms.com for lists of health clubs that are in or near many U.S. and Canadian airports. Airports **Airline and Airport Links.com** www.airlineandairportlinks.com has links to many of the world's airlines and airports. **Jean Lesage International Airport** 418/640–2600 www.aeroportdequebec.com. **Montréal-Pierre Elliott Trudeau International Airport** 800/465–1213 or 514/394–7377 www.admtl.com.

Airline Security Issues **Transportation Security Agency** www.tsa.gov/public has answers for almost every question that might come up.

CARRIERS

Of the major U.S. airlines, American, Continental, Delta, Northwest, United, and US

Airways serve Montréal; Continental and Northwest fly to Québec City.

Regularly scheduled flights from the United States to Montréal and Québec City as well as flights within Canada are available on Air Canada and the regional airlines associated with it, including Air Canada Jazz (reservations are made through Air Canada), Air Creebec, and Air Transat. Air Canada has the most nonstop flights to Montréal and Québec City from some 30 U.S. cities.

Major Airlines **Air Canada** ☎ 888/247-2262 🌐 www.aircanada.ca. **American Airlines** ☎ 800/433-7300 🌐 www.aa.com. **Continental Airlines** ☎ 800/231-0856 🌐 www.continental.com. **Delta Airlines** ☎ 800/241-4141 🌐 www.delta.com. **Northwest Airlines** ☎ 800/447-4747 🌐 www.nwa.com. **United Airlines** ☎ 800/538-2929 🌐 www.united.com. **US Airways** ☎ 800/622-1015 🌐 www.usairways.com.

Smaller Airlines **Air Creebec** ☎ 800/567-6567 🌐 www.aircreebec.ca. **Air Transat** ☎ 866/847-1112 🌐 www.airtransat.com.

CHECK-IN & BOARDING

Double-check your flight times, especially if you made your reservations far in advance. Airlines change their schedules, and alerts may not reach you. Always **bring a government-issued photo ID to the airport** (even when it's not required, a passport is best), and **arrive when you need to and not before.** Check-in usually at least an hour before domestic flights and two to three hours for international flights. But many airlines have more stringent advance check-in requirements at some busy airports. The Transportation Security Agency (TSA) estimates the waiting time for security at most major airports and publishes the information on its Web site. Note that if you aren't at the gate at least 10 minutes before your flight is scheduled to take off (sometimes earlier), you won't be allowed to board.

Don't stand in a line if you don't have to. Buy an e-ticket, check in at an electronic kiosk, or—even better—check in on your airline's Web site before you leave home. If you don't need to check luggage, you could bypass all but the security lines. These days, most domestic airline tickets are electronic; international tickets may be either electronic or paper.

You usually pay a surcharge (up to $50) to get a paper ticket, and its sole advantage is that it may be easier to endorse over to another airline if your flight is canceled and the airline with which you booked can't accommodate you on another flight. With an e-ticket, the only thing you receive is an e-mailed receipt citing your itinerary and reservation and ticket numbers. Be sure to carry this with you as you'll need it to get past security. If you lose you receipt, though, you can simply print out another copy or ask the airline to do it for you at check-in.

Particularly during busy travel seasons and around holiday periods, if a flight is oversold, the gate agent will usually ask for volunteers and will offer some sort of compensation if you are willing to take a different flight. **Know your rights.** If you are bumped from a flight *involuntarily,* the airline must give you some kind of compensation if an alternate flight can't be found within one hour. If your flight is delayed because of something within the airline's control (so bad weather doesn't count), then the airline has a responsibility to get you to your destination on the same day, even if they have to book you on another airline and in an upgraded class if necessary. Read your airline's Contract of Carriage; it's usually buried somewhere on the airline's Web site.

Be prepared to quickly adjust your plans by programming a few numbers into your cell: your airline, an airport hotel or two, your destination hotel, your car service, and/or your travel agent. Bring snacks, water, and sufficient diversions, and you'll be covered if you get stuck in the airport, on the tarmac, or even in the air during turbulence.

Trudeau Airport offers self-serve check-in and boarding passes at electronic kiosks throughout the airport. Make sure you arrive at the airport two hours before your flight's scheduled departure.

Security measures at Canadian airports are similar to those in the United States.

CUTTING COSTS

It's always good to **comparison shop.** Web sites, consolidators, and travel agents can have different arrangements with the airlines and offer different prices for exactly the same flight and day. Certain Web sites have tracking features that will e-mail you immediately when good deals are posted. Other people prefer to stick with one or two frequent-flier programs, racking up free trips and accumulating perks that can make trips easier. On some airlines, perks include a special reservations number, early boarding, access to upgrades, and more roomy economy-class seating.

Check early and often. Start looking for cheap fares up to a year in advance, and keep looking until you see something you can live with; you never know when a good deal may pop up. That said, **jump on the good deals.** Waiting even a few minutes might mean paying more. For most people, saving money is more important than flexibility, so the more affordable nonrefundable tickets work. Just remember that you'll pay dearly (often as much as $100) if you must change your travel plans. Check on prices for departures at different times of the day and to and from alternate airports, and look for departures on Tuesday, Wednesday, and Thursday, typically the cheapest days to travel. Remember to **weigh your options,** though. A cheaper flight might have a long layover rather than being nonstop, or landing at a secondary airport might substantially increase your ground transportation costs.

Note that many airline Web sites—and most ads—show prices *without* taxes and surcharges. Don't buy until you know the full price. Government taxes add up quickly. Also **watch those ticketing fees.** Surcharges are usually added when you buy your ticket anywhere but on an airline's own Web site. (By the way, that includes on the phone—even if you call the airline directly—and for paper tickets regardless of how you book).

Online Consolidators **AirlineConsolidator.com** www.airlineconsolidator.com; for international tickets. **Best Fares** www.bestfares.com; $59.90 annual membership. **Cheap Tickets** www.cheaptickets.com. **Expedia** www.expedia.com. **Hotwire** www.hotwire.com is a discounter. **lastminute.com** www.lastminute.com specializes in last-minute travel; the main site is for the United Kingdom, but it has a link to a U.S. site. **Luxury Link** www.luxurylink.com has auctions (surprisingly good deals) as well as offers at the high-end side of travel. **Onetravel.com** www.onetravel.com. **Orbitz** www.orbitz.com. **Priceline.com** www.priceline.com is a discounter that also allows bidding. **Travel.com** www.travel.com allows you to compare its rates with those of other booking engines. **Travelocity** www.travelocity.com charges a booking fee for airline tickets but promises good problem resolution.

ENJOYING THE FLIGHT

Get the seat you want. Avoid seats on the aisle directly across from the lavatories. Most frequent fliers say those are even worse than the seats that don't recline (e.g., those in the back row and those in front of a bulkhead). For more legroom, you can request emergency-aisle seats, but only do so if you're capable of moving the 35- to 60-pound airplane exit door—a Federal Aviation Administration requirement of passengers in these seats. Seats behind a bulkhead also offer more legroom, but they don't have under-seat storage. Often, you can pick a seat when you buy your ticket on an airline's Web site. But it's not always a guarantee, particularly if the airline changes the plane after you book your ticket; check back before you leave. SeatGuru.com has more information about specific seat configurations, which vary by aircraft.

Fewer airlines are providing free food for passengers in economy class. **Don't go hungry.** If you're scheduled to fly during meal times, verify if your airline offers anything to eat; even when it does, be prepared to pay. If you have dietary concerns, request special meals. These can be vegetarian, low-cholesterol, or kosher, for example. It's a good idea to pack some healthful snacks and a small (plastic) bottle of water in your carry-on bag.

Ask the airline about its children's menus, activities, and fares. On some lines infants and toddlers fly for free if they sit on a parent's lap, and older children fly for half price in their own seats. Also inquire about policies involving car seats; having one may limit where you can sit. While you're at it, ask about seat-belt extenders for car seats. And note that you can't count on a flight attendant to automatically produce an extender; you may have to inquire about it again when you board.

HOW TO COMPLAIN

If your baggage goes astray or your flight goes awry, complain right away. Most carriers require that you **file a claim immediately.** The Aviation Consumer Protection Division of the Department of Transportation publishes *Fly-Rights,* which discusses airlines and consumer issues and is available online. You can also find articles and information on mytravelrights.com, the Web site of the nonprofit Consumer Travel Rights Center.

Airline Complaints **Canadian Transportation Agency** ✉ Air Travel Complaints, Ottawa, ON K1A 0N9 ☎ 888/222-2592 📠 819/953-5686 🌐 www.cta-otc.gc.ca. **Federal Aviation Administration Consumer Hotline** ☎ 866/835-5322 🌐 www.faa.gov. **Office of Aviation Enforcement and Proceedings** (Aviation Consumer Protection Division) ☎ 202/366-2220 🌐 airconsumer.ost.dot.gov.

GROUND TRANSPORTATION

In Montréal, a taxi from Trudeau International to downtown costs about C$35. All taxi companies must charge the same rate for travel between the airport and downtown.

La Québecoise shuttles are a much cheaper alternative for getting to and from Trudeau International. Shuttles leave from Montréal Central Bus Station and pick up and drop off passengers at the downtown train station, as well as at major hotels. Shuttles run every 20 minutes from 4 AM to 11 PM and cost C$13 one-way, C$22.75 round-trip.

In Québec City, private limo service is expensive, starting at C$65 for the ride from the airport into the city. Try Groupe Limousine A-1. Taxis are available immediately outside the airport exit near the baggage-claim area. A ride into the city costs about C$30. Two local taxi firms are Taxi Coop de Québec, the largest company in the city, and Taxi Québec.

Montréal Contacts **Aéroports de Montréal** ✉ 1100 René-Lévesque blvd. Ouest, Suite 2100 ☎ 514/394-7200 🌐 www.admtl.com. **Montréal-Pierre Elliott Trudeau International Airport** ✉ 975 Roméo-Vachon blvd. Nord, Dorval ☎ 514/394-7377. **La Québecoise** ☎ 514/842-2281 🌐 www.autobus.qc.ca.

Québec City Contacts **Groupe Limousine A-1** ✉ 361 rue des Commissaires Est, St-Roch ☎ 418/523-5059. **Taxi Coop de Québec** ✉ 496 2e av., Limoilou ☎ 418/525-5191. **Taxi Québec** ✉ 975 8e av., Limoilou ☎ 418/522-2001.

BUSINESS HOURS

Business hours are fairly uniform throughout the province. Businesses don't close on the following Monday when a holiday falls on a weekend.

BANKS & OFFICES

Most banks in the province are open Monday through Thursday from 10 to 3 and Friday from 10 until 5 or 6. Some banks are open longer hours and on Saturday morning. All banks are closed on national holidays. Most banks (as well as most self-serve gas stations and convenience stores) have automatic teller machines (ATMs) that are accessible around the clock.

Government offices are generally open weekdays 9–5; some close for an hour around noon. Post offices are open weekdays 8–5 and Saturday 9–noon. Postal outlets in city pharmacies—of which there are many in Montréal—may stay open as late as 9 PM, even on Saturday.

MUSEUMS & SIGHTS

Hours at museums vary, but most open at 10 or 11 and close in the evening. Some smaller museums close for lunch. Many museums are closed Monday; some stay open late on Wednesday, often waiving admission.

The days when all churches were always open are gone; vandalism, theft, and the drop in general piety have seen to that. But the major churches in Montréal and Québec City—the Basilique Notre-Dame-de-Montréal, for example—are open daily, usually about 9–6.

PHARMACIES

Most pharmacies in Montréal and Québec City are open until 10 or 11 PM, but a few stay open around the clock. In the rest of the province, pharmacies are generally open 9–5.

SHOPS

Stores and supermarkets usually are open Monday–Saturday 9–6, although in Montréal and Québec City, supermarkets are often open 7:30 AM–11 PM and some food stores are open around the clock. Most liquor stores are closed Sunday. Shops often stay open Thursday and Friday evenings, most malls until 9 PM. Convenience stores tend to stay open around the clock all week.

BUS TRAVEL

The bus is an essential form of transportation in Québec Province, especially if you're not driving but want to visit out-of-the-way towns that don't have airports or rail lines.

Approximately 10 private bus lines serve the province. Orléans Express is probably the most convenient, as it offers regular service between Montréal and Québec City with a fairly new fleet of clean, comfortable buses. Limocar, another bus line, serves the ski resorts of the Laurentians and Eastern Townships. Greyhound Lines and Voyageur offer interprovincial service and are timely and comfortable, if not exactly plush. Smoking isn't permitted on any buses.

Most bus companies offer discounts if you book in advance, usually either 7 or 14 days ahead. Discounts are also often available for kids (children ages 15 and under can travel for free on most bus lines if tickets are booked three days in advance).

FARES & SCHEDULES

Bus terminals in Montréal and Québec City are usually efficient operations, with service all week and plenty of agents on hand to handle ticket sales. In villages and some small towns, the bus station is simply a counter in a local convenience store, gas station, or snack bar. Getting information on schedules beyond the local ones is sometimes difficult in these places. In rural Québec, it's a good idea to **bring along a French-English dictionary,** although most merchants and clerks can handle a simple ticket sale in English.

PAYING

In major bus terminals, most bus lines accept at least some of the major credit cards. Some smaller lines require cash or take only Visa or MasterCard. All accept traveler's checks in U.S. or Canadian currency with suitable identification, but it's advisable to exchange foreign currency (including U.S. currency) at a bank or exchange office. Be prepared to use cash to buy a ticket in really small towns.

RESERVATIONS

Most bus lines don't accept reservations for specific seats. You should plan on picking up your tickets at least 45 minutes before the bus's scheduled departure time.

Bus Information **Central Bus Station** ✉ 505 blvd. de Maisonneuve Est, Montréal ☎ 514/842-2281. **Gare du Palais Bus Station** ✉ 320 rue Abraham-Martin, Québec ☎ 888/999-3977 or 418/525-3000. **Greyhound Lines** ☎ 800/231-2222, 800/661-8747 in Canada 🌐 www.greyhound.ca. **Limocar** ☎ 866/692-8899 or 450/681-3111 🌐 www.limocar.ca. **Orléans Express** ☎ 514/395-4000 🌐 www.orleansexpress.com. **Voyageur** ☎ 514/842-2281 🌐 www.greyhound.ca.

CAR RENTAL

Request car seats and extras such as GPS when you book, and make sure that a confirmed reservation guarantees you a car. Agencies sometimes overbook, particularly for busy weekends and holiday periods. Rates are sometimes—but not always—better if you book in advance or reserve through a rental agency's Web site. There are other reasons to book ahead, though: for popular destinations, during busy times of the year, or to ensure that you get a certain type of car (vans, SUVs, exotic sports cars).

Rates in Montréal run from about C$34 to C$50 a day for an economy car with air-conditioning and unlimited kilometers. If you prefer a manual-transmission car, check whether the rental agency of your choice offers stick shifts; many agencies in Canada don't.

You must be at least 21 years old to rent a car in Québec, and some car-rental agencies don't rent to drivers under 25. Most rental companies don't allow you to drive on gravel roads. Child seats are compulsory for children ages five and under. In Québec, drivers under age 25 often have to pay a surcharge of C$5 a day.

CUTTING COSTS

Really weigh your options. Find out if a credit card you carry or organization or frequent-renter program to which you belong has a discount program. And check that such discounts really are the best deal. You can often do better with special weekend or weekly rates offered by a rental agency. (And even if you only want to rent for five or six days, ask if you can get the weekly rate; it may very well be cheaper than the daily rate for that period of time.)

Price local car-rental companies as well as the majors. Also investigate wholesalers, which don't own fleets but rent in bulk from those that do and often offer better rates (note you must usually pay for such rentals before leaving home). Consider adding a car rental onto your air/hotel vacation package; the cost will often be cheaper than if you rent the car separately on your own.

When traveling abroad, **look for guaranteed exchange rates,** which protect you against a falling dollar. With your rate locked in, you won't pay more, even if the price goes up in the local currency. (Note to self: not the best thing if the dollar is surging rather than plunging.)

Beware of hidden charges. Those great rental rates may not be so great when you add in taxes, cancellation penalties, dropoff charges (if you're planning to pick up the car in one city and leave it in another), and surcharges (for being under or over a certain age, for additional drivers, or for driving over state or country borders or out of a specific radius from your point of rental).

Note that airport rental offices often add supplementary surcharges that you may avoid by renting from an agency whose office is just off airport property. Don't buy the tank of gas that's in the car when you rent it unless you plan to do a lot of driving. Avoid hefty refueling fees by filling the tank at a station well away from the rental agency (those nearby are often more expensive) just before you turn in the car.

Rentals at the airports near Québec City and Montréal are usually more expensive than rentals elsewhere in the area.

Automobile Associations U.S.: **American Automobile Association** (AAA) ☎ 315/797-5000 🌐 www.aaa.com; most contact with the organization is through state and regional members. **National Automobile Club** ☎ 650/294-7000 🌐 www.thenac.com; membership is open to California residents only.

Major Rental Agencies **Alamo** ☎ 800/522-9696 🌐 www.alamo.com. **Avis** ☎ 800/331-1084 🌐 www.avis.com. **Budget** ☎ 800/472-3325 🌐 www.budget.com. **Hertz** ☎ 800/654-3001 🌐 www.hertz.com. **National Car Rental** ☎ 800/227-7368 🌐 www.nationalcar.com.

Local Rental Agencies **Discount Car Rentals** ✉ Montréal ☎ 800/263-2355 or 514/849-2277 🌐 www.discountcar.com. **Enterprise** ✉ Montréal ☎ 800/325-8007 or 514/844-9794 🌐 www.enterprise.com. **Via Route** ✉ Montréal ☎ 888/842-7688 or 514/871-1166 🌐 www.viaroute.com.

INSURANCE

Everyone who rents a car wonders about whether the insurance that the rental companies offer is worth the expense. No one—not even us—has a simple answer. This is particularly true abroad, where laws are different than at home.

If you own a car, your personal auto insurance may cover a rental to some degree, though not all policies protect you abroad; always read your policy's fine print. If you don't have auto insurance, then seriously consider buying the collision- or loss-damage waiver (CDW or LDW) from the car-rental company, which eliminates your liability for damage to the car. Some credit cards offer CDW coverage, but it's usually supplemental to your own insurance and rarely covers SUVs, minivans, luxury models, and the like. If your coverage is secondary, you may still be liable for loss-of-use costs from the car-rental company. But no credit-card insurance is valid unless you use that card for *all* transactions, from reserving to paying the final bill. All companies exclude car rental in some countries, so be sure to find out about the destination to which you are traveling.

Some countries require you to purchase CDW coverage or require car-rental companies to include it in quoted rates. Ask your rental company about issues like these in your destination. In most cases, it's cheaper to add a supplemental CDW plan to your comprehensive travel insurance policy than to purchase it from a rental company. That said, you don't want to pay for a supplement if you're required to buy insurance from the rental company.

Note that you can decline the insurance from the rental company and purchase it through a third-party provider such as Travel Guard (www.travelguard.com)—$9 per day for $35,000 of coverage. That's sometimes just under half the price of the CDW offered by some car-rental companies. Also, Diners Club offers primary CDW coverage on all rentals reserved and paid for with the card. This means that Diners Club's company—not your own car insurance—pays in case of an accident. It *doesn't* mean your car-insurance company won't raise your rates once it discovers you had an accident.

CAR TRAVEL

Canada's highway system is excellent. It includes the Trans-Canada Highway, which uses several numbers and is the longest highway in the world—running about 8,000 km (5,000 mi) from Victoria, British Columbia, to St. John's, Newfoundland, using ferries to bridge coastal waters at each end. It passes through Montréal and Québec City.

Distances in Canada are always signed in kilometers.

FROM THE UNITED STATES

The U.S. Interstate Highway System leads directly into Canada: I–91 and I–89 from Vermont to Québec and I–87 from New York to Québec. Many smaller highways also connect Québec with New York, Vermont, New Hampshire, and Maine.

Drivers must carry owner registration and proof of insurance coverage, which is compulsory in Canada. Québec drivers are covered by the Québec government no-fault insurance plan. Drivers from outside Québec can obtain a Canadian Non-Resident Inter-Provincial Motor Vehicle Liability Insurance Card, available from any U.S. insurance company. The card is accepted as evidence of financial responsibility in Canada, but you're not required to have one. The minimum liability in Québec is C$50,000. If you are driving a car that isn't registered in your name, carry a letter from the owner that authorizes your use of the vehicle.

Insurance Information **Insurance Bureau of Canada** ☎ 514/288–4321, 877/288–4321 in Québec 🌐 www.ibc.ca. **Société de l'assurance automobile du Québec** ☎ 800/361–7620, 514/873–7620, or 418/643–7620 🌐 www.saaq.gouv.qc.ca.

EMERGENCY SERVICES

Dial 911 in an emergency. Contact CAA, the Canadian Automobile Association, in the event of a flat tire, dead battery, empty gas tank, or other car-related mishap. Automobile Association of America membership includes CAA service.

Emergency Services **CAA** ☎ 800/222–4357 or 514/861–7111 🌐 www.caa.ca.

GASOLINE

Gasoline is always sold in liters; 3.8 liters make a gallon. At this writing, gas prices in Canada are fluctuating considerably, ranging from C$0.84 to C$1.12 per liter (this works out to about $2.35 to $3.80 per gallon U.S.). Lead-free gas is called *sans plomb* or *ordinaire* (gas stations don't sell leaded gasoline). Fuel comes in several grades, denoted in Montréal by bronze, silver, and gold colors and in other areas of the province as *regulière* and *supérieure*.

Major credit cards are widely accepted, and often you can pay at the pump. Receipts are provided if you want one—ask for a *facture*.

ROAD CONDITIONS

In Montréal and Québec City, the jumble of bicycle riders, delivery vehicles, taxis, and municipal buses can be chaotic. In the countryside at night, roads are lighted at exit points from major highways but are otherwise dark. Roads in the province aren't very good—be prepared for some spine-jolting bumps and potholes, and check tire pressure once in a while. In winter, be aware of changing road conditions: Montréal streets are kept mostly clear of snow and ice, but outside the city the situation deteriorates. Locals are notorious for exceeding the speed limit, so keep an eye on your mirrors.

RULES OF THE ROAD

By law, you are required to wear seat belts even in the backseat. Infant seats also are required. Radar-detection devices are illegal in Québec; just having one in your car is illegal. Speed limits, given in kilometers, are usually within the 90–110 kph (50–68 mph) range outside the cities.

Right turns on red signals are allowed in the province, excluding the island of Montréal, where they're prohibited. Driving with a blood-alcohol content of 0.08% or higher is illegal and can earn you a stiff fine and jail time. Headlights are compulsory in inclement weather. Drivers may use handheld cell phones.

Ministère des Transports du Québec 888/355-0511 www.mtq.gouv.qc.ca.

CRUISE TRAVEL

Although many operators offer cruises along sections of the 3,058-km (1,900-mi) St. Lawrence River as it flows from Lake Ontario to the Gulf of St. Lawrence and then the Atlantic Ocean, only three companies offer cabin cruises. Two—Navigation Madeleine (C.T.M.A.) and Relais Nordik—offer cargo cruising between Montréal and the Îles-de-la-Madeleine and between Rimouski and Blanc-Sablon. Celebrity Cruise Lines, Holland America, Regent Seven Seas, and Crystal Cruises all offer cruises departing from the U.S. East Coast, with Montréal and/or Québec City as their final destinations.

Cruise Lines **Celebrity Cruise Lines** 800/647-2251 www.celebrity.com. **Crystal Cruises** 800/804-1500 www.crystalcruises.com. **Holland America** 877/724-5425 www.hollandamerica.com. **Navigation Madeleine (C.T.M.A.)** 888/986-3278 or 418/986-3278 www.ctma.ca. **Regent Seven Seas** 877/505-5370 www.rssc.com. **Relais Nordik** 800/463-0680 or 418/723-8787 www.relaisnordik.com.

CUSTOMS & DUTIES

You're always allowed to bring goods of a certain value back home without having to pay any duty or import tax. However, there's a limit on the amount of tobacco and liquor you can bring back duty-free, and some countries have separate limits for perfumes; for exact figures, check with your customs department. The values of so-called "duty-free" goods are included in these amounts. When you shop abroad, save all your receipts as customs inspectors may ask to see them as well as the items you purchased. If the total value of your goods is more than the duty-free limit, then you'll have to pay a tax (most often a flat percentage) on the value of everything beyond that limit.

U.S. Customs and Immigration has preclearance services at Dorval International Airport, which serves Montréal. This allows U.S.-bound air passengers to depart their airplane directly on arrival at their U.S. destination without further inspection and delays.

American visitors may bring in, duty-free, for personal consumption 200 cigarettes; 50 cigars; 7 ounces of tobacco; and 1 bottle (1.5 liters or 40 imperial ounces) of liquor or wine or 24 355-milliliter (12-ounce) bottles or cans of beer. Any alcohol and tobacco products in excess of these amounts are subject to duty, provincial fees, and taxes. You can also bring in gifts up to a total value of C$750.

A deposit is sometimes required for trailers (refunded upon return).

Cats and dogs must have a certificate issued by a licensed veterinarian that clearly identifies the animal and vouches that it has been vaccinated against rabies during the preceding 36 months. Certificates aren't necessary for Seeing Eye dogs. Plant material must be declared and inspected. There may be restrictions on some live plants, bulbs, and seeds. You may bring food for your own use, as long as the quantity is consistent with the duration of your visit and restrictions or prohibitions on some fruits and vegetables are observed.

Canada's firearms laws are significantly stricter than those in the United States. All handguns and semiautomatic and fully automatic weapons are prohibited and cannot be brought into the country. Sporting rifles and shotguns may be imported provided they are to be used for sporting, hunting, or competing while in Canada. All firearms must be declared to Canada Customs at the first point of entry. Failure to declare firearms will result in their seizure, and criminal charges may be made. Regulations require visitors to have a confirmed Firearms Declaration to bring any guns into Canada; a fee of C$25 applies, good for one year. For more information, contact the Canadian Firearms Centre.

Information in Canada **Canada Border Services Agency** ✉ 2265 blvd. St-Laurent, Ottawa, ON K1G 4K3 ☎ 800/461-9999 in Canada, 204/983-3500, 506/636-5064 🌐 www.cbsa-asfc.gc.ca. **Canadian Firearms Centre** ☎ 800/731-4000 🌐 www.cfc-ccaf.gc.ca.

U.S. Information **U.S. Customs and Border Protection** 🌐 www.cbp.gov.

EATING OUT

Was the service stellar or not up to snuff? Did the food give you shivers of delight or leave you cold? Did the prices and portions make you happy or sad? Rate restaurants and write your own reviews in Travel Ratings or start a discussion about your favorite places in Travel Talk on www.fodors.com. Your comments might even appear in our books. Yes, you, too, can be a correspondent!

French-Canadian fast food follows the same concept as American fast food, though roasted chicken is also popular. Local chains to watch for include St-Hubert, which serves rotisserie chicken, and La Belle Province, Lafleur, and Valentine, all of which serve hamburgers, hot dogs, and fries. As an antidote, try the Montréal chain Le Commensal—it's completely vegetarian, and it's excellent.

The restaurants we list are the cream of the crop in each price category. Properties indicated by a ✕🏨 are lodging establishments whose restaurant warrants a special trip.

MEALS & MEALTIMES

Unless otherwise noted, the restaurants listed in this guide are open daily for lunch and dinner.

PAYING

Major credit cards are widely accepted in both Montréal and Québec City. For guidelines on tipping *see* Tipping.

RESERVATIONS & DRESS

Regardless of where you are, it's a good idea to make a reservation if you can. In some places, it's expected. We only mention specifically when reservations are essential (there's no other way you'll ever get a table) or when they are not accepted. For popular restaurants, book as far ahead as you can (often 30 days), and reconfirm as soon as you arrive. (Large parties should always call ahead to check the reservations policy.) We mention dress only when men are required to wear a jacket or a jacket and tie.

WINES, BEER & SPIRITS

Beer lovers rejoice at the selection available from highly regarded local microbreweries, such as Unibroue (Fin du Monde, U, U2), Brasseurs du Nord (Boréale), and McAuslan (Griffon, St. Ambroise). You may find these and other microbrews bottled in local supermarkets and on tap in bars. The local hard cider P. O.M. is also excellent. Caribou, a traditional concoction made from red wine, vodka (or some other liquor), spices, and, usually, maple syrup, is available at many winter events and festivals throughout the province, such as Québec City's winter carnival. Small bars may also offer the drink in season.

The province's liquor purveyor, SAQ, stocks a wide choice of wines and is also the only place you can buy hard liquor; most SAQ stores are open regular business hours. Supermarkets and convenience stores carry lower-end wines, but they can sell wine and beer until 11 PM all week (long after SAQ stores have closed). The minimum legal age for alcohol consumption is 18.

EMERGENCIES

All embassies are in Ottawa. Emergency information is given at the end of each chapter. The U.S. consulate in Montréal is open weekdays 8:30–noon; additionally it's open Wednesday 2–4.

Embassies & Consulates **U.S. Consulate General** ✉ 1155 rue St-Alexandre, Montréal, QC H27 1Z2 ☎ 514/398-9695 ✉ 2 pl. Terrasse Dufferin, behind Château Frontenac, Québec, QC G1R 4T9 ☎ 418/692-2095. **U.S. Embassy** ✉ 490 Sussex Dr., Ottawa, ON K1N 1G8 ☎ 613/238-5335 🌐 www.usembassycanada.gov.

HOLIDAYS

Canadian national holidays are as follows: New Year's Day (January 1), Good Friday (late March or early April), Easter Monday (the Monday following Good Friday), Victoria Day (late May), Canada Day (July 1), Labour Day (early September), Thanksgiving (mid-October), Remembrance Day (November 11), Christmas, and Boxing Day (December 26). St. Jean Baptiste Day (June 24) is a provincial holiday.

INSURANCE

What kind of coverage do you honestly need? Do you even need trip insurance at all? Take a deep breath and read on.

We believe that comprehensive trip insurance is especially valuable if you're booking a very expensive or complicated trip (particularly to an isolated region) or if you're booking far in advance. Who knows what could happen six months down the road? But whether or not you get insurance has more to do with how comfortable you are assuming all that risk yourself.

Comprehensive travel policies typically cover trip-cancellation and interruption, letting you cancel or cut your trip short because of a personal emergency, illness, or, in some cases, acts of terrorism in your destination. Such policies also cover evacuation and medical care. Some also cover you for trip delays because of bad weather or mechanical problems as well as for lost or delayed baggage. Another type of coverage to look for is financial default—that is, when your trip is disrupted because a tour operator, airline, or cruise line goes out of business. Generally you must buy this when you book your trip or shortly thereafter, and it's only available to you if your operator isn't on a list of excluded companies.

Expect comprehensive travel insurance policies to cost about 4% to 7% of the total price of your trip (it's more like 12% if you're over age 70). A medical-only policy may or may not be cheaper than a comprehensive policy. Always read the fine print of your policy to make sure that you are covered for the risks that are of the most concern to you. Compare several policies to make sure you're getting the best price and range of coverage available.

Insurance Comparison Sites **Insure My Trip.com** 🌐 www.insuremytrip.com. **Square Mouth.com** 🌐 www.quotetravelinsurance.com.

Comprehensive Travel Insurers **Access America** ☎ 866/807-3982 🌐 www.accessamerica.com. **CSA Travel Protection** ☎ 800/873-9855 🌐 www.csatravelprotection.com. **HTH Worldwide** ☎ 888/243-2358 or 610/254-8700 🌐 www.hthworldwide.com. **Travelex Insurance** ☎ 888/457-4602 🌐 www.travelex-insurance.com. **Travel Guard International** ☎ 800/826-4919 or 715/345-0505 🌐 www.travelguard.com. **Travel Insured International** ☎ 800/243-3174 🌐 www.travelinsured.com.

Medical-Only Insurers **International Medical Group** ☎ 800/628-4664 🌐 www.imglobal.com. **International SOS** ☎ 215/942-8000 or 713/521-7611 🌐 www.internationalsos.com. **Wallach & Company** ☎ 800/237-6615 or 504/687-3166 🌐 www.wallach.com.

LANGUAGE

Although Canada has two official languages—English and French—the province of Québec has only one. French is the language you hear most often on the streets here; it is also the language of government, businesses, and schools. Only in Montréal, the Ottawa Valley (the area around Hull), and the Eastern Townships is English more widely spoken. Most French Canadians speak English as well, but learning a few French phrases before you go is useful. Canadian French has many distinctive words and expressions, but it's no more different from the language of France than

North American English is from the language of Great Britain.

LANGUAGES FOR TRAVELERS

A phrase book and language-tape set can help get you started. *Fodor's French for Travelers* (available at bookstores everywhere) is excellent.

LODGING

In Montréal and Québec City, you have a choice of luxury hotels, moderately priced modern properties, and small older hotels with perhaps fewer conveniences but more charm. Options in small towns and in the country include large, full-service resorts; small, privately owned hotels; roadside motels; and B&Bs. Even outside the cities you need to make reservations at least on the day on which you plan to pull into town.

Expect accommodations to cost more in summer than in the colder months (except for places such as ski resorts, where winter is high season). When making reservations, ask about special deals and packages. Big-city hotels that cater to business travelers often offer weekend packages, and many city hotels offer rooms at up to 50% off in winter. If you're planning to visit Montréal or Québec City or a resort area in high season, book well in advance. Also be aware of any special events or festivals that may coincide with your visit and fill every room for miles around. For resorts and lodges, remember that winter ski season is a period of high demand, and plan accordingly.

The lodgings we list are the cream of the crop in each price category. We always list the facilities that are available, but we don't specify whether they cost extra; when pricing accommodations, always ask what's included and what costs extra. Properties are assigned price categories based on the range between their least and most expensive standard double rooms at high season (excluding holidays). Properties marked ✕🏨 are lodging establishments whose restaurants warrant a special trip.

Most hotels and other lodgings require you to give your credit-card details before they will confirm your reservation. If you don't feel comfortable e-mailing this information, ask if you can fax it (some places even prefer faxes). However you book, get confirmation in writing and have a copy of it handy when you check in. If you book through an online travel agent, discounter, or wholesaler, you might even want to confirm your reservation with the hotel before leaving home—just to be sure everything was processed correctly.

Be sure you understand the hotel's cancellation policy. Some places allow you to cancel without any kind of penalty—even if you prepaid to secure a discounted rate—if you cancel at least 24 hours in advance. Others require you to cancel a week in advance or penalize you for the cost of one night. Small inns and B&Bs are most likely to require you to cancel far in advance. Most hotels allow children under a certain age to stay in their parents' room at no extra charge, but others charge for them as extra adults; find out the cutoff age for discounts.

Assume that hotels operate on the European Plan (**EP,** no meals) unless we specify that they use the Breakfast Plan (**BP,** with full breakfast), Continental Plan (**CP,** Continental breakfast), Full American Plan (**FAP,** all meals), Modified American Plan (**MAP,** breakfast and dinner), or are **all-inclusive** (all meals and most activities).

APARTMENT & HOUSE RENTALS

The *Gazette* (🌐 www.montrealgazette.com), Montréal's English-language daily, has the best rental listings in town. *Hour* (🌐 www.hour.ca), a good weekly free paper in Montréal, also has rental listings.

BED & BREAKFASTS

B&Bs can be found in both the country and the cities. For assistance in booking these, be sure to check out B&B Web sites (🌐 www.gitesetaubergesdupassant.com is an excellent resource for B&Bs throughout the province). Room quality varies from house to house as well, so **ask to see a few rooms before making a choice.**

Reservation Services **Bed & Breakfast.com** ☎ 800/462-2632 or 512/322-2710 🌐 www.bedandbreakfast.com also sends out an online newsletter. **Bed & Breakfast Inns Online** ☎ 800/215-7365 or 615/868-1946 🌐 www.bbonline.com.

BnB Finder.com ☎ 888/547-8226 or 212/432-7693 🌐 www.bnbfinder.com.

HOME EXCHANGES

With a direct home exchange, you stay in someone else's home while they stay in yours. Some outfits also deal with vacation homes, so you're not actually staying in someone's full-time residence, just their vacant weekend place.

Exchange Clubs **Home Exchange.com** ☎ 800/877-8723 🌐 www.homeexchange.com; $59.95 for a 1-year online listing. **HomeLink International** ☎ 800/638-3841 🌐 www.homelink.org; $80 yearly for Web-only membership; $125 with Web access and two directories. **Intervac U.S.** ☎ 800/756-4663 🌐 www.intervacus.com; $78.88 for Web-only membership; $126 includes Web access and a catalog.

HOTELS

Weigh all your options (we can't say this enough). Join "frequent guest" programs. You may get preferential treatment in room choice and/or upgrades in your favorite chains. Check general travel sites and hotel Web sites as not all chains are represented on all travel sites. Always research or inquire about special packages and corporate rates. If you prefer to book by phone, note you can sometimes get a better price if you call the hotel's local toll-free number (if one is available) rather than the central reservations number.

If your destination's high season is December through April and you're trying to book, say, in late April, you might save considerably by changing your dates by a week or two. Note, though, that many properties charge peak-season rates for your entire stay even if your travel dates straddle peak and nonpeak seasons. High-end chains catering to businesspeople are often busy only on weekdays and often drop rates dramatically on weekends to fill up rooms. **Ask when rates go down.**

Watch out for hidden costs, including resort fees, energy surcharges, and "convenience" fees for such things as unlimited local phone service you won't use and a free newspaper—possibly written in a language you can't read. Always verify whether local hotel taxes are or are not included in the rates you are quoted, so that you'll know the real price of your stay. In some places, taxes can add 20% or more to your bill. If you're traveling overseas **look for price guarantees,** which protect you against a falling dollar. With your rate locked in, you won't pay more, even if the price goes up in the local currency.

Canada doesn't have a national rating system for hotels, but Québec's tourism ministry rates the province's hotels; the stars are more a reflection of the number of facilities than of the hotel's performance. Hotels are rated zero to three stars, with zero stars representing minimal comfort and few services and three stars being the very best. All hotels listed have private bath unless otherwise noted.

Discount Hotel Rooms **Accommodations Express** ☎ 800/444-7666 or 800/277-1064. **Hotels.com** ☎ 800/219-4606 or 800/364-0291 🌐 www.hotels.com. **Quikbook** ☎ 800/789-9887 🌐 www.quikbook.com. **Turbotrip.com** ☎ 800/473-7829 🌐 w3.turbotrip.com.

MAIL & SHIPPING

In Canada you can buy stamps at the post office or from vending machines in most hotel lobbies, railway stations, airports, bus terminals, many retail outlets, and some newsstands. If you're sending mail to or within Canada, **be sure to include the postal code** (a combination of six digits and letters).

The postal abbreviation for Québec is QC.

POSTAL RATES

Within Canada, postcards and letters up to 30 grams cost C$0.51; between 31 grams and 50 grams, the cost is C$0.89; and between 51 grams and 100 grams, the cost is C$1.05. Letters and postcards to the United States cost C$0.89 for up to 30 grams, C$1.05 for between 31 and 50 grams, and C$1.78 for up to 100 grams. Prices include GST (goods and services tax).

International mail and postcards run C$1.49 for up to 30 grams, C$2.10 for 31 to 50 grams, and C$3.49 for 51 to 100 grams.

RECEIVING MAIL

Visitors may have mail sent to them c/o General Delivery in the town they are visiting, for pickup in person within 15 days, after which it is returned to the sender.

SHIPPING PACKAGES

Many shops ship purchases home for you; when they do, you may avoid having to pay the steep provincial taxes. By courier, a package takes only a few days, but via regular Canada Post mail, packages often take a week—or longer—to reach the United States. Be sure to address everything properly and wrap it securely.

MONEY MATTERS

Throughout this book, prices are given in Canadian dollars. The price of a cup of coffee ranges from less than C$1 to C$2.50 or more, depending on how upscale or downscale the place is; beer costs C$3 to C$7 in a bar; a smoked-meat sandwich costs about C$5 to C$6; and museum admission can cost anywhere from nothing to C$15.

ATMS & BANKS

Your own bank will probably charge a fee for using ATMs abroad; the foreign bank you use may also charge a fee. Nevertheless, you'll usually get a better rate of exchange via an ATM than you will at a currency-exchange office or even when changing money in a bank. And extracting funds as you need them is a safer option than carrying around a large amount of cash. Note that PIN numbers with more than four digits are not recognized at ATMs in many countries.

ATMs are available in most bank, trust-company, and credit-union branches across the province, as well as in most convenience stores, malls, and self-serve gas stations.

CREDIT CARDS

Throughout this guide, the following abbreviations are used: **AE,** American Express; **D,** Discover; **DC,** Diners Club; **MC,** MasterCard; and **V,** Visa.

It's a good idea to inform your credit-card company before you travel, especially if you're going abroad and don't travel internationally very often. Otherwise, the credit-card company might put a hold on your card owing to unusual activity—not a good thing halfway through your trip. Record all your credit-card numbers—as well as the phone numbers to call if your cards are lost or stolen—in a safe place so you're prepared should something go wrong. Both MasterCard and Visa have general numbers you can call (collect if you're abroad) if your card is lost, but you're better off calling the number of your issuing bank since MasterCard and Visa usually just transfer you to your bank; your bank's number is usually printed on your card.

If you plan to use your credit card for cash advances, you'll need to apply for a PIN at least two weeks before your trip. Although it's usually cheaper (and safer) to use a credit card abroad for large purchases (so you can cancel payments or be reimbursed if there's a problem) note that some credit-card companies *and* the banks that issue them add substantial percentages to all foreign transactions, whether they're done in a foreign currency or not. Check on these fees before leaving home so that there won't be any surprises when you get the bill.

Before you charge something, ask the merchant whether or not he or she plans to do a dynamic currency conversion (DCC). In such a transaction the credit-card *processor* (shop, restaurant, or hotel, not Visa or MasterCard) converts the currency and charges you in dollars. In most cases you'll pay the merchant a 3% fee for this service in addition to any credit-card company and issuing-bank foreign-transaction surcharges.

DCC programs are becoming increasingly widespread. Merchants who participate in them are supposed to ask whether you want to be charged in dollars or the local currency, but they don't always do so. And even if they do offer you a choice, they may well avoid mentioning the additional surcharges. The good news is that you *do* have a choice. And if this practice really gets your goat, you can avoid it entirely thanks to American Express; with its cards, DCC simply isn't an option.

Reporting Lost Cards **American Express** ☎ 800/992-3404 in the U.S., 336/393-1111 collect from abroad 🌐 www.americanexpress.com. **Diners Club** ☎ 800/234-6377 in the U.S., 303/799-1504 collect from abroad 🌐 www.dinersclub.com. **Discover** ☎ 800/347-2683 in the U.S., 801/902-3100 collect from abroad 🌐 www.discovercard.com. **MasterCard** ☎ 800/622-7747 in the U.S., 636/722-7111 collect from abroad 🌐 www.mastercard.com. **Visa** ☎ 800/847-2911 in the U.S., 410/581-9994 collect from abroad 🌐 www.visa.com.

CURRENCY & EXCHANGE

Even if a currency exchange booth has a sign promising no commission, rest assured that there's some kind of huge, hidden fee. (Oh . . . that's right. The sign didn't say no *fee*.) And, in terms of rates, you're almost always better off getting foreign currency through an ATM or exchanging money at a bank.

U.S. dollars are accepted in much of Canada, especially in communities near the border. Traveler's checks (some are available in Canadian dollars) and major U.S. credit cards are accepted in most areas.

The units of currency in Canada are the Canadian dollar (C$) and the cent, in almost the same denominations as U.S. currency ($5, $10, $20, 1¢, 5¢, 10¢, 25¢, etc.). The $1 and $2 bill are no longer used in Canada; they have been replaced by $1 and $2 coins (known as a "loonie," because of the loon that appears on the coin, and a "toonie," respectively).

At this writing, the exchange rate is US$1 to C$1.13.

Exchange Rate Information **Oanda.com** 🌐 www.oanda.com also allows you to print out a handy table with the current day's conversion rates. **XE.com** 🌐 www.xe.com. **Yahoo Finance** 🌐 http://finance.yahoo.com/currency.

TRAVELER'S CHECKS & CARDS

Some consider this the currency of the cave man, and it's true that fewer establishments accept traveler's checks these days. Nevertheless, they're a cheap and secure way to carry extra money, particularly on trips to urban areas. Both Citibank (under the Visa brand) and American Express issue traveler's checks in the United States, but Amex is better known and more widely accepted; you can also avoid hefty surcharges by cashing Amex checks at Amex offices. Whatever you do, keep track of all the serial numbers in case the checks are lost or stolen. It's not essential to have traveler's checks in Québec.

American Express now offers a stored-value card called a Travelers Cheque Card, which you can use wherever American Express credit cards are accepted, including ATMs. The card can carry a minimum of $300 and a maximum of $2,700, and it's a very safe way to carry your funds. Although you can get replacement funds in 24 hours if your card is lost or stolen, it doesn't really strike us as a very good deal. In addition to a high initial cost ($14.95 to set up the card, plus $5 each time you "reload"), you still have to pay a 2% fee for each purchase in a foreign currency (similar to that of any credit card). Further, each time you use the card in an ATM you pay a transaction fee of $2.50 on top of the 2% transaction fee for the conversion—add it all up and it can be considerably more than you would pay for simply using your own ATM card. Regular traveler's checks are just as secure and cost less.

American Express ☎ 888/412-6945 in the U.S., 801/945-9450 collect from abroad to add value or speak to customer service 🌐 www.americanexpress.com.

PASSPORTS

We're always surprised at how few Americans have passports—only 25% at this writing. This number is expected to grow when it becomes impossible to reenter the United States from trips to neighboring Canada or Mexico without one. Remember this: a passport verifies both your identity and nationality—a great reason to have one.

U.S. passports are valid for 10 years. You must apply in person if you're getting a passport for the first time; if your previous passport was lost, stolen, or damaged; or if your previous passport has expired and was issued more than 15 years ago or when you were under 16. All children under 18 must appear in person to apply for or renew a passport. Both parents must accompany any child under 14 (or send a notarized statement with their permission) and provide proof of their relationship to the child.

There are 13 regional passport offices, as well as 7,000 passport acceptance facilities in post offices, public libraries, and other governmental offices. If you're renewing a passport, you can do so by mail. Forms are available at passport acceptance facilities and online.

The cost to apply for a new passport is $97 for adults, $82 for children under 16; renewals are $67. Allow six weeks to process the paperwork for either a new or renewed passport. For an expediting fee of $60, you can reduce the time to about two weeks. If your trip is less than two weeks away, you can get a passport even more rapidly by going to a passport office with the necessary documentation. Private expediters can get things done in as little as 48 hours but charge hefty fees for their services.

Before your trip, make two copies of your passport's data page (one for someone at home and another for you to carry separately). Or scan the page and e-mail it to someone at home and/or yourself.

As of January 1, 2008, all travelers will need a passport or other accepted secure documents to enter or reenter the United States. Currently, citizens and legal residents of the United States don't need a passport or visa to enter Canada, but other proof of citizenship (a birth certificate) and some form of photo identification is requested. Naturalized U.S. residents should carry their naturalization certificate. Permanent residents who aren't citizens should carry their "green card." U.S. residents entering Canada from a third country must have a valid passport, naturalization certificate, or "green card."

U.S. Passport Information **U.S. Department of State** ☎ 877/487-2778 🌐 http://travel.state.gov/passport

U.S. Passport Expediters **A. Briggs Passport & Visa Expeditors** ☎ 800/806-0581 or 202/464-3000 🌐 www.abriggs.com. **American Passport Express** ☎ 800/455-5166 or 603/559-9888 🌐 www.americanpassport.com. **Passport Express** ☎ 800/362-8196 or 401/272-4612 🌐 www.passportexpress.com. **Travel Document Systems** ☎ 800/874-5100 or 202/638-3800 🌐 www.traveldocs.com. **Travel the World Visas** ☎ 866/886-8472 or 301/495-7700 🌐 www.world-visa.com.

SAFETY

Distribute your cash, credit cards, IDs, and other valuables between a deep front pocket, an inside jacket or vest pocket, and a hidden money pouch. Don't reach for the money pouch once you're in public.

Montrealers are keen to boast they can walk the streets of their city at any time of day or night without fear of incident. And although both Montréal and Québec City are among the safest cities in North America, travelers should nevertheless be on their guard for pickpockets and other petty criminals, especially when traveling on Montréal's often-crowded Métro system.

TAXES

A goods and services tax (GST) of 6% applies on virtually every transaction in Canada except for the purchase of basic groceries. In addition to imposing the GST, Québec levies a sales tax of 6% to 12% on most items purchased in shops, at restaurants, and on hotel rooms.

Departing passengers in Montréal pay a C$17 airport-improvement fee that's included in the cost of an airline ticket.

GST REFUNDS

You can **get a GST refund** on purchases taken out of the country and on short-term accommodations of less than one month, but not on food, drink, tobacco, car or motor-home rentals, or transportation. Rebate forms, which must be submitted within 60 days of leaving Canada, may be obtained from certain retailers, duty-free shops, customs officials, or from the Canada Customs and Revenue Agency. Instant cash rebates up to a maximum of C$500 are provided by some duty-free shops when you leave Canada, and, in most cases, goods that are shipped directly by the vendor to the purchaser's home aren't taxed. Refunds are paid out in U.S. dollars for U.S. citizens. In order to receive a refund be sure to have all your receipts, barring those for accommodations, validated at Canada Customs before leaving the country. Always save your original receipts from stores and hotels (not just the credit-card receipts), and be sure the name and address of the establishment are shown on the receipt. Original receipts aren't returned, unless you request them. To be eligible for a refund, receipts must total at least C$200, and each receipt must show a minimum purchase of C$50.

Canada Customs and Revenue Agency ✉ Visitor Rebate Program, Summerside Tax Centre, 275 Pope Rd., Suite 104, Summerside, PE C1N 6C6 ☎ 800/668-4748 in Canada, 902/432-5608 🌐 www.ccra-adrc.gc.ca.

TIME

Montréal and Québec City are both in the Eastern Standard Time zone. Los Angeles is three hours behind local time and Chicago is one hour behind.

TIPPING

Tips and service charges aren't usually added to a bill in Canada. In general, tip 15% of the total bill. This goes for waiters and waitresses, barbers and hairdressers, and taxi drivers. Porters and doormen should get about C$2 a bag. For maid service, leave at least C$2 per person a day (C$3 to C$5 in luxury hotels).

TRAIN TRAVEL

Amtrak has daily service from New York City's Penn Station to Montréal, although the train sometimes arrives too late to make any connecting trains that evening. Connections are available, often the next day, to Canadian rail line VIA Rail's Canadian routes. The ride takes up to 11 hours, and one-way tickets cost $55 to $68. VIA Rail trains run from Montréal to Québec City often and take three hours. Smoking isn't allowed on these trains.

CUTTING COSTS

To save money, **look into rail passes.** But be aware that if you don't plan to cover many miles, you may come out ahead by buying individual tickets.The 30-day North American RailPass, offered by Amtrak and VIA Rail, allows unlimited coach-economy travel in the United States and Canada. You can either indicate your itinerary when purchasing the pass or confirm it as you travel. The cost is C$899 from early June to mid-October, C$637 at other times. VIA Rail also offers a Canrail pass (for travel within Canada) and a Corridor Pass (for travel anywhere between Windsor, Ontario, and Québec City). Senior citizens (60 and older), children (18 and under), and students are entitled to an additional 10% discount off all rates.

Train Information **Amtrak** ☎ 800/872-7245 🌐 www.amtrak.com. **VIA Rail Canada** ☎ 888/842-7245 or 514/989-2626 🌐 www.viarail.ca.

TRAVEL AGENTS

If you use an agent—brick-and-mortar or virtual—you'll pay a fee for the service. And know that the service you get from some online agents isn't comprehensive. For example Expedia or Travelocity don't search for prices on budget airlines like JetBlue, Southwest, or small foreign carriers. That said, some agents (online or not) *do* have access to fares that are difficult to find otherwise, and the savings can more than make up for any surcharge.

A knowledgeable brick-and-mortar travel agent can be a godsend if you're booking a cruise, a package trip that's not available to you directly, an air pass, or a complicated itinerary including several overseas flights. What's more, travel agents that specialize in a destination may have exclusive access to certain deals and insider information on things such as charter flights. Agents who specialize in types of travelers (senior citizens, gays and lesbians, naturists) or types of trips (cruises, luxury travel, safaris) can also be invaluable.

A top-notch agent planning your trip to Russia will make sure you get the correct visa application and complete it on time; the one booking your cruise may get you a cabin upgrade or arrange to have a bottle of champagne chilling in your cabin when you embark. And complain about the surcharges all you like, but when things don't work out the way you'd hoped, it's nice to have an agent to put things right.

In Québec, all travel agencies have to pay a bond to obtain a permit from the Office de la protection du consommateur (consumer protection office), which in turn protects travelers if they become stranded.

Agent Resources **American Society of Travel Agents** ☎ 703/739–2782 www.travelsense.org.
Online Agents **Expedia** www.expedia.com. **Onetravel.com** www.onetravel.com. **Orbitz** www.orbitz.com. **Priceline.com** www.priceline.com. **Travelocity** www.travelocity.com.

VISITOR INFORMATION

There are major tourism offices in both Montréal and Québec City.

Tourist Information **Canadian Tourism Commission** ✉ 1055 Dunsmuir St., Suite 1400, Four Bentall Centre, Box 49230, Vancouver, BC V5P 1L2 ☎ 604/638–8300 www.travelcanada.ca. **Infotourisme Québec** ✉ 1255 rue Peel, Bureau 400, Montréal, QC H3B 4V4 ☎ 877/266–5687 or 514/873–2015 www.bonjourquebec.com.

WEB SITES

We're really proud of our Web site: Fodors.com is a great place to begin any journey. Scan Travel Wire for suggested itineraries, travel deals, restaurant and hotel openings, and other up-to-the-minute info. Check out Booking to research prices and book plane tickets, hotel rooms, rental cars, and vacation packages. Head to Talk for on-the-ground pointers from travelers who frequent our message boards. You can also link to loads of other travel-related resources.

After your trip, be sure to rate the places you visited and share your experiences and travel tips with us and other Fodorites in Travel Ratings and Talk on www.fodors.com.

Currency Conversion **Google** www.google.com does currency conversion. Just type in the amount you want to convert and an explanation of how you want it converted (e.g., "14 Swiss francs in dollars"), and then voilà. **Oanda.com** www.oanda.com also allows you to print out a handy table with the current day's conversion rates. **XE.com** www.xe.com is a good currency conversion Web site.

Weather **Accuweather.com** www.accuweather.com is an independent weather-forecasting service with especially good coverage of hurricanes. **Weather.com** www.weather.com is the Web site for the Weather Channel.

INDEX

D

E

F

G

H

M

N

O

P

Q

R

S

T

PHOTO CREDITS

Cover Photo (Grande Allée, Québec City): Yves Tessier. 7, *Rubens Abboud/age fotostock*. 8, *Walter Bibikow/viestiphoto.com*. 12, *budak.blogs.com*. 13, *Jon Arnold/age fotostock*. 14, *Andre Jenny/Alamy*. 15 (left), *Blaine Harrington III/Alamy*. 15 (right), *Rubens Abboud/Alamy*. 16, *Walter Bibikow/viestiphoto.com*. 17 (left), *Rubens Abboud/Alamy*. 17 (right), *Hemis/Alamy*.

NOTES

NOTES

NOTES

NOTES

NOTES

NOTES

NOTES

NOTES

NOTES

ABOUT OUR WRITERS

Native Montrealer **Chris Barry,** who writes a weekly column for the *Montréal Mirror,* has contributed to scores of publications over the years. He updated Smart Travel Tips, the Laurentians and Eastern Townships sections, and portions of Montréal.

Originally from Nova Scotia, **Michèle Thibeau** has called Québec City home for 13 years. She's spent the last eight discovering the English-speaking community, its people, news, history, and culture through her work as a journalist and assistant editor of the *Québec Chronicle-Telegraph*. She updated the Québec City and Québec City Side Trips chapters.

Paul Waters, a journalist and veteran travel writer, grew up on Canada's east coast. His wife and travel-writing partner, **Julie Waters,** is a native Montrealer with deep Loyalist roots in Québec's Eastern Townships. They both spent several years living in each of Canada's two metropolises—Toronto and Vancouver—but concluded that neither of those cities can match Montréal for charm, culture, and sheer livability. Paul is on the editorial board of the Montréal *Gazette* and Julie writes for several trade publications. This year they coauthored the Montréal chapter along with Chris Barry.